REGNUM EDINBURGH CENTENARY SERIES
Volume 14

Mission Spirituality and Authentic Discipleship

REGNUM EDINBURGH CENTENARY SERIES

The Centenary of the World Missionary Conference of 1910, held in Edinburgh, was a suggestive moment for many people seeking direction for Christian mission in the twenty-first century. Several different constituencies within world Christianity held significant events around 2010. From 2005, an international group worked collaboratively to develop an intercontinental and multi-denominational project, known as Edinburgh 2010, and based at New College, University of Edinburgh. This initiative brought together representatives of twenty different global Christian bodies, representing all major Christian denominations and confessions, and many different strands of mission and church life, to mark the Centenary.

Essential to the work of the Edinburgh 1910 Conference, and of abiding value, were the findings of the eight think-tanks or 'commissions'. These inspired the idea of a new round of collaborative reflection on Christian mission – but now focused on nine themes identified as being key to mission in the twenty-first century. The study process was polycentric, open-ended, and as inclusive as possible of the different genders, regions of the world, and theological and confessional perspectives in today's church. It was overseen by the Study Process Monitoring Group: Miss Maria Aranzazu Aguado (Spain, The Vatican), Dr Daryl Balia (South Africa, Edinburgh 2010), Mrs Rosemary Dowsett (UK, World Evangelical Alliance), Dr Knud Jørgensen (Norway, Areopagos), Rev John Kafwanka (Zambia, Anglican Communion), Rev Dr Jooseop Keum (Korea, World Council of Churches), Dr Wonsuk Ma (Korea, Oxford Centre for Mission Studies), Rev Dr Kenneth R. Ross (UK, Church of Scotland), Dr Petros Vassiliadis (Greece, Aristotle University of Thessalonikki), and coordinated by Dr Kirsteen Kim (UK, Edinburgh 2010).

These publications reflect the ethos of Edinburgh 2010 and will make a significant contribution to ongoing studies in mission. It should be clear that material published in this series will inevitably reflect a diverse range of views and positions. These will not necessarily represent those of the series' editors or of the Edinburgh 2010 General Council, but in publishing them the leadership of Edinburgh 2010 hopes to encourage conversation between Christians and collaboration in mission. All the series' volumes are commended for study and reflection in both church and academy.

Series Editors

Knud Jørgensen	Areopagos, Norway, MF Norwegian School of Theology & the Lutheran School of Theology, Hong Kong. Former Chair of Edinburgh 2010 Study Process Monitoring Group
Kirsteen Kim	Leeds Trinity University College and former Edinburgh 2010 Research Coordinator, UK
Wonsuk Ma	Oxford Centre for Mission Studies, Oxford, UK
Tony Gray	Words by Design, Bicester, UK

REGNUM EDINBURGH CENTENARY SERIES
Volume 14

Mission Spirituality and Authentic Discipleship

Edited by

Wonsuk Ma and Kenneth R. Ross

Copyright © Wonsuk Ma and Kenneth R. Ross, 2013
First published 2013 by Regnum Books International

Regnum is an imprint of the Oxford Centre for Mission Studies
St. Philip and St. James Church
Woodstock Road
Oxford OX2 6HR, UK
www.ocms.ac.uk/regnum

09 08 07 06 05 04 03 7 6 5 4 3 2 1

The right of Wonsuk Ma and Kenneth R. Ross to be identified as the Editors of this Work has been asserted in accordance with the Copyright, Designs and Patents Act 1988.

All rights reserved. No part of this publication may be reproduced, stored in a retrieval system, or transmitted in any form or by any means, electric, mechanical, photocopying, recording or otherwise, without the prior permission of the publisher or a licence permitting restricted copying. In the UK such licences are issued by the Copyright Licencing Agency, 90 Tottenham Court Road, London W1P 9HE.

British Library Cataloguing in Publication Data
A catalogue record for this book is available from the British Library

ISBN: 978-1-908355-24-9

Typeset by Words by Design

Painting by Wisnu Sasongko, used by kind permission of the Overseas Ministries Study Center, New Haven, CT, USA. Wisnu Sasongko, an Indonesian, was OMSC's Artist in Residence in the 2003-04 academic calendar year.

Printed and bound in Great Britain for Regnum Books International
by TJ International LTD, Padstow, Cornwall

The publication of this title is made possible through the generous financial assistance of The Commission on Theological Education of Evangelisches Missionswerk in Deutschland (EMW, Dr. Verena Grüter), Hamburg, Germany, and Youngnak Presbyterian Church (Rev. Chul-shin Lee), Seoul, Korea.

Contents

Foreword
  Lalsangkima Pachuau — vii

Introduction: The Spiritual Dimension of Mission
  Wonsuk Ma and Kenneth R. Ross — 1

'The Promise is for You and Your Children':
Pentecostal Spirituality, Mission and Discipleship in Africa
  J. Kwabena Asamoah-Gyadu — 10

Doing Mission at the Margins of Society:
Harnessing the Resources of Local Visions
  Nicta Lubaale — 28

Spirituality and Historic Mission Christianity in Africa:
Ghanaization in Roman Catholicism
  Michael Perry Kweku Okyerefo — 38

African Spirituality, Socio-Political Experience and Mission
  Matthews A. Ojo — 47

Mission Spirituality and Authentic Discipleship:
An African Reflection
  Serah Wambua — 62

A Mission To and From the Youth
  Rosauro Lopez Sandoval — 74

The Dream of Unity in Bolivia
  Moses Morales — 87

The *Kenosis* of Christ and His Redefinition of Nationalism
as a Way Towards Reconciliation in Israel/Palestine
  Andrew. F. Bush — 98

Mission in an Orthodox Christian Context:
Witnessing to Christ as Pastoral Responsibility
  Valentin Kozhuharov — 110

Mission According to the Catholic Church in Asia:
A New Way of Being Church
  Clemens Mendonca — 127

Sunder Singh and NV Tilak:
Lessons for Missiology from Twentieth Century India
    David Emmanuel Singh   139

Mission in the Context of Filipino Folk Spirituality:
***Bahala Na* as a Case in Point**
    Tereso C. Casiño   157

The Back to Jerusalem Movement: Mission Movement
of the Christian Community in Mainland China
    Kim-kwong Chan   172

The Holy Spirit and Mission Spirituality:
The Case of Yoido Full Gospel Church
    Younghoon Lee   193

Spirituality and Christian Mission: The Journey of Youngnak
Presbyterian Church, Seoul, Korea
    Chul-shin Lee   203

Grace Korean Church, California, USA: Mission from the Margins
with Little Notice (Of Course!)
    Wonsuk Ma   209

Conclusion: Spirituality as the Beating Heart of Mission
    Kenneth R. Ross and Wonsuk Ma   225

Bibliography   235

List of Contributors   247

FOREWORD
Lalsangkima Pachuau

Spirituality is either acknowledged or presumed to be at the centre of Christian faith. But it is not an easy topic. Because it relates to an experience of God in human life, spirituality can be deeply personal and vastly tradition-influenced. The term itself can evoke very different images and thoughts among Christians of different times, faith traditions, and cultural settings. What an African Christian woman in Ghana meant and what a Franciscan Priest in Canada has in mind by spirituality could be quite different.

Among the various facets of Christianity that modernity has challenged and subdued, Christian spirituality is a prominent one. The Cartesian rationalism and Baconian empiricism that came to define the Western Enlightenment movement left no room for something as mysterious and obscure as spirit and spirituality in its tradition. The Enlightenment tradition came to induce the Protestant Church deeply as it became the main carrier of modernity. As a result, the Western Protestant Church gradually lost its grip on the work of the Holy Spirit in its faith and became divested of a clear understanding and practice of spirituality. A well-known German theologian of the nineteenth century David Friedrich Strauss is probably right when he declared the doctrine of the Holy Spirit to be "the Achilles heel of Protestantism."[1] Had it not been for the rich Orthodox tradition of the East and some faithful Catholic and Anglican Christians who upheld the spiritual tradition, both the tradition and the concept of Christian spirituality could have suffered a much harsher modernist blow.

Among the Protestants, most historians have now acknowledged the contribution of the Pentecostal-Charismatic movement in stimulating Christian belief in, and practice of, spirituality. The movement reinforced thoughts on the doctrine of the Holy Spirit and enlivened discussions on Christian spirituality among Protestant families. Contrary to its understanding in a narrow denominational sense, we now understand the Pentecostal-Charismatic movement to be rich and diverse global phenomenon across denominational lines. Like some other religious movements in history, this spiritual movement began at the margin of the Christian Church. In fact, its marginality obscures knowledge of its history of origin. Some early historians of the movement narrowed its origin to the

---

[1] Quoted from George S. Hendry, *The Holy Spirit in Christian Theology* (Philadelphia: Westminster Press, 1956), 12.

Azusa Street revival (Los Angeles, California, USA) in 1906. These historians then surmised that most of the spiritual awakenings in different parts of the world had originated from there.

However, through recent heightening global interconnection of knowledge and new historical investigations, we learn of similar significant spiritual awakenings around the same time in different parts of the world. Dana Robert describes the remarkable spiritual awakening in different corners of the world in the first two decades of the twentieth century in a lively way as follows: "... news of spiritual awakenings also seemed to pour from every corner of the globe during the first decade of the twentieth century: from Wales in 1904; Los Angeles in 1906; Kedgaon, India, in 1906; Pyongyang, Korea, in 1907; Valparaiso, Chile, in 1909, and rolling revivals in in different parts of western Africa throughout the decades."[2] This list can easily be expanded with lesser-known awakenings such as the revivals in Wonsan, Korea, in 1903, Khasi Hills of Meghalaya, India, in 1905, and in Mizoram, India, from 1906. It is no wonder that Christianity in the non-Western world today is largely funneled through spiritual movements that came out of these awakenings. For lack of a better term, we have popularly called it Pentecostal-Charismatic movement.

The prophetically induced charismatic-driven nature of Christian spirituality in the global South and the global East is not limited to Pentecostal and independent Charismatic Churches. Be it the Anglicans or Baptists in Sub-Saharan Africa, or the Methodists or Presbyterians in Asia and Latin America, churches are gaining strength through charismatic spiritual movements. The boundaries between mission-founded churches and charismatic Christianity have been blurred in many parts of the world. Mission is strongly believed to be a spiritual matter and to be done through spiritual strengths and power. Similar phenomena are seen among some Catholic congregations, which profoundly enrich the movement. Global migrations in recent decades have also heightened the impact of the movement through further interactions.

The charismatic spirituality of Christians in the non-Western world adds to the richness of Christian spirituality. It does create tension with the morally conscious and rationally driven modern Western Christianity largely influenced by the Enlightenment. If Western Christians are often appalled by the lack of rationality in the spiritual experience of non-Westerners, it appears preposterous for many non-Western Christians not to believe in the existence of active and engaging spirits, among whom the Holy Spirit is supreme. A holistic spirituality created by this tension may provide the needed richness to world Christianity.

Right from the beginning of its discussion, the study project on Mission Spirituality of Edinburgh 2010 aspired to a holistic engagement with

---

[2] Dana L. Robert, *Christian Mission: How Christianity became a World Religion* (Chichester, West Sussex, UK: Wiley-Blackwell, 2009), 62.

spirituality in Christian mission. The motivation was first spurred by non-Western scholars who wish to engage with the spirituality of mission at the grass roots of world Christianity. As an academic engagement in the context of world Christianity, mission spirituality is a new frontier in missiology and is crucial for deeper understanding of mission and world Christianity. The project requires intellectuals with knowledge, empathy, and commitment to take on the strenuous task of relating the tensive forms of Christian spirituality. As exacting a project as it is, its outcome contained in this book is rich and formative for missional spirituality in world Christianity.

Lalsangkima Pachuau, Ph.D.
J. W. Beeson Professor of Christian Mission
Dean of Advanced Research Programs
Asbury Theological Seminary, Wilmore, KY, USA

INTRODUCTION:
THE SPIRITUAL DIMENSION OF MISSION

Wonsuk Ma and Kenneth R Ross

The Spirituality Study Track: Its Origins

The centenary of the Edinburgh 1910 World Missionary Conference proved to be a focal point for considering the meaning and direction of Christian mission in the twenty-first century. Far from being a nostalgic evocation of the heyday of the western missionary movement one hundred years earlier, it turned out to be an opportunity for an analysis and re-evaluation of contemporary missionary engagement which was unusual both in its width and in its depth. In 2004 Birger Nygaard made the prescient comment: "The unique potential of Edinburgh 2010 is bringing together a number of traditions that do not normally interact. The meeting of various traditions holds the potential of creating some new *perspectives* – and the possibility of creating/sustaining missionary *movements* for this century. For sure a number of paradigms have shifted since 1910. And I think many of us are struggling to find a sustainable foothold in this new century."[1] This potential was certainly fulfilled in Edinburgh 2010 which brought together probably the broadest representation of world Christianity ever to be assembled at one event. Every major stream of Christian witness from Eastern Orthodox to African Independent was represented both at the centenary conference and in the study process which prepared for it. It also achieved a remarkable depth of analysis which is being unpacked in the substantial series of volumes being published, like this one, in the Regnum Edinburgh Centenary Series.

If there was one moment of inspiration from which Edinburgh 2010 sprang, it was a planning meeting hosted by the Church of Scotland in Edinburgh in June 2005. At this stage there was no formal structure to support the preparations for the centenary but twenty mission leaders and scholars, from around the world and from across the denominational spectrum, came together to dream of what might be possible. Present in Edinburgh on this decisive occasion were: Kwame Bediako, Steve Bevans, Nico Botha, Ruth Bottoms, Frans Dokman, Rose Dowsett, Tormod Engelsviken, Kofi deGraft-Johnson, Michiko Kyoko Ete-Lima, Sebastian Kim, Moonjang Lee, Carlos Linera, Wonsuk Ma, Fergus MacDonald, Jacques Matthey, Nestor Miguez, Philomena Mwaura, Birger Nygaard, Lalsangkima Pachuau and Miguel Palomino.

---

[1] Birger Nygaard to Kenneth Ross, 7 December 2004.

Their task was inspired by one of the distinctive features of the Edinburgh 1910 World Missionary Conference: the eight Commissions which prepared substantial reports on the crucial mission issues of the day.[2] Could something similar be attempted in the run-up to the 2010 conference? This was the challenge faced by the 2005 planning meeting. Remarkably, in the short space of a three-day meeting they identified the themes which, with one subsequent addition, would run through the entire Edinburgh 2010 process. These themes proved to have the capacity to excite the imagination and attract the participation of mission scholars and practitioners from all over the world and from every ecclesiastical tradition. They provided the shape and content of the study process which informed the conference preparations, energised the gathering itself, shaped the Common Call issued by the conference and are now finding their full expression in the volumes which elaborate the thinking of Edinburgh 2010.

For these twenty people, who had never met together before, in the space of just three days to define the themes around which mission thinking and action revolve today seems little short of miraculous. Perhaps it is significant that their starting point as they came together was 'the emphasis that was placed, especially by contributors from the south, on undergirding the whole exercise with prayer. Given the fundamental reality that it is the Holy Spirit who is truly the agent of mission, there is need for the Edinburgh 1910 centenary to have a spiritual character if it is to play a part in Christian mission. All the discussions need to take place in the awareness that "the kingdom of God is not a matter of talk but of power" (1 Cor 4:20).'[3]

In offering an Introduction to a volume concerned with mission spirituality, it is perhaps important to recognise that its very inception occurred in a development which would be hard to explain without reference to the breath of the Holy Spirit on a meeting which consciously looked for God's guidance and inspiration.

The planning meeting worked in four 'cluster groups' each of which had a clutch of loosely related issues which has been raised in prior discussions and consultations. Each of the four were invited to identify the two salient topics to which a Commission or study track might be devoted. It was the fourth 'cluster group' which seized on 'mission spirituality' as a topic which stood out as carrying exceptional importance for mission in the twenty-first century and which therefore deserved to be the subject for the consideration of a dedicated study track. They defined the assignment in the following terms:

---

[2] For systematic analysis of the 1910 Commissions see David A Kerr and Kenneth R Ross (ed), *Edinburgh 2010: Mission Then and Now* (Oxford: Regnum, 2009).
[3] Kenneth R Ross, 'The Centenary of the Edinburgh 1910 World Missionary Conference, Planning Meeting 2-5 June 2005, Working Paper', May 2005, 2.

Mission Spirituality for the Kingdom of God

The Commission on Mission Spirituality will seek to articulate a motivation and dynamic for mission that is rooted in the kingdom of God. It will draw on the experience of Christians in the south and will seek to understand mission in relation to such concepts as new creation, spiritual gifts, renewal, reconstruction, identity, service and holism. It will explore the role of the Spirit and of the church as signs and portents of the goal of all endeavour in the glory of God.

Key issues and questions
1. What shape does Christian mission take when it has the kingdom of God as its ultimate horizon?
2. What is the proper place of the natural order in a mission spirituality?
3. Prophetic witness: challenging the 'principalities and powers' of human institutions with 'signs and wonders' and God-given spiritual authority.
4. Love of enemies; reconciliation through the power of the cross, and witness through self-emptying, humility, and sacrifice.
5. Can we form new relationships with Christians of all traditions, given our diverse understandings of mission; and with all human beings?
6. How can we be faithful to our Christian confession while being open, adventurous and discerning in encounter with representatives of other religions?[4]

Through discussions among stakeholders over the following year the title of the study track was slightly amended so that it would read: 'Mission Spirituality and Authentic Discipleship'. A further international consultation in 2006 laid the foundations for a General Council to be formed to take overall responsibility for the Edinburgh 2010 project. Much work was done in 2006-07 to launch the General Council and establish the Secretariat. With the organisational apparatus in place, the time was ripe for the study tracks to be launched.

Key Questions: What Motivates? What Sustains?

When the General Council of Edinburgh 2010 met in early 2008, the sponsoring bodies for each study theme were reported, often two or three institutions jointly hosting a theme. The Mission Spirituality theme, however, was still without any taker. Wonsuk Ma, of the Oxford Centre for Mission Studies, was present as he travelled there with his wife, Julie Ma, who served as a General Council member. Ma and Cathy Ross, of the Church Mission Society of Oxford, decided to jointly host the study

---

[4] Kenneth R Ross and Tony Maclean-Foreman, 'Towards 2010: Proposals for Commissions', June 2005, 6.

process and became co-convenors of the study process. In their subsequent meetings, a small study committee was formed drawing two additional members from two different organizations: Naomi Rose (CMS) and Thomas Harvey (OCMS). The four-member committee planned and managed the entire study process. Towards the conference, and ultimately towards the publication of a volume on the theme, the convenors divided their tasks: Ma would organize a consultation, and be responsible for the production of the book, while Ross would take leadership during the 2010 conference programmes.

As a late starter, the committee strongly felt that it should organize a consultation to bring initial presentations. The Youngnak Presbyterian Church of Seoul became the gracious host, while the committee identified almost a dozen presenters for the March 2009 Consultation. Rev Chul-shin Lee (Senior Pastor) and Rev Dr. Andrew Choong-hyup Hah (Mission Pastor) acted as the main hosts, while the well-organized missions committee of the church (Chair: Elder Jung-ho Lee) and its staff served the consultation beyond all expectation. The church, through the efforts of Elder Lee, organized a press session with Christian media where the programmes of Edinburgh 2010 were briefed. The presenters were intentionally selected to represent the voices that were not present in the 1910 conference. They ranged from Catholic and Orthodox to Pentecostal, and almost every church in between. Geographically, Asia, Africa and Eastern Europe received conspicuous attention. These studies now form the core cluster of this volume. As much as the studies bring diverse mission experiences from a variety of contexts, fellowship among the participants and the host church was equally rewarding. The church leadership also felt that their heavy investment in human and financial resources was richly rewarded by encouragement the consultation brought to the church towards their role in global mission.

The Edinburgh 2010 conference, held in June of that year, provided a wide forum for lively encounters with various Christian traditions from all four corners of the globe. Two parallel sessions were dedicated to this study theme and two sessions were divided into each of the pairs of the theme: mission spirituality (or 'what motivates you in mission') and authentic discipleship (or 'what sustains you in mission'). Although these two cannot be separated as if they are two independent realities, the short-hand version of the theme proved to be practically useful. The sessions brought two important dynamics to the study process. The first were voices from far beyond the Seoul gathering. Of course, presentations came from each presenter's unique spiritual and social context: a Romanian Orthodox on Bible and mission, subaltern voices and ecological perspectives; a Jamaican Protestant on theological transparency in the context of such challenging social contexts as poverty, terrorism, HIV/AIDS and exploitation of creation; a Tanzanian on economic justice; a New Zealand Anglican on the spirituality study of the World Council of Churches Commission on World

Introduction 5

Mission and Evangelism; a Bolivian Catholic on the Edinburgh 2010 research project in Bolivia; a Ghanaian charismatic on the West African regional Edinburgh 2010 conference; an American Methodist on the Christian revitalization project; and an Indian Orthodox on the meaningfulness of the Christian message in the Hindu context. The second contribution came from the lively group discussions, which by design, were meant to be the primary focus of the parallel sessions. They provided excellent contributions to the understanding of mission spirituality and discipleship, as illustrated below.

Several studies from the two regional Edinburgh conferences in Latin America and West Africa were fed into the formation of the volume. The Bolivian contributions were important as the Seoul consultation lacked any contribution from Latin America. They also strengthen the Catholic input. Originally prepared in Spanish, a Honduran Pentecostal offered her talent for translation, while a Spanish Catholic provided editorial help. The West African studies also brought another unique dimension to the study process. They are deliberately 'focused on the nature of African Christian spirituality... something that has been shaped by the encounters with indigenous or primal spirituality and other transnational church movements of the last century'.[5]

In early 2012, Kenneth Ross, of the Church of Scotland, replaced Cathy Ross whose new professional responsibilities forced her to reassess her involvement in the editorial process. Ken has been an 'Edinburgh insider' who initiated the Towards 2010 process in Scotland in 2001, long before Edinburgh 2010 was formally established as an international project. He had closely followed the Mission Spirituality study track from its inception and had provided a summary of its work in the study guide he wrote for the Edinburgh 2010 conference.[6]

Mission Spirituality: Its Significance Today

Growing interest in spirituality is unmistakable, but how to define spirituality has not been a simple matter. From the beginning, the study committee struggled to have a good grasp of the concept of mission spirituality. The members tried to make sense out of the guide questions, but concluded that they would need to take a journey of discovery. In fact, the committee concluded that the study process was meant to provide a space in various settings for this discovery. Therefore, from the very beginning, this would be a community walk. The committee, therefore, understood itself as a facilitating agent for various participants to discover

---

[5] Cathy Ross and Wonsuk Ma, 'Theme 9: Mission Spirituality and Authentic Discipleship', in Kirsteen Kim and Andrew Anderson (eds), *Edinburgh 2010: Mission Today and Tomorrow* (Oxford: Regnum, 2011), 188.
[6] Kenneth R Ross, *Edinburgh 2010: New Directions for Church in Mission* (Pasadena: William Carey International University Press, 2010), 29-38.

the meaning of mission spirituality and authentic discipleship. We expected that not only the meaning or meanings, but also various aspects or components of this, would surface through interactions, reflections and exchanges.

At the same time, as a starter, the convenors and the committee felt that there was a need for a short-hand version of the theme. The members concluded that mission spirituality and authentic discipleship would be a response to the following question: 'What motivates and sustains us in mission?' The biggest handicap of such an approach is reductionism, as if spirituality is only understood in visible expressions. As the study process discovered and is still discovering, Christian spirituality goes much deeper than anything that is externally discernible. Mission is a natural outcome or expression of the understanding of what it means to be Christian, be it individual or corporate. With this uncertain starter, the journey of discovery began and it took us to Seoul, Edinburgh and Oxford. But they are only meeting places: it was the wide spectrum of Christian traditions and incredibly varying social contexts that enriched everyone who was part of the process. The following quotations may illustrate this journey.

The Seoul consultation informed all the participants of the significance of mission spirituality:

> Christian spirituality is shaped not only through the understanding of a community, but also through its lively interaction with cultural and social context, and its response to human needs. Many studies agree that the main impetus for mission comes from the combination of the biblical call to serve others and the immediate needs presented by society, especially in the context of suffering. Worship, word, liturgy, and prayer are critical parts of Christian spiritual discipline which sustains mission, and they are practiced in a community context.[7]

Then a further reflection emerged towards the conference:

> So it could be said that mission spirituality is essentially Christian spirituality lived in and fuelled by awareness of the *missio Dei*, and that, mission spirituality results in tangible mission practice in the world. Yet... it is more than awareness that prompts global mission, which brings us to the key question for this study. At the heart of this study on mission spirituality and authentic discipleship is the desire to begin to answer the query: 'What motivates and sustains mission?' It was a question put to the diverse group of participants for this consultation and their answers, coupled with internal and external observations of mission past and present, should lead us to some helpful conclusions.[8]

The committee's report to the conference volume further elaborates that,

---

[7] Ma and Ross, 'Theme 9', 285-86.
[8] Wonsuk Ma and Cathy Ross, 'Theme Nine: Mission Spirituality and Authentic Discipleship', in Daryl Balia and Kirsteen Kim (eds), *Edinburgh 2010: Witnessing to Christ Today* (Oxford: Regnum, 2010), 223.

Mission spirituality involves discerning 'the spirits... in order to discover the movement of the Spirit of God in the world and join with it.[9] A mission spirituality...recognises that God is already working, has been working within all cultures, revealing Godself.'[10]

The same report raises several questions on authentic discipleship:

What should an authentic discipleship path look like? What sort of spirituality will it embrace? This will of course in some ways vary from culture to culture, and yet, we can glean some seeds of commonality. We have seen that discipleship should be holistic. Categories (sacred and secular, physical and spiritual, religious and ordinary) and compartmentalizing do not seem to work in the long term; they do not make for sustainable mission. To speak about spirituality is to speak about living a life oriented toward the fulfilment of God's purposes for all creation.[11]

Mission spirituality is shaped by listening to the scriptural call for mission and the work of the Spirit in the world, especially in the context of suffering. The Spirit guides us into the deep understanding and conviction of the Scripture, and also helps us to experience his work in the world. However, discernment becomes critical as there are many different spirits at work. The study process has suggested several discernment instruments, such as spirituality that is 'Christ-centered and biblically grounded' and also discipleship that 'calls us to be inclusive, yet authentic with each other'.[12]

This learning process experienced a climatic moment during the parallel sessions of the conference. The discussion groups were asked to produce one succinct description of mission spirituality and authentic discipleship.[13] A few samples are worth repeating:

Mission spirituality is experience of God, lived out as persons in communities through the empowerment of the Holy Spirit for witness and service, following Christ's way in the hope of reconciliation with the whole of creation.

Mission spirituality is the ongoing inspiration of the Holy Spirit that moves us to witness to the good news of God's love in Jesus Christ's life, suffering, death and resurrection with the aim to bring together God's family in a loving household, share a sense of God's call, live life in humility and fulfil God's will on earth.

Mission spirituality is responding to Jesus' sacrificial love for us empowered by the Holy Spirit, in joyful obedience in crossing boundaries to live attentively to others in a shared search for the fulfilment of God's purposes.

---

[9] Ma and Ross, 'Theme Nine', 223. The inner quotation is from Kirsteen Kim, 'Mission Spirituality', in *Religion in Geschichte und Gegenward* (4th ed, Tübingen: Mohr Siebeck, 2007).
[10] Ma and Ross, 'Theme Nine', 241.
[11] Ma and Ross, 'Theme Nine', 241.
[12] Ma and Ross, 'Theme Nine', 241.
[13] Ma and Ross, 'Theme 9', 184.

At the end of the sessions, a statement on the theme was adopted:

> Remembering Jesus' way of witness and service, we believe we are called by God to follow it joyfully, inspired, anointed and empowered by the Holy Spirit, nurtured by Christian disciplines in community, to bring God's transforming and reconciling love to the whole creation.[14]

And this was later modified to become the ninth point of the historic Common Call:

> 9. Remembering Jesus' way of witness and service, we believe we are called by God to follow this way joyfully, inspired, anointed, sent and empowered by the Holy Spirit, and nurtured by Christian disciplines in community. As we look to Christ's coming in glory and judgment, we experience his presence with us in the Holy Spirit, and we invite all to join with us as we participate in God's transforming and reconciling mission of love to the whole creation.[15]

While the study process took its own journey of discovery, the report of the listening group during the centenary conference also provided its own observation of the process, and captured the essential elements of mission spirituality discussed throughout thematic sessions.

> We realise that there cannot be one prescribed discipline for a missional spirituality. Our spirituality has also to be context-sensitive. Although critical analysis and reflection are always needed, we still learn and share the riches of our diverse spiritual traditions and practices.... But neither Christian spirituality in general nor mission spirituality in particular are solitary enterprises: they have to do with a spiritual life lived in community, rooted in common worship and sustained by the prayer and encouragement from our local Christian communities. Transformations that we are privileged to see in the lives of others grow out of the same source of sustenance. Today we are discovering anew the significance of spiritual direction or companionship: two persons walking and talking together in the presence of God, seeking his will and direction for their lives....

Rene Padilla is quoted in the conference book:

> 'Contemplation without action is an escape from concrete reality; action without contemplation is activism lacking a transcendent meaning'. Both contemplation and action take place in our various contexts. In Africa this implies addressing issues like the HIV and AIDS, and responding to conflict with biblical peacemaking principles, and in many regions it expresses itself in a concern for the environment. Discipleship and the call to discipleship are the gifts of grace from God, and from God alone, and mission spirituality recognises that God is already at work, and that we may join in on what he is doing. Mission spirituality has to do with living.[16]

Perhaps the most far-reaching conclusion of this study process is that spirituality is not an additional dimension of mission to be considered when

---

[14] Ma and Ross, 'Theme 9', 185.
[15] 'Edinburgh 2010 Common Call', in Kim and Anderson, *Edinburgh 2010*, 2.
[16] 'Listening Group Report', in Kim and Anderson, *Edinburgh 2010*, 319.

all the doctrinal and practical apparatus is already in place. Rather, the spiritual dimension is the first thing around which everything else ought to revolve. Since God is the primary agent of mission and God works through the power of the Holy Spirit, it is through openness to the Spirit that mission takes effect in human life. More than was expected when the study track began, it has led to the claim being made, through the essays assembled in this volume, that it is through awareness of the work of the Holy Spirit that Christian mission finds its true character and has its authentic impact.

From this perspective much of the western missionary movement appears to have had an excessively cerebral understanding of faith and an inflated confidence in its own ability to manage its work. Principally through the influence of movements of Christian faith in the global south, new attention to the spiritual dimension is stamping the character of mission in our time. This generates mobile, flexible, adaptable and convincing expressions of faith which carry the good news to the heart of communities in every part of the world. This volume cannot claim to be comprehensive in demonstrating the many ways in which such an understanding of mission is taking effect but it does offer a broad representative sample.

The book should be read not so much as the progressive elaboration of a logical argument but more as a kaleidoscope where each chapter sheds light on a particular form of mission spirituality so that, by the time the reader reaches the end, a comprehensive global picture has come into view. It follows a broadly geographical arrangement with chapters first on Africa and then on Asia being followed by those concerned with Latin America, Europe and the Middle East. Some chapters offer academic analysis from a critical angle while others bring the immediacy of the practitioner perspective. Others again achieve a creative blend of the two. A brief concluding chapter draws out the salient points which have been made but the topic is such that we cannot claim to have arrived at a final conclusion. In fact, what we have gleaned through the process so far is the 'early fruit'. The essays collected in this book are meant to introduce the richness of mission spirituality and authentic discipleship in such a way as to whet the appetite. This volume is only a beginning. Fasten your shoe strings: you are about to embark on an exciting journey!

'THE PROMISE IS FOR YOU AND YOUR CHILDREN': PENTECOSTAL SPIRITUALITY, MISSION AND DISCIPLESHIP IN AFRCIA

J Kwabena Asamoah-Gyadu

This chapter aims to illustrate the importance of religious experience to mission and discipleship focusing on Pentecostalism in contemporary Africa. There are different streams of Pentecostalism but they share certain common phenomenological and theological characteristics. Based on those shared 'family resemblances', I understand Pentecostalism and its historically younger progenies, that is, the various charismatic movements as consisting of:

> Christian groups which emphasise salvation in Christ as a transformative experience wrought by the Holy Spirit and in which pneumatic phenomena including 'speaking in tongues', prophecies, visions, healing and miracles in general, perceived as standing in historic continuity with the experiences of the early church as found especially in the Acts of the Apostles, are sought, accepted, valued, and consciously encouraged among members as signifying the presence of God and experiences of his Spirit.[1]

To whichever category they belong, current studies generally acknowledge the Pentecostal/charismatic movement to be the fastest growing stream of global Christianity. Thus Harvey Cox writes that the growth of Pentecostalism worldwide 'holds within it a host of significant clues to the meaning of the general global spiritual resurgence we are now witnessing.'[2] What defines Pentecostalism is the experience of the Holy Spirit in transformation, radical discipleship and manifestations of acts of power that demonstrate the presence of the kingdom of God among his people. To that end, the Pentecostal movement deserves credit for its reminder to the traditional churches that the non-rational dimensions of religion, in this case the experiences of the Spirit, are important in Christian faith, life and witness. The movement has taught us that the experience of the Spirit as a non-negotiable element in Christian mission and discipleship

---

[1] J. Kwabena Asamoah-Gyadu, *African Charismatics: Current Developments within within Independent Indigenous Pentecostalism in Ghana* (Leiden: EJ Brill, 2005), 12.

[2] Harvey Cox, 'Foreword' in Allan H Anderson and Walter J Hollenweger (ed), *Pentecostals After a Century: Global Perspectives on a Movement in Transition* (Sheffield: Academic Press, 1999), 8.

'is ignored to our common peril and impoverishment' as a world church desiring authentic spirituality in discipleship and mission.[3]

Experience of the Holy Spirit

The basic argument of this chapter is that the reasons accounting for the phenomenal success of global Pentecostalism may be located in its emphasis on the experience of the Holy Spirit and the pursuit of a mission agenda that takes seriously the authority of Scripture, active witnessing, discipleship, and the mediation of the Word of God in powerful, tangible and demonstrable ways. This is what defines the character, spirituality and mission of the church. Christine Leonard's book, *A Giant in Ghana* is a mission history of 'The Church of Pentecost' (CoP) in Ghana and it underscores the presence of these points in the ministry of that African Pentecostal denomination. She for instance makes the following observation on the reasons for the growth and success of the CoP:

> The main reason the church has grown is that its people love Jesus – they have been set on fire for him. It shows in their worship and in their lives. The church has never allowed compromise – they treat sin and reversion to cultic religious practices as seriously as each one takes his responsibility to Jesus Christ and the church.[4]

This means Christian discipleship cannot be divorced from an affirmation of the Lordship of Christ and a life of holiness. Additionally the emphasis on the power of the Spirit means that Pentecostalism functions as a movement that provides ritual contexts within which ordinary people may experience God's presence and power in very forceful ways.

Religious Experience

It is noteworthy that Pentecostals point to Scripture, particularly Pauline thought, as the primary source of authority in matters of faith. Anytime St Paul uses the expression 'spiritual', it refers to the workings of the Holy Spirit. Thus the critical phenomena in the discussion on Pentecostalism and spirituality, as far as the Holy Spirit is concerned, are 'experience', 'manifestation' and 'ministry'. In Pentecostal discourse and practice the Holy Spirit, in keeping with biblical promises is expected to be experienced first, as present day reality. Second, he manifests himself in acts of power and transformation and third, the Holy Spirit empowers the believer and the

---

[3] James DG Dunn, 'A Protestant response to Juan Sepúlveda, "Born Again: Baptism Baptism and the Spirit"', in Jürgen Moltmann and Karl-Josef Kushel (eds), *Pentecostal Movements as an Ecumenical Challenge: Concilium*, 3 (1996), 110.

[4] Christine Leonard, *A Giant in Ghana: 3,000 Churches in 50 Years. The Story of James McKeown and the Church of Pentecost* (Chichester, England: New Wine Press, 1989).

church to serve God's purposes in the world. This is where the movement differs from historic mission Christianity with its overly cerebral, staid, and silent approach to Christian piety. At the turn of the twentieth century, for example, Rudolf Otto lamented how the marginalisation of the non-rational aspect of religion by 'orthodoxy' or institutionalised Christianity had resulted in the 'idea of the Holy' being apprehended only in one-sidedly intellectualistic terms:

> So far from keeping the non-rational element in religion alive in the heart of the religious experience, orthodox Christianity manifestly failed to recognise its value, and by this failure gave to the idea of God a one-sidedly intellectualistic and rationalistic interpretation.[5]

In the preface to the first edition of *Ecstatic Religion,* IM Lewis also submitted that 'belief, ritual, spiritual experience are the cornerstones of religion' and that the greatest of these is 'spiritual experience'.[6] In my thinking, personal experience of the subject of theology, God, is a pre-requisite to viable God-talk and ministry that seeks to bring others to serve and worship this God. Pentecostalism, as a stream of Christianity as my definition shows, is identified by its emphases on the experience and manifestations of the Holy Spirit in acts of power. Mindful of the dynamic nature of Pentecostal spirituality, Allan H Anderson has captured the phenomenal impact that independent indigenous Pentecostal movements have had on Christianity in Africa in terms of an 'African Reformation'.[7]

In spite of achievements in education and medical missions, missionary work in Africa has been criticised for its inability to present a holistic gospel in Africa, a concern that the Ghanaian feminist theologian, Mercy Amba Oduyoye captures in the following observation:

> Needs were stimulated in light of the European lifestyle. They were not the needs of the people of Africa. Thus the structures created to meet these needs were European, and Africans were ill at ease with them. Why the schools and the hospitals? These institutions were more in line with the work of salvation among Europeans than among Africans. But it seemed that being literate was one of the marks of being Christian. In terms of development, a government hospital or school could have achieved and often did achieve the same aims as the Christian hospital or school.[8]

For those who have followed developments within African Christianity, one of the major setbacks of the missionary approach of the traditional churches was the way they marginalized and underemphasized pneumatic phenomena. Africans reacted against the over-cerebral and rationalistic

---

[5] Rudolf Otto, *The Idea of the Holy* (Oxford: University Press, 1923), 3.
[6] IM Lewis, *Ecstatic Religion: A Study of Shamanism and Spirit Possession* (2nd ed, ed, London: Routledge, 1989).
[7] Allan H. Anderson, *African Reformation: African Initiated Christianity in the Twentieth Century* (Trenton, NJ: Africa World Press, 2001).
[8] Mercy Amba Oduyoye, *Hearing and Knowing: Theological Reflections on Christianity in Africa* (Maryknoll, NY: Orbis Books, 1986), 42.

nature of western forms of being Christian. This inability of western Christianity to integrate charismatic experiences, particularly healing and prophecy into worship in Africa, led in time to the rise of a plethora of independent indigenous church movements under various local charismatic figures. William Wade Harries of Liberia also known as the 'Black Elijah of West Africa', Isaiah Shembe of South Africa, Simon Kimbangu of the Democratic Republic of Congo and Garrick Sokari Braide of the Niger Delta, also known as Elijah II, are some of the leading names.

Pentecostalism and the Primal Imagination

In the African context, what is primarily real is the spiritual and as Kwame Bediako argues:

> Primal religions generally conceive of religion as a system of power and of living religiously as being in touch with the source of and channels of power in the universe; Christian theology in the west seems, on the whole to understand the Christian gospel as a system of ideas.[9]

Thus Pentecostal spirituality has found fertile soil in the African religious imagination partly because like primal religiosity, Pentecostalism is a religion that advocates immediate experiences of the supernatural and an interventionist theology. In Africa, religion is a survival strategy and so prayer and ritual often aim at achieving such practical ends as health, fertility, rain, protection, or relational harmony. Much of such experiential spirituality does not only cohere with biblical patterns, but also strikes a response cord with the primal religious orientation of traditional African societies like that of Ghana. Walter Hollenweger is a strong advocate of the view that Pentecostalism is doing well in Africa because its spirituality resonates with primal piety. That may be so, but as a movement dedicated to Christian mission, I argue that the single most important reason for Pentecostal/charismatic renewal in Africa is that the Holy Spirit, the chief agent of mission and renewal, has chosen to do something new on the continent. JV Taylor explains:

> In Africa today it seems that the incalculable Spirit has chosen to use the Independent Church Movement for another spectacular advance. This does not prove that their teaching is necessarily true, but it shows they have the raw materials out of which a missionary church is made – spontaneity, total commitment, and the primitive responses that arise from the depths of life.[10]

Experiences of spiritual renewal that generate 'spontaneity and total commitment' raise questions regarding ecclesiastical, liturgical and theological traditions that have failed to deliver those experiences for many

---

[9] Kwame Bediako, *Christianity in Africa: The Renewal of a Non-Western Religion* (Edinburgh: Edinburgh University Press; Maryknoll, NY: Orbis Books, 1995), 106.
[10] John V Taylor, *The Go-Between God: The Holy Spirit and the Christian Mission* (London: SCM, 1972), 54.

African Christians. Serious questions have been asked concerning the theology and *modus operandi* of some of the many indigenous Pentecostal movements in Africa that attracted masses of spiritually hungry and disenchanted people from the traditional mainline denominations. In sub-Saharan Africa, the excessive deployment of prophylactic substances as extensions of faith for healing by the older independent churches and the articulation of the gospel of Jesus Christ almost entirely in terms of promotion, success, health and wealth by new charismatic waves tend to make their spiritualities appear somewhat myopic. In spite of such deficiencies, there is no gainsaying the fact that the overall impact of Pentecostalism on Christianity in Africa has been positive.

The Church of Pentecost

Within our lifetime, indigenous classical Pentecostal denominations including William F Kumuyi's Deeper Christian Life Church, Enoch A Adeboye's Redeemed Church of God and the Church of Pentecost, established as a collaborative mission enterprise between Peter Anim of Ghana and James McKeown of the UK, have all developed into major Christian denominations with branches in Africa and beyond. In the rest of this article, we will see how the Church of Pentecost (CoP) in particular continues to have such a great impact on African Christianity because of its keen emphasis on the experience of the Holy Spirit and the outflow of the relationship that Christians develop with him. As an African classical Pentecostal church with a transnational ministry, the CoP holds tenaciously to the doctrine of initial evidence, which advocates that after new birth there must follow the subsequent experience of 'Baptism in the Holy Spirit'. This subsequent experience, it is taught, must lead to the speaking of tongues or glossolalia. The 'doctrine of subsequence' or the doctrine of 'initial evidence' flows from the conviction that when the Holy Spirit baptised the disciples at Pentecost, they spoke in new tongues (Acts 2).

In keeping with its classical Pentecostal orientation, the CoP holds that:

> All believers in Jesus Christ are entitled to receive, and should earnestly seek the Baptism of the Holy Ghost and fire according to the command of our Lord. This is the normal experience of the early church. With this experience comes power to preach and bestowment of the gifts of the Spirit. The believer is filled with the Holy Spirit; there is a physical sign of 'speaking in other tongues' as the Spirit of God gives utterance. This is accompanied by a burning desire and supernatural power to witness to others about God's salvation and power.[11]

---

[11] Emmanuel Kingsley Larbi, *Pentecostalism: The Eddies of Ghanaian Christianity* (Accra: Center for Pentecostal and Charismatic Studies, 2001), 278.

Pentecostalism, wherever it has appeared, tends to emphasise the need to exercise strong faith in God in the face of adversity, a belief that is born out of its experience of the felt presence of God.

Robert and William Menzies, in their remarkable work *Spirit and Power*, list 'strong faith' as an important feature of Pentecostal spirituality: 'Overwhelmed by the sense of God's immediate presence among them, Pentecostals were quick to believe in the fact of divine intervention in the affairs of this life. They prayed for the sick, expecting God to deliver the afflicted from suffering.'[12] Charles F Parham, whose Bethel Bible College in Topeka, Kansas, is cited as one of the cradles of the modern Pentecostal movement at the dawn of the twentieth century also held a 'strict and life-long opposition to medicine and vaccination.'[13] In keeping with its faith-healing philosophy, Apostle Peter Anim believed that Christians should look only to Jesus for healing; or they risked perishing in hell fire.[14] Anim's group therefore felt let down when James McKeown, a Pentecostal missionary they had invited from the UK who was expected to exercise stronger faith, sought hospital treatment during a severe bout of malaria.[15]

Experience and Discipleship

Taylor defines Christian mission to mean recognizing 'what the Creator-Redeemer is doing in his world and doing it with him.'[16] Whether it is used with reference to the church as the 'body of Christ' or to the individual Christian, mission begins with an experiential encounter with God. At the beginning of this century, those interested in the demographics of Christian mission in Africa were astounded that the CoP has grown to become the single largest denomination in Ghana after the Catholic Church. Its most distinctive characteristic is the emphasis of experience as a mark of genuiune discipleship. So from its origins, Pentecostal Christianity understood its experience, particularly the experience of the baptism of the Holy Spirit, as an empowerment for mission. Growth through 'conversion' has been identified as the most sustainable kind of church growth.[17] To that

---

[12] William W Menzies and Robert P Menzies, *Spirit and Power: Foundations of Pentecostal Experience* (Grand Rapids: Zondervan, 2000), 23.

[13] Walter J. Hollenweger, *Pentecostalism: Origins and Developments Worldwide* (Peabody: Hendrickson Publishers, 1997), 21.

[14] Leonard, *A Giant in Ghana*, 23.

[15] For briefs on this incident as narrated by Apostle Anim, see Robert W Wyllie, 'Pioneers of Ghanaian Pentecostalism: Peter Anim and James McKeown', *Journal of Religion in Africa* 6:2 (1974), 114-115; Leonard, *A Giant in Ghana*, 23.

[16] This is a slight modification of a definition by John V. Taylor who writes that 'mission ... means to recognise what the Creator-Redeemer is doing and try to do it with him.' See Taylor, *The Go-Between God*, 37.

[17] Richard Foli, *Church Growth in Ghana* (Accra: Methodist Book Depot, 2001), 11.

end, one of the most unique characteristics of the CoP has been its emphasis on personal experience in the process of incorporation into church membership. This is a heritage that has enabled the CoP to maintain its missionary focus and discipleship agenda. This focus on the fundamentals of mission and discipleship has helped the CoP to avoid the clericalism and nominal spirituality associated with the Christianity of the older mission denominations.

Nominal Christianity

'In much of Africa', Maia Green observes of the Christianity of the older churches, 'the widespread adoption of Christian religious affiliation was a direct consequence of mission over-schooling. ... Often, Christian religious affiliation as an aspect of a person's identity is explicitly concerned with the presentation of an exterior state, not an internal one.'[18] So among the Pogoro people of Southern Tanzania, Green notes that conversion to Christianity was not the result of the aggregate choices of individuals attracted by the "message" of Christianity, but a direct consequence of colonial education policy.[19] As with the situation of the Pogoro Catholics, in which baptism became the first stage of becoming 'officially' Christian, many have been baptised in Ghanaian churches without knowing what it actually means to be a Christian. Parents scarcely know the significance of baptism and thus are hardly able to give their children any education in accordance with it. Confirmation has all but lost its value as a means of personally affirming a faith that was affirmed on one's behalf as an infant in baptism. For many candidates the confirmation rite only replaced the puberty rite frowned upon as backward by the urban folk and those with some education. Not only do those who feel that they could get on in life without necessarily passing through the portals of the church stay away from it, but also a lot of those who affiliated with the church became nominal Christians.

The processes of joining the ordained ministry of the traditional churches do nothing to help the high rate of nominal Christianity associated with the historic mission churches. The standards, unlike that of a typical Pentecostal church, are mainly academic. There are numbers who seek ordination as an indirect means of pursuing academic and professional careers in ministry rather than vocations in which they serve in a ministry meant to proclaim salvation in Christ and make disciples of all nations. As corrective measures to these developments, the CoP for example, does not consider lack of formal education as a hindrance to ordination because it is

---

[18] Maia Green, 'Why Christianity is the "Religion of Business": Perceptions of the Church among Pogoro Catholics in Southern Tanzania', *Journal of Religion in Africa* 25:1 (1995), 26.
[19] Green, 'Pogoro Catholics', 29.

believed that where the Holy Spirit is at work, he is the Great Teacher who can teach and even use illiterates once they have come to a personal knowledge of Christ and received the baptism of the Spirit. In its ministry in Ghana and abroad, the CoP has not relied on theologically sophisticated clergy and lay leaders. Pastors are very often simple ordinary Christians who having received a calling into ministry, have mostly been trained on the job. The CoP considers theological knowledge important, but over the years this has not been allowed to determine the choice of people for ministry.

It is revealing that, in the missionary enterprise of the Lord Jesus Christ, those he used were at some point referred to as 'unschooled ordinary men' whose only credential for mission was the fact that 'they had been with Jesus'. In short, they were perceived to have personally encountered and experienced the Lord of mission, Jesus the Christ. James McKeown, the missionary figure behind the formation of the CoP cites 'waiting on God', and not education, as the means of growth for the church: 'if we follow education, we will get what education gives.... We have to seek the Lord and wait on him – this is the secret of the church's success and expansion.'[20] All this is to make the point that pneumatic experience is not everything as far as Christian spirituality is concerned. But clericalism that sacrifices vital religious experience as fundamental to discipleship for ecclesiastical authority and theological propriety is one of the main impediments to such discipleship, mission and renewal in the body of Christ.

Experience and Spirituality

Thus to understand Pentecostal spirituality, experience may be considered critical. Writing about the Pentecostal contribution to the mission of the church in Latin America, Juan Sepúlveda names two common recognisable features of this type of Christianity that are useful for our purposes:

1. To become Pentecostal almost always invariably involved a conflict between a religiosity centred on the 'objectivity of dogma', in which faith consists of formal, conscious and rational acceptance of determined beliefs or doctrines, and a religiosity which gives primacy to the subjective experience of God, in which faith is a response to a kind of possession of one's being by the divine.
2. To become Pentecostal almost always represents a conflict between a religion mediated by specialists of the cultured classes... and a religion in which the poor, simple people have direct access to God

---

[20] Leonard, *A Giant in Ghana*, 45-46.

in which the relationship can be communicated in the language of feeling and the indigenous culture.[21]

Gerlach and Hine also identify the high degree of *commitment* that religious experience engenders as a crucial factor that accounts for the growth of Pentecostalism. Pentecostals themselves verbalise one of the rewards of the Baptism of the Holy Spirit experience as the power to witness effectively. So in the CoP, the most obvious reason for growth, according to Christine Leonard, 'is that their top priority has always been evangelism... every member counts sharing their faith as their own responsibility – not just the leaders.'[22] Personal conversion and Spirit Baptism, Gerlach and Hine submit, are 'bridge-burning' and 'power-generating' acts that constitute for Pentecostals 'a highly motivating religious experience' which generates or sustains religious commitment.[23] On the relationship between religious experience and participation, the two authors conclude as follows:

> Effective participation in a movement involves just such an act that sets the believer apart in some way from the larger social context, cuts him off from past associations, identifies him with other participants in the movement, and provides high motivation for changed behaviour.'[24]

The other important aspect of Pentecostal spirituality is its reliance on oral theology. Music is one oral theological form through which Pentecostals verbalize their experiences. It is an essential ingredient of Pentecostal worship and in the CoP, members have composed local choruses out of their own experiences of the Spirit that are easy to memorise and sing. In several of these choruses the Holy Spirit, as Apostle Michael Ntumy of the CoP points out, is referred to as *Onyame Sunsum* (Spirit of God) and *Sunsum Kronkron* (Holy Spirit). As in biblical imagery, He is also 'fire', 'wind', and in one chorus *Adom Nsu* (Water of Grace) that restores life to dry deserts and parched land resulting from drought. The testimonies of life-changing encounters with God that participants are prepared to share, accounts in large measure for the success of Pentecostalism in Christian mission. Cox recounts his experience with Pentecostals even as a researcher:

> I rarely had any trouble getting Pentecostals to tell me about their faith. They talk about it at the slightest provocation.... Part of what made my work so

---

[21] Juan Sepúlveda, 'Reflections on the Pentecostal Contribution to the Mission of the Church in Latin America', *Journal of Pentecostal Theology* 1 (1992), 95.
[22] Leonard, *A Giant in Ghana*, 7.
[23] Luther P Gerlach and Virginia H Hine, 'Five Factors Crucial to the Growth and Spread of a Modern Religious Movement', *Journal for the Scientific Study of Religion*, 7:1 (1968), 32.
[24] Gerlach and Hine, 'Growth of Pentecostalism', 32.

easy and enjoyable is that Pentecostals tend to be very happy about their faith and they want you to share that happiness.[25]

Taylor also makes this profound observation on the importance of the global Pentecostal resurgence for mission:

> Anyone who has a concern for the church to the six continents must come to terms with the fact that the vast majority of mankind is not going to find God through such a cerebral religion as the Christianity it has so far encountered. That is what the revival movements, the Zionist sects, the whole Pentecostal third section of the world-wide church, are saying to us.[26]

The CoP has very rigorous evangelistic programmes in both urban and rural Ghana. The CoP Witness Movement, the Pentecost Students' Association (PENSA) and the Women's Fellowship are all evangelistic groups that target specific constituencies for mission. Spiritual warfare, a ministry that is very much cherished in African Christianity as a result of the spiritually precarious world in which people live, is part of the missionary method of the CoP. As Andrew F Walls argues, the church as a movement of the kingdom calls people to repentance and to alertness to the presence of Christ within. But the presence of the church, the first test of Christian expansion, does not itself guarantee 'the continuing influence of Christ.' To guarantee the continuing influence of Christ through the church, Walls points out, 'the signs of the kingdom' must also be present through the ministry of the church. These 'signs of the kingdom', as evidenced through the ministry of Jesus, include the triumph of God over principalities, powers and demonic influences.[27] That the power of Christ is effective to heal and deliver is one of the greatest lessons that Pentecostal Christianity teaches the church of Christ today in its attempt at continuing his mission and discipleship in the world.

Community and Discipleship

One of the hallmarks of the life of the early church, as chronicled in the Acts of Apostles and the epistles of St. Paul, was the strong sense of community that bound the members on account of their common experience of the Spirit. In many places, Paul speaks of the various Christian communities in terms of a single family. So the Thessalonians for example, are addressed as 'brothers beloved by God' and mention is made of the 'joy of the Holy Spirit' associated with their conversion (1 Thess 1:4, 6). In an insightful study on the formation of the *ekklēsia*, Wayne Meeks

---

[25] Harvey Cox, *Fire From Heaven: The Rise of Pentecostal Spirituality and the Reshaping of Religion in the Twenty-First Century* (Reading, Massachusetts: Addison-Wesley Publishing Company, 1995), xvii.
[26] Taylor, *Go-Between God*, 221.
[27] Andrew F Walls, *The Cross-Cultural Process in Christian History* (Maryknoll, NY: Orbis Books, 2002), 15.

also shows how the spirit of hospitality including care for the poor and needy was among the virtues that characterised the lives of the early churches as stressed in the traditional admonitions of Paul in some of his letters (cf. Rom 12:13).[28] Such communal bonds have also been known to be one of the most stabilizing factors in African traditional societies as Kwesi Dickson indicates:

> It is a commonplace that the sense of community is strong in Africa. A society is in equilibrium when its customs are maintained, its goals attained and the spirit powers given regular and adequate recognition. Members of society are expected to live and act in such a way as to promote society's well-being; to do otherwise is to court disaster, not only for the actor but also for society as a whole.[29]

Spirituality and a sense of community move together in African religiosity. Thus it is noteworthy that, as an African church, one of the reasons for the massive presence of the CoP across the length and breadth of Ghana and beyond is its community-based methods of church planting and discipleship. The church encourages people to fellowship in their communities and this is a far cry from the situation where certain historic mission church congregations have acquired an elitist character because it is the place for the learned theologian to serve as pastor to the rich, powerful and famous. The CoP community-based approach to church planting not only makes assemblies within the same geographical area accessible to people, but also fosters stronger communal bonds as members are likely to be staying shorter distances from each other. Community-oriented congregations engender meaningful fellowship, discipleship and prompt pastoral care. The Greek word that describes the 'fellowship' or 'communion' that characterised the life of the early church is *koinonia*. This fellowship, which came into being at Pentecost, was more than the deepening of human intercourse. It was the expression of vertical-horizontal relationships that combined sharing with others what one shared with Christ. In other words, the new fellowship gave practical expression to the belief that to experience Christ is to belong to him as a disciple and to belong to Christ is to share his love in communion with others.

Liturgy and Vernacularization

The CoP has a very simple outlook and this is partly evident through its very informal liturgy and vernacularization policy that creates the space and atmosphere for the Spirit to operate during worship. Corporate worship provides the highpoint for the experience of the Spirit through his

---

[28] Wayne A Meeks, *The First Urban Christians: The Social World of the Apostle Paul* (New Haven and London: Yale University Press, 1983), chapter 3.
[29] Kwesi A Dickson, *Theology in Africa* (London: DLT; Maryknoll, NY: Orbis Books, 1984), 62.

manifestations in tongues, prophecies, visions and the expressions of emotional sensibilities. Informality creates the atmosphere for this to happen. The move away from written and stereotyped liturgical formulae ensures that Pentecostal worship is characterised by spontaneity and expectancy, for during worship, God through his Spirit is expected to come and 'inhabit the praises of his people.' Pentecostals are thus able to make room for participatory worship in which people are able to worship God in languages that come naturally to them. The last segment of worship is dedicated to the sermon, the offerings and then an altar call. In Africa the use of the vernacular for prayer, singing, preaching and reading of the Scriptures in particular allows indigenous Pentecostal assemblies to function in contexts with low levels of literacy.

Holiness Ethic

There is a definite relationship between personal experiences of the Spirit and commitment to the cause of Christ and his mission through the church. Such commitment arises out of a sense of belonging that develops within the individual as a result of that intense encounter with the Holy Spirit. Heribert Mühlen compares the relationship that emerges between the Christian and God after an experience of the Spirit to the love between married people. In bodily intercourse, married people offer to one another, not only something such as a physical gift, 'but themselves, their whole persons.'[30] This act of self-giving was initiated by Christ because he loved the church and gave himself for her.

The comparison of the relationship between the Christian and the Spirit to self-giving love, as in marital intercourse, is not unfamiliar to the African context. Among both the Yoruba and Akan peoples for example, spirit possession uses the idiom of sexual intercourse.[31] Here the traditional priest, whether male or female, is quintessentially the 'wife' of the deity possessing him or her. The Akan expression *sunsum afa no*, used to describe spirit possession, literally means a spirit has taken over the executive faculties of the candidate for priesthood. The critical word here is *fa*, 'to take'. This is the same expression that is used for sexual intercourse, particularly when it takes place without the full consent of the woman. In other words, *afa no* (has taken) is used when a woman's privacy has been invaded without consent. What takes place when the Spirit of God takes hold of a person could to a limited extent be explained in terms of the invasion of one's privacy. The candidate, as with the making of prophets in the Christian context, is conscripted for service in a way that involves an

---

[30] Heribert Mühlen, *A Charismatic Theology: Initiation in the Spirit* (London: Burns and Oats, 1978), 119.
[31] JDY Peel, 'The Pastor and the *Babalawo*: The Interaction of Religions in Nineteenth-Century Yorubaland', *Africa* 60:3 (1990), 344.

intense emotional commitment demanding that a person's whole being is yielded to God.

Spirit and Morality

In both the African and Pentecostal Christian contexts the experience of the Spirit is associated with holiness. In the minds of the generality of African Christians, the mainline churches are thought to be too permissive in their ethical standards, but not the church under study here, the CoP. According to the constitution of the CoP, the following deviations attract sanctions: going to questionable places (such as visiting shrines as some Christians do to supplement their faith), falling into such sins as adultery, fornication and alcoholism. Divorce, embracing false doctrines, or not keeping the Lord's Day holy, may all attract sanctions from church authority. The disciplinary sanctions include suspension from full membership for ordinary members, demotion (with or without suspension) for those in leadership, and outright dismissal for pastors. A member on suspension may attend church services but is not allowed to preach or give testimony in church. He or she is also not allowed to join the congregation in 'open-floor' dancing and when in church must sit at the back. Suspended members do not receive Holy Communion.

The seriousness of CoP, as far as Christian morality is concerned, elicits a very high level of membership commitment evident in the intensity of participation in church life. Rodney Stark proposes that in order to grow, religious movements among other things must offer a religious culture that sets them apart from the general secular culture. This means, according to Stark, that movements must be distinctive and impose strict moral standards.[32] Stark uses 'strictness' in reference to the degree to which a religious group maintains 'a separate and distinctive life style or morality in personal and family life, in such areas as dress, diet, drinking, entertainment, uses of time, sex, child rearing and the like.'[33] In Christian terms, drinking and other such indulgences may be interpreted as being worldly, and this is in the light of Paul's counsel to Christians to avoid conformity 'to the pattern of this world' (Rom 12:2). According to Stark such strictness makes religious groups strong by screening out those he refers to as 'free-riders'. Free-riders are those who may want to share in the benefits of the movement without 'contributing' to the collective enterprise. When free-riders are excluded, the average level of commitment increases, and this in turn greatly increases the credibility of the religious culture as well as generating a high degree of resource mobilisation.[34]

---

[32] Rodney Stark, 'Why New Religious Movements Succeed or Fail: A Revised General Model', *Journal of Contemporary Religion* 11:2 (1996), 137.
[33] Stark, 'Why New Religious Movements Succeed or Fail', 137.
[34] Stark, 'Why New Religious Movements Succeed or Fail', 137.

The Ghanaian public image of the CoP and of Pentecostalism generally is that of a religious organisation that is making up for some of the failures and weaknesses – particularly in the area of morality – that have come to be associated with Christianity in Africa. In keeping with its ethos as a Pentecostal denomination, CoP is serious with religious experience and things of the Spirit, and as a religious organisation it pursues a strict and uncompromising stance in what the church perceives as biblical ethical and moral standards. The CoP maintains a very conservative outlook that sets the church apart as an organisation that refuses to be drawn into worldliness. On the relation of such strictness to church life and growth, Leonard observes that the CoP is particularly strict in dealing with matters of marital infidelity and even more so when this occurs among church elders or pastors.[35] In traditional African religiosity, the maintenance of high moral standards in response to prescriptions by the gods is well known. Religion functions as a means of social control.[36] After nearly two centuries of existence in Africa and with the benefit of the translated Scriptures, traditional communities are by no means oblivious of standards required by the God of the Bible presented by the missionaries. If their own deities, which are discounted by the Christian church as powerless and inferior, expect such high moral standards, then converts have good reason to expect the Christian God to demand even higher standards issuing in a more venerable and passionate commitment on the part of worshippers.

Tithing

Giving in the form of tithes and offerings is an important part of Pentecostal spirituality and discipleship. The dictum is that when the Spirit of God touches you, he touches everything you have, including your finances. It is theologically revealing that in 2 Corinthians 8:1-7, St Paul refers to the spirit of giving as an 'act of grace'. That was because in giving towards the needs of the saints, Christian workers and the church, the believer was only appreciating God's ultimate sacrifice in Christ on behalf of all who believe and accept him as Lord and Saviour: 'For you know the grace of our Lord Jesus Christ, that though he was rich, yet for your sakes he became poor, so that you through his poverty might become rich' (2 Cor 8:9; also Phil 2:6-7). In Ghana the spirit of giving in the CoP has become a point of reference for other churches in encouraging their members to give. 'Giving' as an 'act of grace' has been translated into tithing in the CoP, a church which has been financially self-supporting since its emergence some five decades ago. It is said that the intention of McKeown from the inception of the church was 'to build an indigenous church with Ghanaian

---

[35] Cf. Leonard, *A Giant in Ghana*, 110.
[36] See Edmund Ilogu, *Christianity and Ibo Culture* (Leiden: EJ Brill, 1974), 63-64, 201.

culture, Ghanaian ministers and finances generated from within the church.'[37] The members of CoP tithe with zeal and understanding. Thus tithing has become part of the spirituality of the church. In a deprived economy like Ghana where institutions including the government continues to rely heavily on foreign donor assistance, it is to the credit of the CoP that it integrates the experiences of Christian discipleship and making one's financial resources available for supporting the mission of the church.

Patriarchy, Gender, Discipleship

In the African context, as Mercy Oduyoye notes in her work, 'women are religion's chief clients.'[38] The survival of the church in Africa has been made possible to a very large extent by the active role that women in particular have played in her life and work. The older independent churches of Africa broke the male hegemony in Christian ministry because a large number of the founders were prophetesses. The role of women as founders and patrons of independent churches in Africa is cited by Lamin Sanneh as one area where missionary tutelage was overthrown with dramatic effect. I share Sanneh's submission that this timely intervention of women as recipients of spiritual gifts and as possessors of spiritual power saved Christianity from suffering a moribund fate in much of Africa.[39] The CoP is a very patriarchal church that does not ordain women but they remain faithful as disciples. In fact men and women do not even sit or dance together in church. Wives are supposed to refer to and address their husbands as *me wura*, 'my Lord' as a sign of submission and respect. This patriarchal outlook, regrettable as it may be, does not however deny women full participation in the life of the church.

One of the major strengths of the CoP is its strong women's movement and their participation dates back to the origins of the church. Sophia McKeown provided leadership for the local women who were at the frontlines of mission to work. In the words of James McKeown himself, in sharp contrast to his experience in the UK Apostolic Church, in Ghana 'it was women who came and were baptised in the Holy Spirit; women who gave money and committed their time and women who prayed.'[40] One woman, Mrs Helena Obo, is described as 'a real rock in the foundation of the church.' Mrs Obo, in times of real financial need, was said to have sold her personal jewellery and other valuable items to support James McKeown for whom she also served as an interpreter. Mrs Obo also organised the women at Saltpond in the Central Region for Bible study, prayer and

---

[37] Ntumy, 'Growth and Development', 24.
[38] Mercy Amba Oduyoye, *Daughters of Anowa: African Women and Patriarchy* (Maryknoll, NY: Orbis Books, 1995), chapter 5.
[39] Lamin Sanneh, 'The Horizontal and Vertical in Mission: An African Perspective', *International Bulletin of Missionary Research* 7:4 (1983), 7.
[40] Leonard, *A Giant in Ghana*, 54.

evangelism. She was a leader in the women's movement of the CoP from its inception in 1938 until 1974.[41] Women are found in the various assemblies as prophetesses and interpreters of preachers where the latter cannot communicate in the mother tongue of the area. In other words, the spiritual gifts of women are recognised in the local congregations.

Afua Kuma: A Church of Pentecost Grassroots Woman Theologian

Kwame Bediako and Philip Laryea have pointed us to Afua Kuma as a useful example of the sort of contribution that women have made to the dynamic presence of the CoP in African Christianity. She was a member of the CoP. The Pentecostal church background of Afua Kuma, to my mind, is very significant to her oral theological thinking. Although an illiterate woman, it is highly significant that in the work of both Bediako and Laryea, Afua Kuma is referred to as a 'grassroots theologian' who has played a significant role 'in the development of Christian thought' and whose theology 'is foundational for Christian theology in the twenty-first century.'[42]

In Afua Kuma's prayers, which I submit are born out of her Pentecostal experience, Jesus is imaged as *Obaatanpa* (Capable Mother), *Kronkron* (Holy One), *Otumfo Nyankopon* (Almighty God), *Ohene* (King) and *Nyansabuakwa* (Custodian of Wisdom). For our purposes I single out Afua Kuma's application of the Akan expression *Obaatanpa* for God. As Laryea rightly points out, the image is derived from the natural and biological roles of women as mothers with exceptional qualities of emotional attachment and care for children. The expression is however not restricted to the feminine gender in usage. It is also used for males and for any human institutions that perform the functions of caring and emotional support. The theological import of Jesus as *Obaatanpa* lies in the fact that 'although the Jesus of history comes to us as a male, our conception of him as Jesus of faith transcends gender. ...To invest the Jesus of faith with the *Obaatanpa* image is to attest to the fact that in him both genders cohere.'[43] As a grassroots theologian, Afua Kuma gained prominence during CoP conventions in which she was invited to mount the evangelistic crusade platform and through her oral theological skills in the Akan language narrate the nature of God in her prayer. Hers was a unique ministry not unlike the women in the traditional churches who use *ebibindwom* (African lyrics) to recount the mighty deeds of God as outlined in the Scriptures and experienced in the daily life of the African Christian.

---

[41] Leonard, *A Giant in Ghana*, 43.
[42] Philip T. Laryea, 'Mother Tongue Theology: Reflections on Images of Jesus in the Poetry of Afua Kuma', *Journal of African Christian Thought* 3:1 (2000), 50-60.
[43] Laryea, 'Images of Jesus', 50.

Wilbert Shenk outlines the relationship between the experience of the Spirit and the novel ministries of Pentecostal women like Afua Kuma succinctly:

> The sense of the immediacy of the Holy Spirit in the life of the faith community has fostered an ethos in which women are free to acknowledge and exercise their gifts, including leadership roles in the churches. Pentecostal/charismatic churches have long recognised the leadership of women. Indeed, numerous prophetesses have founded churches. Now a shift is under way as women in these churches are being encouraged, in the freedom of the Spirit, to forge their own style of ministry rather than fitting into the conventional patterns of ministry of the past.[44]

It is definitely very significant that Kwame Bediako reveals Afua Kuma's prayers as paradigmatic of 'grassroots' or oral theology in action. Prayer, as an oral theological form and the medium of communication with the object of worship, provides access to the belief and theology of worshippers. In the assessment of Bediako, the prayers of this Pentecostal woman are 'an illustration of that spirituality which gives a clue to the vibrant Christian presence... which forms the true basis of African theology.' In these prayers, as Bediako further reflects, Jesus is presented not only as Lord, but also as a living reality, Protector, Provider, and Enabler who has conquered the ubiquitous forces and mysterious powers whose activities would have made it difficult for the Christian to come to a full appreciation of abundant life in Christ.[45]

Conclusion

In this chapter I have attempted to discuss spiritual experience as a non-negotiable element of Christian mission using Ghana's Church of Pentecost as a paradigm. African churches are now at the forefront of mission and most of these churches are Pentecostal in nature. Mission in African hands has ceased to be defined in terms of the overseas activity of western mission agencies; and mission frontiers, if lessons in modern African Christianity have anything to teach us, have also ceased to be geographical. Pentecostal churches are thriving in African and among African communities in western context primarily because of their emphases on belief, experience, conviction and commitment to what the Spirit of God is doing in the world. The CoP, as an example of this new paradigm in mission, possesses a strong prophetic and healing ministry; an uncompromising holiness ethic; a wider demographic appeal with an equally extensive geographic spread; a community-oriented approach to church planting; a diversified ministry including provision for children and

---

[44] Wilbert R Shenk, 'Recasting Theology of Mission: Impulses from the Non-Western World', *International Bulletin of Missionary Research*, 25:3 (2001), 102.

[45] Kwame Bediako, *Jesus in Africa: The Christian Gospel in African History and Experience* (Akropong, Akwapim, Ghana: Regnum, 2000), 9.

youth; and a strong women's movement. These are the factors that have made the CoP one of the most popular churches in the West Africa sub-region. Among African churches establishing in Western Europe and North America at the present time, the CoP is also the one with the best organised network. With the features characterising its spirituality, the CoP stands for what is widely perceived in Ghana to be a more accessible and 'more respectable option' in indigenous Pentecostalism.

One of the most important lessons that the need for personal experience teaches is that in Pentecostalism, religion is expected to be a matter of personal choice rather than of institutional presence.[46] Pentecostalism is an experiential religion *par excellence*. Although the early Pentecostals revelled in the glory of spiritual experience, most of them readily organised their lives around the principle of reaching out to a lost world and touching lives for God.[47] Those who will work for God in mission must first come to an experiential knowledge of him. That is why Pentecostals take serious exception to the routine manner in which people become Christian in the mainline churches through the processes of infant baptism and confirmation. These routine processes of incorporation into the church have not been helped by the approach of Christian mission conducted through the provision of educational facilities and social services, important as these may be. So in spite of the major contributions that the older mission churches have made to the life of the Christian church in Africa, the urgent call to return to the fundamentals of Scripture through experience must be considered a major lesson in mission and discipleship that God is teaching his church through the Pentecostal movement.

---

[46] Bryan R Wilson, 'The Functions of Religion: A Reappraisal, *Religion* 18 (1988), 199.
[47] Menzies, *Spirit and Power*, 22.

DOING MISSION AT THE MARGINS OF SOCIETY: HARNESSING RESOURCES OF LOCAL VISIONS

Nicta Lubaale

Introduction

At the time of Edinburgh 1910, a century ago, Christians met to strategize on how to evangelize the unreached world. At that time the Holy Spirit was beginning to speak in a new way, unrecognized by the mission delegates gathered in Scotland. The Azusa Street Pentecostal experience in the United States of America, and the emergence of African Independent Churches on the African continent, were distinct manifestations (though historically linked) of a new and revolutionary movement of the Spirit. This brought a fresh understanding of mission – the Spirit of God was beginning to speak from the margins. In this chapter we focus specifically on African Independent Churches (AICs) as one case of a new vision emerging from the margins to offer resources for contemporary mission.

In the Organization of African Instituted Churches (OAIC) – which is the continental umbrella body for AICs – an African Independent Church is defined as a church that acknowledges Jesus Christ as Lord, and which has either separated by secession from a mission church or an existing African independent church, or has been founded as an independent entity under African initiative and leadership.[1] OAIC recognizes three broad types of AICs:

1. *Nationalist* – those churches that were founded as part of a broader movement to seize political power from the Europeans;
2. *Spiritual* – churches in which the power and gifts of the Holy Spirit are central, and which are close to African culture. These churches often created alternative 'counter' communities of the Holy Spirit in opposition to colonial or missionary models of society;
3. *African Pentecostal churches,* founded after political independence, influenced by the global Pentecostal movement, strongly oriented towards the future but retaining roots in African culture.

African Independent Churches are also called 'African Instituted Churches', 'African Indigenous Churches' and 'African Initiated Churches' – even, since the spread of AICs into the Diaspora, 'African International

---

[1] Slightly modified from David B Barrett's definition, in *Schism and Renewal in Africa* (Oxford: Oxford University Press, 1968), 50.

Churches'. Without entering into the discussions over which name to use, we prefer to use here the simple acronym 'AIC'.

This chapter attempts to locate the mission of AICs in the concept of their founding visions and explores how these visions have motivated people at the margins of society to play their role in different eras of the past century and how they can continue to serve as resources for Christian mission today and tomorrow. We understand 'vision' here in two, connected, ways. Vision is an experience where a person gets divine guidance about the present and the future. At the same time (and from a sociological perspective), vision can be seen as an individual or collective construction of a future or desired state of society that is different from the current state. In both senses of the word, a vision is something that moves people to action.

I understand marginality in two ways that are intrinsically related: (1) being on the sidelines of dominant movements and activities in society due to social status i.e., being financially poor, unemployed, non-literate, living in the slums, or in poor rural homesteads; (2) doing mission in a way that challenges the established understanding of mission. Someone's capacity to do mission in this way (i.e. their methods and values) is usually derived from that person's origins in, or identification with, the visions of those who are socially at the margins. It usually results in the rejection of the missioner by the sections of society and the institutions that have given themselves the power to define acceptable models of mission. Whatever your social status is, these received values will push you to the sidelines as someone or a community of people who have erred. From their foundation, this has been their experience of the AICs and many of the Pentecostal churches – and continues to be so to the present day. It is this second category of marginality which the Holy Spirit uses to breakdown the wall between the resource-poor and the resource-rich.

Characteristics of African Instituted Churches

In the OAIC we have been engaging with the concept and reality of the founding vision for the last 13 years. The OAIC defines the founding vision as what the people of faith hear God telling them to do (often through the leadership and guidance of a prophet or preacher), what they believe about the world around them, and how they understand their call to live out their faith in the particular society to which they belong.[2] At first we used the term 'founder's vision', but we later realized that this was seen as limiting. Christians who are involved in mission in the contemporary environment – as for example, care givers and educators on HIV and AIDS, trainers in

---

[2] More technically, a 'founding vision' can be defined as the reality that is constructed by the founding members of the faith by which they interpret events around them and which shape their reactions and guide their decisions.

sustainable agriculture, church planters, evangelists, and dramatists – felt excluded as the concept was understood to refer to people who had worked in a specific era which is past. With such challenges from the present day 'founders' we decided to redefine the concept so that 'founding' can also be seen as an ongoing process, because the Holy Spirit who is our chief missioner has never stopped inspiring, equipping and empowering fresh founders in each generation.

Historically, the AICs' founding visions were created at a time of crisis in the lives of Africans. It was a period when African Christians were faced with a three dimensional challenge of what they considered to be cultural domination, political domination and spiritual domination. Colonialism was taking root, and its impact was being increasingly felt in every aspect of life. The gospel of Jesus Christ was being spread – churches, hospitals, and schools were being built.

At the same time people were beginning to read the Bible for themselves, in their own mother tongues. They found Jesus Christ the healer, and the Holy Spirit who dwells in their midst, who can reveal the future, who guides and gives power to overcome evil.

The context and the Christian gospel provided AIC Christians with a variety of resources for action. The African worldview understands reality in terms of both the spiritual and the physical. Blessings, misfortunes, sickness, success and failure are deemed to emanate partly or fully from the unseen spiritual world. Therefore the AICs sought (and seek) to act in both physical and spiritual realms in order to deal with the challenges that faced them.

The missionary churches had not put adequate emphasis on the role of the Holy Spirit in the lives of individuals and communities. Healing was confined to the medical clinics, yet people were struggling with their understanding of reality that looked at causes of illness or suffering in ways which went beyond the terms in which they are defined by modern medicine.

Prayers for the removal of the colonialists were said continuously throughout this early period, and prophecies confirmed their impending departure. Symbols were developed which were spiritual but also carried political messages. For example, in western Kenya the churches carried flags identifying their own denominations. At a time when 'raising a flag' was a political act in defiance of the colonial Union Jack, the denominational flag asserted people's loyalty to another reality – to the kingdom of God, not the British Empire.

Prophecy from the margins, overcoming fear, inspires people to speak to power. Both historically and at the present time, key to the growth and development of AICs have been the verses from Joel 2:28-29: 'And it shall come to pass afterwards, that I will pour out my Spirit on all flesh; your sons and your daughters shall prophesy, your old men shall dream dreams, and your young men shall see visions. Even on the male and female servants in those days I will pour out my Spirit.' In the contemporary situation, young people are starting their ministries, and women are founding churches. Even in local cultures where women are not allowed to be in leadership, they bring their contribution through prophecy, visions and dreams. In the AICs it is not uncommon for a young girl to stand in the midst of the congregation and to deliver a message of rebuke to church leaders for their sins. Through these means women gain the courage to speak to power in their local environments.

The AICs thus carried out both a priestly and a prophetic role in the community. They identified evils in the present, and prospected for the future, hunting for resources in the scriptures, and in their own society (occasionally, too, borrowing from colonialist social structures such as schools and churches), with which they could begin to build their alternative vision of society.

Even if there were specific individuals who were recognized leaders in the AICs during the founding period, members in these movements value and operate on the principle of the priesthood of all believers. This is what empowers groups of women, men and young people to propagate the gospel of Jesus Christ in their workplaces and neighborhoods. It is out of this understanding of mission that common people or people who are of low status in society can hold senior positions in their churches. What matters is the calling and the evidence of the Spirit of God and the commitment to live out the values of a specific community of missioners. People in the AIC movement regularly get visions or dreams and warn their communities about what is going wrong. The congregations and fellowships also spend a lot of time praying and fasting over the issues that have been predicted that might have an adverse impact on the community. Prayer is a major part of the mission at the grassroots. Collective prayer is also a process of collective reflection. It leads to a collective or common understanding of the issues at hand and agreement on possible actions that arise out of that understanding.[3]

Another important feature of AICs is their ability to build cohesive communities at the margins of society, where people care for each other. In the early twentieth century the AICs were building alternative communities. The Spirit of God enabled them to critique and reject the individualism and secularism which was coming with modernity. In the founding vision AIC members linked these alien values to colonialism and to the presence of the missionaries. Together, these new alien forces were introducing Africa to the pressure of the market. AICs understood that it was the attraction of new consumer items that made colonial rule acceptable to many, and as a result in some instances refused to buy the newly imported goods. In the same way they rejected witchcraft and the

---

[3] See Paulo Freire, *Education for Critical Consciousness* (New York: Continuum, 1981).

ritualistic and clan demands of African traditions which were heavy on individuals. So these new AIC communities 'of the Spirit' moved to the middle and became counter-cultures to both the western model of society and also to some aspects of African local cultures. It is this resourcefulness in community-building that the OAIC develops today to enable the member churches to support people living with HIV and AIDS, children in need, and people struggling with unemployment to mention a few.

People develop their understanding of mission through listening to the voice of the Spirit and reading the scriptures in the situations in which they are placed. This is done both individually and collectively in fellowships. For example, the women in Nyamarimba congregation of Africa Israel Nineveh Church started praying over the issue of the increasing number of orphans in their community. Out of this process of prayer they felt guided to start a ministry to support orphans and other children affected by HIV and AIDS. To date they have formed an organization which is caring for 1,200 orphans and other children in need in Kisumu District in Kenya.

AICs carry out training through informal processes. Training and nurturing takes place in the context of small groups where there is mutual encouragement, rebuke and peer advice. This mode of training is used to mobilize and train missioners in their own environments. The training continually focuses on the realities in which the churches operate. This enables the emerging leaders to appreciate the challenges in their mission field even before they are ordained or given bigger responsibilities. This mode of training can also be adopted and used to increase the number of theologically trained ministers in informal urban settlements and rural areas where church workers cannot easily take up full time training schedules. This process of informal training creates a critical mass – which is needed to move people from reflection and dreaming to action and to advocacy. Books, seminars and conferences, radio and TV are also sources of knowledge for this process. Learning how to understand these sources of information is made easier by the fact that the information is read ideologically – that is, from the position of a counter-culture.

Critique of AICs

Movements on the margins continue to grapple with the inability of powerful theologies to understand popular Christian movements. To many they are simply not respectable. The accepted methods of engaging with civic issues are always outside the spirituality of the AICs. So they have to take on the dominant model of civic education which hardly recognizes the motivation of the Holy Spirit to speak to power. The received models of civic education weaken the conscientization process that takes place through the reading of the word, prayer and listening to the voice of the Spirit individually and communally.

The fact that the visions are passed on through oral processes i.e. song, preaching, dreams, prophecies and sermons and are not written down means that the resourcefulness of the AICs cannot be communicated to the wider church. It also hinders some of the churches from dealing with some of the issues that act as barriers to abundant life in the lives of individuals and communities.

The economic inequalities that women in Africa suffer and the AICs' patriarchal models of leadership still hold women back from realizing their full potential as compared to the men even if they are working in the same environments with access to the same empowerment of the Holy Spirit. It is also expected that a young man can start a church but not a young woman. So women are mainly found in the social ministries (Miller and Yamaori).[4] This implies that these churches' understanding of the working of the Holy Spirit is still confined to local and cultural perceptions of gender roles.

There are inadequacies which come with an attempt to use methods in mission which were relevant for a different era but are no longer relevant. Restraining the younger generation from dreaming, visioning and acting in relation to the demands on mission in their era leads to frustration and departure of young people.

Protecting the founding vision in some cases is used to entrench values which marginalize those who are weak i.e. the place of women, young people and children in society. Many churches which emphasize the role of the Holy Spirit slide back into local cultural restrictions and prejudices when they come face to face with present day issues like HIV and AIDS, and the rights and well-being of women, children and young people. It is common to find people who say the Holy Spirit has not told us to talk about HIV and AIDS yet. Some may turn simply to a call for repentance and others understand it as a problem caused by demons such that if expelled from a person, healing will come. This has not been giving the missioners the results they want. Many of the ministers and missioners in these churches are challenged by the enormous problems in the environment in which they are operating. Their ideological base is confronted by problems whose causes they do not understand fully. The reality of HIV and AIDS is rooted in the spiritual, social, political and economic realities of Africa and in the unequal relationships between the rich and poor countries.

When someone's ideological understanding is challenged in this way it can be described as 'bafflement'. "The knowledge which should be capable of giving guidance, of resolving perplexities, of pointing a way out of the labyrinth, meets an intractable problem which will not yield to this knowledge. Now the knowledge appears less potent than we had believed it

---

[4] See Donald E Miller and Tetsuano Yamamori, *Global Pentecostalism: The New Face of Christian Social Engagement* (Berkeley and Los Angeles: University of California Press, 2007).

to be. As a result we are baffled. We do not know what to do next."[5] Many of these churches in the AIC movement are continuously finding themselves in this situation as they progress in their work and ministry.

Even where theological training is taking place, in most cases it is not linked to the values and principles found in the founding visions of the churches. Frequently the theology is borrowed from evangelical or ecumenical sources, and little attempt is made to integrate it into the popular theology of the AICs at the grassroots. This leads to a two-level theology where what is most deeply believed by many people cannot be properly articulated; and what is 'respectable' in theological circles is not deeply felt. This is a significant constraint on contemporary AIC mission.

The use of the prophetic gift in AICs in most cases is focused on local evils – at family levels, in the local church, the denomination and communities where people live. It leaves out the national and the global issues unless they are interpreted in the local sense. There is an unconscious attempt to build a local community that reflects the kingdom of God where all are well and this wellness is achieved through the resolution of the spiritual problems and the physical, spiritual and social needs of the community members. This is necessary but it is only part of the solution.

'Come ye out of them.' The call to come out of the world and to distinguish between the people of the Spirit and the people of the world has been a key element in the founding of Spiritual and Pentecostal AICs. This can lead to a failure to understand God's work in the community. In a workshop which the author was facilitating, a Pastor Waiswa from Uganda mentioned that he had to break barriers because he had been using a language like 'they out there', 'the Egyptians', the 'lost', the 'sinners' just to mention a few terms he had been accustomed to use to describe outsiders. I had to tell my church that we have been wrong and ignorant in the way we were alienating ourselves from the people we are supposed to minister to. We stopped using such statements and now we can get out and work with others as we deal with issues of HIV and AIDS, vulnerable children and food security.

AICs have spread to Europe and North America as part of the Diaspora. There they have founded many flourishing churches. But how can AICs in these contexts move beyond ethnic divides and still work towards establishing a place in which Africans can feel at home? While many African missioners from Pentecostal and Spiritual churches are beginning to reach out to their local host communities, many are still building congregations where they operate on levels of organization where doctrinal differences and ethnic exigencies do not serve as the most vital reference points. More important is the fact that these churches are simply places to

---

[5] John M. Hull, *What Prevents Christian Adult Learners From Learning?* (London: SCM Press, 1985)

share similar sentiments, places to feel at home.[6] This type of community building is critical for the immigrants, migrants and students who find themselves in new cultures where the understanding of community and the place of an individual in society is different from what they have always known. The shortcoming of this type of community-building is that it excludes the host populations from benefiting from the enormous spiritual resources which the African migrants carry with them. In a conversation with the author, Peter Sleebos, the General Superintendent of the Assemblies of God, said 'Who will help the African Pentecostal Churches in the Netherlands to realize that we need them? We need their way of worship but most of them are keeping it to themselves.' The missioners in this case are in similar circumstances to their counterparts who struggle to earn a living at the margins of society in Africa, and focus on building mission strategies which focus on meeting the needs and aspirations of their own social class. This is necessary, but by itself it prevents the church from reaching out to other social classes.

Engaging this Spirituality in Holistic Mission

In order to facilitate AICs to be more effective in mission, OAIC needs to undertake a long-term programme of engaging positively with the spirituality of its member churches. This programme will include the following activities.

Documenting the founding visions, and tracking the changes in the visions that have taken place in the various eras through which the AICs have passed. Without documentation the founding visions will be lost or will be changed imperceptibly over time as the churches absorb influences from the surrounding environment. In this way the founding visions can become a resource not only for AICs – and even for contemporary 'founders' – but also for the wider church.

It is clear that the historical founding visions were created to deal with the challenges of their day. Many AIC missioners have continued with values which were developed in resistance to the dominant model of development and church that was brought by the colonialists and missionaries. Some of the symbols and practices were relevant to this specific era but in a radically different environment, are no longer so. For example, the original resistance was directed to foreigners. The contemporary situation may require AICs to challenge their fellow Africans. This requires creating space for the present day missioners to dream and see visions in their own generation. It requires a process of training and remobilizing and enabling the missioners to read the word, listen to the Holy Spirit and scan the environment they are operating in.

---

[6] See Ogbu Kalu, *African Pentecostalism: An Introduction* (Oxford: Oxford University Press, 2008).

In this situation the OAIC has adopted a policy of walking alongside churches and church leaders in a position of 'critical solidarity'. *Solidarity* requires commitment to a particular community, and to its faith or ideological stance, and is often costly. *Critical* solidarity demands an attempt to be honest to reality – both the reality of the partner (who may have a more 'objective' understanding of the challenge that the church faces) and of the church members (whose 'spiritual' perception of the situation may be profoundly true). A recent example of the process was a meeting where OAIC sought to enable AIC leaders from Kenya to reflect on the political situation. An 'objective' overview was given by a political journalist, and then leaders were facilitated to discuss and reflect on the spiritual meaning of the political realities presented, and the resulting challenge to prayer and to action.

Using Participatory Learning and Action (PLA) tools which have been created to illuminate the social realities of grassroots communities, links can be made with the scriptures. James, a grassroots development facilitator from Uganda, tells this story:

> I used to go to the churches to train them in development but people were not enthusiastic at all because they felt that we were bringing worldly things to the church. I went back and studied the scriptures. I got the relevant scriptures and used them alongside the participatory learning and action tools. Out of the discussions generated in this process Christians who were at the beginning opposed to development training realized that they were practicing their faith against the scriptures they believe in. We also as facilitators learnt that we need to recognize the place of the Bible in social transformation. This resulted in the transformation of their understanding of the link between their faith and development. It is about people and communities being well and not focusing on amassing wealth.

Through processes like this, access to reality is illuminated by using sociological tools which have been developed over a period by development scholars and practitioners. Another example is the use of the access and control tools on resources by gender and age groups. The author has used these tools which reveal the great disparity in access to resources and power between women and men, and elders and young people. The results in most cases have not been different among the people of the 'Spirit' and those of the 'world'. This usually leads to a more informed debate in the church on these issues after congregations have been taken through the process of analyzing the causative factors of the unwanted situations in the lives of individuals, families and communities. It is this process that brings the people in the church and the rest of the community to work together to transform their lives for the better.

Conclusion

God is concerned about the people at the margins of society and through the Holy Spirit and the scriptures, God will continue to empower them in

Doing Mission at the Margins of Society

unique ways. This empowerment leads to action which may sometimes be disruptive to our accepted models of mission. Unlike Christ's disciples who said 'we saw a man driving out demons in your name and we told him to stop because he is not one of us' (Mark 9:38), we should start looking at those in mission, especially those at the margins, and say we found people who are doing things in a different way and we would like to enable them to sharpen their mission so that they can be more effective.

SPIRITUALITY AND HISTORIC MISSION CHRISTIANITY IN AFRICA: GHANAIZATION IN ROMAN CATHOLICISM[1]

Michael Perry Kweku Okyerefo

Introduction

The Second Vatican Council was a watershed in the life of the Roman Catholic Church. The Council's emphasis on the intention of the revealed word to be incarnate in every culture paved the way for inculturation in the church as a conscious effort in every time and space. *Sacrosanctum concilium*, the Vatican II document on *The Constitution on the Sacred Liturgy* particularly asserts that the liturgy, especially the Eucharist through which 'the work of our redemption is accomplished', is the source of the spirituality of the church. The liturgy makes members of the church a 'holy temple of the Lord, a dwelling-place for God in the Spirit'. That is why the Council saw the need to reform the liturgy to enable the faithful 'to express in their lives and manifest to others the mystery of Christ and the real nature of the true church' wherever it is present in this world.[2] It is within this crucible that the church's evangelising mission (mission *ad gentes*) in the modern world should be situated in the African experience, with the African experience receiving its mission and, in turn, engaging in that same mission.

This chapter presents the lived African Christian (Roman Catholic) spirituality from a Ghanaian perspective. It draws on the liturgical life of the church by capturing the salient liturgical developments championed by local churches (dioceses). The liturgical life of the church is derived from the model with which the local church particularly identifies, and within which its 'lived religion' (experience spirituality) is expressed.

The chapter, therefore, addresses how Ghanaian culture gives expression to Catholicism. This expression is the lived experience of Ghanaian Catholics by means of the church's liturgical life, which itself is derived from the model of the Catholic Church in Ghana as a 'Family of God'.

---

[1] Its German version was published in M.P.K. Okyerefo, 'Spiritualität und christliche Missionsgeschichte in Afrika: Ghanaization in der römisch-katholischen Kirche', *Protokolle zur Liturgie – Veröffentlichung der Liturgiewissenschaftlichen Gesellschaft Klosterneuburg*, Band 3 (Oct 2009), 268-281.

[2] Austin P Flannery (ed), *Vatican Council II Vol. 2: More Post Conciliar Documents* (Collegeville, MN: The Liturgical Press, 1982), 1.

Using the Basic Christian Communities (BCCs), the feast of Corpus Christi, and the 'outdooring'[3] or naming ceremony of children as examples, this study will depict inculturated Catholicism in Ghana. The aim is to show how Catholic spiritual life and Ghanaian culture 'reciprocally inform, transform, and reinforce each other'.[4] The purpose of the liturgy of the Eucharist is to transcend the rites in the church in order to encapsulate the active living out of the love and unity therein celebrated, and serves as the crucial spiritual life of the Roman Catholic Church. This life is given expression in the church as the 'Family of God' to which the BCCs and the entire community of believers at worship during other liturgical activities attest in an acculturated fashion. The BCCs are neither unique to Africa, nor did they originate here. In fact, the BCCs today are much more characteristic of the Catholic Church in South America where, according to Penny Lernoux, the new message of 'liberation', 'temporal as well as spiritual, is transmitted through experimental forms of communal worship that share striking similarities with the primitive Christian communities of the pre-Constantine, missionary church, unfettered by power and riches'.[5] The difference, however, between the BCCs in Latin America and Africa (Ghana) lies in the 'spirit' that moves them. While liberation theology is ostensibly the live-wire of the church in Latin America, the church in Africa, having the 'Family of God' as its model, has BCCs that represent the ideal family built on love and sharing. The difference is steeped in a church that finds itself in diverse socio-political conditions. The BCCs, therefore, form the foundation on which the other liturgical innovations previously referred to will be discussed. The study will draw on examples in the Catholic dioceses of Accra, Kumasi and Ho to show how Catholics articulate the faith in specific contexts, giving authentic Ghanaian expression and comprehension to the Roman Catholic faith.

The Universal Mission

Under the title 'Outback Mass available only once a fortnight' *The Tablet* of 19 January 2008 carries a story on Australia, which is said to be experiencing a shortage in the number of clergy. Declining numbers 'of clergy and dwindling rural communities' are said to be 'forcing priests to travel several hundred miles to say Mass'. The liturgy of the Eucharist cannot be celebrated without a priest.

---

[3] 'Outdooring' is a Ghanaian term commonly used for the celebration of the naming of a child. It is a literal term to express the act of bringing the infant outdoors for the first time.
[4] J Pashington Obeng, *Asante Catholicism: Religious & Cultural Reproduction Among the Akan of Ghana* (Leiden: EJ Brill, 1996), 1.
[5] Penny Lernoux, 'The Latin American Church', *Latin American Research Review* 15:2 (1980), 2012.

The Australian experience reflects the trend in most of Western Europe and the US, which is often reported in the media. New pastoral strategies and approaches have, therefore, become necessary. Or, perhaps, even a general re-thinking on a workable model of the church that will be more appropriate in such circumstances. Models are, sociologically speaking, mental constructs with which the reality on the ground can be measured. Such thinking may well be easier in relation to society; however, the church cannot be visualised in mere sociological terms. Although peopled, members of the church are qualified in the sense that they are the people of God. The church consists of society but transcends it at the same time. Therefore, models of the church must be primarily theological even as they are sociological. But as a community of believers whatever model the church assumes at any one time is coloured by the social context within which the church operates.

In view of this, the complaint about the declining number of clergy, particularly in the western World, sometimes fails to recognise that never in the history of the church have there been adequate numbers of clergy. Even in those regions of Africa and South America that appear to have a boom in vocations the situation is not uniform. Therefore, it is unlikely that there will ever be enough priests anywhere or in the entire church. The older church in Europe, for example, has been used to certain *modus operandi* such as having priests mostly resident in single parishes and administering to the people of God in that particular parish. Where such a model has been practised for centuries, it is difficult to visualise a different model, such as the main station/outstation model in Ghana.

Mission in Ghana

When it is suggested that vocations in Africa are in superabundance, it is important to note that many individual African parishes are collections of several towns and villages. A priest in Ghana typically lives in the parish centre, what is called the main station, and strives to serve that station as well as the adjoining outstations. Some parishes have as many as 20 communities or more. The population of such parishes varies from a few hundred to many thousands of people. Priests typically serve these churches under trying conditions such as bad roads and lack of adequate transport. In fact, they sometimes have to walk several kilometres to the outstations they serve. They do not have the luxury of the one-station parish model, where priests both live and work, which typifies the church in the west.

However, it is under the trying circumstances described above that the church seems to be thriving, even vibrant in certain places in Africa. Priests have never and cannot single-handedly build parishes or the church. Vital though their position is, their work thrives only in collaboration with the laity. In this light, one cannot envisage pastoral success in priests' work in Ghana without the many catechists and other laity who keep the church alive in our communities. As the church expands, so also is it more difficult for priests to know their flock personally. The new Pentecostal/charismatic churches springing up take advantage of this weakness of the Catholic Church to recruit some Catholics. What is more, some of the new churches are also beginning to establish institutions such as schools, hospitals and even universities, providing the very services the Catholic Church provides as part of its evangelization strategy.[6] The original establishment and significant growth in membership of the Catholic Church since 1880, the official date for the inception of the church in Ghana – meant that teaching was historically left to catechists who were trained to do so by missionaries – a practice which is currently upheld, particularly when priests are not always present. The contemporary call to a 'new evangelisation' is making the church in Ghana re-examine this model in view of the ministries and practices that promote effective evangelisation. Rather than a radical departure from this model, the church wishes to build on it by promoting the model of the 'Church as Family of God'. Members participate in the life of this family by meeting frequently to break the word, sometimes bread (Eucharist) as well, thereby administering to each other and to themselves.

In an interview with *The Tablet* Cardinal Peter Turkson, primate of the Catholic Church in Ghana, outlined this concept of evangelization in Ghana and Africa.[7] The Church as Family of God underscores the church as eternally rooted in the nature of the Trinitarian God. The family of God subsists in the unity of God. Each individual family, each family of the Christian community in an outstation, a parish, a chaplaincy, a diocese, a nation, indeed in the entire the world, finds meaning and gives expression to itself through its rootedness in this family of God. Love, compassion and sharing are characteristic of this family. The important point about inculturation regarding this model is that it takes its clue from the proverbial African family. It paints an ideal picture of the family that, steeped in the liturgy of the Eucharist, shares a life of unity and solidarity in society. It is not to say that the ideal family exists anywhere. It exists, neither in Africa, which is plagued by wars, ethnic conflicts, greed, bad governance and disease, nor in the west, which is devoured by greed, materialism and relativism. Modernization and the secularization of the African society are also beginning to take their toll on the Christian family. But shortcomings constitute precisely the reason for the existence of the church, a family that should bring hope to a people even on the verge of brokenness.

---

[6] See further Michael PK Okyerefo, 'The Gospel of Public Image in Africa', in Harri Englund (ed), *Christianity and Public Culture in Africa* (Athens: Ohio University Press, 2011), 204-16.
[7] R James, 'Mission Possible: The Tablet Interview', *The Tablet*, 10 November 2007, 14-15.

By modelling parish communities on families, therefore, the church calls for healing relationships, offering each individual and groups a place in it. Consequently, the pastoral work cannot depend on priests and religious alone. Priests and religious together with the numerous catechists and laity who offer themselves in unpaid service to the church in Africa are responsible for its growth. In normal human families the work of family members, which sustains these families, is unquantifiable and cannot be paid for. And each member's contribution is important. The challenge today, however, is that to renew the church, families have to be renewed. It is not enough to be running around saying mass. Catechesis should be a notable part of the work of the priests, religious and catechists, while these pastoral agents, particularly priests, visit the homes of their faithful to share in their lives as family members, sometimes bringing several members together.

Concretely then, the BCC concept proves adequate to sustain the lived religion in our parishes; however, it is not widely entrenched in Ghana. In the Accra archdiocese, the concept is widespread in Tema. The BCCs certainly added to revitalizing the University of Ghana Catholic Community. The church in the university consists of a chaplaincy for students and a parish for workers. When in 2005 the Parish Pastoral Council recognized that members of the parish merely attended mass Sunday after Sunday without really participating in a life in common (not a family), it initiated the BCCs, dividing the parish community into small families according to proximity. This was in recognition of the fact that the students have been operating this model for a long time, what they refer to as Cells. The Cells or BCCs meet together to pray and discuss the Bible as well as their welfare. Members begin to know each other better, thereby reaching those who would otherwise be left on the fringes. Hence, when any members are sick, bereaved or have an occasion to celebrate, this comes to the notice of the entire church (the bigger family) through the smaller family of the BCC. The model has made the priests' work more effective. They visit the various BCCs to participate in their meetings, celebrate the liturgy of the Eucharist with them, thereby getting to know their members better. The entire pastoral strategy is built on the principle of winning people by love. People want to feel wanted. Where this is lacking, they leave the church for some novel religious group that seems to fulfil this need. Thanks to pastoral adaptation the African family, in both its nuclear and extended forms, gives impetus to the lived religion of the church in the spirit of the Second Vatican Council. Such a pastoral strategy has been made possible through Vatican II in view of the conscious awareness about inculturation the Council has awoken in the church in Africa.

Pashington Obeng notes that following the Second Vatican Council the church in the Council's document *Gaudium et Spes* (The Church in the Modern World) is well aware of the new demands our changing world makes of it.[8] Such demands include the Catholic Church's 'relations to other religions', *Nostra Aetate*, as eternally belonging to 'the nature and mission of the church', *Lumen Gentium*. Consequently, unlike the pre-conciliar attitude of missionaries frowning upon inculcating indigenous cultural practices into the church, the post-conciliar spirit is one of encouraging dialogue with the same indigenous cultures and religions. It is this novel spirit that makes it possible for the Asante Diocese (Kumasi archdiocese), for example, which Obeng studies in great detail, to embark upon the indigenization of the faith. Inculturation, then, becomes naturally understood as the intention of Jesus Christ, the Word of God, to be incarnate in every human culture whose authors he came to save. Such understanding would empower the Kumasi Archdiocese, led by Archbishop Sarpong, to launch into a project of inculturation aimed at making the Catholic faith more intelligible to its adherents. Kumasi is not the only local church that is engaged in this initiative. In fact, the recognition of *Nostra Aetate* that 'Christians and non-Christians are firmly rooted in their respective cultural and historical contexts', thereby living out their faiths 'from those particular social conditions' makes inculturation a worldwide imperative.[9] The church itself 'is by its very nature missionary', *Ad Gentes Divinatus*.[10] It means that the internal nature of the church must initiate a move to encounter people and be relevant to them in their life situations. One of the main means by which Vatican II makes this possible is the move away from Latin as the only language of the mass to the use of the vernacular. So in Kumasi, not only is the liturgy celebrated in Twi (a variant of the Akan language in Ghana), the liturgy is replete with numerous attempts at inculturation. The Kumasi archdiocese's way of celebrating *Corpus Christi* is an example of the significant liturgical innovations Obeng terms the 'Asantesization of Catholicism'.

Corpus Christi is the feast of the body and blood of Christ commemorating the Eucharist. Traditionally it falls on the Thursday following Trinity Sunday, although in some regions of the church it is translated to the following Sunday. On that day the body of Christ, tucked in a monstrance, is carried in procession after the liturgy of the Eucharist. By this means the Lord Jesus is adored in the full view of the public at a number of altars erected for the purpose. In this way Catholics show Jesus Christ to the world as their priest, prophet and king.

In Kumasi the kingship of Christ appears to receive a rather nuanced impetus in view of the position occupied by the *Asantehene* (king of Asante) and other chiefs in that society. On the feast of Corpus Christi the monstrance with the body of Christ is 'carried in a palanquin under a large *Gye Nyame* (Except God) umbrella', just as the king or chief is carried on

---

[8] Obeng, *Asante Catholicism*, 124.
[9] Obeng, *Asante Catholicism*, 126.
[10] Flannery, *More Post-Conciliar Documents*, 814.

special occasions.[11] The bishop, representative of Christ (*alter Christus*), 'processes under an umbrella like an *ohene*, but the bishop does not sit in a palanquin. He walks, in deference to Christ the King'.[12] Obeng observes that the Asante ritual symbols on display, such as the drumming and ceremonial sword-bearing, are the 'condensed expressions of Christ's royal power which' is 'above and beyond the local political and religious authority of the Asante king'.[13]

In the same vein of making the Catholic faith more intelligible to adherents in a local church, Ho diocese has an entire office devoted to 'faith and culture'. One of the significant rites it has produced, among others, is that of the naming ceremony of children. The naming ceremony is quite widespread in Ghana, with many ethnic groups celebrating the occasion on the eighth day after the birth of a child. On that day the child is brought out of the room (to be 'outdoored') to see the light of day for the first time and it is given a name. The rite of naming or 'outdooring' is performed in similar but different fashion by diverse ethnic groups in Ghana. For example, among the Bakpεle, an ethnic group in the Volta Region of Ghana, the child is brought out of the room early in the morning when the family and invited guests are gathered. Emergence from the room would signify leaving darkness into light. The elder in the family who will perform the rite raises the child with its face upwards to see the light of day that the child may learn to tell the difference between darkness and light, evil and good. A number of other symbols are used including splashing water unto the roof of the house in front of which the assembly is gathered that it may drip on the child. This action means the child should learn the difference between fair weather and rain. Salt and alcohol are put separately on the child's tongue accompanied by the words, 'if it is salt, say salt; if it is alcohol, say alcohol', indicating honesty is an imperative virtue. Peter Sarpong outlines some other symbols employed by the Asante, some specifically when naming a girl, others when naming a boy.[14]

It is this traditional Ghanaian celebration that has been Christianized in the Ho diocese; what can be referred to in the spirit of Pashington Obeng's work as 'Eweization' of the rite of reception (baptism) into the Christian (Catholic) fold. Thus, the rite is an amalgamation of the traditional naming ceremony and the Catholic rite of infant baptism. The naming or 'outdooring' ceremony can, therefore, be celebrated by a priest leading the rite, employing some of the symbols enumerated above, which Ghanaian culture shares in common with Christianity such as that of darkness and light or sin and goodness. The priest may administer baptism to the child at the same time or leave it for a future date in church. Where baptism is

---

[11] Obeng, *Asante Catholicism*, ix.
[12] Obeng, *Asante Catholicism*, 130.
[13] Obeng, *Asante Catholicism*, ix.
[14] Peter Sarpong, *Ghana in Retrospect: Some Aspects of Ghanaian Culture* (Tema: Ghana Publishing Coorporation, 1974), 91.

performed, the water that is used as a symbol of cleansing and new life in the Christian rite reinforces the traditional virtue of honesty required by traditional culture.

The examples depicted in this work (church as family of God epitomised in the BCCs in Accra archdiocese, Corpus Christi in Kumasi archdiocese, and the Naming or Outdooring Ceremony in the Ho diocese) have been made possible by Vatican II. The Council's Constitution on the Sacred Liturgy, *Sacrosanctum Concilium*, encourages local churches (dioceses) within the Catholic Church to tap cultural resources of their societies, albeit within the boundaries of liturgical experimentation. More Post-Concliliar documents continue to entrench the position of the Council. On the tenth anniversary of the Council Pope Paul VI issued an exhortation on Evangelization in the Modern World, *Evangelii Nuntiandi*. One of the main preoccupations of *Evangelii Nuntiandi* is to address the methods and approaches that should be employed in preaching the gospel to make it more effective in our times. Following *Gaudium et Spes*, *Evangelii Nuntiandi* asserts that the 'gospel must impregnate the culture and the way of life of man' because 'in the building up of the kingdom it is inevitable that some elements of these human cultures must be introduced'.[15] The exhortation recognizes that although the gospel and evangelization are not specifically related to any culture, they are not necessarily incompatible with them. 'On the contrary, they can penetrate any culture while being subservient to none'.[16]

By relating the gospel to the actual personal and social lives of people, all human cultures can be regenerated through contact with the gospel. This is the task, which the Council and its Post-Conciliar exhortations set local churches (dioceses) within the Universal (Catholic) Church. In fulfilling this goal, however, individual churches should be united to the Universal Church even as the former seek to inculturate the gospel. Consequently, Catholics from different cultural backgrounds visiting the dioceses of Accra, Kumasi and Ho would be able to participate in the parochial (parish) family life and recognize the inculturated liturgical celebration of Corpus Christi and the reception of children into the family of the church without these rites being radically different from those of the same celebrations in their own local churches.

Conclusion

As the Ghanaian examples of attempts at inculturation illustrated in this chapter show, the dialogue with indigenous cultures and other religions, which Vatican II promotes, has the potential of enriching the Catholic Church. The process of inculturation may be arduous, involving

---

[15] Flannery, *More Post-Conciliar Documents*, 719.
[16] Flannery, *More Post-Conciliar Documents*, 719.

accommodation, innovation, modification and sometimes even conflict, but there is no doubt that it is rewarding.

By promoting the use of the vernacular in the liturgy, Vatican II makes human beings and their culture the centre, which the gospel seeks to penetrate. Human beings can, thus, develop models of the church that best make the gospel more intelligible to them. Hence, as models of the church as Family of God, the BCCs in the University of Ghana Catholic Chaplaincy, for example, present members with homes in which they can share common anxieties, hope and love. Members can rely on each other's support, thereby re-enacting and actively participating in the life of the church redeemed by the Saviour's love, which members emulate. A model presents an ideal with which reality is to be measured. What a model seems to say is that it is possible to achieve this ideal. Individuals and groups are urged to look to the ideal and implement it in their lives, taking their respective circumstances into account. So a model can enhance reality and raise reality to a lofty level.

The cultural reality, in which Ghanaian Catholics live, therefore, can be a means of their rendering the Catholic faith meaningful to themselves. The various attempts at inculcuration then, such as those spelt out in this chapter, are essentially an encounter with Christ who is incarnate in these cultures. Surely he intends the subjects of these cultures to live their religion in them and propagate it to others. That will fulfil the exhortation of *Evangelii Nuntiandi*, which asserts that evangelization should constantly relate 'the gospel to men's actual lives, personal and social...' and 'deal with community life in society, with the life of all nations, with peace, justice and progress'.[17]

---

[17] Flannery, *More Post-Conciliar Documents*, 723.

AFRICAN SPIRITUALITY, SOCIO-POLITICAL EXPERIENCE AND MISSION

Matthews A Ojo

Introduction

Christianity in Africa has changed demographically and structurally compared to the early decades of Christian missions in the nineteenth century. For almost a hundred years, the Roman Catholic Church and the mainline Protestant denominations, offshoot of the western missionary endeavours, largely dominated the religious scene. However, this monopoly was broken with the emergence of the African Independent Churches from the last decade of the nineteenth century, and this religious independence accelerated in the early decades of the twentieth century. Nevertheless, the ongoing revitalization of doctrines and practices within Christianity which began with the emergence of the African Independent Churches and progressed substantially from the 1970s with the Charismatic Renewal, has continued to make Christianity a dominant social force in the continent as the lives of millions of Africans continue to revolve around religion, even amidst the deterioration of the quality of life on the continent – largely due to inept governance by many governments. Concomitantly, other religions, such as Islam and African Traditional Religion, have also witnessed some kind of renewal and have expanded their spaces into the public sphere. By the 1980s, the three major religions were already competing for attention and social relevance. Subsequently, religion began to feature prominently in the public sphere and in popular culture (video films, novels, gospel songs, etc.) and thus activated the sentiments of millions of Africans.

On the political scene, religion became a tool for political negotiation and manipulation, and a marker of ethnic and social identities within the religious pluralistic environment. In fact, despite the inclusion of clauses(s) on the de-establishment of religion in the constitutions of many African nations, various governments continue to promote religion in various ways, and some political leaders continue to project their religious faith into the performance of their official functions. For example, President Frederick Chiluba's declaration of Zambia as a Christian nation in October 1996 provided Charismatics and Pentecostals a moral platform to penetrate the country's political sphere and become a relevant social force. However, this Pentecostal identity could not prevent corruption and intolerant attitudes to political opposition; neither did it eventually provide a high quality of governance in the country. Nonetheless, Africans have taken the presence of religion in the public sphere as normal and desirable.

Although this public image of Christianity looked encouraging in the post-independence era from the 1960s, it was obvious that there is a concern about the quality of the spirituality of Christians in modern Africa. It was this ambiguity in African spirituality that informed Kwesi Dickson's opinion in 1984 that, 'for several decades discerning African Christians have raised questions regarding the validity of the expression of Christianity in Africa'.[1] From its formative years in the missionary era of the nineteenth century, African Christian spirituality was strong, dynamic and transforming such that it was able to confront and displace African Traditional Religion in many societies. It was this same spirituality that triumphed over the evil forests where early African Christians were consigned to build their churches, and also displaced the political dominance of Islam in some places. This same spirituality was further reflected in the emergence of the African Independent Churches as a revivalist movement and in the divine call of their leaders as prophet-healers. This African Christian spirituality was built on prayer, visions and dreams, power manifestation and the immediate experience of the supernatural as a transforming power. However, by the 1980s this spirituality has been unable to offer any meaningful social and religious discourse to address the deteriorating economic and political life of many countries. Indeed, one can draw a preliminary conclusion that contemporary African Christian spirituality in the twenty-first century lacked creativity and was unable to present any redemptive option that would engage substantially and critically with the state and governance in Africa. There is urgent need for a critical awareness of the inept socio-economic and political systems and a willingness to undertake the task of conscientisation that will awaken Christians to finding solutions to pressing political problems.

It may therefore be obvious that there is a crisis within Christianity in Africa. Never before has the relevance of Christianity and indeed Christian spirituality been questioned in the socio-economic and political arena as it is at present. This crisis stems from the realisation that there are disconnections between Christianity and governance in the African states. That the centre of gravity of Christianity has shifted from the western world to Africa, Asia and Latin America is obvious. What remains to be addressed is the impact of Christianity in the governance of Africa in the post independence era from the 1960s. The track record of mainline churches in the democratic struggles from the late 1980s to the early 1990s, and also in conscientizing their members on their civic responsibilities, have not been sustained for any extended period of time. Undeniably, the social action fostered by the Justice, Development and Peace Commissions

---

[1] Kwesi A Dickson, *Theology in Africa* (London, DLT, 1984), 2.

of the Roman Catholic Church has not been matched by other denominations. The public profiles of church leaders such as Archbishop Desmond Tutu of South Africa, Cardinal Anthony Okogie of Nigeria, Dr Matthew Kukah of Nigeria, Bishop Peter Kwesi Sarpong of Ghana, to mention a few, have not translated into a successful project of nation building or of redeeming the society from its ills.

Therefore, questions that ought to be asked include the following: why are there frequent and deep-rooted moral failures and corruption among Christians who hold political power and are in leadership positions? Why do contemporary African Christians holding political offices not strive to lead good and exemplary lives in the belief that they are preparing for the final events of this age and Christ's return? Or why has African Christian spirituality been unable to find answers to problems of governance? A critical analysis of the problem reveals that five points of disconnection between Christian spirituality and the nation state may be observed.

First, there is a disconnection between spirituality and morality in the continent. African spirituality has always been boosted by revival movements. The African church movement in the late nineteenth and early twentieth century provided an alternative spirituality to the mainline Protestant churches as they sought new ways of self-expression under African leadership. By the second decade of the twentieth century, the prophet-healer movements became the dominant forms of the African Independent Churches and the claims that the power of God could address all human problems raised African spirituality to a new height. The commitment of members to prayers and chastity, and their denunciation of idolatry, won the administration of traditional rulers and the mainline Protestant churches, where most of the early members had come from. By the 1960s, evangelical awakening on the university campuses provided new impetus leading to the Charismatic Renewal. However, in recent times, particularly from the 1980s, we are constantly faced with failures of Christians in public office and the corruption and mismanagement in the system. The question then is why has the spirituality of Christians not been channeled positively into accountability and morality in the public sphere?

Secondly, there is a disconnection between African spirituality and development praxis in Africa. Most of the development thinking has come from the West but most of those needing aid and development has been from the global South and Africa in particular. Beginning from the 1960s, development issues first arising from economics acquired some kind of profile as goals and targets were set to reduce the gap between the rich nations of the West and the less-developed countries of the global South. However, while there were Christian institutions in the West such as Christian Aid, Tear Fund, World Vision, etc., not much development thinking has come from African Christianity. While scholars have claimed originality to African spirituality, yet there has been little African input into development praxis on the continent.

Thirdly, there is a disconnection between African spirituality and governance on the continent. Although mission education of the nineteenth and early twentieth century produced the early African political leaders, there is no evidence that the quality of governance of the state and its people has ever been substantially influenced and affected by the spirituality of these leaders. In situations where committed Christians have become leaders of nations, they have in most cases not been able to provide quality governance. All too often, they have been accused of corruption and mismanagement as soon as they leave office. The conviction and sentencing of Mrs Regina Chiluba in Lusaka, Zambia to 18 years imprisonment for converting state property to personal use clearly illustrates the ambiguity of the morality of African Christian political leaders.[2]

Fourthly, there is a disconnection between African spirituality and the quality of education offered and received by Africans from church-operated institutions, be they elementary, secondary, or colleges and universities. Missionary education in the nineteenth century provided substantial stimulus for socio-economic change in African societies and fostered in some Christians a commitment to be change agents in the emerging Africa of the twentieth century. However, although mission or church-run schools still exist in many African nations under various rubrics, those graduating from these Christian-operated schools have not demonstrated distinctive qualities that could be attributed to their mission education.

Fifthly, there is a disconnection between Christian spirituality and the quest to provide quality leadership for the continent and thus offer hope to millions of hopeless Africans. Leadership in Africa, with few exceptions, has not been exemplary or sacrificial. It has not been the Nehemiah model nor the Jesus model nor the Pauline model. Rather it has resembled the traditional African tribal chieftaincy structure with all its privileges and power but lacking in trust and accountability.

Unless the above disconnections are addressed, it is doubtful if Christianity can impact positively and substantially at the national and social levels in the twenty-first century. Therefore, I will argue that Africans, upon their conversion and enlistment into the Christian church and in the process of their spiritual formation, make selections of biblical and spiritual values such as success, power, health, etc. which are in congruence with African traditional worldviews which are essentially this-worldly. At the same time they deselect or confine to secondary roles those fundamental biblical principles of self-discipline, sacrifice, self-denial, obedience, holiness, which are Christ-centred and other-worldly. This conscious selection and de-selection, which resembles the traditional African propensity to worship a variety of gods at different times and for

---

[2] For details see http://news.bbc.co.uk/1/hi/world/africa/7921415.stmc (accessed 20/3/2009).

situation-restricted benefits, invariably produces Christians who behave ambivalently depending on time and situation. Consequently, Africans prioritise spiritual values into primary and secondary ones, and their spiritual formation follows this listing. Therefore, it is often possible to find a Christian serving as a public official who takes bribes but who will defend the faith against any Islamic onslaught; or a Christian man who despite the church's constant insistence on monogamy will marry not two but four wives, but who will gather every member of his household regularly to daily prayers and will give generously to the church every Sunday and during special occasions.

Ethnicity, Corruption and Political Instability

Self-determination came to Africa on the heel of the withdrawal and collapse of colonialism from the mid-twentieth century. Between 1956 and 1980, 43 African countries gained their independence bringing in political transformation and ushering unlimited hope for millions of Africans as they looked to the future. However, by the early 1970s, it was becoming glaringly obvious that African political leaders lacked the capacity to bring any substantial transformation to the continent. First, there was the prevalence of regional conflicts, which were traceable to the nature of politics in post-colonial Africa. Much of the politics of post-independence African nations has been characterised by a pattern of power competition among ethnic groups and political parties, and also by corruption.[3] Political leaders were self-centred and ruled their countries as personal fiefdom. The military coups from the mid-1960s which were supposed to be corrective soon atrophied into the same ineptitude that characterised the civilian governments that succeeded the colonial powers. The forecast was gloomy, such that a writer in 1983 recorded his impression that in many ways Africa is,

> a continent where events have conspired against progress, where the future remains a hostage of the pasts.... As setback followed setback and each modest step forward was no more effective than running in place, black Africa became uncertain of its own identity and purpose, divided by ideology and self-interests, perplexed by the demands of nationhood and as dependent militarily and economically on foreign powers as it was during the colonial era. It moves through the 1980s as a continent in crisis, explosive and vulnerable, a continent where the romance of revolution cannot hide the frustration and despair that tears at the fiber of African society. ...The irony of Africa's misfortunes is that this is the place when mankind originated and

---

[3] Corruption means lack of moral principles, impairment of integrity, and inducement to wrong and evil disposition. Its manifestation is majorly the giving and receiving of bribes, and it also includes embezzlement, favouritism, financial mismanagement, theft, etc. See Felecia I Uwechue-Omoregbe, *Fight Corruption (Be Reasonable)* (Benin City: Bendel Newspapers Corporation, n.d.), 1-2.

this was a center of culture and sophistication long before the Europeans arrived.[4]

This impression has not changed much, or perhaps has worsened, amidst the many regional conflicts in Sudan, Ethiopia, Uganda, Rwanda, Congo, Chad and Zimbabwe. One then needs to enquire into those factors that made independent Africa of the 1960s and 1970s so backward and that inflicted so much pain on its citizens, despite the presence of a large Christian population.

One issue that has continued to bedevil Africa is ethnicity. It has been a constant factor in wars and power struggles. Ethnicity is interest-oriented, and it is of political significance because many ethnic groups in Africa are not only based on common culture or historical experience but also upon co-residence in a region. For example, the Yoruba, the Igbo, the Kikuyu and the Ngoni occupied fixed geographical areas in their respective countries. Therefore, the tendency has been for each group to promote its own political and economic interests, regardless of the overall national interests. Ethnic loyalties are so strong that one's allegiance is supposed to go to one's ethnic group before the nation. Hence, channelling the nation's wealth to one's ethnic group by whatever means is deemed desirable and necessary. Therefore, for a political leader there is rarely any distinction between money privately earned or dishonestly removed from the public coffers, as long as some close relations gain from such 'non-economic' earnings. Access to and manipulation of the government's finances has become the surest gateway to fortune. In short, politics is seen as way of gaining access to instant wealth for private and sectional benefits. Consequently, ascendancy to political power has become nothing more than the process of gaining control of the state's economic resources for the betterment of one's ethnic group. Such competition highlights ethnic dichotomy and results in political instability. Although military coups have ostensibly been carried out to rid countries of corruption, regrettably military governments have at times been worse than their civilian counterparts.

By the mid-1970s, corruption in Kenya was high among government officials. For example, driving licence racketeering was commonplace. The police force was not much better. There were instances of vital documents being removed from prosecution files to weaken police cases. In Uganda, corruption played a prominent part in the allocation of shops and economic properties left by the expelled Asians in 1972.[5] It was only in Tanzania that the country's rigorous socialist policies somehow lessened the incidence of corruption.

---

[4] David Lamb, *The Africans* (New York: Vintage Books, 1983), 5, 7.
[5] Henry Okullu, *Church and Politics in East Africa* (Nairobi: Uzima Press, 1974), 35-36.

The churches in the post-independence era did not fare better. There were quarrels involving embezzlement of church funds, of pastors caught in adulterous relations with their church members, of collusion of church leaders with government officials, etc. For example, in Uganda President Obote gave a gift of a new car to every bishop appointed during his time, and these cars were accepted![6] In Nigeria, the crisis of leadership in the Methodist Church in the 1980s was so bitter that several court cases were instituted by the laity against the church's Primate.

Some political leaders have denounced corruption, but few actions have been taken to root out this rot. The few actions proposed lacked the moral vigour to enforce them. For example, in November 1971, a motion was passed in the Kenya National Assembly to set up a commission to enquire into tribalism, nepotism, and corruption, but the resolution was soon vetoed by the KANU Parliamentary Group.[7] No wonder, we continue to hear about the reported cases of 'disappearance' from Kenya's banks of huge sums of money meant for development purposes.

It is in Nigeria that corruption really gained ground. In 1961, the Christian Council of Nigeria included corruption and ethnicity among the ills of the society that must be eradicated.[8] However, the enormous wealth brought into the country in the mid-1970s by the oil boom rather encouraged practices that were more corrupt. There were widely reported cases of corrupt charges against government officials in 1974-6. The first major sensational case was the resignation of Joseph S Tarka, the Federal Commissioner of Communication in August 1974. His friend, Mr Godwin Daboh, wrote letters to the police and the Civil Service accusing Tarka of corruption, yet nothing was done. He then went to court to swear to an affidavit, and the press reported the case. Yakubu Gowon, a Christian and then Head of State, instead of investigating the corrupt charges hounded journalists who sustained the anti-corruption campaign.[9]

However, the regime of Murtala Mohammed that overthrew Gowon made a drive against corruption in public life as an essential part of the renewal of political activity in Nigeria. Consequently, many aspects of government activity were investigated in 1975 and 1976. For example, one governor was accused of treating the State's Mercantile Bank as his 'personal property', while all ex-Governors (military officers) under Gowon except two were dismissed with ignominy from the Armed Forces and the Police.[10] A 1993 survey on Nigeria in *The Economist* noted that bribes and kickbacks were entrenched in almost everything – obtaining

---

[6] Okullu, *Church and Politics*, 38.
[7] Okullu, *Church and Politics*, 40.
[8] Christian Council of Nigeria, *Christian Responsibility in Independent Nigeria* (Ibadan, 1961).
[9] Colin Legum (ed), *African Contemporary Record 1974/75* (London, 1975), B742-3.
[10] *African Contemporary Record 1974/75*, B669-70.

permits, clearing customs inspection, getting treatment in hospital and so on.[11]

Corruption, ethnicity and political instability are organically linked in a vicious circle. Corruption harms the broadest society. It encourages inefficiency, rids the government of income, and its costs include loss of political credibility, distortion of people's values, and creation of tensions within society. Moreover, corruption clearly undermines national stability and sets asides the principles of good governance and stability.

To minimise and eradicate corruption, a more determined approach must be made by the churches. It is not enough to adopt resolutions condemning corruption in church synods or annual assemblies. It ought to be undertaken as a persistent campaign by every denomination. The churches must take the initiative and lead in a worthwhile campaign against corruption. The church cannot stand idly by, and assume as a western scholar did, that corruption will be eradicated with the passage of time, when education becomes widespread, when public opinion becomes stronger, when loyalties moved from the family or tribe to the nation-state, etc.[12] The crusade against corruption must begin now.

The Power of Renewal

Happily, amidst the political turbulence in the continent, there is still hope of a renewal because a new generation of Christians are now re-ordering Christian experience and fostering a new spirituality that is focusing on the ills of the society, which they believe could be eradicated by the power of the gospel as Christians live as salt and light in the world. The emerging Charismatic movements in Africa offer the continent the possibility of renewal and hope. Charismatic movements emerged in the 1970s and by the 1980s they had assumed much social prominence partly due to the attention given to them by the media, and also due to the multitudes of new churches and 'ministries' that were emerging and erecting signboards all over the major cities of Africa. Their emergence has marked the beginning of a substantial Christian awakening in the continent.

The Pentecostal and charismatic movements have changed the pace and direction, and enlarged the scale, of communicating the gospel. They continued to utilize mass media and communication technologies for carrying out evangelism, mobilizing human and material resources, and re-packaging a new spirituality. Consequently, they reconstruct religious life and Christian spirituality through specific biblical ethics. As the old missionary era ended, Pentecostals have invented a new spirituality and morality that focuses on contemporary issues. Charismatic movements have

---

[11] *The Economist*, 21-27 August, 1993, 5-6.
[12] Ronald Wraith & Edgar Simpkins, *Corruption in Developing Countries* (London: George Allen & Unwin Ltd, 1963), 208.

been one of the great African realities in the twentieth century. They exhibit an awareness of the deteriorating situation in the continent and seek to change it. This power to remedy is so intrinsic to the Charismatic movements that almost every publication emanating from them offers some answers to some prevailing problem. A reflection from a Pentecostal literature comments thus:

> We must not be content to chant our hymns and say prayers while the crisis deepens.... There must be a change of thinking and attitude towards life and our responsibility for the condition of our nation and society. The great need of Christians in Nigeria is to realise that *they are responsible* for the present crisis because of their indifference and inactivity when they have the mighty *Gospel to solve* the *crisis*.[13]

The crisis was understood to include problems of poverty, ignorance and illiteracy, corruption and under-development. Covertly, they seek to change historical events and redeem the public space on their knees. They critique the responsibility of power because they accept Chinua Achebe's argument that the trouble with Nigeria and indeed Africa is leadership. The difference between Pentecostals and other Christians might be found in their diagnosis of Africa's problems: are these primarily spiritual or political or socio-economic? Does individual salvation inform public morality? Consequently, Pentecostals and Charismatics share the optimism and the ideology of the 'African Renaissance' and further claim to have heard God declare, through a number of messages, the recovery of Nigeria, and indeed Africa. It may tarry but will surely come to pass. Nigeria will become great again! It is an important tool in God's design for the liberation of Africa![14] One of their publications puts it thus:

> We must realise that the present revival and move of the Holy Spirit all over Nigeria is not only for Nigeria, but God has chosen Nigeria as the base from which he is going to invade other West African countries with the gospel of liberation and deliverance.[15]

Elsewhere, it said,

> God intends that Nigeria should be the beacon of the gospel in Africa. The mantle of leadership in *Africa*... falls on the *church* in Nigeria. It is for this reason we are a little bit prosperous.... This is for no other purpose than to enable the *church* champion God's ultimate will for Africa.[16]

Charismatics are mindful that socio-economic and political prescriptions are not enough to 'cure' Africa of her problems, so they are turning to a more vibrant spirituality. For example, the passage, 'If my people shall pray, and seek my face, and turn from their wicked ways; then I will

---

[13] *Herald of the Last Days* (Ilesha, Nigeria), No. 34:4.
[14] Part of correspondence from Professor Ogbu Kalu in late 2004 on the debate about Pentecostalism and Governance in Nigeria.
[15] *Herald of the Last Days*, No 32, 9.
[16] Christian Students' Social Movement of Nigeria, '*The Way Out*', 6.

forgive their sin, and will heal their land' (2 Chron 7:14), an often quoted verse by Charismatics, has become a potent text sustaining the commitment to renewal and to solving the problems of the continent. It prompted calls like the following:

> However, more than the internal factors *that weigh on our economy is the fact that our woes are due to our national transgression against God*.... For how long will these continue? It would continue, so long as the church permits it to continue, so long as the *church* remains insensitive, so long as the *church* forgets she is the light of the world.... The church in *Nigeria* is grossly delinquent on this prophetic ministry or warning and judging the nation. Rather than do this, some of us legitimise the actions of men who go and plunder the state treasury and run to us for help and prayers....[17]

Overall, Pentecostals are working towards moral responsibility and sensitivity as they pray and undertake what they call 'land cleansing prayer walks'. They insist that though evil may be holding Africans in bondage, they reject the associated pessimism but foresee renewal for the future.

The Missionary Agenda for the Present and the Future

The question still needs to be asked: what kind of African spirituality will address African socio-economic and political problems and how can we promote any meaningful connection between spirituality and governance in Africa? Indeed, looking back, Christianity has had tremendous impact on nineteenth century nationalism, on the making of the educated and political elite, and in the socio-political transformation of many countries. Even in the post independence era, there was a brief period of Christian active participation in the political sphere. For example, beginning from the late 1980s and through the mid-1990s, a number of African countries witnessed a period of democratisation fervour and agitation in which the Christian church played significant roles. In Benin Republic, Togo, Gabon, Cameroon, South Africa, Togo, Ghana, etc., Catholic bishops and the Protestant churches played significant roles in fostering political changes that tried to move these countries forward from dictatorial regimes to democratic ones. This changing religious context and its impact on politics and governance in Africa partly informed the conference on 'The Christian Churches and Africa's Democratisation' that was held in Leeds in September 1993, and which was coordinated by Paul Gifford.[18]

Following this democratisation fervour, African countries entered the 1990s with great prospects, but by the late 1990s, these hopes were dashed. A reference has already been made to Frederick Chiluba's declaration of Zambia as a Christian nation in October 1996 and the subsequent problem

---

[17] CSSM, 'The Way out of Our Present Predicament: A Clarion Call on the Church', a pamphlet, issued in December 1983 as an advertisement in the national dailies, 2-3, 8.
[18] The publication that resulted from this conference is Paul Gifford (ed), *The Christian Churches and the Democratisation of Africa* (Leiden, EJ Brill, 1995).

of governance in the country. It would appear that Chiluba only exploited the support of Pentecostals and Charismatics for sectional interests. In Ghana, the Pentecostal and charismatic churches moved close to the government of President Jerry Rawlings and provided the regime with a religious and moral legitimacy; however by 2000, no substantial socio-economic improvement had taken place. In Togo, the democratization agitation created more space for religious organizations leading to the registration and recognition of more than the initial seven churches,[19] but the totalitarian government of President Eyadema, who held power for almost 40 years, was unable to move the country forward in any significant way. In Nigeria, there was a great hope with the stepping down of Ibrahim Babangida as the country's president in August 1993, but the authoritarian regime of Sanni Abacha caused much oppression and anxiety in the country.

Even in 1999, after Pentecostals and Charismatics adopted Chief Olusegun Obasanjo as a symbol of the Christian control of the political sphere, believing that he was an answer to prayers about the ending of oppression and mis-governance and the ending of a Muslim political dominance, nothing has changed substantially for good in the country. Looking back now, in February 1999 the Pentecostal constituency felt elated about the election of a political leader who had publicly claimed a dramatic conversion experience, but eight years later the country was still torn apart by religious conflicts and sectional interests. In Ghana, the same scenario has begun to be reenacted. Upon winning in the second re-run of the keenly contested election in Ghana in January 2009, President John Atta-Mills held a much publicized thanksgiving service in the Mountain of Pure Fire and Miracles, an independent Charismatic ministry founded by a Nigerian, Enoch Aminu. This was actually a second service, having held a similar one in Nigeria in the Synagogue Church of All Nations, Lagos under the leadership of Prophet TB Joshua.

In view of the above, the church in Africa should not only seek to align with politicians but must seek to promote a spirituality that will influence society and thus offer solutions and remedy to the geo-political problems in the continent. First, the church represents an amalgam of diverse cultures and background but which are solidly united, hence this reconciling power of the gospel can be extended outside the Christian fold.

The church's mission must involve dealing with evil in the society and the transformation of the community. In this regard, the church has a prophetic responsibility to speak to the nations in the light of God's Word. Such a prophetic responsibility should be directed first in condemning the ills of the society – the perversion of justice, the oppression that is becoming institutionalised, and the sins that are being glossed over. Like

---

[19] These churches were the Roman Catholic, Baptist, Methodist, Anglican, Seventh Day Adventist, Presbyterian and the Assemblies of God.

the Old Testament prophets, the church must awaken itself from slumber and condemn every evil and self-righteousness. The prophetic ministry must also be directed towards revealing God's will and message to the people. Messages of renewal and hope ought to come out forcefully from the church. Moreover, the church has a pastoral responsibility to undertake amidst the contemporary difficulties and helplessness that has afflicted many Africans. Through counselling, teaching and social support, the church should endeavour to reduce and minimise the fear, anxieties and hopelessness that have characterised the African scene for the last 30 years.

The church must widen its scope of activities and seek to carry its witness to the economic and socio-political arena. We are aware that the church is in a precarious position. As a social institution, it equally suffers from the weakness of its society, but unlike the society that must search for economic and ideological answers from the IMF and other western countries, the church has a ready-made answer in the Scriptures. The pietist, *keep-free-from-politics* missionary teaching rarely produces critical Christian leaders who see the relevance of Christianity to the common socio-political life; therefore, this theology must be re-assessed. First, it is rather difficult to stand aloof from the very system that is oppressing and doing injustice to one. Personally, I do not consider suffering with fortitude and resignation as a Christian virtue. In reality, the experience of the Early Christians does not support such complacency. The Apologists of the second and third centuries wrote forcefully to defend Christianity and to launch attacks on the Roman system that was persecuting them.

Christians' involvement in politics must be sustained by the church in such a way that politics should not be the privilege of some 'political misfits' who are satisfied with what wealth they can amass for themselves or their ethnic groups, but politics ought to be a continuous struggle for the realisation of what ought to be. There ought to be a condemnation of extreme wealth on one hand and extreme poverty on the other; a condemnation of the socio-economic set-up that allows one African, whether a political office holder or a founder and pastor of a mega Pentecostal church, to go to Paris or London or New York to give birth or be treated for appendicitis while millions of other Africans die daily in ill-equipped hospitals. In sum, Christians must witness to God's demands for justice and a meaningful life. In essence, politics ought and must reflect the expression of Christian belief that African Christians expect the advent of the Lord every day.[20] It is in such a situation that the church in Africa can effectively carry out its mission.

The churches can influence governance and public morality in the country because they have large congregations, and hence they have an

---

[20] Chris U. Manus, 'New Testament Theological Foundations for Christian Contribution to Politics in Nigeria', *Bulletin of Ecumenical Theology* 2:1 (1989), 25-26.

existing power base. In addition, they can mobilize their large constituency drawn from diverse cultures and backgrounds for both religious and political actions. More important, the Pentecostal churches' unique role of having constant contact with the grass roots can help them implement changes easily. Such changes could be lasting if incorporated into Bible studies and sermons. However, most Christian churches still shy away from politics, labeling it as the domain of sinners. Certainly this perception must change. Furthermore, the trust that the congregations have in the pastors can be used in passing down religious and social values.

The church must promote certain values such as accountability, transparency, discipline, diligence, trust, etc. – values that will impact not only on individual lives but on governance as well. Accountability as a religious and democratic imperative should not only be about giving reports, but is it must be construed as a process to be guided by transparency, awareness of the expectation of others, awareness of one's statutory responsibilities, and the promotion of discipline. Indeed, what we need is a comprehensive appetite for accountability, i.e. a practical commitment to holding one another mutually responsible for our actions.

As pointed by John W de Gruchy in his theological reflection on democratization in Africa, the electoral process is not enough to usher in and sustain democracy; rather the society must cultivate democratic values which are imperative in the sustenance of any constitutional democracy.[21] Within the present framework in Nigeria and other African countries, it is certain that democratic values are lacking. Hence, the need for the churches, with their multi-ethnic composition, a microcosm of the larger society, to foster and promote democratic values in the continent. For example, the churches can teach tolerance, dialogue, discipline, etc. and sustain such with their own examples. What we need is value-formation within the Pentecostal constituency, in the churches as a whole as well as in the civil society. Pentecostal churches already have within their institutions, though informal, such structures as home cells, or house fellowships, through which democratic values can be taught and experienced.

Particularly as I have argued in 2004, Pentecostalism with its participatory ethos can overcome the individualism of greed, avarice and corruption that is endemic in the Nigerian society.[22] Alexis de Tocqueville has recognized how participation has enhanced the value of democracy in

---

[21] John W de Gruchy, 'Theological Reflections on the Task of the Church in the Democratisation of Africa', in Paul Gifford (ed), *The Christian Churches and the Democratisation of Africa* (Leiden, EJ Brill, 1995), 47-60.

[22] Matthews A Ojo, 'Pentecostalism, Public Accountability and Governance in Nigeria', a paper presented for discussion at the workshop on 'Pentecostal-Civil Society Dialogue on Public Accountability and Governance' organised by CLASA on 18 October 2004 in Lagos, Nigeria.

the United States.[23] Therefore, the Pentecostal constituency can contribute to the quality of governance as it teaches its membership to jettison individualism, a trap for corruption and ethnicity, and seek a conducive environment where all citizens recognize themselves as part of the community with civil responsibilities. It is through participation that we can speak and listen to ourselves and emphasise the reciprocity of our actions. Tocqueville believed that as a result of participation, people learn values that transcend self and enhance pluralism. The Pentecostal faith as a revivalist tradition has often centred on participation and associational life. Thus, the civic value of Pentecostal faith can be brought to bear on governance.

Lastly, there is need to strengthen the church hierarchy in Africa. Presently, the clergy are not trained to fulfil functional political roles in modern Africa. It is no longer adequate in the contemporary world to train a person in a two-year Bible college and expect him to function effectively in the competitive modern world. Even in the Pentecostal-charismatic churches, the pastors hardly have any theological training but only rely on the in-house Bible teaching from teachers who themselves are not trained but only rely on their spiritual gifts. Therefore, the churches must seek ways of broadening the outlook and orientation of their ministers either by recommending training in secular post-secondary institutions as a prerequisite for admission to seminaries and pastoral training institutions, or by affiliating their training institutions to secular ones. Broad-based secular training is necessary as a tool for advancement in the present competitive world. In order to counter the political domination of Islamic fundamentalism, the church must have capable leaders to speak out on its behalf and to mobilise church members for effective actions.

Conclusion

In contemporary times, it is impossible to live in Africa and be indifferent to political issues. Not only in terms of cataclysmic events such as the government clamp-down on missionaries in Southern Sudan in the late 1950s and 1960s; the government-inspired assassination of Anglican Archbishop Jamani Luwum of Uganda in February 1977; the religious riots in Nigeria in the 1980s, 1990s, 2000, 2003, 2006 and 2008; the attempted compulsory registration of churches in Ghana by the government of Jerry Rawlings in 1989; the massacre of worshippers in an Anglican church in Johannesburg in July 1993; ethnic massacre in Rwanda in 1994-5; the political crisis and ethnic conflict in Kenya in 2008; the deep political

---

[23] James T Kloppenberg, 'Built by Association: What Tocqueville saw in the Ethic of Reciprocity' in Centre for the Study of Values in Public Life, Harvard Divinity School *Religion and Values in Public Life* (Cambridge, Harvard College, 2000), 16-21.

cleavage and structural collapse in Zimbabwe in 2008 and 2009; *but* even in apparently peaceful times, the churches in Africa are increasingly confronting the discrimination of political power. Therefore, African Christian spirituality ought to be re-modelled to confront modern challenges.

There is no reason to believe that Africa will within a short time break from its circle of poverty, backwardness and disintegration on its own strength or solely through political and economic means. But the churches can do much to change the situation and accelerate progress towards better governance. At least the churches can end their complicity in the crisis, and thus, as Charismatics have prescribed, minister the gospel of renewal to their own members. In addition, the churches must face the geopolitical realities in the continent with forceful challenge. Certainly, there are no effective alternatives to that. Can the churches continue to maintain a distance from politics considering the present geopolitical realties of the continent? Or as Ka Mana puts it, 'What type of evangelisation should be undertaken to create innovative societies and personalities' in Africa?[24]

Finally, Christianity as a major social force in the continent can set the pace for good governance when it brings a lively and redemptive spirituality to bear on the lives of its members and on the fabric of the society. However, the church must first remove the contradictions between what it preaches in the form of values and what it does in reality. Thereafter, it will be in a better position to carry out its missionary and prophetic mandate to the society.

---

[24] Kä Mana, *Christians and Churches of Africa Envisioning the Future* (Akropong, Ghana: Regnum Africa, 2002), 84.

MISSION SPIRITUALITY AND AUTHENTIC DISCIPLESHIP: AN AFRICAN REFLECTION

Serah Wambua

Historical Perspective of the African Church

The 1910 World Missionary Conference met to evaluate and plan the evangelization of the 'non-Christian world', including Africa, which was then termed 'the dark continent'. A century later, the 2010 Conference addressed the subject of mission from a different premise. Today mission is 'from everywhere to everywhere'. One of the significant realities today is the recognition that the centre of Christianity has shifted from the global north to the global south. Yet there remains an urgent need for concerted effort globally and locally to do God's mission in a world that is in even greater need than it was in 1910. In a world today that is diverse and with a population of six billion people, the harvest today is indeed plentiful and the laborers few!

This chapter looks at the wholistic mission of the church in Africa that has been championed by the Anglican Church Mission Society-Africa with sister agencies. We will start with a historical overview of the church in Africa, introduce the African worldview as directly connected to African spirituality, assess the current challenges in the continent and then focus on two key strands in the CMS-Africa's response to the African predicament.

The African church has been in the continent for nearly two thousand years. Western missionaries zealously spread the gospel throughout the continent in the nineteenth and twentieth centuries. The recent history of the Christian church in Africa is linked to the period when colonialists occupied Africa in search of resources such as land and cheap labour.[1] Christian missionaries arrived on the African soil almost hand in hand with the colonial masters, and although they worked in consultation they were not always in agreement. Missionaries questioned certain colonial practices including the slave trade, exploitation of the locals and such oppressive practices. The one belief that both missionaries and colonialists held in common was that African social and cultural systems were primitive and animistic and hence needed to be replaced with European values. In essence, missionaries understood their mandate as being to evangelize the

---

[1] Mvume Dandala, Speech at the National Council of Churches of Kenya National Pastors Conference, 2008.

heathen Africans, including civilizing them to make them the exact replica of the European or American.[2]

The evangelization of Africa which is credited to the missionary movement of the nineteenth century was a sacrificial move on the part of missionaries called to do God's mission. It is on record that on their journey out from Europe some missionaries packed their belongings in their coffins, and indeed many of them died of tropical diseases even before they reached their destinations. This sacrifice has eternal value for the kingdom of God and the African church owes much to our western brothers and sisters. Apart from sharing the gospel and planting churches in Africa, missionaries are applauded for their contributions in education, health and agriculture in African countries where they had a presence. Indeed mission schools produced African leadership that was later to take the front stage in the struggle for independence of Africa.

It is noted that before the coming of missionaries and even after, Africa was religious. Otieno asserts that the typical African worldview is driven by religion. He states 'the interdependence between these life sustaining forces in the universe constitute the very essence of African spirituality, it is how these forces are mediated and managed that promote the abundance of life.'[3] Most traditional African societies believed in a Supreme God. Another important feature of many African religions is the belief in ancestral spirits who mediate between the living and the spirit world. Community life as opposed to individualism is another salient feature of the African worldview. Burnett emphasizes this when he quotes the famous African statement, 'I am, because we are'.[4] This statement in essence summarizes what community life is like in Africa, although this is now changing and what was referred to as traditional African religion is today a mix of African traditional religion and other belief systems.

One of the criticisms levelled against the western missionary movement was the failure by missionaries to acknowledge or even understand the social and cultural values and systems of the African people. Their perception was that the existing cultural practices and beliefs were evil and had no place in the kingdom of God. This presentation of the gospel seems to have confused many in Africa who equated civilization to Christianity, a perception that still lingers on

The missionary movement brought a gospel to Africa that was dualistic and the root causes of dualism can be traced back to Greek influence on early Christianity. The Greek theory dichotomizes the world into two spheres of sacred and secular. This left its mark on the western Christianity

---

[2] Sulaiman Z Jakonda, *Your Kingdom Come: A Book on Wholistic Christian Development* (Jos: RURCON, 2001).
[3] Nicholas Otieno, *Human Rights and Social Justice in Africa: Cultural, Ethical and Spiritual Imperatives* (Nairobi: All Africa Conference of Churches, 2008), 18.
[4] D Olumbe, 'Introduction to African Worldview', paper presented to the AIM ABO Conference, 2007, 63.

which was brought to Africa where a much more wholistic view of life had prevailed. This perhaps explains why Christianity has not found much depth in the continent despite the presence of the churches over many years. The notion of the sacred and the secular has influenced the churches and the mission field to this day.

It is acknowledged that missionaries did a commendable job before passing on the baton to Africans. Mission stations across Africa, typically with a school, a medical centre and a church, were well managed. When missionaries started handing over these institutions to Africans, the process often lacked careful planning.[5] Africans seemed ill-prepared to handle the responsibilities that soon became theirs. This is evident in most African countries including Kenya, Uganda and Nigeria.

The African Context

The African church has been in the hands of Africans for several decades since independence. Some of the evangelistic mission organizations in the continent include the African Evangelistic Enterprise serving across the continent since 1960 when Billy Graham preached in Nairobi. AEE is a child of the East Africa Revival. This ministry focuses on evangelism of African cities and has made a mark on the continent.[6] The East Africa Revival, despite its legalistic attributes, made an impact on the spirituality of the greater East African region. The transparency, accountability and oneness of this movement left a mark that lingers on in church life in East Africa today.

Several surveys by church-related agencies have placed the rate of church growth in Africa at 3% annually.[7] This growth has been phenomenal, both within the ecumenical and the Pentecostal movements. Yet despite this impressive growth there are underlying issues in African spirituality that need to be addressed. The African church is commonly referred to as 'a mile long and an inch deep'. Although this statement arouses negative emotions among many African church leaders, it is largely true. The growth of the church in Africa will become wasted if proper and effective discipleship is not applied. There is an urgent need to raise genuine disciples of Christ to do mission in obedience to Christ's command. A key aspect of the African people that has not been addressed, especially by Africans themselves, is the African worldview which places religion and spirituality at the core. It helps define who they are. While analyzing Reinhard Bonnke's theology and its undoubted appeal in Africa, Frank Kursechner-Palkmann points out that the Pentecostal movement is

---

[5] Jakonda, *Your Kingdom Come*, 42-43.
[6] Darku Amoo Nii, *Holistic City Evangelism: Accra Perspective* (Accra: Eshcolit, 2005), 112.
[7] Darrow L Miller and Scott Allen, *Against All Hope: Hope for Africa* (Nairobi: All Africa Conference of Churches, 2005), 42-43.

the fastest growing Christian force in the world.[8] The theology of Bonnke revolves around Satan, demons, healing and the Holy Spirit. This doctrine appeals to an African audience that has had real experiences with the spirit world.

Islam has been present and active in Africa for several centuries now, but more recently the strategy seems well calculated to Islamize Africa. The turning point can be traced to the 1979 Medina conference when Muslims took stock of their mission in Africa and consequently re-positioned themselves to seek more converts in the continent. Recent statistical analysis places Christians at 48.37% while Muslims were at 41.32%.[9] Most cities and towns in Africa today are woken up by the Islamic call to prayer. Today many of the key business sectors in the continent, including communication and tourism, are run or being earmarked for purchase by Muslims.

Traditionally, Islam and Christianity co-existed, but more recently there have been conflicts between the two religions, particularly in Sudan and Nigeria. The church in Africa is becoming increasingly aware of the challenge of Islam. This awareness is crucial since it presents numerous opportunities for dialogue and evangelism. The traditional attitude on the part of Christians has been lacking the great commission message to 'disciple all nations'. Today most of us are convicted that we need to reach out to our Muslim brothers as 'Christ also died for them'.

Poverty has been a perennial challenge in sub-Saharan Africa. While other continents, particularly Asia and Latin America, have made positive progress in this regard, Africa has remained stagnant. The United Nations Millennium Development goal number one addresses poverty and points particularly to sub-Saharan Africa with increasing numbers still living on less than a dollar a day. Political conflicts, climatic changes, famine, diseases such as HIV/AIDS and global economic recession have deepened the poverty challenge in Africa. The church is slowly recognizing that God's mission is irrelevant in Africa without addressing poverty as a primary concern.

Unemployment is yet another challenge in Africa. This is compounded by a youthful population, with 60% under 25 years of age.[10] This situation presents multiple challenges including crime, idleness, opportunistic diseases and political unrest, with young people being used by politicians in conflict areas. Child soldiers have been a significant feature of political strife in Africa, including in northern Uganda, the Democratic Republic of Congo and more recently in the Kenyan crisis of 2008. The South African case of xenophobia in 2008 involved this same youthful population who

---

[8] Frank Kürschner-Pelkmann, *Reinhard Bonnke's Theology: A Pentecostal Preacher and His Mission – A Critical Analysis* (Hamburg: EMW, 2004).
[9] Patrick Johnstone and Jason Mandryk, *Operation World: 21st Century Edition* (Carlisle: Paternoster, 2001), 21.
[10] Dandala, Speech at National Pastors Conference.

out of their own vulnerability targeted their own brothers 'on the basis of borders that were not even of our own making as Africans'.[11]

Other challenges in our context include ethnic tensions, secularism, gender imbalances, child abuse, corruption and related injustices. In the midst of all this, the one question asked by both Christians and by members of other faiths is: 'Where is the church?' This question is obviously based on the premise that Christians form the majority in Sub-Saharan Africa, and yet what has been their social and economic impact? The reality is that the church is visible on Sundays in Africa but the question is: where is the church from Monday to Saturday?

The Paradox – Africa's Resources verses Africa's Woes

The Church Mission Society (CMS-Africa) has been accompanying the church in Africa addressing the above question. CMS has a history of over 200 years in Africa – sending missionaries, planting churches and evangelizing. Earlier on, CMS understood mission as 'from the west to the rest' of the world. Today CMS acknowledges with gratitude to God that mission is 'from everywhere to everywhere'. CMS-Africa, has its mission motivated by the conviction that Africa is blessed. This empowering message is rooted in the belief that the church is God's principal agent of social and cultural transformation. We believe that this century is indeed the defining moment for the church and CMS is envisioning the church in Africa to address the area of wholistic discipleship, an area that has not been seen as an integral ministry of the church. The five marks of mission as defined by the Anglican Communion and adopted by CMS-Britain calls the church to preach the gospel, make disciples, serve the poor, tackle injustice, and save the planet. This broadly summarizes the mission of the church.

The heartbreaking paradox is that, despite her problems, Africa is indeed endowed with resources that can be exploited to make a significant difference in the continent. Miller and Allen assert that despite Africa's brokenness, she is blessed with unimaginable abundance.[12] Africa is the second largest continent on earth. It is home to over 874 million people, forming about 14% of the world population. Africa is the world's richest continent in terms of natural resources.

In terms of agriculture, it has been argued that Zambia, Zimbabwe and the Democratic Republic of Congo combined have the potential to feed the entire continent. Farming, herding, ranching and commercial crops mark the African landscape. Besides, the African continent is home of some of the greatest rivers of the world. Deposits of some of the world's known minerals exist in Africa: cobalt, platinum, diamonds, gold and copper, to

---

[11] Dandala, Speech at National Pastors Conference.
[12] Miller and Allen, *Against All Hope*.

mention but a few. Besides, Africa's energy potential is almost unlimited. Libya, Nigeria and Angola are among the world's top ten oil producers. On solar potential, Dr Adeyemo writes, 'The Sahara desert alone covers a solar energy field area of about 9,065,000 kilometers, which holds more potential to produce more than Africa's energy needs for all her domestic electrical appliances.'[13]

Not only is Africa's rich heritage remarkable, but the scripture makes a lot of reference to Africa. It was the Middle East and Africa that served as the birthplace and early homeland of Judeo-Christian faith. Africa played a vital role in the life of Jesus. Africa was the place of refuge for Jesus when King Herod threatened his life.[14] There are many more references in the scripture affirming that from the beginning God's eye was on Africa, to bless her and not to curse her. This is the Biblical message that is inspiring and giving hope to us in Africa.

Yet, the people of Africa are the greatest source of wealth in Africa. They are made in God's image and are gifted by God in diverse ways to bless the continent. Africans form 3,500 ethnic groups speaking some 2,110 languages. Africans are renowned for their culture, music, celebrations, colours and art. They are respected for their generosity, perseverance, respect for elders and strong sense of family.

The Root Problem

Today many Africans are convinced that the African worldview is the root cause of our problems. Dennis Tongoi, in, the Foreword to the book *Against All Hope: Hope for Africa*, asserts that the numerous development initiatives in Africa will fail unless the worldview of the African people is identified, acknowledged and addressed.[15] Sulaiman Jakonda affirms this position when he states 'Despite all modernization, the typical African worldview has always been governed by religion.'[16] This indeed is the gap that both the missionary church as well as the current church has failed to address. The African indigenous church movement largely grew out of this failure by the church to address pertinent issues rooted in African culture and religion. African cultural practices such as polygamy, witchcraft, veneration of ancestral spirits, clan and communal responsibility left African Christians hanging, and the result has been Christians torn between the two worlds.

We recognize that, for one to do God's mission, it has to be within a cultural setting and consequently the value systems and beliefs inevitably

---

[13] Tekouboh Adeyemo, *Hope for Africa: Against All Hope* (Nairobi: Samaritan Strategy Africa, 2005).
[14] Miller and Allen, *Against All Hope*.
[15] Adeyemo, *Hope for Africa*.
[16] Jakonda, *Your Kingdom Come*.

come into play. Christian workers and missionaries therefore need to study and understand the worldviews of the people they work with. It has been observed for instance that some of the strongest Christian countries in Africa have experienced the worst injustices. Rwanda, which was home of the East Africa revival movement, suffered one of the worst cases of genocide. The African worldview for instance teaches, 'My tribe is better than yours, men are superior to women, fatalism and witchcraft,' among other unbiblical and disempowering views of life in Africa.[17]

Miller and Allen have correctly argued that the key to social and cultural transformation lies in the worldview of the people.[18] This is true anywhere, but more so in Africa where traditions and cultural practices are so deep-rooted. We are convinced that churches as well as governments and development experts in Africa need to address this crucial aspect of human beings for any sustainable development to take place.

We argued earlier that Africans are religious people and that religion and worldview inform each other. The concept of worldview refers to the total set of beliefs or assumptions that comprise the mindset of an individual, consequently determining how they view reality.[19] Worldview is the underlying set of ideas that enables people to cope with life in a given culture.[20] Darrow and Allen have argued in their book that ideas have consequences and that indeed as the Bible states we reap what we sow (Gal 6:7). Tokunboh Adeyemo of the Centre for Biblical Transformation affirms this school of thought when he states the 'Faith is processed in the mind and acted out in the visible... world after the mind had approved of it.'[21]

The Africa working group, convinced that a paradigm shift in Africa is necessary in order for the church in Africa to make a difference, have designed a comprehensive training on worldview specifically aimed at invoking the Biblical worldview in the African context. CMS-Africa is part of the Africa working group. We believe that the church is God's principally ordained agency for social and cultural transformation. We recognize the brokenness of the church in Africa, yet we know that Christ sees the church as his bride continuously being made perfect. The church is perhaps the single most important indigenous sustainable institution, with members in virtually every sphere of society (arts, music, business, governance, education, farming etc). The time is therefore ripe for the African church to present the whole gospel so that the kingdom of God may be experienced in Africa.

---

[17] Miller and Allen, *Against All Hope*.
[18] Miller and Allen, *Against All Hope*.
[19] Miller and Allen, *Against All Hope*, 39.
[20] Charles H Kraft, 'Culture Worldview and Contextualization', in Ralph D Winter and Steven C Hawthorne (eds), *Perspectives on World Christian Movement: A Reader* (3rd ed, Pasadena: William Carey Library, 1999), 385, 87.
[21] Adeyemo, *Hope for Africa*.

Mission Spirituality and Authentic Discipleship: An African Reflection

God's intentions for us in Africa as for the rest of the world are echoed in the Book of Isaiah 65:20:

> Never again will there be an infant who lives for a few days
> Or an old man who does not live out his years;
> He who dies at a hundred will be thought a mere youth;
> He who fails to reach a hundred will be considered accursed.

In a continent experiencing the very opposite of Isaiah's message, we are catalyzing the church to dream, a dream that is coming to reality. Yet, for the church to effectively advance God's intentions, its leadership requires fresh vision and equipping. Since 1999, a group of passionate and gifted men and women have been envisioning church leaders across the continent, providing them with a fresh vision for the church as God's primary agent of wholistic transformation across the spheres of human existence, social, cultural, spiritual, political, economic and environmental.

Churches that have received this worldview training are making remarkable contributions to the transformation of their communities. They are effectively and practically addressing issues like the HIV and AIDS pandemic, responding to conflict with Biblical peacemaking principles, and effectively engaging in social, political, business and environmental concerns using their local recourses. Unsurprisingly, they are also more effective in their evangelistic outreach. They are realizing how powerful the Christian message becomes when the church both proclaims and demonstrates the good news of the kingdom.

Today, these African trainers, referred to as 'Samaritan Strategy' are advancing this tested wholistic Discipleship training program into every corner of the continent. Since 1999, this network of trainers has empowered over 3,000 churches and over 100,000 church leaders in 35 African countries. The partnership between CMS-Africa with the Africa Working Group has been strategic for God's mission in Africa. The history of the CMS in evangelism, church planting and community development in Africa for over two hundred years has created strong links with churches in the continent. We are humbled to see God at work as we hear many stories (like the one below) from across the continent where Christians and churches are reaching out to those in need – bringing the kingdom of God to them.

The Vision Conference in 2002 was a day of awakening for Pastor Luke and three other members of the Power Revival Centre. It gave birth to a new vision of changing his church and surrounding community for the glory of God by sowing a seed of love. This seed grew to become the Sheep Care Community Centre, a registered local self-help group. At the conference organized by CMS and facilitated by Dennis Tongoi they were challenged that human lives and success largely depend on the worldview they hold. They sat together and listed their resources: an empty *mabati* (iron sheet) church which was only used for few hours on Sunday and a group of young jobless people.

A simple survey in Nairobi's Soweto slums revealed that many school-age children were not in school. The majority were roaming the streets and/or scavenging for food. Pastor Luke met them and challenged them to do something for nothing, instead of doing nothing for nothing – that by loving God, themselves and others they would realize their destiny and bring change in their community and beyond.

Sheep Care was the centre's response towards the findings of the survey and the first ministry to be implemented. They offered to teach the children for free. After some weeks, two children were brought by their guardians and they started teaching them in the church hall. Later the team came across street children and after interacting with them it emerged that their greatest needs were for love and food. Pastor Luke began by dividing the maize flour in his house to make porridge for some 20 children. Breakthrough came when some of the hard-core street children were rehabilitated and reunited with their families. From then on, parents and guardians began to bring their children to the centre.

To date the school has 350 children. The school takes care of baby class pupils to class seven. The Lord has enabled the school to build twelve classrooms as church members and others were touched by the ministry. They now have enough desks as opposed to children sitting on the dust. There are eight volunteer teaching staff. Their biggest challenge is feeding these children.

Subsequently four other seeds have been planted. The BISAK Ministry offers: balanced ecosystem, improved nutrition and income generation, social development, alternative agriculture and kitchen gardening. The formation of BISAK ministry was triggered by deteriorating environmental standards in Soweto slums. The ministry strives to realize a healthy and sustainable environment for God's creation. In addition the ministry seeks to address the increasing malnutrition and orphans in the area due to HIV/AIDS

Other ministries include the Sheep Care School of Computer Studies which strives to bring computer training and services to Soweto community. It is also an income generating activity for the centre. The Water and Sanitation Ministry is bringing water nearer to the residents at an affordable rate. God has worked through his servants and now there is a borehole in the centre. The borehole has impressive yields and they intend to use the water to plant trees, run the alternative agriculture project, fish farming, meet all the centre's water needs and share with the community at an affordable rate. The Art and Design Ministry identifies and exposes the art talent in the community. It concentrates only on art that glorifies God. The products are sold, thus generating some income while creating employment opportunities through utilization of such talents.

Pastor Luke and his church, whose Motto is 'care and feed the flock', have indeed risen to the challenge by demonstrating love to their neighbors. This is a church with a clear mission to its community, utilizing available local resources from within the community and wholistically reaching out in word and in deed. This indeed is the teaching given by the Samaritan Strategy training which is a mindset transformation as churches and Christians like Pastor Luke become agents of hope in their own communities.

Business as Mission

On the economic front, we realize the challenges in the continent are equally complex, with both historical and contemporary factors coming into play. Africa stands today as the poorest continent with only 1.7% of the world's GNP. Yet as has been pointed out, there are abundant and untapped resources in the continent which can transform the continent into an economic power base.

During the Lausanne World Evangelization meeting in Thailand in 2004, a new strategy for doing God's mission, namely Business as Mission (BAM), was born and endorsed as one key strategy for the twenty-first century. BAM was found particularly strategic for encouraging business people and entrepreneurs to engage in mission, especially in the least developed countries and among the un-reached people groups. For the last four years, a passionate group of African leaders have been envisioning the church and Christians in Africa to embrace business as mission as a viable missionary strategy in Africa. BAM is calling on the African church to release entrepreneurs and business professional within the church to transform the world through their business activities.

Lausanne 2004 defines Business as Mission as a movement of kingdom-minded business people whose emphasis is to transform communities through their businesses with the intention of making Jesus known, encountered and followed. BAM recognizes that the daily work of doing and being in business is one way of engaging with society, bringing the kind of transformation desired by the Christian faith.[22]

Business as Mission is part of the worldview training specifically developing the business sector. The context for this strategy is the tendency for our churches to be dichotomized, basically marginalizing business people and professionals and inviting them to church only during fundraising events. It is now getting increasingly accepted that this dichotomy is both unbiblical and counter-productive for the great commission. We are therefore calling the church to embrace business people, affirm them and then release them to the market – their mission field. BAM is a wholistic mission with a conscious evangelistic engagement with the business world as a place where the Lordship of Christ and the kingdom of God is worked out in decisions, culture, structures and systems of commercial life. BAM recognizes business as a

---

[22] Business as Mission (BAM) Lausanne Forum, 2004.

calling, business people as fulltime ministers – not just as mission supporters – and the market place as a prime mission field. BAM is about real business. In Africa, BAM aims at what we are referring to as the quadruple bottom-line, seeking financial, social, spiritual and environmental outcomes.

The BAM seed is now planted in several countries in the region including Kenya, Uganda, Rwanda, Burundi and Ghana, with growing and passionate teams championing the movement. We see BAM as the entry point for poverty reduction in Africa as gifted entrepreneurs within churches resonate with this new mission thinking and begin to address community transformation in and from the market place. BAM is empowering and inspiring businessmen in Africa to create jobs and make wealth strategically dealing with the poverty challenge. We see BAM as a timely mission strategy given the trends in the world economy as well as the trends in Islam. New opportunities are emerging as business people find unique and more dignifying avenues of doing God's mission. We have businesses in place (see below) demonstrating that BAM is working. We are using the CMS platform to connect best practices for learning as well as connecting entrepreneurs with capital to enhance business as mission in Africa.

Herbal Garden (HG) was established in 2006 with the primary purpose of addressing mass poverty through sustainable solutions, thereby, expressing our BAM core values of fulfilling economic, social spiritual and environmental responsibilities. HG aims to contribute to poverty alleviation in Kenya through foundational principles of a solid work ethic. HG has its vision to economically empower families, bring sufficient nutrition, and uplift communities to live in dignity. The vision of HG is to enable strategic partnerships that add value to integrated agribusiness in marginalized communities.

The Aloe Vera project was the first where farmers are growing Aloe Vera and the company is processing the various products and marketing them locally and internationally. Already the company has its flagship product (Aloe Vera soap), with high aloe content, which is successfully helping to treat a variety of skin ailments. Additionally, HG has formulated 'Pruna Essential Tea' made from Pruna-Africanas which helps in the management of various cancers. HG is partnering with farmers in training other farmers, income generation, and crop management extension in consultation with the Ministry of Agriculture. We are encouraging farmers to use the added income to plant other crops such as pyrethrum for insecticides and maize for bio fuels.

Conclusion

Wholistic ministry is about transformation of those who are disciples of Jesus to bring the kingdom of God to their communities. The African church is increasingly responding to the call of God to do integral mission incorporating both proclamation and demonstration of the good news of Jesus. It is becoming apparent that wholistic mission is not an option if the church is to be relevant to society. Churches are beginning to realise that the gospel is about the kingdom of God This wholistic mission approach is transforming society as dualism is addressed and the whole church is equipped for works of service. This kingdom-based mission seeks to engage all the human and material resources at the disposal of the church. It is equipping more disciples as businessmen and professionals realize that they are fulltime ministers of the gospel and that the market place is indeed their mission field. This is multiplying the Christian witness and resources at the disposal of the church.

At the same time, churches are beginning to engage with their own worldview and relating it to the Biblical worldview in addressing pertinent issues such as HIV and AIDS, fatalism and governance. There are parallels that can be drawn between the African worldview and the Biblical worldview, and as the church engages in these teachings, Christians are gaining insight into biblical truths. Relevant materials are now in the market for use by the African church, including an African Bible commentary written by Africans. Yet we know that transformation is the work of the Holy Spirit moving the body of Christ from where we are to where God intends us to be.

A MISSION TO AND FROM THE YOUTH

Rosauro Lopez Sandoval
(translated by Michelle Alvarez)

Introduction

Although the population of Bolivia is not as large as that of other Latin American countries, the life conditions of its major cities in relation to young people is similar to that of other countries. One can see young people struggling to survive, longing to have better days, and to be taken into consideration. What characterizes the young Bolivian city dwellers today is their desire to be able to live more comfortably. As a result they have chosen education, hoping to secure a fixed income for their lives. Some seek admission into colleges of education to secure teaching positions in order to secure a government salary which, although it is not much, is a fixed allotment they can count on every month. Others look for college degrees to gain social status and to negotiate a job, since the situation of poverty and joblessness leads many professionals to act in this way due to the lack of youth policies.[1]

In addition another element that affects Bolivia's youth is the impact of globalization and the world of technology which makes many young people live in uncertainty, since they do not have the ability to cope and compete in various job opportunities. This is a reflection of the existent educational poverty in Bolivia, since academic schooling and training do not respond to the need of most small businesses.[2]

Through the previous description, one can see the situation faced by many young people today. Deficient government policies are partly the product of unorganized societies in which everyone seeks their personal interest thus increasing a mind-set of survival, no matter what. The reality and the insecurity lived many young people, is not knowing what will happen to them tomorrow.

Another factor that characterizes young Bolivians is the issue of gangs in remote areas of the city outskirts. These consist of young people looking to take centre stage and be heard. Unfortunately their behaviour causes damage to society and to themselves, but the reality of life in different social sectors has led them into this lifestyle. There are also young

---

[1] A. López, 'What do the youth want?', in Garza Azul (ed), *Opinion and Analysis* (la Paz-Bolivia, 2003), 65-67.
[2] López, 'What do the youth want?', 74-77.

environmentalists who seek prominence in order to be heard by the adult society. In the same manner, there are those who campaign for human rights.

If we attempt to examine in depth why there are young people who become violent and disrespectful in society, one could simply cite examples taken from articles, showing young people living in abuse, discrimination, imposition, and violence. This is the reality faced by young men and women in society, on the street, in the family, in schools, at work, anywhere and at anytime. If these are the conditions that youth face, no other type of behaviour can be expected from them, since the reality of their surroundings becomes their actions. Consequently one sees a youth that strongly portrays a global society in ways that it would not like to be portrayed.[3]

Due to this vision, we must take a look at the social contexts where young people live and operate. At this point, the church environment also comes in and we could ask ourselves: how is it helping today's youth in the development of values?

In this chapter we will look into the different attitudes and skills of young people who participate in church communities, specifically in urban and peri-urban areas. We will demonstrate the skills they possess and how these can be utilized, working closely with them in order to help them in this process of growth within their spiritual world. It is also of interest to discover what moves a youth group to come into being and to participate in the life of the church. We will consider different types of groups and how they can be apostles among other youth, in their families, schools, colleges, and throughout the social environment where they move.

Announcement of the Gospel, Incarnate in Life, as a Witness to Contemporary Society

Firstly, we must clarify that 'the word *mission* comes from the Latin word *missio* or from the verb *mittere*, meaning to send. Now this word covers two things: the act of sending and content of what is sent, or if you prefer, the relationship between the sender and the one sent. These two concepts must be included in the concept of mission. The mission is, then, sending and the missionary a messenger or apostle (from the Greek verb *apostello*, 'send'). Apostleship entails sending, mission, delegation or embassy.'[4]

This present mission has to start from life, the concrete acts given in the various social and cultural milieus. For this, it is necessary to think in terms of relationships in an interpersonal and cultural dialogue which helps to

---

[3] Julio Benites Balladares, Reinaldo Pazmiño Arbelaéz and Juan Bautista de Oliveira, 'An insight into youth violence', *Spíritus Magazine* 47:182 (March 2006).
[4] R Alonso de Linaje, *Mission is the Life of the Church in America* (2nd ed, Guatemala: Temas de Catequesis), 35.

grow and humanize the diverse societies. To do this we must shed all prejudice in order to reach a dialogue where reciprocity between people exists, where we are not dogmatic in our fundamental postures which provoke rejection from the other side, since these are perceived as hostility towards their identity and their culture.

In this respect mission with and from today's youth should be oriented to dialogue, where the youth feel part of the struggle for life. In the same manner a young Jesus must be presented, that is, one who walks with them, where they can talk to him as one more of their own age, where there is mutual confidence. To meet this challenge we must work from the different institutions that are engaged in pastoral care and mission to the youth.

In the preparation of the Fifth Bolivian National Missionary Congress the conviction emerged that all the baptized are called to be missionaries – they have to go from being evangelized to be evangelizers.[5] On one hand, priests as witnesses and disciples of Christ are called to be instruments of forgiveness and reconciliation, committed to the service of the faithful according to the Spirit of the gospel. Furthermore they must be attentive to the challenges of today's world and sensitive to the suffering of people. Priests must try to discern the charisms of the faithful through listening and dialogue, so that they can contribute to the encouragement of a community.[6]

Among the challenges posed to the priest by the document of the Conference of Aparecida, is the current culture in which he operates and one he should understand, in order for Jesus' message to be relevant for the life of the community and especially for the youth. To meet this challenge priests must have a human, spiritual, intellectual, and pastoral formation. For the work of priests to be coherent and convincing, they should love their pastoral work and be in communion with the bishop and other priests of the diocese.[7]

The laity are also called to be witnesses and disciples of Christ. The teaching of the Second Vatican Council emphasizes the common dignity of the baptized and this also refers to the mission. The laity must be aware of their worth. The shepherds must value the spiritual work of the laity, which leads other sisters and brothers to encounter Jesus.[8] To achieve this goal it is necessary that the laity have a strong faith formation, experience in

---

[5] Pontifical Mission Societies. Instrument of participation for the Missionary Regional Congress of Bolivia. Path towards the Fifth National Missionary Conference of Bolivia. CAM 3 (Third American Missionary Congress). COMLA 8 (Eight Latin American Missionary Congress), La Paz-Bolivia, 64-65.
[6] John Paul II, Apostolic Exhortation *Ecclesia in América*, and the Saints and the faithful deacons and the encounter with Jesus, path toward conversion, communion and solidarity in America (January 22, 1999), n. 39.
[7] V Latin American Episcopal Conference and the Caribbean (CELAM), in Aparecida – Brasil, May 13 – 31, 2007, *The Life of Our Peoples Today*, n.196-197.
[8] John Paul II, *Ecclesia in América*, n. 44.

prayer and a witnessing life. In this way lay people will feel like missionaries in the place where they are, whether in the family, work, neighbourhood or in politics. The task of the laity in the church is important for the church, both in the inter-ecclesial environment, as well as in the social environment where they operate.[9]

The document of the Fifth Conference of the Latin American Episcopate (held in Aparecida), also refers to the laity as 'men of the church in the heart of the world and men of the world in the heart of the church.'[10] This is the environment to which lay people are called, the world of politics, economy, culture, science and the arts. In the same manner, they bear witness by their love for their family and love for their children. At the same time, the laity are called to bear witness to life.[11]

The Santo Domingo Conference highlights the call Jesus continues to make to young people in order to make sense of their lives. It also shows that youth are the future and therefore must be prepared to assume responsibility, both in the social and cultural as well as in the ecclesiastical sphere. They must actively express their responsibility and be guided by the Holy Spirit, so they can shape society in a more humanitarian and Christian direction.[12]

Taking into consideration what has been said so far, we can now gather the thoughts of young people that participate in groups within the church, in regards to their missionary commitment, and the challenges they face as young people in the present world.

How Young People Perceive their Missionary Commitment

At this point we want to show the experiences of young people in being the church today. We refer to the Bolivian reality. These views were collected from young people who participate in groups in the Catholic Church. The purpose of this field work is to discover the experience of the youth arising from their being part of the church of Jesus. It seeks to reveal the concerns that move them to participate in the different groups, the difficulties they have as young people in this commitment to Jesus, what they see that needs to be worked out within the ecclesiastical institution to improve the work with young people themselves, and the challenges they face as young people committed to the church. The age range for the surveys in parishes was 15 to 25 .

---

[9] Pontifical Mission Societies. Path towards the Fifth Nacional Missionary Conference of Bolivia, 64-65.
[10] *The life of our peoples today*, n.209.
[11] *The life of our peoples today*, n.210-211
[12] *The life of our peoples today*, n.111

a) What young people understand by mission; where the mission of Jesus should be carried out today; how the mission is actually carried out in different communities.

On the subject of mission, young people understand the term as having a plan for their lives, thus demonstrating with this personal attitude that their personal growth is based on sound values.[13] In the same manner they conceive the mission as following Jesus, going where he sends them, announcing the good news that is the gospel, beginning from the heart of the home, and being available in the service of others. And they also understand that this mission should be carried out in all places of society, especially among the poorest, in remote places among people who are spiritually lacking, 'as this mission is an experienced proclamation, where the presence of God is discovered in the world and his love for humanity is made known.'[14]

As for the practice in parish communities, on the one hand young people express their mission for Jesus through the preaching of the word, through prayer and meditation. They make it clear that these parishes are living cells of the church, where the faithful have an experience of relationship with Christ.[15] But others claim that in their parishes more organization is needed as it relates to the mission, because they are only involved a sacramental ministry, where the priests are more interested in the participation of people in the Mass. These young people think that a parish is a school in which we experience formation for evangelization and catechesis. They believe also that the parish is a place of encounter and bond of communion which should be open to different people, cultures and groups as an integrative core of ministries and charisms. In summary, a parish must be characterized by communion and missionary participation: liturgical, ecumenical, prophetic and transformative.[16]

b) From his baptism, how young people feel called to follow Jesus.

The young people surveyed expressed the view that the mission is for everyone, especially for those who have embraced the faith since baptism. This is the reason why they perceive themselves as missionaries and want to put their mission into practice, from wherever they are, in any social context. They also emphasise the importance of providing assistance to

---

[13] R. Cuadrado, *Values for the Youth, Called to be Happy* (Madrid: Covarrubias), 153.
[14] First meeting with Youth Missionaries, 'Memory we have come to worship and announce', Tolata, Cbba, Bolivia, January 4-8, 2005, 20.
[15] *The life of our peoples today*, n.170, 171.
[16] Pontifical Mission Societies, 'Our Parish to the Missionary Challenge' (Buenos Aires: New Age), 8-9.

others, showing love to the simplest. And this they want to carry out as a lay movement.

The mentality of these young people involved in the communities is due in part to the existing values in Bolivian families. In nuclear families, who live out solidarity among their members, there is a profound religiosity, respect for life, and marriages where there is still fidelity. Community support also exists, especially among the poor. The oral tradition of the grandparents is preserved and passed on from parents to children.[17] The conjugal love of the spouses provides the basis for the procreation and education of children, creating a family community. With the love that spouses give each other, they become co-operators with the God of life and the children become a reflection of this love.[18]

The mentality is also due to the good reception that young people can find in parish groups, where young people feel good about themselves, without rejection by others, where there is an atmosphere of mutual understanding. Besides being with others of the same age, the experience of parish groups is an opportunity to create bonds of friendship and bring their skills into play. But all this will last to the degree that mechanisms are created in which a young person can feel attracted not only to persons his age, but more importantly feel the stimulus of the community to work for a Christian commitment, where each young person feels the call of Jesus who invites them to be disciples and apostles.

At the same time we must consider the fact of difficulties, especially the material ones, in which other families live. In recent years many families have been disrupted because of migration to cities and other countries, seeking better living conditions, leaving their children in the hands of family members and in other cases with a brother or sister. This has led to other kinds of training for the children, which often has not been the right one, given the importance of paternal and maternal influence. The situation of poverty remains in many Bolivian families where parents have to work all day, leaving their children alone at home; situations where economic problems and abuse of alcohol affects many couples, causing the disintegration of their homes.

c) *The various issues affecting young people to pursue a true commitment to Jesus and his church*

Just as young people feel the call of Jesus to carry out his missionary work, they also realize that they face obstacles on account of their youth. Among these is the economic factor, as some have to work and study for some

---

[17] P Romero, *Family and Human Development in Bolivia* (Cochabamba: Divine Word, 2002), 50-51.
[18] Episcopal Bolivian Conferencia, Pastoral Letter from the Bolivian Episcopal leadership to families, 22 April 1983, 33-34.

time, leaving little time for religious activities. This excuse among young people is quite understandable, but there is also the fact of non-attraction to church activities. Just as they expressed that the time factor prevents their commitment, they recognize that they have time for other non-academic university events which is a major cause of their withdrawal from parish groups they once attended. There is also the fact that universities do not provide an education with positive community values. On the contrary, values of individual competence are promoted in the quest to excel in a professional sphere.[19] Since the university should be the centre of leadership training, it becomes necessary for the church to participate in that environment, to build a new society. This requires that the church participates in this environment, illuminating scientific research through appropriate pastoral encouragement services, while respecting academic freedom.[20]

Some of these young people see the ecclesiastical institution closed in relation to their thinking, so they are not attracted to participate in their communities. Perhaps this is mostly due to the lack of interest to know the reality of young people in different parish communities, or the type of training provided, which does not reflect the reality experienced by young people in Latin America and much less in neighbourhoods or communities where there is an influx of young people.[21] To change this mentality, it is necessary for priests to take into account the current challenges of society. They must dialogue and listen to people so there will be lay people who help with missionary encouragement within the community and beyond, in the wider society.[22] Here I name Pope Paul VI who expressed the importance of the lay person, since their life unfolds in different fields of the social world: politics, economics, culture, science, media, as well as family and the educational field of children and youth.[23]

However, just as there are young people who find it difficult to practise their faith, there are others who have no problem spending time on church activities. With this attitude young people put into practice what was expressed in the preparation towards the Fifth National Missionary Congress, which affirms that all the baptized are called to be missionaries. They have to go from being evangelized to evangelize. But for the laity to

---

[19] National plan of formation for the university national pastoral of Bolivia, May 2005, 3.
[20] Third General Conference of Latin American Bishops, Puebla de los Angeles, Mexico, January 27 to February 13, 1979, 'Evangelization in the Present and the Future of Latin America', 1054.1057, in *General Conferences of Latin American Episcopal Churches, Río de Janeiro, Medellín, Puebla y Santo Domingo* (Santa fe de Bogota: Kimpres, 1994).
[21] Cochabamba Archdiocese, *Missions Commission, Pastoral Influence of the Archdiocese towards CAM 3 – COMLA8*, Cochabamba-Bolivia. 2007, 2.
[22] John Paul II, Apostolic Exhortation *Ecclesia in América*, 39.
[23] Paul VI, Apostolic Exhortation *Evangelii Nuntiandii*, (December 8, 1978), 70.

fulfil this mission it is necessary that pastors trust them as adults in the faith, encouraging them to fulfil their ecclesiastical task. In the same way, it is necessary that the laity have a strong faith formation, with experience in prayer and a witnessing life. In this way the laity must consider themselves missionaries in the place where they are, whether in family, work, neighbourhood or in political matters. As mentioned, the task of the laity in the church is important, both within the church and in the social environment in which they operate.[24]

Taking into account the views that have been evident from the experience of young people, we see how much thought and behaviour depends on the environment where the person lives, since in diverse societies one can also appreciate diverse forms of cultural expression. It is therefore necessary to take into account the reality of each young person to guide him or her in personal and community growth. It is essential to value the presence of these young people who have faith rooted in their lives, because as young people they can be apostles to their peers. For this, it is necessary to help them in their training as leaders. We encounter the problem of many young people with little religious culture, not just those who do not participate in church activities, but also those who do. Among the latter, active in their parish communities, some expressed the view that the formation received in their communities is not enough. They feel they need to know more about this Jesus of life and that the church needs to open up and adapt to social changes. Others take a positive view of the teaching of the church, while recognizing the changes she experiences.

From the vision expressed by the young people who seem to show a convincing faith in their lives, some of them think that the influences of other youth cultures do not bring about any changes in their lives. Others, however, affirm that they do feel affected somehow in their life and behaviour, being pulled into another lifestyle through the social environment in which they live.

This way of thinking of these young people is also due to the fact that at this age and stage of life they are in a process of growth and maturation. During this growth they develop self-esteem in the group in which they are embedded and in the culture where they move. It should be noted also that at their age, society can be perceived as offering wonders, with abundant opportunity for consumption and unlimited access to information. If they are not orientated at young people find it difficult to build a strong personal identity that helps their personal and social life.[25] We also have to consider that at this time, many young people rely more on friends than parents.

---

[24] Pontifical Mission Societies, Path towards the Fifth Nacional Missionary Conference of Bolivia.
[25] A. Goic, 'Option for the youth: visions of Medellin and Puebla. Visions of the church today', in Peter Hünermann and Margit Eckholt (ed), *Latin American Youth in the processes of globalization, option for young people* (Buenos Aires: University of Buenos Aires), 89-91.

They do not confide so much in adults as in people of their own age, the friends with whom they can share their concerns.[26]

This diverse way of seeing reality makes us, on the one hand, find ourselves with a group of young people who see that the training provided in their parishes responds well to the reality in which they live, as the issues presented to them are adequate so far as their formation is concerned. On the other hand, there are other young people who have expressed the view that there is no concrete training in their communities, since the subjects taught do not respond well to the reality in which they live. This is due, they say, to the material taught which is not taken from the grassroots but from other places which are unfamiliar to them. This is what the young people gathered in Vinto, Cochabamba said when they responded that the training material being taught in their communities did not respond to their felt needs.[27]

All this reinforces the conclusion that the different views of young people depend on their family culture and the kind of society where they operate in their development process, whether school, college or friends. But there is also the fact that at this time young people live in situations of contradiction in their way of life. Nevertheless, this stage of life has its own values, although it is mediated by the influence received from the social environment where one lives and grows. This way of living and growing in a social environment explains the variety of noticed behaviours. It is necessary and crucial to consider the lives of young people in the reality of the society in which they live, as this influences their social action.[28]

Among the difficulties that young people see as a problem affecting their missionary commitment are a lack of conviction and consistency in the lives they live in their community, who perceive a double morality. Nonetheless they feel they are doing the best they can to put into practice the gospel of Jesus. Other young people express the view that in their communities there is coherence of life and teaching by the pastoral agents, whom they consider to be an example to follow. They genuinely live the gospel, giving an example of life, evangelizing other young people, fulfilling their obligations as young people.

To conclude this point, one can say that there is a lack of relevant engagement with the social sectors where young people are found. In other words, we need to make alive the life of Jesus in different environments, taking into account the different youth cultures that are present in different social environments, with consequent influence on the home environment, friends, school, college and in many cases the workplace.

---

[26] D Cusilaime. R Ordonez, 'The Escape Adolescent Behaviours Familiar Spread Alarm' (Bachelor of Psychology thesis, Universidad Mayor de San Simón, 2000), 33.
[27] Cochabamba Archdiocese, *Missions Commision*, 2.
[28] Pontifical Missionary Work for Youth, 'Youth Missionaries', http://www.misionesceb@entelnet.bo, (2007).

d) The challenges that young people propose to the church to work with and from the young people today.

After understanding their different ways of thinking and seeing the social world in which these young people move and develop their life, it is also fitting to rescue and mention the various challenges they consider necessary to carry out a mission from and with the young people. First note that every young person lives in a particular society. By knowing the situation of the young person we can learn more about their personality, their conflicts and therefore be able to better help them. This requires that the church care about what the youth really want, rather than just criticizing them. Young people express themselves collectively in society through different lifestyles, thus creating youth cultures.[29]

Given these views, it is important to recognise that youth are known for being rebellious and demanding. This represents a stage in their development and often, as their experience grows, they become able to form more mature judgements. This is easier for some than others but it needs to be recognised that all young people are in the process of reaching maturity, while experiencing various models of life. The support these young people receive in their growth should start from the family. Parents should provide a closer interaction with their children because at this age children tend to distance themselves from parents if they find no approval. This support should be given from the intellectual, emotional and spiritual aspects.[30] But these young people also look to the church to assist them in the growth and maturation of their faith. In particular, they ask the priests of their local churches for accompaniment and support in their activities.[31]

If we take into account the various authors who have spoken about young people, we might say that those who form part of the church communities, ask to be heard, seen and understood. So do the young of various parishes in the city of Cochabamba. We can reaffirm the need to be aware of the diverse influences that, to a greater or lesser extent, can affect young people.

It is also important to take into account youth language, knowing how to discover and interpret it as a form of self-expression, through words, music or aesthetics, to identify and relate to their peers. Young people look for an identity in each group they join which will set them apart from others.[32] They yearn for priests and pastoral agents to tune in to their identity and to

---

[29] J Baeza, *Juvenile Culture*, 3-4 (CD ROM), Pastoral Juvenil ITEPAL.
[30] L Guy, *The Cycle of Life* (Thomson Internacional, 2001), 347-348.
[31] Fourth Episcopal Latin American Conference, Santo Domingo, Dominican Republic, October 12-28, 1992, 'New evangelization, humana promotion and Christian culture', 112-113 en *General Conferences of the Episcoplian Church of Latinoamericano, Río de Janeiro, Medellin, Puebla y Santo Domingo* (Santa fe de Bogotá: Kimpres, 1994).
[32] Baeza, *Juvenile Cultures*, 3-4.

come to understand their language. They do not appreciate being treated simply as passive recipients of the ministry of the church and long to be trusted to advance the witness of the church through initiatives geared to connect with their peers.

The views and comments that we have collected from many young people show their concern that the church should be on the wavelength of different ways of thinking and acting found in various youth cultures. Diverse groups with different languages can gather true followers of Jesus Christ, since these young people are involved in parishes. Notwithstanding their diversity of languages, they also experience Jesus in their lives in different ways, feeling he helps them at all times, considering him a friend.

The need for encouragement is perceived by young people in different ways. Some indicate the need to be accompanied by an adult, as the experiences of others can help their lives. Others suggest that given the diversity of their own concerns, this support be offered by friends, people with whom they have an affinity. All agree that there is need to provide open spaces for communion, spiritual formation and moral training to transform their lives. Again, notice the insistent need to overcome the problems of communication and to understand the world of young people – the language and youth-sensitivity codes they use. It is also necessary to be aware of the cultural changes taking place among the young and the instability that results. This causes the journey alongside young people in their growth and maturation to be much more complex.[33]

Everything points to the importance of strengthening the missionary awareness. In this twenty-first century the problems and challenges facing youth are new. A solid spiritual formation, not just academic, is needed for priests and for those who play a leadership role in youth ministry. This missionary consciousness must reach a critical level and global level, involving the whole person. Spirituality must be Christ-centred, and the communion of the priest and Christ must be lived out in order to offer a vital expression of evangelization.[34]

To refer to a lived experience as something of the past can provoke rejection or acceptance in communication with the youth. What adults can do is to demonstrate the meaning of faith by living it out. Any suggestions made to the youth must be authenticated by a way of life.

To get young people to commit themselves to be apostles to other youth it is necessary to begin by listening. They are voicing their view that there is a lack of commitment, knowledge, Christian life and missionary formation. They need to be assured that adults and youth are facing these

---

[33] Latin American Episcopal Counsil, Youth Department – SEJ, *Civilization of Love, Work and Hope, Orientations for a Pastoral of Youth in Latin America* (Santa fe de Bogota: Kimpres, 1995), 62.

[34] J. Sarabia, 'Missionary formation of Sínodo Light Priests of 1990 y de la Pastors Dabo Vobis', en *Pontificia Missionary Union, Missionary Training Course, Missions for the third millennium*, Rome, 14-15.

challenges together, as parts of the one body. The patience needed for listening and mutual sharing in this journey must not cease. We can always look at Jesus. His commitment took him to the cross. Death did not move him away from humanity. On the contrary, he remains with us all of our days until the end of time.

Conclusion

The stage of youth is marked by a growth process where monitoring, support and guidance for life are required. It is a process that deals with physical and psychological changes, the search a person experiences for new ways of conducting their interpersonal relationships. This involves facing questions and doubts about one's own personality which will gradually be resolved through social interaction.

In light of this, a closer accompaniment is necessary by parents, by adults who have contact with them, as it happens in the parish communities where there is an influx of young people. It is necessary to enter into dialogue with young people, taking an interest them. This does not mean being deprived of the freedom of social development but implies a fraternal dialogue and listening, where you create an environment of friendship and reception that will strengthen mutual trust and facilitate stepping into their world.

Considering the various answers given by young people in this study, who are involved in the activities of their parish communities. We see in their reviews, that they often perceive the adult world as being very confined, having out-dated ideas regarding the reality of the world of youth. This is understandable if we look at the world that surrounds the youth and their lack of experience of life. These young people ask to be heard and understood by others. They also ask to be helped in life. This attitude shows that they are willing to listen to others, to be guided. But this work of knowing how to reach young people will largely depend on the various community leaders in the parishes. Each community and each social sector lives and expresses their cultural experience according to the environment in which they grow and live. For this reason it is essential to take into account the cultural context of young people.

Taking into consideration the traits that characterize young people will help us to work better with them, since every environment that inspires acceptance and dialogue helps the person feel safe in the place where he is, without feeling any sort of rejection. For this reason we see the need to work with young people involved in parish communities, as their presence is already a favourable point. What is required is to work with them, to help them understand that Jesus has a mission for them. It is essential that the various pastoral agents be convinced of the importance of young people themselves becoming apostles to other young people who are far from any church activity, including those involved in the same community.

We have mentioned the fact that youth are characterized by trusting people their own age. It is therefore important for young people from diverse communities to move from being evangelized to evangelizing. For this we must help them discover they are important in the church. It is necessary to accompany their growth process, from the family crib when this is possible and from church communities where diverse pastoral agents support their various stages of growth. And if there were no pastoral agents prepared to work with young people, it is necessary for the priest to look out for those who have charisma to work with youth. Likewise, as part of his pastoral work, it is necessary that priests encourage the laity to practise missionary commitment.

For this it is necessary that the laity understand that simply by the fact of being a Christian they are also responsible for missionary work in the society in which they live. It is also important to help in the various parish activities as one parish makes the entire people of God. Correspondingly, the priests must remember that the laity are not their assistants, but through baptism and confirmation, are also missionaries, who may not have understood their missionary calling and therefore fail to put it into practice. For this reason, we insist on taking into account the suggestions of young people when they say that they do not feel prepared to assume their missionary work and need training. If we want a committed Christian church, a sincere commitment is needed from the various pastoral agents who are involved in church activities.

THE DREAM OF UNITY IN BOLIVIA

Moses Morales

Introduction

Everyone in some way or another has a dream. A dream of a better world, where everyone has equal opportunities, where there is work and wages for all. Others dream of a world of peace, justice, fraternity, brotherhood, unity. There are people who dream about their own welfare and happiness. Despite the reality that we live, we all dream! But the first Grand Dreamer is God, his own dream has become a reality. Early in the course of history, God has created a home for all human beings, but today, unfortunately, human sin caused this place not to be a livable home.

In recent years, we have begun to live in a new century. The last century was characterized by scientific and technological breakthroughs that no one imagined before. But it was also a time that violently knocked down the hopes of individuals, peoples and communities. We live in a time of much noise and clutter that does not help many people to keep dreaming or living in hope. Dialogue, as a way to share dreams, is slowly being lost. Despite the fact that media have become more and more sophisticated in providing new means of communication (computers and the internet), somehow human beings live more isolated from each other. Only God does not give up and continue dreaming. God, playing with the fate that humanity has itself set, reveals his dream and gives us new hope.

God's great dream is this: '*that all may be one*'. Of the many dreams of God, this one was revealed to us through the prayer of his Son Jesus, who on the eve of his death prayed for the unity of his own and all those who through his word would one day believe in him: 'That all may be one as Thou, Father, are in Me and I in you. Also be one in us: that the world may believe that thou hast sent me.' (Jn 17:21)

This dream has affected the journey of the church for 20 centuries. It has inspired and challenged many men and women throughout history to break down walls and build bridges of dialogue and understanding. Today, it is this dream that fuels many missionary disciples of the Lord to continue to build roads of unity in a society that is ever more cracked, split, and polarized for ideological, political, economic, cultural and unfortunately, religious reasons. In the midst of this world, Jesus' dream must go from desire to reality. Today it is not possible for us, as Christians, to continue living as indifferent to God's call: 'Let us all be one.' There is a challenge for those believers in Christ who doubt and question God's dream, believing that humanly speaking, unity is not achievable in this world and will only be a reality in the end of times.

This chapter, inspired by the dream 'that they all be one' and motivated by my experience of working for over 15 years as head of the Secretariat for Ecumenical and Interreligious Dialogue of the Bolivian Episcopal Conference, is intended to reflect, taking into account the various roads to unity built up in recent times, about a very important aspect of unity and ecumenism we should not forget – the training of the ecumenical person in all dimensions. Without this, ecumenism will not be deepened or advanced for another hundred years.

So far, things related to the ecumenical movement have theoretically gone well. As can be seen, many events have taken place in the world in favour of ecumenism. There are a variety of documents produced as a result of reflections, thoughts, meditations, etc. on ecumenism. There are signed agreements of mutual recognition on the sacrament of baptism. Bilateral and multilateral dialogues between Rome and the World Council of Churches and between Rome and the Christian churches, in particular with regard to specific issues, have led to mutual agreements. In addition, programmes have been scheduled, such as the Week of Prayer for Christian Unity in 2008, which gave us the opportunity to celebrate 100 years of prayer for unity. Every day new ecumenical events and meetings are developed worldwide and on the different continents. Finally, the list of everything that is accomplished in ecumenical dialogue around the world seems to be endless. So what is missing? Failure to make a reality of ecumenism in each local church, in every Christian community, in every baptized Christian![1] Failure to live in unity in our everyday lives. Being ecumenical is not limited or reduced to a global event, such as a week of prayer that involves a certain group of people, or a study of current issues, or a meeting or a celebration. To be ecumenical is much more than that; it is to live all initiatives in a particular way that help make God's dream a reality: 'may they all be one.'

Many pastors, priests, nuns and lay people acknowledge that ecumenism in Bolivia is very important for the life of the churches in general. But to make of it a specific commitment, as a personal and communal responsibility in the practice and experience of ecumenical dialogue, is still a long way ahead of us. Sometimes indifference is the attitude that takes over instead of an ecumenical attitude and commitment. So what has gone wrong? From our experience we believe that it is a neglect of training the person (man and woman) in ecumenism.

---

[1] By 'local church' in this chapter is meant the Catholic Churches in each country.

The Formation of the Ecumenical Person in Bolivia

Is there a way forward in the formation of the ecumenical person in all dimensions? A person with open awareness and a hospitable heart (2 Thess 2:8), who truly loves others (Jn 13:34-35) as the guiding principle of their relationship with them (Ephesians 4:1-3), can testify to that wonderful communion of faith, hope and charity that God wants to be 'put at the service of mankind for the gospel of peace'.[2] Ecumenical formation of every Christian disciple is, therefore, a serious education on the principles of faith, love and hope.[3] This encourages in the heart of every Christian community an ongoing process of internal Christian conversion, without which there is no true ecumenism.[4] In fact, this person would be ready to lead his or her life according to the gospel in communion with the Father through the Son in the Spirit and will also be more prepared to live in community with other believers and to promote Christian unity.[5] The ecumenical movement is, therefore, based on listening to the word and on the Trinitarian communion.[6]

The path to unity begins with a pedagogy of communion, which shows trust in the human capacity to overcome one's own shortcomings and to learn how to grow. This pedagogy needs to be applied to the fabric of life of every church in order to be implemented later beyond its own limits. If someone has not experienced love and forgiveness, it is more difficult for him or her to love and forgive. If a Christian does not live this reality in ecclesial communion with the closest brothers, how can he or she enter into communion with brothers and sisters of other Christian churches? Ecumenical hope is to build up capacity to avoid injury and to help others to pursue of the gospel.[7] The challenge is to make all ecclesial reality a school of forgiveness and fellowship.

---

[2] *Unitatis Redintegratio* (UR), 2.

[3] *UR*, 2.8.

[4] *UR*, 7, John Paul II, Encyclical Letter *Ut Unum Sint*, 15.

[5] *UR* 7.

[6] 'This mutual help in the search for truth is a sublime form of evangelical love' (John Paul II, Encyclical Letter *Ut Unum Sint*, 78).

[7] John Paul II clearly explains what it means to promote a spirituality of communion: 'spirituality of communion indicates above all to look at the heart to find the mystery of the Trinity who lives within us, and whose light we also welcome the faces of the brothers and sisters. A spirituality of communion also means an ability to think of the brother and sister of faith within the profound unity of the Mystical Body, therefore, as 'one who belongs to me,' able to share their joys and sufferings, to sense their desires and fulfill their needs, to provide a true and deep friendship. Spirituality of communion is also the ability to see the positive in the other, to welcome it and appreciate it as God's gift: a 'gift for me', rather than the brother who has received it directly. In other words, spirituality of communion is to 'make room' for a brother and sister, carrying 'the weight of each other' (Gal 6:2) and resisting the selfish temptations which constantly beset us and generate competition, races, distrust and jealousy. Our illusions, unless this spiritual path,

The formation of an ecumenical conscience and heart is driven by a spirit of reconciliation. This spirituality involves three stages: recognizing one's own poverty and weakness,[8] asking for forgiveness of sins against unity,[9] and finally experiencing the gift of love, which is the ability to love with the love that comes from God. Thus, unity will be the expression of the love that God gives us.[10]

When God gives a vision, a responsibility is attributed also. Therefore, the main effort of the ecumenical pastoral today will be to develop instruments of communion. First, this effort aims to promote mutual understanding, that is, trying to gain 'a better awareness of doctrine and history, spiritual and liturgical life, the psychology of religion and culture of brotherhood.'[11] Many prejudices are born out of ignorance. Everyone within a particular Christian community must try to answer the main question: who are my other Christian brothers and sisters? How do they believe, celebrate and proclaim the Gospel?

To this end it may be useful to create small study groups. This ecumenical study involves three levels. A first level is one of information, explaining the status of the issue; a second level is one of training in order to deepen – with the help of experts – the main topics of doctrinal dialogue; and a third level is the one of relationship in community, or interpersonal, where reciprocal encounters are favoured, essential as they are to let trust and friendship be born.[12]

Promoting awareness and recognition that what unites us is much stronger than what divides us is another fundamental dimension of ecumenical pastoral. Ecclesial communion is given first through the word that becomes flesh and bread. In fact, the Word, which existed in the beginning, is what unites, reconciles and redeems us. The Word has the power to uncover the roots of violence and deception, providing for us the

---

serve a few external instruments of communion. Objects would be soulless masks of communion rather than ways of expression and growth.' (John Paul II, Apostolic Letter at the end of the Great Jubilee Year 2000, *Novo Millennio Ineunte*, 43).

[8] The ecumenical journey begins with the recognition of one's weaknesses and limits, it is the awareness of our own weakness that leads us to seek and see the wealth that is beyond ourselves.

[9] *UR* 7. In fact, 'if we have no sin, we make God a liar and his word is not in us' (1 Jn 1:10).

[10] Christian *agape* is a spiritual rather than a pastoral way of being, rather than a way of doing. Every person is loved and this shows the love God has for him. The only serious thing is that Christian love is a 'transparency' – clear, credible and compelling – of God's love. Nothing else. (B. Maggioni)

[11] *UR* 9.

[12] Bruni says rightly that 'the road to unity is not only reserved space for meetings or only for official theological dialogue of the various committees, but free access to a wide open reciprocal attendance a deep understanding of the ways of thinking, feeling and living Christianity, by the churches of the east and west.' (G Bruni, Communion Service, 6).

food that sustains and nourishes our action in the world. Finding the time and place where many Christians gather around the Word of God so they can grow and mature together in the knowledge of their faith, can be very fruitful for the ecumenical movement.

Ecumenism is also a crosscutting theme in the pastoral activity of the whole Christian community. Prayer for peace and unity of the church may be present, for example, in worship and in Sunday Eucharist. Those with training positions within the community should be careful about the methods of expression of faith, avoiding any language that 'in some way can be an obstacle to dialogue with the others.'[13] Also, when explaining in theology courses, for example, the Petrine ministry, one must take into account the ecumenical debate. The important thing is that the ecumenical movement is not an extracurricular activity, a kind of appendix, less than an option, but an element of every day pastoral care. This might help to enable grassroots receptivity of ecumenical theology.

Every community must clarify how to behave and what to say from the ecumenical point of view. First we must address a given argument from a theological perspective, knowing its origin and keeping always in mind the will of the Father: 'that all may be one in Christ.' It is also necessary to know *how* to make possible, under the inspiration and grace of the Holy Spirit, 'coming together interpersonally'. Third, we need to develop a new interiority, the purification of historical memories and the rereading of the divisions, to care about theological language, to enhance the ability to forgive, to welcome others and to accept their differences,[14] as well as sharing in prayer and service.[15]

So what's left? We find an answer once again in the Letter of John Paul II *Novo Millennio Ineunte*: 'We certainly are not seduced by the naïve belief that to the great challenges of our time, we may learn a magic formula. No, it is not a formula what will save us, but a person and the certainty that he gives us: I am with you! The answer is not, then, to invent a 'new program'. The program is the one that is summed up in the gospel and in the living tradition. And that is centralized in the final analysis, Christ himself, to know him, love him, imitate him, to live in the Trinitarian life and with him transform history until its fulfillment in the heavenly Jerusalem.'[16]

---

[13] *UR*, 11. The way John Paul II observed that the term 'separated brethren', tends now to be replaced by 'more careful words that evoke the deep communion – linked to the baptismal character – which the Spirit fosters in spite of historical and canonical breaks. He speaks of 'other Christians', the 'other baptized', the 'other Christian communities'. (John Paul II, Encyclical Letter UUS, 42).
[14] The Christian is one who hosts (2 Cor 6:11-12, 2 Thess 2:8).
[15] *UR*, 8. 12; *UUS*, 43.
[16] John Paul II, Apostolic Letter at the end of the Great Jubilee Year 2000 *Novo Millennio Ineunte*, 29.

Dialogue and Mission: An Inseparable Interdependence

The implementation of the Edinburgh 1910 Conference of Protestant Missions, and the celebration of the Vatican II Council, were motivated primarily by the theme of the Mission. The church is essentially missionary. But how do we carry out this challenging task among all Christians today without damaging the cause of the gospel?

We need to remember that our work is common to all Christians: the gospel message and call to change the 'scandal of division' with the good news of unity. To achieve this goal we must let ourselves be challenged. We remember the words of one delegate from Asia: 'You sent missionaries to evangelize. We thank you. But along with the missionaries you have also sent division...' which after a hundred years are still there. We must also be challenged by the teachings of Vatican II, which said 'missionary activity and the restoration of Christian unity are closely linked by the need of mission that requires all who are baptized together in one fold, to give unanimous testimony of Christ our Lord before all the people. But if you still cannot fully give witness to one faith, it is necessary, at least, to encourage mutual appreciation and love.'[17]

Unity and harmony are gifts from God, which every human being can enjoy by grace, while division and discord are human inventions and a result of sin. The church, whether in the Protestant or Catholic or other traditions, in listening to the Word of God, suffers the disintegration that comes from the heart of the person, even if baptized, when the call to remain united to Christ is ignored. This tension is manifested throughout the history of Christianity from its very origin.

Dialogue is primarily an ecclesial attitude, a way forward in mission that must be manifested in respect, appreciation, collaboration and meeting together to discover worth in each other. It is grounded in the mystery of God who took the initiative to start when the 'dialogue of salvation was opened spontaneously by divine initiative: he loved us first; we shall ourselves take the initiative to extend the same dialogue to everyone without waiting to be called.'[18] Dialogue in mission is like a crossroads, because the good news is not imposed, it is announced. For this reason, the Catholic bishops meeting in Aparecida (Brazil) reaffirmed their ecumenical commitment, noting that 'the relationship with the brothers and sisters baptized in other churches and ecclesial communities is an indispensable way for the disciple and missionary.'[19] There is no other alternative.

---

[17] Decree *Ad Gentes*, 6.
[18] Paul VI, Encyclical *Ecclesiam Suam*, 52.
[19] V Latin American Episcopal Conference and the Caribbean, Aparecida, Brazil, 2007, No. 227.

To Carry out the Mission, it is Necessary to Be in Communion with the Master

The characteristic of every Christian, a follower of the Lord, is love. Catholic bishops in Aparecida, said, 'To be in communion with the Master, it is really necessary to assume the centrality of the commandment of love, which he called his own when he said: 'Love one another as I have loved you' (Jn 15:12). This love, which is Jesus' total self-giving, in addition to being the hallmark of every Christian, cannot fail to be the hallmark of his church, his community and his disciples who testify that 'everyone will know that you are my disciples' (Jn 13:35).[20]

Love is the essential requirement for all pastoral activity, including ecumenical dialogue; therefore, it is the ingredient that adds flavour to things we do for the glory of our Lord Jesus Christ. Without love, serving means nothing. 'If I have no love,' says St Paul, 'I am nothing.'[21] Therefore, dialogue requires us above all to be in communion with the Master, to tune in and do whatever he asks of us and to eliminate the human desire to prevent God's dream that all be one be alive among us.

To get in tune with the Master, pastoral conversion is necessary. This means 'to abandon old structures that no longer favour the transmission of faith.'[22] Indeed, among the old structures we Christians have retained in our pastoral ministry, there is the proclamation of the gospel accompanied by the anti-testimony of division. What matters to the churches and to many missionaries sometimes is to 'win converts' to their own 'church' and not helping people to whom they announce the good news of the Lord and Savior to become authentic disciples and missionaries.

Being in communion with the Master means to assume the learning and practising of the beatitudes of the kingdom: 'the lifestyle of Jesus Christ himself: love and faithful obedience to the Father, his intimate sympathy with human suffering, his proximity to the poor and the least of these and his faithfulness to the mission entrusted to him through the gift of his life.'[23] We also have 'to know what he did and to discern what we should do in today's circumstances.'[24]

One of the challenges that Christians currently face is ecumenical dialogue. We do not live alone and isolated. We are part of a society and of the world, and 'pastoral conversion requires from ecclesial communities to be communities of missionary disciples who are Christ-centered and find in him the source of openness, dialogue and readiness to promote

---

[20] Document of Aparecida (DA), 138.
[21] 1 Cor 13.
[22] DA, 365.
[23] DA, 139.
[24] DA, 139.

responsibility and effective participation of all the faithful within Christian communities.'[25]

Let us remember that the essence of evangelization is not so much preaching as the testimony of life. So let's get to work so that our message may become more believable.

The Objective of Mission is the Kingdom of God

The goal of the mission and the work of evangelization is building the kingdom of God on earth. Churches are instrumental for building up the kingdom. The constant temptation in mission is to reverse things that cause a change in direction. When this happens, the mission is no longer serving the kingdom, but the church itself. Therefore, it is easier to proselytize than to build God's kingdom on earth. But this can mean allowing the sin of division among us.

The Christian churches of the Latin American continent, in particular of Bolivia, are invoked today by the poor and oppressed, and God hears this cry of unity around a goal greater than the defence and growth of our own churches. Greater is the defence of life – the greatest gift we receive from God through the construction of just and humane social structures free from the threats of hunger, violence and marginalization. 'To be disciples and missionaries of Jesus Christ so that our people may have life in him – Catholic bishops tell us – leads us to assume the gospel from the perspective of the kingdom's priority, assuming the tasks that contribute to the dignity of every human being and working along with other citizens and institutions for human well-being.'[26]

To the extent to which Christian churches live and proclaim the gospel of liberation of Jesus Christ, and unite around common goals, is the extent to which people of good will, witnesses and heralds of God's love can be recognized by all. A hundred years after the Edinburgh Mission Conference (1910) officially launched the ecumenical movement in the world, it is time for Christian churches to no longer be selfish, but ask for and offer each other forgiveness and reconciliation and unite around the great cause of the kingdom of God. They must unite in building new relationships and just socio-economic, political and cultural structures, as signs of the kingdom of God and allow a decent life for all people, because they are all sons and daughters of God.

Conclusion

Mission and ecumenism go together, not separately. That is a truth that we cannot deny. This was suggested by the Asian delegates through a letter

---

[25] DA, 368.
[26] DA, 384.

sent to the Protestant missions in 1910. In addition, the documents of the Catholic Church after Vatican II have reinforced this truth. In recent times, various documents of the World Council of Churches and the Pontifical Council for Promoting Christian Unity reaffirm it. Similarly, the Latin American Council of Churches (CLAI) and the Latin American Episcopal Conference (CELAM) have recognized again that we cannot be proclaiming the gospel while being divided Christians. The bishops of the Catholic Church have said that mission must be carried out in ecumenical dialogue with the Christian churches, because this is an indispensable way to eliminate one of the worst evils of the present century.

I want to conclude my reflection, indicating some specific areas that can help deepen ecumenical dialogue to realize God's dream in our midst: 'that all may be one.'

In 1959, John XXIII, the ecumenical pope very wisely said, 'It is much more that unites us than divides us.' Despite our differences, all Christians have fundamental aspects of unity: the Bible, the creed, God who sent his son Jesus Christ and in him we are redeemed (justified), baptism, renewal-conversion and faith reflected in works through charity.

What makes us alike and at the same time different from everyone is what makes us humble, and humility is the source of unity for mutual service and true brotherhood. Whoever believes themselves to be superior to others, presumably possessing all without the other, carries within him or her elements of separation and division. On the contrary, whoever is last and serves all, believes there is still much to learn, receive, and offer. Whoever is convinced that he or she can grow only in conjunction with others, this person becomes an instrument of unity and peace.

Relations among Christians are to be based on the model of relationships that exists between the Father, the Son and the Holy Spirit. This same spirit among Christians establishes a new type of relationship like the relationship between Jesus and his Father – let us love one another just as the Father loves the Son and the Son loves all mankind. This is the love which the Holy Spirit pours into our hearts. Therefore, to love 'the way' Christ loves us means to live out the same love. [27] Jesus is not so much a role model, but a source of life within us and among us. The risen Lord gives us his Holy Spirit as a fountain that springs alive in our hearts forever. Therefore, it is more than a simple imitation. It is following Jesus. It is real and vital participation in his paschal mystery. 'The glory that you gave me, give it to them to be one, as you and I are one. So I'll be in them and you in me and they will be perfect in unity. Then the world will recognize that you sent me as I have loved them like You love me.'[28]

---

[27] Jn 13:34.
[28] Jn 17:22-23.

'...And the love with which you loved me will be in them and I'll be in them'.[29] This is the unity that Jesus wants for us.

The basis of dialogue that leads to unity is conversion to the God of life, the Father of our Lord Jesus Christ in the grace and presence that the Spirit gives. It is a conversion that we must deepen day by day and that is to be lived out in love.

Regarding the question of spiritual identity, dialogue asks for a clear expression and manifestation. We recognize who we are, what makes us live and in whom our faith is centered. This leads us to recognize what unites us deeply with other Christians and what marks our differences. It also helps us discover whether these differences touch the essential, or just identify different ways of feeling and expressing the Christian experience. In affirming our way of being witnesses to the risen Christ and sharing our Christian experience, we enrich each other.

Identity and proclamation. The dialogue at this level should be essentially the experience with God that the brother or sister describes, while also conveying our own experience with God in Jesus Christ. Here, there is a foundation: respect for others and acknowledgement of the Holy Spirit already at work in the other. This 'offers everyone the possibility that, in the way known only to God, be associated with the paschal mystery.'[30] There is also an explicit announcement of what makes us think and live, so there is dialogue and proclamation. The announcement is in the same communication of our experience of God in Jesus Christ. In addition, humility, which accepts and acknowledges the other's experience, is what leads to the proclamation of Jesus Christ and the Spirit's action in all.

The importance of mutual understanding. Overall, we know very little indeed about the history of other Christian churches. A better mutual knowledge places us before God and his revelation, especially with those churches and ecclesial communities who have Christ as the foundation of life. With them we discover what unites us more deeply and what still divides us. Many of the differences that separate us are explained through the history of our church, the Christian churches and ecclesial communities, that question us and invite us to a fuller conversion. For example, the case of those who see the Pope's role more as a demonstration and centralism than as a visible sign of unity, invite us to distinguish between what is essential from what is simply a historical contribution. Against all types of stiffness and triumphalism, which may come from both sides, our following of Jesus Christ teaches us to become humble before Christ and servants of all for universal salvation, which springs from the Paschal Mystery.

Prayer puts us in an attitude that makes us available to God in Christ and that enables us to discover what he says and do what he wants us to do. Prayer places us in a searching attitude, in the loving acceptance and

---

[29] Jn 17:26.
[30] Documents of Vatican II: *Gaudium et Spes* (GS), 22.

implementation of the will of God: his plan of salvation and our holiness.[31] Personal and shared prayer with other Christians puts us in the living environment of faith and communion among all.

Finally, despite all the prejudices and obstacles against the search and fulfillment of God's dream, the unity of Christians, one thing is for sure: ecumenism, which was born in an evangelical environment and as a manifestation of Holy Spirit, is one of the greatest gifts of the twentieth century that God has given it to all his people. Thanks to ecumenism, many Christians live a new culture and new forms of mutual relations. Mutual appreciation and mutual understanding prevail, changing personal and community attitudes. Prejudices and mutual condemnations fall away. That is the experience of many members of Christian ecumenical groups in our country.

---

[31] See Heb 1.

THE *KENOSIS* OF CHRIST AND HIS REDEFINITION OF NATIONALISM AS A WAY TOWARDS RECONCILIATION IN ISRAEL/PALESTINE

Andrew F Bush

Introduction

The bitter divisions and hostility between the Israeli and Palestinian peoples appears to be intractable as the apparently endless cycle of violent attack and retribution continues without abatement. The tensions are not limited to the violence of one state against the other, but also plague relations between Jewish and Arab communities within Israel and between Christian and Muslim communities in Palestine (the West Bank including East Jerusalem and Gaza). Peace negotiations are destroyed by militant violence, only to be revived and shattered again. The possibility of reaching an agreement that would satisfy all communities and end the violence appears a distant hope but must be sought in view of the suffering of both Palestinians under occupation and Israelis who live with the persistent threat of terrorism. For some Christians their eschatological expectations reject the possibility and even the legitimacy of peace; nevertheless, speculative interpretation of biblical prophecy must never be allowed to override the definitive ethical teachings of Christ to be a peace-maker (Matt 5:9) and to love one's neighbours.

For Palestinian Christians who have courageously maintained a witness for Christ peace means the difference between living in a vortex of violence and hatred in which their children find diminishing prospects for a meaningful future, and the opportunity to build productive lives in an environment free from militarism and violence. I recall a conversation with an elderly Palestinian Christian on the day that Israeli forces were shelling the headquarters of the Palestinian Authority in Ramallah one hundred metres from where we were speaking. 'My whole life has been war,' she said, 'Why can't there be peace?'[1]

This chapter will explore the possibilities for reconciliation between the communities in Israel/Palestine through an emphasis on an essential shared human identity and a renewed nationalism drawn from Christ's *kenosis*, or self-emptying (Phil 2:5-8). Both Israeli and Palestinian nationalism is an

---

[1] The author has been serving on the West Bank since 1998 with the Palestinian Bible Society. There he founded Living Stones Student Center, an outreach to students at Bir Zeit University and surrounding villages.

essential part of individual and communal identity and is embraced as a means of ethnic survival. At the same time this nationalistic emphasis fuels the conflict between Israelis and Palestinians. If the *kenosis* of Christ is affirmed as a model for reconciliation through emphasis on shared human identity, how does this model respond to the intertwining of human identity and nationalism? Is this model indeed useful in the Palestinian/Israeli context?

This chapter will propose that the self-emptying of Christ of the prerogative of power and of the consequent rude triumphalism which was the Satanic temptation and his subsequent embracing of radical servanthood offers the possibility of a human identity based upon a transformed nationalism. Such a transformed nationalism is defined by an inclination towards the well-being of others instead of a nationalism bent towards individual and communal uniqueness and privilege. Christ did not deny his national identity, but rather redefined what that identity could be in the midst of the violence of Roman occupation and the corruption of the religious institutions. The example of Christ points to the unique opportunity for the Palestinian Christian community to assume a prophetic role in Israel/Palestine. If Palestinian Christians will make the radical decision to stay in the land, enduring the violence, and embracing the vulnerability of Christ in his servanthood, they may speak a profound word to their Palestinian Muslim and Israeli neighbours.

The Possibility of a Theology of Humanity for Reconciliation in Palestine and Israel

In their critical situation Palestinian Christians are actively reflecting upon theologies which will be useful in helping their community address the crisis of Israel and Palestine.[2] Mitri Raheb, an important Palestinian Christian leader and pastor in the Evangelical Lutheran Church of Jerusalem, emphasizes the importance of a theology of humanity in Palestinian society as a basis for dialogue among Christians, Muslims, and Jews. He states:

> A theology of humanity can be very important to us in Palestine, where three religions and two nations have to exist. Such a theology holds that every human being, no matter what his religion or nationality, is created in the image of God. To protect a human being's rights is therefore a divine law. To be religious, therefore, means simply to be a true human being. Dialogue

---

[2] Andrew F Bush, 'Palestinian Christian University Students in Interfaith Discussion' (Dissertation, Princeton Theological Seminary, 2004), 52-54.

among all people of good will is essential in creating conditions of maximum justice, tolerance, and development in the region.[3]

The apostle Paul's exhortation in Philippians 2:5-8 to consider the example of Christ's radical *kenosis*, or self-emptying, to share our humanity affirms the importance of human identity:

> Your attitude should be the same as that of Christ Jesus:
> Who, being in very nature God,
> did not consider equality with God something to be grasped,
> but made himself nothing, or
> taking the very nature of a servant,
> being made in human likeness.
> And being found in appearance as a man,
> he humbled himself
> and became obedient to death –
> even death on a cross!

Christ's *kenosis* as an affirmation of humanity is a profound response to dehumanization in contexts of violence. Anecdotally, once within a single day, in speaking with the author both a Jewish Israeli and a Christian Palestinian referred to their respective adversaries as 'animals'. *Kenosis* suggests the most essential *kerygma*. While evangelical proclamation customarily begins with the message 'God loves people', *kenosis* offers a more elemental word of hope: 'you are a person – a person not an animal; a human created in God's image'.

Other voices have explored the treasures of Christ's *kenosis* in relation to reconciliation. Martha Frederiks in her article "Kenosis as a Model for Interreligious Dialogue' emphasizes the value of the shared routines and struggles of life for establishing a foundation for meaningful communication and relationship between very disparate peoples.[4] Frederiks emphasizes that for Christians the crucifixion of Christ remains the central witness on the human pilgrimage and that an emphasis on shared humanity does not imply or necessitate a broad pluralism. Frederiks states:

> In its willingness to seek the other, to respect the other in his/her culture and religion and in the encounter with the other, sharing our deepest convictions about God, the model of kenosis offers a paradigm for a joint human pilgrimage toward God. The Christian testimony on that pilgrimage is that of a God whose love for the world was so profound that he was willing to become human in Christ and die on the cross.[5]

---

[3] Mitri Raheb, 'The Spiritual Significance and Experience of the Churches: The Lutheran Perspective', in Michael Prior and William Taylor (eds), *Christians in the Holy Land* (London: The World of Islam Festival Trust, 1995), 130.

[4] Martha Frederiks, 'Kenosis as a Model for Interreligious Dialogue', *Missiology* 33:2 (2005), 211-222.

[5] Frederiks, 'Kenosis as a Model', 217.

The Kenosis *of Christ*

David Bosch in *Transforming Mission* maintains that in Christ's *kenosis* he identified with those on the periphery.[6] This identification includes those who are made vulnerable by persistent violence. Ed Matthews in his essay 'Christ and Kenosis: A Model for Mission' asserts that identification by self-emptying with those on the periphery implies assuming the risk of laying aside power and status.[7] Miriam Ward in her essay 'The Theological and Ethical Context for Palestinian-Israeli Peace' in the excellent and still relevant book *Beyond Occupation: American Jewish, Christian, and Palestinian Voices for Peace*, argues that a shared theology of humanity created in God's image provides an ethical foundation that is essential for true reconciliation in Israel-Palestine.[8]

Nevertheless, there is dissent concerning the value of a theology of humanity to address the complexities of the conflict between communities in Israel and Palestine. Palestinian academic Andreas Mazawi has stated that this theology of humanity is not particularly helpful to advance the unique relationship of Muslims and Christians, and thus Israelis as well, in Palestine because of its lack of specific reference to the context. In his view, such theology creates,

> ...universalistic interpretations of an anthropological nature regarding human solidarity (which could be true about any place and time), while not conceptualizing their hermeneutical approach in terms of definite areas of Islamo-Christian theological concern. While such an approach proves itself to be symbolically functional in a period of political crisis, it has nevertheless remained limited in its contribution to a genuine Palestinian Christian theology which regards Islam as a reciprocal part of its development.[9]

In support of Raheb, the emphasis on humanity in the face of the destruction of human life is an important protest against violence in the pursuit of nationalistic goals. Nevertheless, Mazawi is correct in his assertion that a theology of humanity lacks sufficient reference to the context of Palestine. Emphasizing shared humanity as a basis for dialogue, understanding, and reconciliation does not address the linkage of identity and nationalism in Israel-Palestine and the difficulties which nationalism produces.

Further, especially from the perspective of liberation theology, self-emptying unto vulnerable servanthood is extremely problematic. How does

---

[6] David J Bosch, *Transforming Mission: Paradigm Shifts in Theology of Mission* (Maryknoll NY: Orbis Books, 1991), 513.
[7] Ed Matthews, 'Christ and Kenosis: A Model for Mission', *Journal of Applied Missiology* 2:1 (1991).
[8] Miriam Ward, 'The Theological and Ethical Context for Palestinian-Israeli Peace', in Rosemary Radford Ruether and Marc H Ellis (eds), *Beyond Occupation: American Jewish, Christian, and Palestinian Voices for Peace* (Boston: Beacon Books, 1990), 171-82.
[9] Andres Elias Mazawi, 'Palestinian Local Theology and the Issue of Islamo-Christian Dialogue', *Islamochristiana* 19 (1993), 107.

one encourage a people such as the Palestinian community who have been dispossessed and stripped of basic human rights to embrace servanthood towards their oppressors? How does one insist that communities under barrage from *qassam* rockets from Gaza embrace the vulnerability of an essential humanity? From another perspective, feminist theologians have also rejected theologies of *kenosis* due to their history as a rationale for maintaining women and other dispossessed peoples in situations of oppression.[10]

To these objections it must be said that *kenosis* in the Palestinian and Israeli context does not necessitate either a rejection of national aspirations or a fatalistic acceptance of abuse and injustice. *Kenosis* in the life of Christ was not only an act of identification with human frailty, but also a profound act of opting for radical dependency upon God, a trusting that the purposes of God will be achieved not by human intrigue or force but by the Spirit of God. From this perspective Aristotle Papanilolaou in 'Person, *Kenosis* and Abuse: Hans Urs Von Balthasar and Feminist Theologies in Conversation' suggests that *kenosis* is essentially an intentional making space for the presence of God, a giving place for the power of God.

Furthermore, the servant-hood that Christ embraces through *kenosis* is servant-hood informed by a vision of God's ultimate victory over the Satanic claims of dominion which scorns any form of weakness. In other words, the victory of Christ is not *in spite of* servanthood, but it is the victory *of* servant-hood. Certainly an appreciation of the life of Christ and the ultimate emptying of the cross is necessary to fully appreciate such an argument for the validity of servant-hood. In any event, further exploration of the possibilities of the *kenosis* of Christ for reconciliation necessitates a recognition of the problem of the impact of nationalism on communal identity in Israel/Palestine.

Human Identity and the Problem of Nationalism in Palestine and Israel

In the Palestinian and Israeli context the difficulty with this emphasis on a theology of shared humanity as a means towards reconciliation is that nationalism is seen as critical for personal and communal identity and even for survival. The competing national claims of Israel and Palestine are both linked to possession of all or part of the land of ancient Palestine. As possession of the land is at least in part based on the authority of ethnic legitimacy, both communities attempt to deny the other as an authentic people group. Of the Palestinians it was said by the earliest Zionist leaders that there never was a people known as Palestinians; the land was either 'empty' or at most inhabited by a motley collection of Arab peoples who

---

[10] Aristotle Papanikolao, 'Person, *Kenosis* and Abuse: Hans Urs Von Balthasar and Feminist Theologies in Conversation', *Modern Theology* 19:1 (2003), 41-65.

did not share a common ethnic identity. Ilan Pappe, a Jewish Israeli historian who disputes the popular narratives of the founding of Israel states in *The Ethnic Cleansing of Palestine*:

> To bring this project to fruition, the Zionist thinkers claimed the biblical territory and recreated, indeed reinvented, it as the cradle of their new nationalist movement. As they saw it Palestine was occupied by 'strangers' and had to be repossessed. 'Strangers' here meant everyone not Jewish who had been living in Palestine since the Roman period. In fact for many Zionists Palestine was not even an 'occupied' land when they first arrived there in 1882, but rather an 'empty' one: the native Palestinians who lived there were largely invisible to them or, if not, were part of nature's hardship and as such were to be conquered and removed. Nothing, neither rocks nor Palestinians, was to stand in the way of the national 'redemption' of the land the Zionist movement coveted.[11]

In spite of its falsehood, this claim continues to be made today both in Israel and by some American Christian Zionists.[12] Besides this ethnic cleansing by the denial of the existence of a Palestinian ethnicity, Zionist leaders at the founding of the nation in 1948 sought to actually ethnically cleanse *eretz* Israel by premeditated forced expulsion.[13] Today some members of Israel's Knesset continue to call for the forcible removal of Palestinians from the land.

---

[11] Illan Pappe, *The Ethnic Cleansing of Palestine* (Oxford: Oneworld, 2007), 11.

[12] Christian Zionism is as fierce or more so in its denial of the very existence of a Palestinian people. In what is perhaps the darkest blemish on evangelical missions today the ethnicity, history, present suffering, and aspirations of Palestinians are explicitly denied. Christian Zionism in a bizarre twenty-first century continuation of raw colonial policies supports the occupation of Palestine by the Israeli Defense Forces as an extension of the efforts by the tribes of Israel under Joshua to take the land. For an in depth discussion of Christian Zionism see Timothy P. Weber's *On the Road to Armageddon: How Evangelicals Became Israel's Best Friend* (Grand Rapids: Baker, 2004). For similar and opposing views from a Messianic Jewish perspective see Wesley H Brown and Peter F Penner (eds), *Christian Perspectives on the Israeli-Palestinian Conflict* (Schwarzenfeld: Neufeld Verlag, 2008). For an extensive discussion of the rise of Palestinian nationalism which preceded any presence of modern Zionism in Palestine see the discussion entitled 'The Emergence and Survival of Palestinian Nationalism' in Rosemary Radford Ruether and Herman J Ruether, *The Wrath of Jonah: the Crisis of Religious Nationalism in the Israel-Palestinian Context* (Minneapolis: Fortress, 2002), 85-130.

[13] Pappe, a post-Zionist Israeli historian, forcefully makes this argument citing sources which establish the plan and execution of the removal of Palestinians from the land. He writes: 'This book is written with the deep conviction that the ethnic cleansing of Palestine must become rooted in our memory and consciousness as a crime against humanity and that it should be excluded from the list of *alleged* crimes.' Illan Pappe, *The Ethnic Cleansing of Palestine* (Oxford: Oneworld, 2007). 5.

Conversely, militant Palestinian movements such as HAMAS[14] deny Israel's national claims to the land and war against Israel's presence by militant attacks on the Israeli Defense Forces and on Israeli civilians.[15] Popular Palestinian media often identifies Israeli leaders by the foreign nationality of their birth; thus, challenging the validity of their ethnicity and claim to the land.

This pressure to deny national identity is also felt within the Palestinian community by Christians whose nationalism is at times challenged by their Muslim compatriots. Khalil al Sakakini, formerly a leading Christian participant in the Palestinian Arab national congresses expressed frustration and bitterness at this sense of imposed social inferiority. He wrote:

> No matter how my standing may be in science and literature, no matter how sincere my patriotism is, no matter how much I do to revive this nation... as long as I am not a Muslim I am nothing (in the eyes of Muslim Palestinians). If you desire to amount to anything, then be a Muslim and that will be peace.[16]

Ultimately then, what is critical for Palestinians and Israelis is that their human identity cannot be separated from their national identity. To mitigate their nationalism is viewed as a grave threat to their existence and is fiercely rejected. How then can a theology of a shared humanity be useful as a means towards reconciliation? How does Christ's self-emptying to share our humanity speak to nationalism in Palestine and Israel?

Christ's Nationalism and the Call to Serve the Nations

The human identity embraced by Christ was not a rejection or denial of his national identity, but rather a radical redefinition of the expectations of that nationalism. This redefinition can be seen as a restoration of Israel to the purposes of their national election. The national calling upon Israel was to be a vehicle for making the knowledge of the Lord accessible to the nations. Their society under God's law was to be unique, reflecting God's justice, mercy and grace. Stanley Hauerwas states: 'For Israel, therefore, to love God meant to learn to love as God loves.'[17] As it is stated in the Book of Deuteronomy:

> Yet the LORD set his affection on your forefathers and loved them, and he chose you, their descendants, above all the nations, as it is today. Circumcise

---

[14] The most prominent of the militant Islamist groups which aspire to the destruction of Israel and the establishment of an Islamic state in Palestine.

[15] The moderate Palestinian political movements such as the PLO/Fatah party founded by Yassir Arafat has officially acknowledged Israel's right to exist and seeks to negotiate a two state solution that would acknowledge both people's claims to the land.

[16] Mazawi, 'Palestinian Local Theology', 52.

[17] Stanley Hauerwas, *The Peaceable Kingdom* (Notre Dame: Notre Dame University Press, 2002), 78.

your hearts, therefore, and do not be stiff-necked any longer. For the LORD your God is God of gods and Lord of lords, the great God, mighty and awesome, who shows no partiality and accepts no bribes. He defends the cause of the fatherless and the widow, and loves the alien, giving him food and clothing. And you are to love those who are aliens, for you yourselves were aliens in Egypt. Fear the LORD your God and serve him. Hold fast to him and take your oaths in his name (Deut 10:15-20).

If Israel complied with God's law by showing mercy to the weak and doing justice with one's neighbour, they would both enjoy rich blessings and also illustrate to the nations the character of God and the prospects of life under his rule. At their best the prophets and psalmists of Israel grasped this missional calling to the nations: 'Give thanks to the LORD, call on his name; make known among the nations what he has done' (Ps 105:1). Walter C Kaiser states, 'The Psalmist longed for and deeply desired that God, the King of Israel, might be acknowledged as Lord and Savior of all the families of the earth.'[18] The end of making the name of the Lord known to the nations would be that the nations also could serve the Lord and be included as the people of God.

Israel's failure was that it lost sight of the unique nation they were called to be: a righteous people, faithful to the Lord, exercising justice and mercy towards the weakest members of its society and generosity towards the stranger. Mistaking election for entitlement, falling into idolatry and forgetting the marginalized among its own, Israel failed in its calling. Its missional calling to the nations became inverted. Instead of fulfilling their call to be the nation through whom the nations would be blessed, Israel understood that the nations were called to recognize its preeminence. These failures brought upon Israel the rebuke of the prophets and ultimately its loss of national status through captivity. Arthur F Glasser in *Announcing the Kingdom* describes this exclusivity:

> Israel reasoned that nothing it might do would jeopardize its standing with God. Their conviction arose from what was judged to be an unconditional promise made to David concerning the security of Jerusalem, the inviolability of the Temple, and the permanence of the Davidic line (2 Sam 7. 8-16). As a result, Israel largely forgot that it was chosen by God for service and that this was both a privilege and an obligation. Only a few sensed with Isaiah that God was concerned that his people be 'a light for the Gentiles' (42:6; 49:6). Almost none of them translated their calling into dynamic outreach. In the postexilic period this concern of the exiles diminished to the point where they sought to preserve their faith and religious practice by living in complete

---

[18] Walter C Kaiser, 'Israel's Missionary Call', in Ralph D Winter and Steven C Hawthorne (eds), *Perspectives on the World Christian Movement* (Pasadena: William Carey Library, 1992), A-33.

withdrawal from the nations... Jewish exclusiveness steadily gained ground during the postexilic period.[19]

Christ Jesus as a prophet to Israel was calling Israel back to its missional purpose to be used by the Lord to bless the nations. Christ reiterated the importance of extending mercy to the weak, the marginalized, and the sinful in Israeli society (Matt 25:31-40). Most notably, Christ also emphatically extended the blessing of God beyond Israel to the nations. Jesus traveled to the region of Tyre and Sidon and there extended healing to the daughter of a gentile, a Syro-Phoenician woman (Matt 15:21-28). In this encounter it is argued that his reference to gentiles as 'dogs' is itself a rebuke of popular Jewish prejudice and meant to be instructive to the disciples as they prepared for their mission to the nations.[20] Finally, through the new covenant Christ heightened Israel's calling to bless and serve the nations, commissioning the Jewish disciples to take the message of God's forgiveness to all nations. Kenton Sparks argues provocatively that this commissioning was a corrective to the Israeli triumphal commission to defeat the nations and possess the land.[21]

We can thus understand Christ's *kenosis* to share in the human experience as including the experience of national identity. He consequently defined through his perfect love and servanthood the highest national purpose which was to care for the marginalized and to serve other nations by extending the knowledge of God's justice and mercy. Arguing then from the ministry of Christ and the nationalism he embodied, human identity moulded by nationalism can be a basis for reconciliation when that nationalism refutes the triumphal and embraces a concern for the welfare of other peoples.

How would this be realized in Israel and Palestine? Identity as a Palestinian or as an Israeli would need to lay aside the motive to destroy the other and rather embrace a consideration of the welfare of the other with forgiveness. It necessitates a willingness to empathize with the fears and injuries of the other. Where can such a radical transformation of nationalism begin? The Palestinian Christian community has the most immediate access and responsibility to the example of Christ, as well as the power through the Spirit of God to follow his example.

---

[19] Arthur F. Glasser, *Announcing the Kingdom: the Story of God's Mission in the Bible* (Grand Rapids: Baker, 2003), 134.
[20] Don Richardson, 'A Man for All Peoples', in Winter and Hawthorne, *Perspectives*, A-105-106.
[21] Kenton L. Sparks, 'Gospel as Conquest: Mosaic Typology in Matthew 8:16-20', *The Catholic Biblical Quarterly* 68:4, 651-63.

Embracing Nationalism as Servanthood

Can it be imagined that the nationalism that is fiercely asserted through war and violence by Israel and Palestine be transformed to a nationalism that seeks the welfare of the other? The Palestinian Christian community *by having the same mind as Christ* as the apostle wrote has the opportunity to be a prophetic voice in the midst of violence and hatred by being an example to their Muslim neighbours and to Israel of servanthood and reconciliation. Such a radically prophetic stance which advocates a Palestinian nationalism characterized by concern for the other – for the people of Israel and for intra-Palestinian harmony – may be found even now in the Palestinian Christian community. Salim Munayer is a professor at Bethlehem Bible College and the president of Musalahah, a Bethlehem based organization dedicated to building bridges of understanding between Palestinian Christians and Muslims and Israeli Jews. He writes:

> If I am called a Christian Palestinian, I have a commitment and obligation toward my Palestinian people and their future and welfare. At the same time I have an obligation to my Lord to love my enemies, to break the circle of hatred and enmity and violence, to be a peacemaker, and to look for practical ways for peace between Jews and Arabs. We as Palestinian Christians can play an important role, and be an avenue of peace.[22]

Palestinian Christian students at Bir Zeit University are a segment of the Palestinian Christian community on the frontlines of dealing with the interface of theology and nationalism. How will their faith inform their nationality, identity, and progress towards peace? In the cauldron of political ferment they have tried to formulate responses to this question. Fuad (a pseudonym), a Palestinian Christian student, describes trying to reason with a Muslim classmate for a different ethic towards the land and Israel:

> The human being is most valuable, the most fruitful thing in the land. We do not need to kill to take the land. And I start talking with him about peace and we have to love each other even if they hate us, even if they persecute us. But for Islam that is like giving in. They say no, we have to struggle to take our rights. I face them with the truth that Jesus told us: you can't struggle evil with evil. You have to be right. You have to pray with people who persecute us. You have to be generous with them. In the opposite way, they are dealing with us. They refuse. They say we are wasting our time with prayers. What is taken by power must be taken back by power also.[23]

Such witness has met intense hostility from militants in Palestine. Rami Ayyad, a native Gazan Christian, was apparently martyred by Islamic

---

[22] Salim J Munayer, 'Relations between Religions in Historic Palestine and the Future Prospects: Christians and Jews', in Michael Prior and William Taylor (eds), *Christians in the Holy Land* (London: The World of Islam Festival Trust, 1994), 149.

[23] Bush, 'Palestinian Christian University Students', 66.

militants on 7th October 2007 for his service to the Gazan community which emphasized peace and the need to love one's neighbour. The Christian voice for reconciliation where it may be found is often regarded as representing an unpatriotic motive manipulated by western Christians who are biased towards Israel.

Palestinian Christians, many working in relief organizations, must endure the harassment of military personnel at the hundreds of checkpoints that choke the West Bank, east Jerusalem and Gaza. Palestinian Christians must endure the loss of their land to settlers and to the building of 'Jews only' settlement roads. In spite of the dehumanizing aspects of occupation the Palestinian Bible Society and its sister office in Israel are joining hearts and hands to work as a united team, to be a prophetic witness to their societies.

For Palestinian Christians to choose to be a radical witness of Christ's humility and servanthood will mean for many the costly decision to stay in the land rather than emigrate. Such a decision is itself a prophetic act. The difficulty of paying such a price is reflected in the demographic survey of Palestinian Christians conducted by Sabeel, the Ecumenical Liberation Theology Center in Jerusalem, which confirms the massive emigration of Christians since 1948.[24]

For Christians in Palestine to walk in the vulnerability of Christ they will need the support of the wider international Christian community. In order for evangelicals who endorse political Zionism to support Palestinian Christians they will have to consider the implications of their nationalistic theology and its inconsistencies with the example of Christ's life. Indeed Christian Zionism needs a radical encounter with the Christ's prophetic ministry to Israel and his renunciation of narrow nationalism. In fairness those who oppose Christian Zionism and Israel's policies towards Palestine often become equally as strident. Their opposition to Israel becomes so intense that their posture appears far from the compassion of Christ for Israel, as when he wept for the nation while gazing on the troubled street of Jerusalem from the Mount of Olives. Palestinian Christians may yet be a prophetic voice to these communities as well, calling them to Christ's radical self-emptying unto servant-hood, even towards antagonists.

Conclusion

The prophet Isaiah spoke of day in which truth would go forth to the world from Zion (Is 2:1-3):

> In the last days
> the mountain of the LORD's temple will be established
> as chief among the mountains; it will be raised above the hills,

---

[24] *The Sabeel Survey on Palestinian Christians in the West Bank* (Jerusalem: Sabeel, 2006), 47, 63.

and all nations will stream to it.
Many people will come and say,
'Come, let us go up to the mountain of the LORD,
to the house of the God of Jacob.
He will teach us his ways, so that we may walk in his paths.'
The law will go out from Zion, the word of the LORD from Jerusalem.

He will teach us his ways. How strange these ways are to peoples striving for dominance, driven by triumphal nationalistic ideologies. A theology of human identity which works towards an appreciation of the commonalities between Israel and Palestine can provide a starting point towards reconciliation if the nationalism that moulds communal and individual identity will learn the ways of the Lord. Could the Palestinian Christians who seek his way be the voice, however frail, of the Word of the Lord from Jerusalem? Could they yet be – in the midst of militant pressure and the temptation to flee – the transformative community? Certainly to do so the wider Christian family must also have the same mind of Christ who emptied himself, moving past the partisan inclinations which erodes the grace of God in the church's attitudes and actions towards Israel and Palestine.

MISSION IN AN ORTHODOX CHRISTIAN CONTEXT: WITNESSING TO CHRIST AS PATORAL RESPONSIBILITY

Valentin Kozhuharov

Orthodoxy and Mission in Eastern Europe

Telling Orthodox believers 'to do mission' means little to them: they would only grasp 'doing/fulfilling ecclesiastical tasks'. Because it is the church community (the ecclesiastical body) that tells them what tasks they must fulfil in order to acquire their own salvation and to help others to come to salvation. This implies that mission has never been well developed in the Orthodox church and that Orthodoxy has never been interested in mission and has always paid special attention to the salvific role of the church in her unity with the source of salvation – the Lord Jesus Christ.[1] Thus the Orthodox church developed the so called 'internal' mission which in actual fact meant building the ecclesiastical body and strengthening each believer in their strict observance of ecclesiastical discipline (complete humility, prayer, worship, fasting, strict keeping to the teaching of the church, deeds of mercy, etc.) which would lead the believers on the path to salvation. It was only a recent trend that the Orthodox churches in some countries became socially active, with a missionary dimension to the social activity. Affirming that the decades of communism (and the five centuries of

---

[1] There are opinions among Orthodox theologians that the Orthodox church did mission in the past and we acknowledge, too, that missionary efforts have been undertaken by Orthodox Christian missionaries since the early centuries of the Christian era until now. See James Stamoolis, *Eastern Orthodox Mission Theology Today* (Maryknoll, NY: Orbis Books, 1986), 1, 19 where he widely considers all pros and cons to the issue of existence of Orthodox mission. We also need to understand that the Orthodox would usually 'do mission' within their own boundaries of Orthodox presence (either national or local). The examples which are usually given (such as those of Cyril and Methodius, the Russian missions of the eighteenth and nineteenth centuries, the missions to Japan and China) represent dual missionary endeavours undertaken by the church and the emperor, the so called ceasaropapist approach to mission. A true Orthodox mission has only been the 'internal mission' of the church which has always been known as witnessing to Christ but not as mission. Today, though we could give examples of church planting by Orthodox churches in various countries of Africa and Asia, this internal witnessing continues to be the main concern of the Orthodox churches and their missionaries.

Ottoman yoke in some of the Orthodox countries) prevented the churches from fulfilling their social tasks seems not true because even in times of freedom and relative concordance between state and church they nevertheless did not pay much attention either to social issues or to mission.

Only the changes at the end of the 1980s made it possible for the Orthodox churches in Eastern Europe to see a period of revival and growth. The first few years saw the churches struggling and claiming their property back from the state in order to restore (and build new) church buildings, monasteries and other ecclesiastical facilities. After this initial 'revival', the churches started restoring their teaching activity and social ministry while the worshiping ministry had started earlier, immediately after the changes took place. In almost all so called 'Orthodox' countries in Eastern Europe, such as Russia, Ukraine, Belarus, Moldavia, Romania, Serbia, Bulgaria and Georgia, the churches were filled with people and the church as a whole grew rapidly. Then in the next several years enthusiasm diminished and those who remained in the church were mostly the believers who were strengthened in their faith and their Christian life. Property, to a large extent, was given back to the churches and this allowed them to engage more seriously with social issues, especially as the churches gathered power and resources.

It was not until the end of the twentieth century that the churches in this part of Europe could focus on social issues. It was first of all the Russian Orthodox church (ROC) that seriously and widely undertook social ministry. The other Orthodox churches only proclaimed social activity as a priority of their ministry by making brief references in documents and in decisions of the Holy Synods. They could not adopt regular, well-grounded and efficient programmes of social activity (though today good examples can be given in Ukraine, Romania, Serbia and Bulgaria). The period between 1990 and 2000 gave the ROC enough strength and power to allow her to undertake wide-spread social activity. The foundation for this was formulated in the 'Basics of the Social Conception of the Russian Orthodox Church', adopted at a Holy Archbishops' Council in August 2000 and put into practice immediately thereafter.[2] Besides outlining the common social task and responsibilities, the document also defined the role which the ROC was expected to fulfil in the Russian society. In fact, some of this document's definitions came from earlier documents on mission which were developed within ROC.

---

[2] 'Osnovy sotsialnoi kontseptsii Russkoi Pravoslavnoi Tserkvi'. V: *Informatsionny bulletin Otdela Vneshnih Tserkovnyh Sviazei Moskovskoi Patriarchii* ('Basics of the social conception of the Russian Orthodox Church'), in *Information Bulletin of the Department of External Ecclesiastical Relations of the Moscow Patriarchate*, Moscow, 8:2000, 3-121. English version of the document can only be found at the official website of the Moscow Patriarchate of the Russian Orthodox church at http://www.mospat.ru/en/documents/social-concepts/ (accessed 16.2.2013).

Seeking Revival of Missionary Activity

It may sound strange to affirm that a new missionary movement of the modern type can appear within Orthodoxy but this is what happened in mid-nineties of twentieth century when the Russian Orthodox church undertook extensive missionary activities on its territory. The Missionary Department of the ROC was established in late 1995 and the Russian Orthodox church initiated a new stage in missionary practice and missionary theology. We should note that ROC first started practically with mission and only then tried to provide a theological formulation of Orthodox mission. It appeared that the theology lying behind the practical mission fully corresponded with the teaching of the Church Fathers and relevant modern Orthodox theological research. This means that the ROC's missionary activity confirmed again the true understanding of mission as interpreted and practised in the Orthodox church for centuries, though it has never been called 'mission' but 'ecclesiastical discipline', 'ecclesiastical tasks', or simply witnessing.

As shown in my earlier research on the missionary activity of the Russian Orthodox Church,[3] three important documents appeared to theologically define the missionary practice which already had been on stream in ROC: the Concept of 1995, the Report of 2004 and the Concept of 2005.[4] The last of the three documents summarised the experience the ROC had acquired during the ten-year period of intensive missionary activity between 1995 and 2005 and formulated the ROC's vision for her mission during the period 2005-2010. The document appeared in April 2005 and was immediately spread to dioceses and churches to urge them to follow its definitions and at the same time to get feedback from the church

---

[3] Valentin Kozhuharov, *Towards an Orthodox Christian Theology of Mission: An Interpretive Approach* (Veliko Tarnovo, Bulgaria: Vesta Publishing House, 2006).

[4] *Kontseptsia vozrozhdenia missionerskoi deyatel'nosti Russkoi Pravoslavnoi Tserkvi*. Moskovskii Patriarchate, Moskva, 6 oktiabria 1995 (*Concept of revival of the missionary activity of the Russian Orthodox Church*). Moscow Patriarchate, Moscow, 6 October 1995.

Doklad Vysokopreosviashtennogo Ioanna, archiepiskopa Belgorodskogo i Starooskol'skogo, predsedatelia Missionerskogo Otdela Moskovskogo Patriarchata na Archiereiskom Sobore Russkoi Pravoslavnoi Tserkvi 3-8 oktiabria 2004 (*Report of His Eminence Ioann, Archbishop of Belgorod and Stary Oskol diocese, Head of the Missionary Department of the Moscow Patriarchate, at the Archbishops' Council of the Russian Orthodox Church, 3 to 8 October 2004*). Moscow Patriarchate, 2004.

Kontseptsia missionerskoi deyatel'nosti Russkoi Pravoslavnoi Tserkvi na 2005-2010 gody. Moskovskii Patriarchate, Moskva, 2005 (*Concept of the missionary activity of the Russian Orthodox Church for 2005 to 2010*). Moscow Patriarchate, Moscow, 2005.

None of the above documents have been translated into English and the quotations and excerpts are given according to the Russian texts as translated by the author of this essay.

leaders so that the document be improved and be in concordance with all previous ROC documents and decisions, principally with the 'Basics of the Social Conception of the Russian Orthodox Church'.

For some two years church leaders at diocesan and parish level considered and discussed the document. Only in April 2007 did the final edition of Concept 2005 appear and it was immediately spread to dioceses for practical implementation. Not that missionary activity had stopped but now the document required that its theological considerations be put into practice in each of the dioceses and parishes of the Russian Orthodox Church. During the ten-year period of the ROC's mission between 1995 and 2005 missionary activity was mainly carried out by clergy and seminary students from the Belgorod region. It is true that the missionary activity embraced not only the 'European' ROC dioceses but also vast territories in Siberia and Russia's Far East. Nevertheless only a small number of believers and church leaders were involved in the work carried out by the missionary department of the Russian church. This department undertook a wide discussion process where Concept 2005 was considered and hotly discussed in many diocesan centres and parishes. This activity aimed not only at getting feedback but also at inspiring the believers to 'go and make disciples'. What is the meaning of 'going and making disciples' as understood by Concept 2005 and by the Russian Orthodox Church as a whole? It is exactly as exposed in the gospel and nothing more. It is in line with the mission which Christianity has been carrying out for centuries. It is about forming and strengthening God's people. Nevertheless, the specific circumstances of a church, or a country, or a territory which 'sends-out' missionaries, always attributes specific meaning to the understanding of the Great Commission. This is the case with the 'Russian' mission: it reflects a specific Russian Orthodox (widely based on all-Orthodox) approach to mission and to proclaiming the gospel.

The 2005 'Concept of Mission'

The vast missionary activity of the ROC in the period between 1995 and 2005 naturally led to the publication of another missionary document to summarise the experience gained during the ten years of mission and to point out the new challenges faced by the Orthodox church in the new millennium. The April 2005 'Concept of Mission' indicated three main areas of consideration when forming the theology of mission: the goals and tasks of mission today, the forms and methods of mission, and the main directions of missionary service today.

Goals and tasks of mission

'Concept 2005' starts with a preamble which defines the ground of mission: 'the mission of the Orthodox church aims at salvation of every human being'. This foundation requires that 'missionaries deeply realise that their activity is of great importance for the church and humanity' and that 'every Orthodox believer is responsible before God, the church and his/her conscience as to proclaiming the Good News to every nation'. The conclusion to this affirmation is almost indispensable: 'all the faithful children of the Orthodox church should take the path of Orthodox Christian witnessing'. In this way the document's preamble clearly states how mission is understood from an Orthodox point of view.

In the first part of the document ('Goals and Tasks of the Modern Mission'), it is clearly defined what mission is: 'it is the fulfilment of the Great Commission of Christ: Go ye into all the world and preach the gospel to every creature' (Mk 16:15). Preaching the gospel brings the ultimate goal of mission, 'theosis of the whole of creation'. Theosis, or divinisation, in Orthodox understanding means the path to salvation and the spiritual struggle to achieve salvation. It does not simply mean divinisation in itself (which is not possible for humans in this life). The ultimate goal of mission is closely connected with the purpose of mission.

'In the Orthodox understanding, the purpose of mission can be rightly grasped only if we consider the three important theological principles of being a Christian: soteriological, ecclesiastical and eschatological.'[5] Without firm grounding in these notions, no right understanding of the Christian mission from an Orthodox perspective can be reached. Without understanding what the soteriological principle means in the lives of the believers, it is not possible to explain the ardent wish for salvation of the ordinary Orthodox Christians in the churches. 'Without understanding the ecclesiastical structure of the church – its hierarchical, sacramental and liturgical constitution,'[6] no proper comprehension of the sacrificial ministry and faithful life of the local churches within the apostolic succession (ecclesiastical hierarchy) of the believers could be achieved. Without understanding the eschatological purpose of the lives of believers and of the church as a whole, no sound understanding of the mission of Christ and the mission of the church could be reached because the mission of the church is 'to announce the *eschaton* – the salvation in Jesus Christ'.[7]

However, this ultimate goal should be more specifically defined by immediate goals of mission, and one of them is 'building up Eucharistic communities by the example of the one founded by Jesus Christ.' This goal can be achieved by fulfilling specific tasks of mission, and in the document

---

[5] Anastasios Yannoulatos, 'The Purpose and Motive of Mission from an Orthodox Theological Point of View', *International Review of Mission* 54:215 (July 1967), 282.

[6] Alexander Schmemann, 'The Missionary Imperative in the Orthodox Tradition', in Gerald H Anderson (ed), *The Theology of the Christian Mission* (New York: McGraw-Hill, 1961), 252.

[7] Schmemann, 'The Missionary Imperative', 254.

seven important tasks are exposed to clearly define how the goals of mission could be achieved.

Forms and approaches to mission

There are four main forms of mission: informational mission, apologetic mission, mission of church upbringing, and external mission. The direction of missionary activity starts with information and then through apologetic witnessing brings people to Christ through catechesis and ecclesiastical discipline. Then the believers, being firmly rooted in the Orthodox faith and practice, can 'go and make disciples' in the external mission of the church.

Main directions of missionary service

Defining the main directions of mission gives the understanding of mission as interpreted by the Russian Orthodox church in her specific circumstances. Ten main directions are defined in Concept 2005:
- Missionary service of lay people
- Missionary commissioning
- Missionary parish
- Missionary worship and services
- Organisation of missionary schools
- Mobile mission
- Establishing missionary camps and stations
- Mission amongst young people
- Mission amongst the immigrants in Siberia and Russia's Far East
- Characteristics and qualities of contemporary missionaries.[8]

All of these spring from the internal organisation of a missionary church in the centre of which are the missionary divine services, with the Holy Liturgy in their core. Special attention is given to immigrants coming mainly from China and Korea and settling intensively in the eastern regions of Russia, bringing change to the ethnic structure of society. This part of the document also defines the main directions of missionary service of the ROC in the near future. Twenty specific 'fields of missionary activity' have been defined to encompass both the internal and the external mission of the ROC, first of all carried out within Russia and its 'territory of pastoral responsibility'.

There is a special paragraph in 'Concept 2005' about spiritual security. Unlike any other type of security, this means missionary activity done in such a way that it secures stable and sustainable development of Russian

---

[8] See further Kozhuharov, *Towards an Orthodox Christian Theology of Mission*, 33-42; cf. Valentin Kozhuharov. *Missionerskata deinost na Ruskata pravoslavna tsurkva dnes* (*The Missionary Activity of the Russian Orthodox Church Today*) (Veliko Tarnovo, Bulgaria: Vesta Publishing House, 2008), 128-33.

society in its movement towards higher spiritual levels of growth as understood in their Orthodox form and content. No illusions are cherished and the ROC's understanding of spiritual security embraces only those 'who have ears to hear', while the other members of the society need to listen more attentively if they want to be saved. The ROC's goal is that every Russian citizen be saved if they believe in Jesus Christ and rightly follow the church's rules of ecclesiastical discipline.

It is all too obvious that the main concern of mission, as defined in the ROC's missionary documents and in its practice of mission, is its internal mission, that is baptising, catechising (education) and living a Christ-like life. This internal Christian growth (both of the church as a whole and of each individual church member) takes place in the so called 'Eucharistic parishes' which lead the believers towards salvation, or more precisely, through theosis to salvation. Only when the Orthodox church and her members feel that their true spiritual struggle bears good fruit, can they 'go forth and make disciples of all nations'. It is often confirmed in Orthodox writings of the Church Fathers that, 'you must first heal yourself and only then heal the others.' Many believers in the Russian Orthodox Church are convinced that if Christianity as a whole gets contaminated with unhealthy teaching and practices, this inevitably creates unhealthy churches which are not able to draw people to Christ and cannot bring people's souls to salvation. This is why spiritual health and security are immutable premises for healthy growth in Christ – a path most efficiently offered by the Orthodox Church. In fact, the Church Fathers often pointed to the Eucharistic communion as the centre of the Christian life, and Orthodox researchers and clergy even point to it as the foundation for missionary activity: the Eucharist is the mission of the church.[9]

'Theologies' of mission as understood by ROC

If we follow the definitions of 'Concept 2005', we can find three main missionary 'visions' (theologies) of the ROC's missionary activity: the theology of catechesis, the Eucharistic theology and the theology of salvation.[10] The three visions give us the understanding that mission means catechisation, Eucharistic participation and a path to salvation.

We have already mentioned that the theological reflection found in 'Concept 2005' arose from the practical missionary activity carried out by the ROC between 1995 and 2005. The new form of mission – the so called 'mobile mission' – enabled the missionaries to practically fulfil the Lord's command: 'go …and preach the gospel' by teaching, Eucharistic participation and salvific struggle in the believers' Christ-like life. What

---

[9] See Schmemann, 'The Missionary Imperative', 254.
[10] Kozhuharov, *Towards an Orthodox Christian Theology of Mission*, 57-67, and Kozhuharov, *Missionerskata deinost*, 253-65.

life is this? It is a life of acquiring the Holy Spirit within ourselves. 'We acquire the Holy Spirit through our celebration of the Eucharist and the reception of Holy Communion, through our participation in the sacraments, through our discipline of daily prayer, of deeds of love, and through the practice of fasting, all of which result in a Christ-like life'.[11]

Mobile mission was carried out in the form of missionary pilgrimages by train at distances of more than 15,000 kilometres to Siberia and Russia's Far East, by so called car-temples (trailer-truck-temples) where again dozens of distant areas of Russia were covered, and also by plane and by ship.[12] In addition, several missionary conventions and conferences discussed and summarised practical issues of missiology, hundreds of missionaries were educated and spiritually prepared, dozens of missionary centres were opened, hundreds of missionary parishes were reorganised to meet the requirements of the ROC Missionary Department in carrying out effective mission among the Russian population. If we take into account the fact that this huge amount of activity was carried out mostly in the 2000-2005 period, we can imagine the vast scale of missionary enterprise undertaken by the ROC and her missionaries on the church's 'territory of pastoral responsibility'.

Third 'Concept of Mission'

The intensive missionary activity in the years between 1995 and the end of 2005 gave the Russian Orthodox Church abundant experience which had to be summarised and properly assessed.[13] The ROC felt she needed a break to

---

[11] John Meyendorff, 'Theosis in the Eastern Christian Tradition', in Louis K. Dupre and Don E Saliers (eds), *Christian Spirituality: Post-Reformation and Modern* (New York: Crossroad, 1989), 473.

[12] For example, four major missionary pilgrimages by train were carried out. The first pilgrimage took place between 19 and 30 October 2000 to Archangelsk region, the second from 6 to 16 March 2001 to Karelia region, the third and largest from 7 August to 2 September 2001 to Eastern Siberia and the Far East (a distance of more than 15,000km), the fourth from 17 to 25 December 2001 to Penzensk region. The car-temple (in fact, this is a trailer truck with an inbuilt temple) undertook several missionary travels between 2003 and 2005, particularly to the Kalmykia republic and the region of Adygeia. The third form of mobile mission – the so called 'missionary camps and field stations' left hundreds of new-built churches and chapels on many of Russia's eastern territories with hundreds of priests serving there. Through this type of mission thousands of people converted to Orthodoxy – both Russians and of other ethnic groups and language communities – and established hundreds of educational centres and schools to further spread the gospel amongst local people. In this way the three theological 'visions' – catechising, Eucharistic participation and salvific spiritual struggle – found their practical implementation within Russia as a result of the ROC's missionary activity.

[13] This was when the last of this first period of missionary pilgrimages, the mission of 7 to 17 October 2005 to the Far East Kamchatka region, took place.

enable her to evaluate the outcomes and to give theological grounding to the practical outworking of mission carried out in the last ten years. The 2005 'Concept of Mission' was examined and hotly discussed in many of Russia's diocesan centres and parishes. A huge amount of work was done by clergy and lay people to summarise the fruits of mission and of missionary research. This finally resulted in a new version of the 'Concept of Mission', published in April 2007.[14]

The character and the spirit of the document remained the same as its predecessor, as did the theological grounds of mission. Nevertheless, the new structure of theoretical definitions of mission in fact shows a considerable reassessment of the missionary activity and its theological foundation. In the 2005 'Concept of Mission', we find the following path of theological reflection concerning mission: first, defining the goals and tasks of mission today, then, on this ground the appropriate forms and method of mission were proposed, and finally, the two were specifically reflected in the practical missionary ministry of clergy and lay people.

The approach of the 2007 'Concept of Mission' is different. First, the battle field, the area of missionary activity, is clearly shown to give Christians the understanding of what means and resources are needed to fulfil their missionary calling; then, the main goals, tasks and methods of mission are defined; and finally, the practical implementation of missionary tasks is presented to show the possible and the immediate forms of mission in practical terms.

In particular, the new vision involves the following considerations.

Mission is clearly defined in the first sentences of the preamble: 'mission is witnessing and preaching that aims to arouse faith in those who listen... and to proclaim the Good News to all the creation', and 'mission aims at sanctifying not only man but the whole world, too.'[15] This spiritual postulate was confirmed by the Church Fathers and by modern theologians: 'Christ has come to save humanity, and through the people Christ saves and redeems the whole world, the whole creation.'[16]

This understanding of mission is practically supported by defining the tasks leading to achieving sanctification and salvation: 'The Orthodox mission aims at teaching peoples to be enlightened in the truths of the faith, at educating people to enable them to live a Christ-like life, and mainly at passing on the experience of communion with God through a personal participation of the believers in the sacramental life of the Eucharistic

---

[14] 'Kontseptsia missionerskoi deyatel'nosti Russkoi Pravoslavnoi Tserkvi na 2005-2010 gody'. V: *Missionerskoe Obozrenie*, No 4. Belgorod, 2007, S. 4-19 ('Concept of the missionary activity of the Russian Orthodox Church for 2005 to 2010'), in *Missionary Review*, Belgorod, April 2007, 4-19.

[15] Kontseptsia... (April 2007), 5.

[16] Schmemann, 'The Missionary Imperative', 256.

community.'[17] Again, the path of 'catechisation-Eucharistic participation-spiritual struggle for salvation' is seen as the main direction of mission.

Mission is also defined in terms of 'gospel and culture': 'The Orthodox understanding of mission sees it as an eschatological event where the gospel will be proclaimed "unto the end of the world" (Matt 28:20), and it is this eschatological perspective that gives us the right understanding of the relations between mission and national cultures... requiring from the missionaries to approach the world, to sanctify and renew it, to transform the way of life of people through accepting local cultures and ways of cultural expression, provided they do not contradict the Christian faith, thus transforming them into means of salvation.' Here comes this essential difference in understanding the issue of 'gospel and culture' as interpreted by the Orthodox church (and by other Christian traditions, as well): local cultures and ways of cultural expressions can be accepted and lived only if they do not contradict your faith and your life as a faithful Christian in a Eucharistic community. Only on this ground can local cultures be transformed into means of salvation. Missionaries need to constantly acquire the Holy Spirit, that is to be spiritual, in order to differentiate between holy and profane, between Christian and pagan, between right and wrong. Spirituality, as well as many other Christian postulates, seems to obtain new characteristics in some Christian denominations, and the Russian Orthodox Church has always affirmed the true meaning of spirituality: 'This is to be spiritual in the Orthodoxy: "being in Christ". This means that we think, feel and wish what Christ thought, felt and wished. And this means that we should have "Christ's mind", "love of Christ"... if Christ wished that "all men be saved and come to the knowledge of the truth" (1 Tim 2:4), then we also must wish the same.'[18]

The first section of the 2007 'Concept of Mission' gives us five characteristics of the missionary field of activity of the ROC today:
- most of the Russian people traditionally belong to the Orthodox culture of this country and nevertheless they remain indifferent to the Orthodox church and the Orthodox culture as a whole and tend to neo-pagan practices or a secular orientation.
- the country experiences a large scale expansion of non-traditional religious and non-religious worldviews, of destructive cults and totalitarian sects that powerfully influence modern Russian people; the ROC needs to bring Russians back into the parish's fence in order to prevent them from perishing.
- the newcomers and the ones who still are not firmly rooted in the Orthodox faith need new approaches and new ways of pastoral work in order to enter and to remain in the church; this requires that new

---
[17] Kontseptsia... (April 2007), 5.
[18] Anastasios Yannoulatos, 'Orthodoxy and Mission', *St Vladimir's Seminary Quarterly* 8:3 (1964), 144.

missionary imperatives be developed in the area of pastoral care and spiritual guidance.
- there is great need to create and develop new teaching materials to help people get acquainted with Christianity and bring them into the Orthodox church.
- Russian society needs unity and a healthier spiritual-moral environment because the new challenges today lead society to reject traditions and traditional moral values.
- The ROC claims that these new challenges erode Russian society today. Each challenge needs a response. Here are the challenges and the missionary tasks:
- Loss of cultural identity, and the task is: seeking ways to Christianise national cultures.
- Social-economic reforms and their consequences for society, and the task is: protection of the people that the state does not protect.
- The advance of the sciences which question issues of morality and the essential foundations of life, and the task is: to oppose and counteract the processes of substitution of science for ideology or occultism and the attempts to divinise science, especially in the field of humanities.
- Informational violence and its influence on people, and the task is: to oppose informational aggression of destructive cults and organisations against the Orthodox church, individuals, family and society.
- The plurality of religions and worldviews, and the task is: to oppose attempts to substitute the absolute and the only truth of Christ for a 'unified and universal' religion.

As we are now acquainted with the battlefield, we need to define the main goals, tasks and methods of mission. This is what the 2007 'Concept of Mission' presents. As in the earlier version of 2005, the ultimate goal of mission again is formulated thus: mission aims at fulfilment of God's primordial provision – theosis of man and of all creation. Unlike the 2005 version, however, the immediate goal of mission is defined in terms of spreading the Orthodox faith: (1) of bringing up people into being active members of the church; (2) of passing on the experience of communion with God; and (3) all the three can only be accomplished through building Eucharistic communities to be spread 'unto the end of the world'. The immediate goal of mission is then achieved through fulfilment of eight primary tasks of mission, as exposed in the document.

Carrying out specific tasks needs organisation and responsibility. The document further defines the responsibilities of the missionary bishops (four main tasks), the missionary priests (five tasks) and the missionary lay people (three tasks).

The forms and the methods of mission are declared as follows:

- Mission of bringing up people to become active members of the church
- Apologetic mission
- Informational mission
- External mission.

And, unlike the 2005 version, in the 2007 'Concept of Mission' we find a fifth important form of mission:
- Mission of reconciliation.

The last one is connected with the task of reconciliation between generations, between political and other type of opponents, between former enemies, both peoples and territories, and between secular and religious culture. For the first time the new Concept defines several types of dialogue: 'dialogue of life', 'dialogue of social responsibilities', and 'mission of dialogue'.[19] It is worth noting that dialogue does not mean retreat but mutual understanding and tolerance.

The second main part of the 2007 'Concept of Mission' concludes with the characteristics and the qualities of the modern missionary where, unlike the previous version of 2005, the characteristics of the synodal missionary and the diocesan missionary are defined. The missionary ministry of the former is closely related to the commissioning tasks the Holy Synod puts on a missionary. That of the latter is closely connected with the commissioning tasks the local bishop puts on missionaries and on missionary centres and organisations.

The practical issues of missionary ministry in the 2007 'Concept of Mission' summarises the first two theoretical parts into a unified specific practice of mission as already found in the ROC's mission in the last ten to twelve years. There are several forms of missionary activity which differ from what we found in the 2005 Concept.

The first concerns the young people of Russia. In the new version, special attention is given to defining different types of young people with a view to enabling missionaries to develop appropriate approaches and methods to work with them. The following types of young people have been identified:
- Youngsters who are church members but still do not take any active role in the life of a parish. The missionary task requires that new ways of individual work with them be found in order to turn their potential into action and use it for the benefit of the church and the believers.
- New believers, or neophytes, who need much catechisation and education. They need to be properly educated through their inclusion in various forms of catechisation, mainly through catechetical courses and Sunday schools for adults.

---

[19] Kontseptsia... (April 2007), 13.

- Non-believers who take a positive view of the Orthodox church but who have never thought of becoming members. The most appropriate work with them would be fulfilling creative tasks or organising their rest and holidays in appropriate way and forms.
- Young people who have chosen to belong to other Christian traditions or to other traditional religions but who still maintain a positive attitude to the Orthodox church and would agree to a dialogue of reconciliation. Such youngsters could be included in associations or programmes focussed on such issues as ecological education or drug rehabilitation.
- Non-believers who are disinterested in any relation to the Orthodox church or to any other type of religious life. These are the majority of young people in Russia and this makes the work with them most important. The missionary tasks lie in breaking their false stereotypes of the Christian church as a whole and on religious life in particular, in opening their minds to new images of life, and in preparing their hearts to accept the truths of the Christian faith.
- Young people who negatively relate to the church. Missionaries should seek dialogue with such youngsters only on the foundation of love and reliance on God's help to turn their hearts.

The second important difference concerns the definition of a missionary parish. Eight main characteristics are suggested:
- the parish organises missionary activity on the territory of its own pastoral responsibility;
- parishioners should be educated in missiology and get experience in missionary work;
- it is recommended that parishioners obtain higher secular education;
- the parochial council should include members who are missionaries in spirit and who understand very well what mission is and how it needs to be fulfilled;
- ecclesiastical social activity (*diakonia*) is also one of the main features of a missionary parish;
- the parish should establish a body of missionary catechists to organise the teaching ministry of the parish;
- divine services should be based on the missionary imperative of accessible worship and serving God;
- the parish should keep constant contact with the Missionary Department of the ROC in order to regularly get methodological and other types of help and support.

3) The third issue of the 2007 'Concept of Mission' concerns the missionary ministry of lay people where, for the first time, the role of women in the field of mission has been clearly defined. The role of women in Orthodox witness is treated as equal to that of men. Women's missionary ministry is understood as having four main areas:
- founding charitable organisations and bodies to serve those in need;

- missionary ministry in hospitals;
- missionary and teaching ministry in social homes, mainly children's homes, nursing homes and boarding schools;
- missionary ministry in prisons for women.

The last main part of the 2007 'Concept of Mission' concludes by defining the most important areas of missionary work of the ROC in the near future. Most of the affirmations concern the future of the Russian nation as a whole and the role of the believers in improving the spiritual climate in the country. One important affirmation seems quite significant in assessing the current situation in Russia (and possibly in the world as a whole): 'For the last 800 years, the Russian Orthodox church has never been exposed to the necessity of apostolic preaching on areas and territories where millions of people, through the violence of the atheistic communist regimes of the past decades, have lost their faith and tradition and have acquired other types of culture and history. Now we have faced the paradoxical situation where Russia needs a second Christianisation of the peoples living on the vast Russian territories.'[20]

Conclusion: Personal Observations

It is not easy to speak in first person singular in a scholarly essay, especially when the essay reflects theological considerations. But my humble experience in doing mission within the context of the Russian Orthodox Church makes me believe that even deep theological concerns can be shared and explained in order to find similarities between our experience and the experience of other missionaries and Christian theologians. Seven years of mission in Russia convinced me in a very practical way that doing mission is not an option but an imperative. Jesus Christ most often used imperatives when talking and preaching, he most often would say 'do this' and 'don't do that' and would not allow for any ambiguity. Obedience used to be one of the most honoured qualities in the past, especially in the Slavic countries where Slavic people were considered to be quite a submissive race. It may be that today it is still honoured in some places but it is all too evident that humility and submission are not the first qualities honoured by people today. Democracy and freedom are often understood as giving us the right not to be humble and not to submit to others. Today imperatives are almost avoided in society, only recommendations and offers are issued.

Nowadays people agree that imperatives seem least acceptable in the area of religion and spiritual growth: love is the foundation of the Christian faith – love towards God and your neighbour. But is it as simple to love your neighbour (not to speak of your enemies)? It is not: love needs efforts, strength, sacrifice, and humility. Love needs submission, and often it needs

---

[20] Kontseptsia 2005 (April 2007), 6.

imperatives to be obeyed and fulfilled. This is at least the experience the Russian Orthodox Church has had in her history and present activity.

Schmemann's affirmation that the Eucharist is the mission of the church, as cited above, has been practically and theologically developed by the Russian Orthodox Church in her missionary activity and in missionary researches. Indeed, it is this most intimate and holy act of communion with God that makes believers wish the same intimate and holy communion for every human being. Communion means unity. As Fr Meyendorff affirms, the real unity of Christians is not in ecumenical gatherings, and not in their common actions, and even not in the witnessing amongst non-believers – the unity is in the eucharist: it is an eschatological celebration which shows the coming of the kingdom.[21]

The Great Commission found in Matthew 28:19-20 tells us that teaching is the first imperative in mission: the original Greek text of the verses uses only 'teach' as an imperative form of the verb, all the other forms, translated as verbs in the modern texts, are participles (that is, literally we could translate them as 'by going [there]... teach all nations, baptising them...'). It is this understanding of mission that makes the ROC's missionary activity put the main focus on teaching (catechising). This is why the three theological visions of mission require first education of people, then bringing them into the church and enabling them to fully participate in the Eucharistic life of the parish, which ultimately should lead them on the path of salvation. The example of the ROC with her thousands of schools and teaching centres and Orthodox gymnasia gives us the understanding that teaching is the core of any missionary work.

But we know that teaching is not just telling people about Jesus and about the church as God's community of faithful followers of Christ: teaching needs to be appropriate and right. If it is inappropriate and wrong, teaching does more harm than not having taught at all.[22] Then, the right

---

[21] John Meyendorff, 'The Orthodox Church and Mission: Past and Present Perspectives', *St Vladimir's Theological Quarterly* 16 (1972), 66.

[22] Defining what is right and what is wrong is a delicate issue, especially if this concerns doctrines and ideologies. In her teaching and ecclesiastical practice, the Russian Orthodox Church has always referred to Christian tradition and to the teaching of the Church Fathers. On 6 April 2006, a document was adopted at a World Russian People's Council: *Declaration on Human Rights and Human Dignity*. Then this declaration was further developed and took the form of Church's Teaching which was confirmed, adopted and sanctioned by an Archbishop's Council on 26 June 2008. The document, with the title *Teaching of the Russian Orthodox Church on Human Dignity, Freedoms and Rights*, was immediately implemented within the various ecclesiastical bodies, the Orthodox Churches and the Orthodox educational establishments throughout the country. It defines the Orthodox understanding of the three foundational human qualities as opposed to the universal declaration of human rights of 1948. The document specifically considers such issues as family, gender and sexual orientation, technological advances, especially biotechnology and the moral and ethical issues deriving from its advance,

teaching is constantly multiplied and reaffirmed in the Holy Communion and in the Eucharistic life of the believers in a missionary parish. In this way the missionary parish should prepare true missionaries to go and teach the others appropriately and rightly, too, by preparing them in their embarking on the path to salvation.

Observing the missionary activity of the ROC, one wonders whether this local church is ready to do mission in the way she proclaimed in documents and showed in her missionary activity. The ROC realises the need of reorganisation, of reassessment, and of transformation. The church needs people transformed in their life and thoughts so that they discover mission in a new way and bring the Good News to people in the most adequate and efficient way. 'We need to discover mission in a new way: we not only need to teach people but to transform ourselves and only then to teach the others…. This is the way the church will be transformed: if each of us discerns God and stays with him.'[23] 'Staying with God' needs obedience to imperatives, and at the same time it needs love and love and love: towards God and neighbour, and towards all the creation, since the Orthodox affirmation of sanctification of nature through sanctification of man lies in the foundation of the Christian understanding of the salvific mission of Christ.

The missionary practice and the theology of mission of the Russian Orthodox church is still to be assessed by the other Orthodox churches and the other Christian traditions, and the other religions, too. It has still not been fully assessed even within the ROC itself and she needs to get responses and to agree theology and practice into one unified Concept capable of transforming people's lives and nature's weakness. My missionary experience tells me that the Russian Orthodox Church could truly fulfil God's commandment of proclaiming his good news to the whole creation only if she interacts with the world and cooperates with the other Christian churches. Still her teaching and ecclesiastical practice seems to remain quite secluded and inward, and she mainly aims to bring people living within Russia into the Orthodox church. Russian Orthodox Christians' poor knowledge of western Christian ways of living a Christ-like life does not help them enter a true all-Christian dialogue and fellowship. My first missionary task in Moscow was to acquaint Orthodox

---

freedom of conscience and freedom from conscience, good and evil in human history and today, truth and 'new truths', etc. All these are still to be assessed and fully comprehended but even now we can see the big abyss between the modern expressions of life and the traditional vision of a Christian church which claims to have remained true to the teaching of the gospel and the early church – see https://mospat/ru/en/documents/dignity-freedom-rights/ (accessed 16.2.2013).

[23] Antonii, mitropolit Surozhskii. 'Missionerstvo Tserkvi'. V: *Missionerstvo Tserkvi*. Sviato-Sergievskoe bratstvo, Moskva, 2005, S.16. (Antony, metropolitan of Surozh. 'Missionary activity of the Church'), in *Missionary activity of the Church*, St Sergius Brotherhood, Moscow 2005, 16.

Christians with western Christianity, more specifically with the Anglican Church.

At the same time, western Christians do not know much about the Orthodox church either. My second missionary task was to acquaint non-Orthodox Christians – mostly in the UK – with the Orthodox Church. A closer cooperation between churches in the west and the east of Europe is very much needed. When we look at the mission as done by the ROC, it is obvious that it is mostly grounded on Orthodox doctrine and dogmatic teaching. We all are quite aware that the doctrines and the theology of the various Christian churches still divide Christians (or more specifically, the ecclesiastical hierarchy and the believers in the 'traditional' churches) in the world and this fact does not help us establish true unity in Christ.

My third missionary task in Russia was to seek ways of reconciliation between the different Christian traditions and practices in the churches. Explaining and teaching an all-Christian attitude to proclaiming the gospel (to mission) can be – and truly is – a painful process. Attempts to reconcile two different Christian traditions can be just as painful. But this is what missionaries would always experience, as we think of whether we are prepared to 'pay the price: weariness, threats, career, family, facing risks, antagonism, embarrassment.'[24] It is my deep conviction that the Russian Orthodox Church has undertaken a truly Christian missionary activity and that her cooperation and agreement with the other Christian churches would make a difference in the world in this new challenging century.

---

[24] Alistair Brown, *I Believe in Mission* (London: Hodder & Stoughton, 1997), 50-57.

MISSION ACCORDING TO THE CATHOLIC CHURCH IN ASIA: A NEW WAY OF BEING CHURCH

Clemens Mendonca

Introduction

Our century is experiencing the emergence of two dominant features in the functioning of our society: the symbolic (that which brings us together, that which unites us) and the diabolic (that which puts asunder, that which divides). On the one hand we are living in an age of spiritual entropy. We realize that the world is on the brink of despair. At such times of hopelessness one naturally looks up to religion to find solace and guidance. Even here in this spiritual domain we have to admit that religions on the whole are going through a testing period in their history. They are losing their dynamism as reconcilers and spiritual guides.

Despite this dark picture, thank God, all over the world there are also people from various religious and secular traditions gradually becoming aware that the way the world functions will only lead to destruction and despair. We experience something like 'world consciousness' for peace and harmony, for justice and equality.[1] What unites all people of good will from diverse cultures and religions today is a common quest:

- The quest for a healthy world – environment;
- The quest for unity in the human family beyond race, colour, caste, religion, gender, politics, nations and continents;
- The quest for meaning in life.

There are various movements these days working to attain this goal. Any movement towards peace, justice, human rights, healing, wholeness and welfare of all is from the Spirit of God, the giver of hope to humanity. It is the Spirit that opens us up to the signs of the times and renews the face of the earth. The Spirit cannot be imprisoned in our ways of thinking and acting for she blows where she will, works when, where, how and in whom she will and moves the hearts of anyone whom she will.

The Spirit then is the primary agent of mission in the world and in the church. The awareness that the church is a reality deeply rooted in this world and among its people diverse in cultures, languages, religious beliefs, and ideologies is a gift of God's Spirit to the modern world. She cannot exist in isolation. But for centuries we have been living in seclusion, in our

---

[1] See C. Murray Rogers, 'A New Millennium – Nearly!', *Hindu-Christian Studies* 8 (1995), 36-37, 36.

own self-made wells. The question of respect for other religions, cultures, and the 'otherness' of the other was not our concern at all. But there seems to be a sweeping change in such a mindset today. Vatican II has brought a radical change in the church's approach towards other religions and cultures.[2]

According to the Catholic Church the understanding of mission is very much 'life' oriented i.e., the fullness of life. What comes afterwards (life after death) begins to strike roots here on earth. This was already there in the teachings of the Catholic Church but Vatican II has expressed it in clearer terms. No doubt social context, church tradition, theological reflection etc. have all contributed towards this kind of approach. The kingdom of God is within us, among us or as Raimon Panikkar often puts it, in between us (in our relationships)! 'This means developing relationships, being open, being involved.'[3] Fullness of life (kingdom of God) is all comprehensive and can be restricted neither to the social nor to the spiritual realm alone. It is holistic.

The Second Vatican Council is experienced as the 'New Pentecost' in the Catholic Church where the 'windows' were opened for the fresh air of the Spirit to flow in freely.[4] The Council's central theme was renewal and updating (*aggiornamento*). The goals of this Council were purely pastoral.[5] It was to meet the challenges of the modern world through dialogue. *Ecclesiam Suam* (ES) of Pope Paul VI summarizes this radical change in the Catholic Church in the following words: 'The church must enter into dialogue with the world in which it lives. It has something to say, a message to give, a communication to make' (ES No.65).[6] The two significant phrases of the encyclical are 'Mission and Dialogue'. The mission of the church is to encounter the contemporary world through dialogue. Similarly, the apostolic exhortation of Pope Paul VI *Evangelii Nuntiandi* (Evangelization in the modern world) and the encyclical letter of Pope John Paul II *Redemptoris Missio* bring out the broader aspects of evangelization. Accordingly, evangelization includes both spiritual

---

[2] See especially Pastoral Constitution on the Church in the Modern World *Gaudium Et Spes* promulgated by His Holiness, Pope Paul VI on December 7, 1965; The Declaration on The Relation of the Church to Non-Christian Religions *Nostra Aetate* Proclaimed by His Holiness Pope Paul VI on October 28, 1965 and The Decree *Ad Gentes* on the Mission activity of the Church, promulgated by Pope Paul VI on November 18, 1965.
[3] Interview of Orlando Furioso with Panikkar, http://dasblauelicht.blogspot.com/2009/04/raimon-pannikar-hindu-christian.html
[4] http://www.highbeam.com/doc/1G1-175443849.html
[5] Dr Marcellino D'Ambrosio, The Unfinished Business of Vatican II http://www.crossroadsinitiative.com/library_article/820/Unfinished_Business_of_Vatican_II.html
[6] *Ecclesiam Suam*, Encyclical of Pope Paul VI on The Church, August 6, 1964, http://www.vatican.va/holy_father/paul_vi/encyclicals/documents/hf_pvi_enc_06081964_ecclesiam_en.html

upliftment and integral human (physical/economic) development.[7] Redemptoris Missio gives directions how to proceed in this new task of mission and dialogue: on the one hand promoting the values of the kingdom such as peace, justice, freedom and brotherhood and on the other fostering dialogue between peoples, cultures and religions.[8]

Mission According to the Catholic Church in Asia

Mission in Asia is inconceivable today if we do not take into consideration Asia's rich cultural diversity and multi-religiosity. Expressions like 'mission, evangelization, and conversion' so vital to Christian faith, are greatly misunderstood in many Asian countries (like India). This should give us a hint that the 'how' of mission is as important as its 'why' and 'what' if it has to be intelligible in Asian soil. For example in presenting the Post-Synodal Apostolic Exhortation *Ecclesia in Asia* (EA) of Pope John Paul II to the Bishops of Asia, Cardinal Paul Shan had pointed out that 'the big question presently confronting us, given the religious and cultural context of Asia, is not why we should proclaim the Good News of Christ's Salvation but how' (EA 29).[9] We need to take our context seriously.

Asia is rich in human resource and human potential. Asians constitute 54% of the world's population and the Christian population is just 2.3%. This is despite the fact that Christianity had its genesis in Asia. Considering the vast population, the percentage of Christians after 2000-plus years is still very small. The rationale behind this poor response to the message of the gospel seems to be the failure of the Asian church in articulating and communicating the Christian faith in a way suited to the Asian genius and

---

[7] See *CBCI (Catholic Bishops Conference of India) Evaluation Report*, 1995, CBCI Evaluation Committee, New Delhi, at 215: 'Thus today there is a shift from the concept of presence amongst people to programmes for and with the people. In other words, evangelization work should be kingdom-centered in which people are important. Hence emphasis should be on spreading and sharing the Good News and its concrete implications to all people of good will. Evangelization, therefore, includes the promotion of peace and justice, the running of educational institutions, hospitals, working for the needy and poor, etc.'

[8] *Redemptoris Missio*: 'The Church's task is described as though it had to proceed in two directions: on the one hand promoting such 'values of the kingdom' as peace, justice, freedom, brotherhood, etc, while on the other hand fostering dialogue between peoples, cultures and religions, so that through a mutual enrichment they might help the world to be renewed and to journey ever closer toward the kingdom' (No.17). And again: 'A commitment to peace, justice, human rights and human promotion is also a witness to the gospel when it is a sign of concern for persons and is directed toward integral human development' (No. 42).

[9] 'Presentation of Ecclesia in Asia in New Delhi by Cardinal Paul Shan', General Relator, Synod of Bishops for Asia in *Boletin Eclesiastico de Filipinas*, vol. LXXVI, No. 816 (Jan-Feb 2000) at 136, quoted in Edmund Chia, 'Interreligious Dialogue in Ecclesia in Asia', *Jeevadhara* 30:177 (May 2000), 301.

relevant to the signs of the times. This is evident in the colonial lifestyle adopted by Christians, the western ecclesial structures, art and architecture, liturgies, music and above all western theological thought patterns, Christological and ecclesiological formulations, etc. It is only after Vatican II that there is a move towards the development of Asian theology – which however is still looked upon with suspicion. For example, the Asian church is afraid of being misunderstood by Rome. Ever since the then Prefect of the Congregation for the Evangelization of Peoples, Cardinal Josef Tomko's description of India as 'the epicenter of certain theological tendencies and Asia their main territory,'[10] there has been a sort of suspicion and mistrust of the Indian/Asian theologians on the part of the Vatican. The church has not taken seriously the specific Asian multicultural and multireligious context.

In Asia great distances are spanned by a multiplicity of races, religions and cultures. Sharp contrasts exist among peoples, cultures, religions and conditions of life from country to country and within the countries of Asia. Positively, Asia is the birthplace of such diverse religious traditions as Hinduism, Buddhism, Judaism, Christianity, Islam, Taoism, Confucianism, Zoroastrianism, Jainism, Sikhism, Shintoism etc. All these religious traditions embody deep-rooted religious values (EA 6).

Seen economically, a number of countries of Asia have made considerable progress, but still to be found are exist degrading and inhuman poverty, widening inequality, unequal distribution of resources and opportunities etc. Poverty is a telling forecast of Asia's future. Regardless of its many positive effects globalization has 'worked to the detriment of the poor, tending to push poorer countries to the margin of economic and political relations. Many Asian nations are unable to hold their own in a global market economy' (EA 39).

Oppressive systems based on class, caste, race and gender disparity are dreadfully rampant in Asian countries and are divisive factors in our societies. Migration within Asian countries and to other countries is also a major problem facing Asia. Migrants, refugees, and asylum seekers are inhumanly treated. There are also a number of life-threatening propensities such as flesh-trade, human rights abuses, institutionalized inequality of women etc. going strong on Asian soil.

Politically Asia is diverse: dictatorship, democracy, and militarization – all these are at home in Asia. Constant political upheaval and uncontrolled corruption at all political levels is common to her. 'In certain countries, the whole of life is politicized, affecting every sector, making implementation impossible. Governments are forced to adopt policies and practices such as the Structural Adjustment Policies (SAP), dictated by the International Monetary Fund, the World Bank and the World Trade Organisation. These

---

[10] Cf., Cardinal Josef Tomko, 'Proclaiming Christ the World's only Saviour', *L'Osservatore Romano* (Eng), April 15, 1991, 4.

policies are devoid of a human face and social concern.'[11] Allegedly militarization is aimed at national security. But despite these apparent security-complexes, nations live in constant threat of wars. Worst of all, terrorism has become an organized body that is spreading seeds of revenge and hatred among people. The effects of militarization are manifested today more than ever in the huge number of refugees. In the face of such militarization we cannot deny the possibility of a nuclear holocaust.

Dialogue with the Asian context is the arena for our mission work in Asia. Asian mission suffered very much from the colonial attitude of 'conquest' i.e., conquering peoples, cultures and religions. Consequently, the missionaries had, generally speaking, a very negative attitude towards the cultures and religions of Asia. The missionary methodology consisted in importing western models of church life and thought patterns rather than initiating processes of inculturating the Christian faith in the cultural and religious forms of the people of Asia. By and large, missionaries were planting churches and increasing church membership as if this alone constituted mission. They were not very much involved in transforming Asian society with the leaven of the gospel.

Today the Catholic Church speaks of 'new evangelization' (EA 29). Pope John Paul II calls this new evangelization a 'prophetic and revolutionary calling' to the Roman Catholic Church: 'Evangelization can be new in its ardour, methods and expression. It must be adapted to the people of our day....' The new evangelization must strive to incarnate Christian values and open the gospel message to human cultures. Evangelization according to John Paul II should lead to, 'a civilization of love' (*Redemptoris Missio*, 51, EA 29).[12]

For Asia this new evangelization is about the churches in Asia taking on the 'face of Asia' so that they respond to the specific needs of Asia and become more meaningful for Asian society, particularly the poor and the downtrodden.[13] Evangelization, inculturation, mission, dialogue etc. are not mere words but worlds in themselves. They presuppose the fundamental disposition of openness of heart and mind. This openness implies the ability to listen and to receive – both built on the attitude of hope! Today's understanding of mission has to include 'listening' and 'receiving' because they embody par excellence openness of our being.

The Asian church has to listen to the Spirit operative within her own life. She should listen to the contemporary prophets/prophetesses both within and outside the church who through their writings, theological reflections and through various movements of the Spirit are pointing to a new direction

---

[11] *For All The Peoples of Asia,* Federation of Asian Bishops' Conferences Documents from 1997 to 2001, Vol.3, Edited by Franz-Josef Eilers, Claretian Publications, Philippines, 2002, 7.
[12] http://www.christlife.org/evangelization/articles/C_newevan.html
[13] Cardinal Julius Darmaatmadja, 'A New Way of Being Church in Asia', *Vidyajyoti Journal of Theological Reflection* 63 (1999), 888.

for a meaningful understanding of mission in Asia. Besides, the Asian church has to listen to the poor and the underprivileged; to the women whose voice is not heard; to the youth who search for meaning in life; to the cry of the earth that is being constantly devastated; to the truth embodied in various religious traditions so that she is able to recognize the workings of the Spirit who gathers and unites. In all these we are opening ourselves to the truth as St Thomas repeated often, 'Every truth by whomever it is said is from the Holy Spirit' (I-II, q. 109, a. 1 ad 1).[14]

The Federation of Asian Bishops' Conferences (FABC), being aware of the Asian context and at the same time true to the Catholic teachings on mission looks at evangelization as an integral activity involving the whole human community, every group, and every person. Thus evangelization is an all-encompassing activity that mutually involves all other activities of the church including interreligious dialogue. It has to do with inculturation, dialogue, the Asian-ness of the church, justice, the option for the poor, etc. Accordingly 'there will be no complete evangelization unless there is dialogue with other religions and cultures. There is no full evangelization if there is no answer to the deep yearning of the peoples of Asia.'[15] Concretely, the focus of the FABC is on the new way of being church in Asia. This 'new way' is the triple dialogue: dialogue with the poor of Asia, dialogue with the religions of Asia and dialogue with Asia's diverse cultures. The dialogue with cultures takes place through the process of inculturation; the dialogue of religions takes place through interreligious dialogue and dialogue with the poor is with a view to facilitate integral human development and liberation. 'These three ministries are mutually involving components of the evangelizing mission of the church and constitute what has come to be referred to as the New Way of Being Church in Asia'[16]

As Asians, we claim harmony as a core value. Our 'new way of being church' is a communion of communities. The triple dialogue to which the Asian church has committed herself, asks us to stretch our capacities for relationships that are more inclusive. To put it succinctly, this triple immersion of the Asian churches into the life of Asia's poor, into Asia's vibrant cultures, and into Asia's living and fertile religious traditions is the need of the hour. If this triple immersion takes place, Asian churches will emerge with vitality, newness and originality. The western church could

---

[14] Card. Giacomo Biffi, Congregation for the Doctrine of the Faith *Catholic Culture for True Humanism*, http://www.vatican.va/roman_curia/congregations/cfaith/documents/rc_con_cfaith_doc_20021124 _card-biffi-politica_en.html#top

[15] Cardinal Julius Darmaatmadja, 'A New Way of Being Church in Asia', *Vidyajyothi* 63 (1999), 891.

[16] Edmund Chia, 'Towards a Theology of Dialogue, Schillebeeckx's Method as Bridge between Vatican's Dominus Iesus and Asia's FABC Theology' (Ph.D. thesis, University of Nijmegen, 2003), 83.

follow this method of dialogue with the context in its venture of evangelization.

Finally, evangelization in Asia requires concrete pastoral action. For this a new method has to be adopted which the FABC calls the pastoral spiral methodology. It consists of 4 steps: (i) exposure and immersion in the Asian realities; (ii) analysis of socio-economic-religio-cultural realities; (iii) theological reflection and prayer on these findings and experiences; (iv) pastoral planning in an ongoing process of praxis.[17] This has to be introduced in the centers of formation and theological education.

In the new understanding of evangelization, liberation, dialogue, and inculturation are seen as essential constituents. However, the Asian church has to keep in mind her triple responsibility while accomplishing this task:

First, she has to take her mission of evangelization seriously – she cannot give it up. She is called to proclaim the good news!

Secondly, this mission of evangelization must be proclaimed in such a way that others (i.e. the other religious traditions) understand it. That implies 'listening' to their spiritual quest and faith-expressions and from there learning to communicate in such a way that they understand our faith-expressions. This is the function of dialogue.

Thirdly, the mission of evangelization has to be relevant in today's context i.e., it must be contextualized and concretized in our commitment tor justice, peace and the well-being of all, inclusive of the earth. This is called diakonia or evangelization in service.

Evangelization in service is a means of sharing the good news of God's kingdom with the whole of creation i.e., the recipient of this good news has to be the whole of creation. This good news is: caring for the poor and the downtrodden, bringing comfort, healing and hope to the broken hearted, freedom to those in bondage, light to those who grope in the darkness of ignorance, and proclaiming peace and reconciliation where hatred, revenge and injustice abound in the whole world (cf. Luke 4:18-19). The church should make brave attempts to work towards this goal. Consequently we need to have some basic understanding of dialogue.[18]

Mission of Dialogue

The Catholic Church from the time of Vatican II with its Decree on *Nostra Aetate* has been gradually opening itself up in the direction of interreligious

---

[17] *FABC Papers 53:* Redemptorist Justice and Peace Secretariat. *The Impact of Tourism: Its Challenge to the Mission of the Church in Asia.* [1989] This FABC number is a report on a 1989 consultation on the topic 'tourism as a religious issue'. The reflection process employed was the FABC 'Pastoral Spiral' methodology (Exposure-Immersion, Social Analysis, Theological Reflection, Pastoral Planning).

[18] Clemens Mendonca, *Dynamics of Symbol and Dialogue: Interreligious Education in India* (Münster: Tübinger Perspektieven zur Pastoraltheologie und Religionspädagogik, Bd.13. LIT Verlag, 2002).

dialogue at various levels (though in a more cautious way!). Hence we have today the document 'Dialogue and Proclamation' issued in May 1991 by the Pontifical Council for Interreligious Dialogue (PCID) and the Congregation for the Evangelization of Peoples. The Council insists on a constructive and positive interreligious relationship between various religious traditions in order to enhance mutual enrichment and understanding. It recommends a fourfold dialogue:

- The dialogue of life, where people strive to live in an open and neighbourly spirit, sharing their joys and sorrows, their human problems and preoccupations.
- The dialogue of action, in which Christians and others collaborate for the integral development and liberation of people.
- The dialogue of experience/testimony, where persons, rooted in their own religious traditions, share their spiritual riches, for instance with regard to prayer and contemplation, faith and ways of searching for God or the Absolute.
- The dialogue of theological exchange, where specialists seek to deepen their understanding of their respective religious heritages, and appreciate each other's spiritual values.[19]

According to the Pontifical Council for Interreligious Dialogue [PCID] 'dialogue is a two-way communication. It implies speaking and listening, giving and receiving, for mutual growth and enrichment. It includes witness to one's own faith as well as openness to that of the other. It is not a betrayal of the mission of the church, nor is it a new method of conversion to Christianity.'[20]

Similarly, Raimon Panikkar points out that in interreligious dialogue there is no merging of religious traditions. The aim is not to merge the world's religions into a universal religion. Nor is it to arrive at a total agreement between religious traditions. Instead the ideal foreseen by interreligious dialogue is: to foster communication between diverse religious traditions and different cultures of the world in order to bridge the gulfs of mutual ignorance and misunderstandings, giving them the chance to speak their own mythical/mystical language, to share the richness of their faith experience.[21]

What we need to avoid is aggression and insensitivity. Mission will suffer if we are aggressive and insensitive in dealing with other religious

---

[19] Pontifical Council for Interreligious Dialogue & Congregation for the Evangelization of Peoples, *Dialogue and Proclamation: Reflections and Orientations on Interreligious Dialogue and Proclamation of the Gospel of Jesus Christ* (1991), n. 42. Also cf., n. 8-9.

[20] The Pontifical Council for Interreligious Dialogue. http://www.vatican.va/roman_curia/pontifical_councils/interelg/documents/rcpcinterelgpro20051996en.html.

[21] Raimon Panikkar, *The Intrareligious Dialogue* (Bangalore: Asian Trading Corporation, 1984), 36-37.

traditions and cultures. In simple terms our mission is: to unite and not to divide; to discern and not to destroy; and to heal and not to hurt. Our path is the path of love (cf 1 Cor 13). The basic principle to be kept in mind in dialogue is: to understand others as they understand themselves so that they understand us as we understand ourselves.[22] However we should be aware of certain prerequisites before entering into such a dialogue.

First, one must be deeply rooted in, convinced of and faithful to one's own religious tradition. One must remain loyal to one's own tradition. Panikkar reminds us that remaining loyal to one's own tradition does not mean obeying blindly without a critical understanding of the beliefs and doctrines that have been handed down by a religious tradition. Neither is it just a mechanical repetition of rituals. Instead tradition in its real sense means 'continuation and growth'. That which is handed over in a tradition for future generations is the 'crystallized experience of what has happened' long ago in a particular context. It can become stagnant and mechanical if it does not cater to the changing situation of the recipients. In fact, tradition has within itself an inner dynamism of growth, open to change to suit the needs of the receivers. A tradition that remains unchanged over the years has no relevance for changing generations and so is bound to degenerate into a dead symbol. In such a case it cannot be called an authentic tradition.[23]

Secondly, one must be genuine and be able to understand rightly the traditions of others.[24] We must not violate other traditions; they (other traditions) must be interpreted according to their own self-understanding i.e., we have no right to interpret the religious beliefs and faith of other religious traditions from our perspective. Doing this would be a great violation of these traditions. Violating these traditions is equal to absolutizing one's own religion. This means that we are called to enter and share in the same myth and its beliefs, sacred as they are to their believers.

Thirdly, one must also be open to the 'new' i.e., to listen to the Spirit of God and be open to be guided and led by the Spirit.[25]

The three common examples of light, salt and leaven in the dough which the gospels give us are powerful symbols of how we need to go about our mission of evangelization in Asia. The light en-lightens so that we can see the lighted objects. No one can see pure light – we only see lighted objects. The salt loses itself in the process of giving taste to the food. It does not convert everything into salt. The leaven is silent in its action and transforms

---

[22] Francis X D'Sa, 'Missionarisch Kirche sein in Asien. Dialog der Religionen als Herausforderung', in André Gerth and Simone Rappel (eds), *Global Message – Weltmission heute* (München: Don Bosco Verlag, 2005), 53-74.

[23] Raimon Panikkar, 'In Christ There Is Neither Hindu Nor Christian: Perspectives on Hindu-Christian Dialogue,' in C Wei-hsun Fu and GE Spiegler (eds), *Religious Issues & Dialogues* (New York: Greenwood Press, 1989), 479.

[24] Panikkar, 'In Christ There Is Neither Hindu Nor Christian'.

[25] D'Sa, 'Missionarisch Kirche sein in Asien'.

the whole dough. It does not convert everything into leaven![26] The Asian church is called to be the light of the world, salt of the earth and leaven in the dough in order to bring about transformation of our societies.

Conclusion

The FABC recognizes the presence of the Spirit of God in history, guiding the salvation of all people. Hence dialogue with other religions, positively recognizing the authentic values present among them, and holding dialogue also with the historical socio-cultural movements is very important. Since the poor masses of Asia are deeply religious, seeking God and longing for spiritual fulfillment, the church has to become the church of the poor catering to their needs and aspirations. The cultural elements that are oppressive should be challenged by the church. Therefore, evangelization of cultures, dialogue with other religions, the challenge of transforming the unjust and inhuman social and political structures are understood today in Asia as the essential aspects of evangelization, and these cannot be separated from the proclamation of Jesus Christ and the gospel.

In view of this, efforts to work out indigenous contextual theologies abound. This does not mean that full fledged theologies of this kind have arrived. It only means that Asian theologians have become more deeply aware of the fact that traditional creedal formulae become meaningless in the cultural contexts of Asia. These formulae were worked out on the cultural and religious background of the Jewish, Greek and Roman worlds. This is the main reason why the salvific story of Jesus has not made any substantial impression on the Asian peoples as a whole. Asia's peoples have admired Jesus enormously but, for example, his 'way of the cross' as the way of salvation doesn't make sense on their religious and cultural horizon. Asian women and men theologians have been absorbed in this enterprise in diverse ways.[27] More contextually, theologians from the 'dalit' (suppressed and oppressed) community are coming up with ideas which will constitute the bricks of a meaningful and relevant dalit theology. Asian theologians have also been articulating their own brand of a theology of liberation which is constructed on the quest for justice and peace. Last but not least, women theologians have been creatively working towards a theology that is more intuitive and meditative, highlighting a dimension that traditional theology either overlooks or neglects or perhaps even denies.

In short, in the context of religious and cultural plurality the Asian church has the responsibility of critiquing, opposing and taking a clear

---

[26] Cf., Raimon Panikkar, *Transforming Christian Mission into Dialogue*, 26.

[27] See, e.g. Francis X. D'Sa, 'Ecclesia Semper Reformanda aus der Sicht anderer Religionen', in Erich Garhammer (ed), *Ecclesia Semper Reformanda. Kirchenreform als bleibende Aufgabe* (Würzburg: Echter, 2006), 231-247.

stand against the oppressive systems that abound in her continent and of inspiring the people to reach their human/communitarian destiny. This mission of the Asian church finally is to collaborate with other religious traditions so that together they can be reconcilers and bridge-builders between God, the world and humans. Propagating hatred and cultural superiority would only worsen our situation. The Asian church can lead the way in such a venture.

Furthermore, the Pontifical Council for Interreligious Dialogue (PCID) appeals for such interreligious collaboration. It points out that interreligious cooperation is no longer an option but a necessity.[28] It expresses the need for dedicated efforts to 'examine how, in a world that is increasingly interconnected, we can find new ways to respect our religious differences while forging peaceful bonds based on our common humanity.'[29] It also states emphatically that, 'Religion will prosper in this century only to the extent that we can maintain a sense of community among people of different religious beliefs who work together as a human family to achieve a world peace.'[30]

We have enough opportunities to collaborate with one another. There are common concerns for which religious traditions need to take responsibility, such as, oppressive and unjust systems that are widespread in our societies; rampant corruption at various levels; the agony of the poor, the marginalized, the downtrodden, women, dalits, tribals, children; religious fundamentalism leading to terrorism and despair; the devastation of mother earth etc. It is the Spirit of God alone that can guide the church to engage in such kingdom-centered activities.

I conclude this chapter with a citation from Patriarch Ignatius on the role of the Holy Spirit in the work of mission:

Without the Holy Spirit –
God is far away,
Christ stays in the past,
the Gospel is a dead letter,
the church is simply an Organization,
authority, a matter of domination,
mission, a matter of propaganda,
the liturgy no more than an evocation,
Christian living a slave morality.

But in the Holy Spirit – the cosmos is resurrected and groans with the birth-pangs of the kingdom, the risen Christ is there, the gospel is the power of life, the church shows forth the life of the Trinity, authority is a

---

[28] Symposium on Interreligious Dialogue held in Rome by the Pontifical Council for Interreligious Dialogue, Jan. 16-18, 2003 (Zenith News).
[29] Symposium on Interreligious Dialogue
[30] Symposium on Interreligious Dialogue

liberating service, mission is a Pentecost, the liturgy is both memorial and anticipation, human action is deified.[31]

---

[31] http://www.orthodoxresearchinstitute.org/articles/dogmatics/harper_holy_spirit.htm

SUNDER SINGH AND NV TILAK: LESSONS FOR MISSIOLOGY FROM THE TWENTIETH CENTURY

David Emmanuel Singh

Introduction

Early centuries of the Christian era were charged with followers of Jesus criss-crossing their world. There are not many parts of the world that can boast of having had a somewhat direct part in the life of Jesus himself. Early disciples travelled to witness to their faith in Jesus. St. Thomas is believed to have come to India. Whether one believes in the tale of St Thomas or not, one can have a taste of a faith that is truly ancient. Christianity by far predates modern missions in several waves and, yet, Christians have remained one of the smallest minorities in the subcontinent.

Why has Christianity done so dismally in terms of numbers in the land of the great world religions? There is no single answer to this but one can advance a possibility: India has had a lot of Chrisianity but not enough of the person of Jesus. This is certainly what Gandhi believed was the fundamental problem with Indian Christianity. There were the usual trappings of a well organised religion with clearly fashioned dogmas, church hierarchy, implicit or explicit displays of power – but not enough of Jesus' likeness in terms of a truly incarnational and vicarious life!

This chapter presents two examples of Indian Christians from the heartland of Hindu India. They bore the marks of the living Jesus and, despite short lives, showed what was possible. Their model of Christian life was consigned to the margins and soon forgotten. A robust (and at times arrogant and triumphalistic) enterprise of missions has gained converts from the among the margins of society but never succeeded in winning the heart of Hindu India. Some may find them inspirational if not for emulation then for further enquiry.

Christian 'Sanyasis': Tilak and Singh[1]

The Indian Railways are the largest public enterprise in India. Today, it employs one and a half million people and generates a revenue of 20 billion dollors. It was not as busy and as profitable in the early twentieth century but was still a popular and happening place then, as it is now. Stories of

---

[1] A *Sanyasi* is one who has either reached and adopted the fourth stage (*ashrama*) of the ideal Hindu life or has embraced it by bypassing the intervening stages.

Tilak and Singh are connected strangely to trains. Tilak was 'saved on' the train whilst Singh was 'saved from' the train!

'Saved on' the train: Narayan Vaman Tilak

Tilak (1862-1919) was a brahmin from an elite sub-group in western India. His father was mostly away on state duties which brought him closer to his mother. But, when his mother passed away he withdrew into his own imaginative world for comfort and security – this seems to have had a rather positive effect on him as it turned him eventually into a great Bhakti poet. His hymns are still sung in Marathi and in Marathi speaking churches.

As a brahmin from the Maratha region, it was not surprising that he spoke Sanskrit and had an intimate knowledge of the key ancient texts. Early on, he chose the life of a wandering *sanyasi* (Hindu mystic) giving religious discourses and performing Puranic recitals. [2] In one of his journeys on a train, he was introduced to Jesus. An unnamed gentlman on the train gave him a copy of the Bible. He read the Bible expecting nothing good to come from it but only because he had promised the geneleman he would. His reading (especially of the Sermon on the Mount) led him to see Jesus naturally in terms of a Guru (teacher) and, subsequently, as his God.

He continued his *sanyasi* and migrant lifestyle. But, in place of giving discourses on the Puranas, he spoke of Jesus. Jesus and his teachings were a natural fulfilment of his aspirations as a Hindu. His enormous corpus of writings includes some 700 hymns which are still widely sung!

'Saved from' the train: Sadhu Sunder Singh

Singh (1989-1929) was born in a Sikh family in the undivided Punjab. He was raised by his mother as a Sikh and a follower of the Hindu Bhakti (devotional) tradition. He was not a brahmin like Tilak but was a khashtriya (another higher caste). It was, thus, strange for him to have learned the Bhagawat Gita (Song of God – second century BCE) by heart. He was familiar too with the Upanishads (scriptures from well before the Gita), and the Qur'an. His mother was a deeply religious person, and often took him to visit *sanyasis* for blessings. He attended an American Presbyterian school where he was introduced to Christianity.

At 14, when his mother died, in despair he turned against Christianity. We know he burned a copy of the Bible in public as a deliberate act of rebellion against Christianity. Being deeply disturbed by his own action however, he fervently prayed to God. But his unrest increased and so he prayed he would commit suicide by throwing himself on the rail track if

---

[2] *Puranas* are literally that which is ancient. These are ancient (post-Vedic) texts containing a mythic history of the universe from creation to destruction, including stories of heroes (gods) and (philosophy).

God did no reveal himself to him. He saw Jesus instead and this changed him.

Singh was denounced by his father when barely 15. He was baptised in Shimla at a public ceremony on his sixteenth birthday. Like Tilak, he had an uneasy relations with institutional Christianity. Although, he attended St John's Anglican theological college in Lahore, he left after eight months of struggling to adapt to the life and not a little distaste for academic theology. Later, he surrendered his preacher's licence to the Anglican Bishop in answer to the call of God to work freely with all people.

Singh became a *sanyasi* and a wandering preacher. He had a special call for Tibet where he went several times on foot over the passes and where he died in 1929. Unlike Tilak, Singh did not write much (seven short tracts and all written towards the end of his life), but his influence has been more widespread than Tilak.

Christo-Centric Sanyasa

Both Tilak and Singh had some association with the mainstream Christianity of their time but, in terms of their ministries, largely operated outside its institutional/social boundaries. They believed they were called to focus on the person of Jesus and direct contact with the people and not to be sidetracked by institutional obligations. So, what is it about Jesus that attracted them?

As is normally the case with individual (as opposed to group or mass) conversions in India, both Tilak and Singh believed they were called by Jesus to a personal and direct life in him. Although they loved their Bible, it was the New Testament and, within it, the gospels, whose narratives they imbibed and identified with the most Their language and thought about God were Christo-centric. They began with their direct experience of Jesus rather than with an unspecific theistic experience or intellectual consideration. For example, Singh says,

> The first time I entered heaven I looked around about and asked, 'But where is God?' And they told me, 'God is not to be seen here any more than on earth, for God is Infinite. But there is Christ, he is God, he is the Image of the Invisible God and it is only in him that we can see God, in heaven and on earth.' And streaming out from Christ I saw, as it were, waves shining and peacegiving and going through and among the Saints and Angels and everywhere bringing refreshment.... And this I understood to be the Holy Spirit.[3]

---

[3] BH Streeter, AJ Appaswamy, JS Welles, *The message of Sadhu Sunder Singh* (New York: The Macmillan Company, 1921), 44.

Experience of Jesus

Thus, the fundamental basis of Singh's and Tilak's faith is the 'direct experience of Jesus'. The Jesus who appeared to his disciples, was alive and this was not something they accepted simply by faith but through what they believed to be their actual encounter and continued spiritual communion through prayer. Their prayer was dialogical and it was set in the context of a real relationship not self-immersion. Jesus was their lord, guru, father and mother. They were merely his disciples-servants, *shishyas/dasas*.

Like most children of the time, both Tilak and Singh were closer to their mother than their father. Fathers were generally considered to be the providers and thus distant from their children. The father represented the notional headship of the family. The mother was the real person children related with and were taught by and not the father. This is where, I suppose, the idea of Jesus being the Mother-Guru comes from! But the ideas of father-mother need to be understood not in the gendered sense but as cultural types representing the characteristics of transcendence-intimacy, wrath-mercy, justice-love.

Jesus: Mother-Guru

Tenderest Mother-Guru mine,
Saviour, where is love like thine
A cool and never-fading shade
To souls by sin's fierce heat dismayed
Right swiftly at my earliest cry
He came to save me from the sky
He chose disciples – those who came
Consumed by true repentence' flame
For me, a sinner, yea for me
He hastened to the bitter tree
And still within me living too
He fills my being through and through
My heart is all one melody
Hail to thee, Christ, all hail to thee.

However, there is always the danger with over familiarity. The mother is also a guru, teacher, and likewise familiarity with Jesus needs to be balanced by reverence for him. The following poem reflects this struggle:

I cannot describe it, O Christ...
At one time I said, 'thou art my guru
I must be careful to behave with thee as a disciple'
I sat at a distance in reverential fear
I tried to gain intellectual comprehension of thee
But you spoilt it all with a smile
...
I jumped up and ran to you and flung my arms around your neck...

O Lord, I cannot keep my proper place with thee

The *dasa* says – how can disunion and friendship ever remain together?

Although there is an assumed notion of God the Father, this Father maintained strict discipline; and he is often also the agent of punishment. Jesus, like the mother, was the face of the Father. Jesus represented that side of God that was beautiful, tender, forgiving, consistently loving, caring and, most importantly, self-sacrificing. But, like the mother, the Jesus of their direct awareness also combined in himself the roles of the what is the best in fatherhood and motherhood and, thus, the struggle to hold both distance and friendship in tension:

> Father and mother both thou art
> Whence may I fonder title seek
> Yet even these are all too weak
> To show the love that fills thy heart.
>
> Love that no man can name in word
> Yet in experience all may prove
> Steadfast, immortal, holy love
> Such is thy nature, soverign Lord.

God's transcendence and his immanence had a human metaphor – a typical Indian family! Even with Jesus, the object of their direct relationship, there was a need to maintain reverence (as the Guru). Jesus as the 'mother' fulfilled their deepest aspiration for actual friendship, intimacy, and loving communion.

Jesus: Master

Both Singh and Tilak also related with Jesus as their Lord and Master. Their writings are full of references to themselves as the *dasa*, slaves or servants.

> As lyre and the musician
> As thought and spoken word...
> As flute and breath accord
> So deep the bond that binds me
> To Jesus my Lord.
> As mother and her baby
> As traveler lost and guide
> As oil and flickering lamp-flame
> Are each to each allied
> Life of my life, Christ bindeth
> Me to his side.
> As lake and streaming rainfall
> As fish and water clear
> As sun and gladdening dayspring
> In union close appear
> So Christ and I holden
> In bonds how dear.

Tilak also thought of Jesus' Lordship in terms of the idea of 'yoga' in Hinduism. In the Hindu Bhakti tradition, the notion of 'union' (*yoga*) is significant both in denoting spiritual practices and gaining experiential intimacy with a personal God.

> But this alone I know, that from that day
> This self of mine hath vanquished quite away
> Great Lord of Yoga, thou has yoked with thee
> Saith *dasa*, even a poor creature like me.

This union is however, not absolute in the monistic or Vedantic sense but it is something that allows the disciple to 'live, move and have his being' in God through Jesus (see Gal 2:20). Jesus has the dominant role in this experience of unity as he replaces what is tarnished in the human 'self'. Singh says,

> If we want to rejoice in God we must be different from him; the tongue could taste no sweetness of there were no difference between it and that which it tastes.

So, despite their emphasis on intimacy, they maintained the need for difference conceived in terms of Lord-servant / Guru-disciple, as explained in Singh's tracts: *At the Master's Feet* (1922), *With and without Christ* (1928), *The Real Life* (1927), and *The Spiritual Life* (1925). This was a natural way of thinking about God within their personalistic Bhakti tradition!

Suffering/Sacrifice of Jesus

Hindu culture has a special place for suffering and sacrifice – not suffering caused by others or accidental suffering, but voluntary suffering. Bhakti is meaningless unless it is single-minded and involves some experience of voluntary suffering. Love of wealth and material possessions do not go with the Sanyasi ideal of self-sacrifice – attachments can distract the disciples from their devotion to God. This is why those that become Sanyasis and accept sufferering for a cause become objects of veneration (e.g. Gautama Buddha, Gandhi, and even ordinary Sadhus and Sanyasis).

The closest Sanskrit word for voluntary sacrifice is *tapas* (literally 'heat'). It is associated with the Sanyasis who are searching for the *yoga* (unity with a personal God). This is the highest form of devotion to God by means of asceticism (also called Bhakti Yoga – as opposed to Karma and Gyana Yoga). It is a way of 'burning off' 'sin', making way towards progressive 'sanctification' and leading to intimacy with one's God.

> Many Examples of Hindu Tapas: Ravana (1,000 years to please Shiva); Vishvamitra (1,000 years) tapas raises his status from Khatriya to Brahmin. Bhagirathi a king brought the river Ganges down to earth! (and a Budhhist Monk who starved himself to death as a mark of self denial and as a sort of community service!).

But this celebration of suffering is not either for its own sake or for the sake of attaining salvation (*moksha*) of one's own self (although, that is an aspect of it); it is primarily to bear witness to Jesus and his sacrifice – the prospect of seeing Jesus face to face was a motivation too (Singh for example, wanted to die young)! Even in extreme persecution, Singh believed Christ's presence turned his suffering into a heaven of blessing. It is easy to see therefore why Indians are especially attracted to Jesus suffering voluntarily and selflessly for others!

Through suffering God strikes us in love. The cross is the key to heaven... the cross will hear those who bear the cross, until it bears them up to heaven, into the actual presence of the glorious Redeemer.

> [W]hy then am I to be great
> With stripes the wicked ones beat your back
> Then don't I want them too?
> They made you lift your heavy cross
> Then who will hinder me?
> On your head they placed a crown of thorns
> Such shall be my glory
> They nailed you at the last upon the tree
> My death shall be the same...
>
> Has thou ever seen the lord
> Christ the crucified?
> Hast thou seen those wounded hands
> Has thou seen his side?
> Has thou seen the cruel thorns woven for his crown?
> Has thou seen his blood dropping down?...
>
> Has thou seen he who came to save
> Suffers thus and dies
> Has thou seen on whom he looks
> With his loving eyes?
>
> Hast thou ever seen
> Love that was like this?
> Hast thou given up thy life
> Wholly to be his?
>
> Come now, let us two together.

In some of Tilak's poems, one can read a certain contempt for this world, not because it is necessarily evil or illusory but because it prevents the actual union of the follower with Jesus. Place/location ceases to have any significance when the encounter does happen – everything else pales into insignificance! There is also a sense of urgency about hastening death so as to actualise the potential meeting with Jesus.

> Laugh and weep and sit and sleep
> Now O Christ, shall mine and thine

> Come to an end forever
> Although this is not possible in body
> That matters not to me
> What joy is more blessed
> Than to be rid of this body
> Saith *dasa* wehen we are one
> Who reckons 'here' or 'there'?
>
> Ah, Love, I sink in the timeless sleep2
> One image stands before my eyes
> And thrills my bosom's deep
> One vision bathes in radient light
> My spirits' palace halls
> All stir of hand all throb of brain
> Quivers and sinks and falls
> My soul fares forth – no fetters now
> Chain me to this world's shore
> Sleep, I would sleep, in pity spare
> Let no man wake me more.

Singh too desired to die young like Jesus – extreme asceticism may have been a deliberate means for this to happen. One can critique this as being typically otherworldly but nothing can be further from the truth. The pursuit of suffering was twofold: emulating the master so as to be with him/in his company even in suffering and to touch lives of others who might be searching God:

> Once on a dark night I went alone into the forest to pray, and seating myself upon a rock I laid before God my deep necessities, and besought his help. After a short time, seeing a poor man coming towards me I thought he had come to ask me for some relief because he was hungry and cold.
>
> I said to him, 'I am a poor man, and except this blanket I have nothing at all. You had better go to the village near by and ask for help there.' And lo! even whilst I was saying this he flashed forth like lightning, and, showering drops of blessing, immediately disappeared.
>
> Alas! Alas! It was now clear to me that this was my beloved Master who came not to beg from a poor creature like me, but to bless and to enrich me (2 Cor 8:9), and so I was left weeping and lamenting my folly and lack of insight.

If we resist evil men, who would do us harm, then neither part is likely to be profited; probably both will be injured, as in the collision of two trains both are shattered. But if, by not resisting, we suffer, then, on the one hand, the cross-bearer is benefited spiritually, and on the other hand, the oppressor will be impressed by the forgiving spirit, and will be inclined towards the truth.

Suspicion of Doctrinal and Institutional Dimensions of Christianity

Both Singh and Tilak chose to be outside the instutitutional boundaries of the organised church (Tilak much later in life than Singh). Singh was baptised as an Anglican but dropped-out of his theological collge, surrendered his licenece to have the freedom to work with all and witness to all. He was not interested in the church as an organisation/institution. For Singh, for example, church was the body of Jesus and he belonged to this body:

> I belong to the Body of Christ, that is the true church, which is no material building, but the whole corporate body of true Christians, both those who are living here on earth and those who have gone into the 'world of light'.

When asked which church he belonged to, he would reply, 'to none. I belong to Christ. That is enough for me.' This way of thinking about the organised church encompassed organised doctrinal/theological positions churches held:

> We Indians do not want a doctrine, not even a religious doctrine; we have enough and more than enough of that kind of thing; we are tired of doctrines. We need the Living Christ. India wants people who will not only preach and teach, but workers whose whole life and temper is a revelation of Jesus Christ.

> It is quite natural that no form of church service can ever satisfy deeply spiritual people, because such persons already have direct fellowship with God in meditation, and they are always conscious of his blessed presence in their souls.

For both Tilak and Singh, it was the Bhakti and not Gyana or Karma that appealed the most.

Discussion

Why do Christians like Singh and Tilak see devotion to Jesus as a way to be Christian in India? And why should we even consider their example as a model for Christian life?

Ninian Smart is perhaps not the sort of scholar from whom one would seek help in missiology. His analysis is helpful, however, because he speaks of the dimensions of religions which resonate with the notion of the *margas*: Bhakti, Gnana, Karma. If one compares Tilak's and Singh's preference for Bhakti against Smart's dimensions they predictably appear 'strong' in the emotional, narrative/mythic, practical/ritual dimensions but 'weak' in social/institutional, doctrinal/theological/philosophical, and material dimensions.

This means great buildings, monuments of human or religious achievements and great theological systems did not impress them as might also be the case with a fair majority of those impacted by the great Hindu culture. Abondonment, seclusion, suffering, lack of wealth, personal experience of God and sacrifice would be instantly recognised and appreciated. An individual who encompasses all of these 'virtues' would be seen as an *avatar* or God-man.

One needs however to add that Singh's and Tilak's example of a culturally rooted faith would not be unproblematic from some perspectives. Depending on one's vantage point, for a start, their faith might seem too much like truncated Christianity. However, the question would be: despite this and several other difficulties, can their examples be appreciated (at least) for the possibilities they might hold for Christian life? I do think this is possible and, so, in critiquing Singh and Tilak I would like to focus on a number of creative tensions.

Non-Material – Material

Both materialist and non-materialist traditions exist in the Hindu culture. Charvaka, for example, is a materialistic and atheistic (*nastik*) philsophy. This is distinct from the traditionally orthodox *shad darshan* (six systems of *astika* or theistic philosophy). Jainism and Buddhism are not materialistic but are in their origins, *nastic*. Such extremes are not seen as problematic. A good number of prominent Indians have been *nastic* and yet no one has ever questioned their identity as Hindus. The mainstream traditions of philsophy, popular Bhakti spiritualities etc. however have been *astika*. The Bhakti cults have essentially always been person or avatar centric. The Puranas dating from the third to fifth centuries CE are theistic and like Mahabharata and Ramayana, have been hugely influential in shaping modern Hinduism.

Astika tradition has similarities with the *nastic* (particularly Buddhist/Jain) but also significant differences. One emphasises god-centreness and the other does not, but both exalt voluntary suffering, sacrifice and renunciation. Astika tradition however incorporates material life and relations in a life consisting of different stages (*ashramas*). Those who deny themselves the stage of *grihastha* (householder fulfilling duties to ancestors, family, society and gods), normally following *brahmcharya* (student marked by chastity and desire for learning), and progress to *vanaprastha* (retirement) and *sanyasa* (absolute renunciation), are honoured as gurus and god-men.

Here, because of the absence of the second stage, material pursuits get completely bypassed. In any case, even with *grihastha ashrama*, material concerns remain only a very small part of life. All of one's investments in material culture, family life etc. get eventually left behind and, thus, are not considered of eternal value. Material objects are often seen in Hindu culture as the sources of attachment and power – both being futile in terms of their effects on the aims of *moksha* (liberation). Power and control replace service and sacrifice as the ideals of a sacred life. Absolute renunciation is like new birth – something that defined the conversion of Siddhartha

Gautama Buddha (c.563-483 BCE), the founder of Buddhism. However, the need for *moksha* is not felt equally by all Hindus. It is associated with the last stage of life. So, unless one renounces the world at an early age, one goes through other stages of life until one naturally reaches the stage of retirement and renunciation.

Jesus-God (Personalistic – Impersonalistic)

Having been deeply influenced by theistic Bhakti traditions, both Tilak and Singh, even as Christians, assume a theology but do not see a need to waste their time in defining its content and providing rational explanations of beliefs and practices. Apologetics (and polemics) are not worthy objectives for them. Life in Christ is to be enjoyed, celebrated and shared, not argued about. Both Tilak and Singh do not dwell on explaining the great Christian mystery of the Trinity. Christ is the only face of God the Bhakta can relate with and so he is the one who is talked most about. Their emphasis is not on 'setting up their booths' but on living as the disciples of Jesus, their Guru and God. They can meet with Jesus in spirit but that is not the same as meeting him face to face. There is therefore a sense of urgency in their mission as they want to be with Jesus. They have had a foretaste of this Jesus in their experience and now they want others to follow him and be blessed by him.

The existence of God as the Absolute and Transcendent (Father) is assumed but this God is fully incarnate in Jesus, the *purna-avatar* (complete incarnation comparable in the Hindu tradition to Rama and Krishna, as opposed to partial avatars such as the *varaha, matasya, narasimha* etc.). God, as the Father is the *nirguna* (God-in-Himself) aspect of Being who can only be known and experienced in his avatar, Jesus. This avatar is the *saguna* (God-for-us) aspect of Being. God relates with people only through Jesus and this is sufficient for the Bhaktas both here on earth and in heaven. In thus distinguishing God-in-Himself and God-for-Us, Tilak and Singh are broadly consistent with the mystical traditions within Christianity and Islam as well.

New Testament – Old Testament

In appraising Tilak and Singh, we must address the issue of the unity of the Bible. It is clear that Singh and Tilak show relatively less interest in the Old Testament, although nowhere in their writings do they ever suggest a truncated Bible containing the New Testament only as the source of inspiration. But there is an unspoken suggestion that Hindu traditions and scriptures point to the Jesus of the New Testament whom they encounter in their experience. This assumes continuity between Indian texts/traditions and Jesus. Thus for example, to them the 'channels' for the appearance of

Jesus were also dug by their sacred traditions/texts who is the complete and final *avatara* of God.

Missionaries to India largely did not have a clue how to relate to a complicated Sanscritic culture with countless ancient religious texts in a number of different classical languages. It almost seemed like there were many different spiritualities all somehow co-existing without central figures of authority, churches/communities and institutions. With the exception of some like D'Nobili, most concentrated on the 'outcastes' and the 'untouchables' with encouraging results! The caste Hindus were largely left alone and they in turn left missionaries to their own devices, nothwithstanding the characteristic disparaging and antithetical attitude missionaries had towards everything to do with the Hindu culture.

The orientalist translations of Sanscritic-Buddhist texts were an eye-opener, but the intellectual attempts at relating with Hinduism were and remain marginal. John Nicol Farquhar's idea of fulfilment was based on his exposition of Matthew 5:17: 'I came not to destroy but to fulfil'.[4] This assumed an evolutionary connection between Hinduism and Christianity – as lower to higher – so what is foreshadowed in Hinduism was fulfilled in Christianity. This took care of the problem of the Old Testament!

Singh and Tilak were contemporaries of Farquhar, and though there are similarities, they stood outside academic developments in mission thinking. They saw themselves primarily not as Christians in the sense of belonging to an institution or denomination, but as the followers of Jesus. They chose to follow Jesus not because someone told them to, but because they believed they saw Jesus and conversed with him. Everything they knew in their own tradition seemed to lead to Jesus and all their needs were met by him through an 'actual' and not simply a 'faith' encounter! Christianity as understood by them was the fulfilment of Hinduism.

> Singh say: Hinduism has been digging channels. Christ is the water to flow through these channels.

Jesus' location within the Jewish / Old Testament context is not attractive to any self-respecting Hindu. There is no room in traditional Christianity for the rich Hindu culture, traditions and scriptures. The submission to the authority of such a Guru/god-man would be tantamount to rejecting one's sacred traditions and one's identity. It would also mean adopting a foreign Jesus culturally remote to the world of the Hindus. Membership of a foreign organisation, such as the churches, would mean severing one's connections with other forms of relations where God is manifested and experienced.

---

[4] See JN Farquhar, *The Crown of Hinduism* (London: Oxford University Press, 1913).

Devotional – Non-Devotion (Extrinsic)

Not everyone is charitable to devotional faiths. Such faiths do come in for a fair bit of criticism because the dominant culture we live in is positivistic. We are often under pressure as people of faith, because we have to negotiate the worlds of faith and reason. This is why often our emphasis on experience tends to get suppressed or looked down upon.

Some might find Tilak's and Singh's emphases on direct experience of Jesus 'outside the boundaries of the institutional church' problematic. We might argue that if there is no clearly defined community and theology, experience can 'get out of hand.'

To be fair to Tilak and Singh, one must say that their experiential spirituality is not without foundation. They were churchmen but resigned their place in the church/mission organisation's hierarchy, not to lynch the concept of the institutional church, but to be free to fulfill their call to mission. Their concept of the church was very New Testament. To them the church was the people – not necessarily believers, but followers of the living Jesus. This was the community of which they were part and to which they were accountable. Their experience was not exactly without foundation. They identified the Jesus with whom they conversed with the Jesus of the New Testament.

Individual – Instititional

Were Tilak and Singh social misfits? They did appear to love solitude but they also enjoyed company. Tilak was a family person and we have stories of close friendships of Singh with others. However, why did they feel the need to distance themselves from institutional Christianity? Hindu society can be seen in many different but inter-related ways. We might not think of Hinduism in this way, but there is a lot of flexibility within the different ways in which individuals group themselves in it. This is the reason why individual conversion will never be comprehensible to Hindus.

The caste system is one way of describing Hindu society. However, too much attention has been given to it. It is undeniably central to Hindu society but is certainly not the only example of social and religious life. One is born into a caste. One cannot convert to it or from it. One's conversion could have two outcomes – it could be seen as a defilement of the place of one's birth and one's sacred station in life, and conversion has the potential of erasing one's identity. It would be easier for the so-called 'untouchables' to give up their identity (as it brings them nothing but pain/suffering) but not a 'caste Hindu'! What one needs to realise is that the Hindu society has internal 'safety valves' which have ensured its survival this long. There are, apart from caste, informal structures or social or religious groups within it – many of which are 'trans-caste'.

Sampradaya (traditions) is one of them. It is a delicate network of individuals from any caste – but these are often for scholars! Likewise, the idea of *satsang* describes another way in which groups form within Hindu society. A *satsang* (*sat* (truth/God) *sang* (fellowship)) is the fellowship of those who worship a personal God. There is no strict system of membership as in an institutional church or religious order. People are free to come and go. There is no competition between them. They are focussed on an individual at the centre of this: a living Guru who is often seen as a representative of God. The *satsang* can thus mean fellowshiping with the Guru or God. The *satsang* can also mean 'devotional speech', 'song', 'dance' or all of it. New *satsangs* are perfectly valid. One can belong to a *sampradaya* or caste to which one is born in and yet choose to be part of a *satsang*.

Darbar (court of the king) is another extremely innovative way of defining internal groupings in Hindu society. We know Tilak experimented with this idea. Sadly, this was not continued after him and so we do not know what could have been achieved. In recent times, Rajinder Lal of the Allahabad Agricultural Institute in Allahabad has revived this model. It deserves to be studied further as various reports suggest it has consistent mass appeal.

Ashram (hermitage) is another age-old model of socio-religious groupings within society. One of the earliest models of an *Ashram* is that of a learning community of *brahmcharies* (student ascetics). Here the *Ashram* parallels the *Gurukul* (the domain of the Guru; a sort of an extended family of the Guru). The *shishyas* (disciples/students) form the main group of members. The disciples live and grow up as part of the extended household. They may have time set apart for formal learning, but their whole life in the *Gurukul* is part of the process of intellectual and spiritual growth. Everyone here is an equal. Jainism, Sikhism and even Buddhism (in various degrees and forms) follows this tradition. A number of Christian *Ashrams* were established in India, some of which continue on the margins of the institutional church – often as mere appendages or exotic experiments. Sat Tal was established by Stanley Jones (1884-1973). He was known to Gandhi and this may have been his version of Gandhi's own experiments with *Ashrams*. In Gandhi's case *Ashrams* replicated simple, slow moving rural idylls but were also powerful centres of spiritual regeneration and of the moral politics of Gandhi. Christian *Ashrams* were never this relevant and soon became rather fossilised into rigid institutions. Most people saw through them as a contrived re-invention of the western churches!

Experience – Knowledge

Knowledge for its own sake or for defence or argumentation was not thought necessary. It was for the specialists who were called to pursue the *marga* of *Gyana* (knowledge). Tilak and Singh were not called be theologians or apologetes. They had an abundance of Jesus and so they simply invited people to experience this for themselves. One needs, however, to bear in mind that Tilak and Singh were not thinking of experience and knowledge as necessarily opposed to each other. Experience too leads to knowledge, but this knowledge is qualitatively different to the knowledge gained from theologising. The Bible reveals God to us and encourages us to enter into a real communion with the living Jesus.

Their choice of an experiential faith was not accidental. They were steeped in their respective traditions before they read the Bible. They were looking for an encounter with God but not Jesus. This was to them the greatest sign of truth that Jesus found them even when they were not looking for him. When in crisis they called on God, but Jesus and not Krishna or Rama appeared to them. They then read about this Jesus in the New Testament. They did not start with reading books – even the Bible, they only read it properly after their encounter with Jesus!

The emphasis on experience also attracts the criticism of being ignorant of the body of knowledge contained in the great historic traditions of Christianity, great developments in theology and scriptural interpretation. To them there was nothing truer than what the living Jesus commanded. They enjoyed great freedom in Christ and were not afraid of being wrong in doctrine/theology. Thus, for example, baptism as a doctrine and practice was problematic. It caused irreparable separation of the converts from their family, society and culture. Tilak spoke of alternative ways of appreciating the import of baptism in terms rooted in the Hindu culture. *Diksha*, for example, was a sort of an initiatory sign offered upon one's induction into the *satsang/sampradaya/darbar* of Jesus, the Guru.

Local – Non-Local

Singh and Tilak raise several significant questions for context-sensitive mission thinking. Today, there are pragmatic reasons for taking the local context seriously. First, mass conversions to Buddhism have been widely publicised. Buddhism is deemed to be an indigenous/local religion! There have been four such conversions since 1957: 1957, 2001, 2006 and 2007. Secondly, consideration must be given to the isolation of Christianity in India where it is still sadly considered a western religion. Christian worship has none of the vitality and flavour of the Indian Bhakti. Its forms are distinctly dogmatic and creedal rather than simple re-lived stories such as the Mahabharata, Ramayana and the Puranas. Thirdly, colonial power is no more and yet Christianity is still associated with power and much real estate. The rapid economic development is a relatively recent phenomenon. Suffering is still seen as a common experience of the majority. Even among those who are benefitting from economic development, the idea of suffering strikes a chord. Even among the rich, self-denial is seen as a godly virtue. In this context too the cross and the suffering ideal of Jesus Christ remains in background.

In writing about Jesus, George says: 'It was Gandhi who made Jesus and his image real to me'.[5] Stanley Jones devoted a chapter to Gandhi to show that here was an example of an Indian who was deeply impacted by Christ (but not through the institutional church which was seen to be too foreign, self-assured and quite above suffering).[6] Gandhi taught Jones a new understanding of the Cross: '...the Cross has become intelligible and vital... with the teaching of Gandhi that they [Indians] can joyously take on themselves suffering for the sake of national ends, there has come into the atmosphere a new sensitiveness to the cross.'

This tradition of sensitivity to the cross continues in some aspects of contemporary Indian Christianity (Dalit) where Gandhi challenges Christians to live like 'Jesus the servant' and not like 'Jesus the Lord' and Christianity to do a serious 'Christology of servanthood' not 'lordship'. Tilak and Singh, like Gandhi, call Christians 'to learn the full meaning of vicarious existence from Jesus and apply it it worship and missionary action.'[7]

The particular institutional/social dimension of Indian Christianity associated with the mission or church compound creates (in some places) a greater degree of opposition and distance than is helpful. It creates a sense of physical distance and enhances cultural and doctrinal separateness that conversions, when they do happen, only serve to exacerbate. Hindu culture is founded on the principles of community, compromise, adaptation, diversity, tolerance. Diversity is appreciated and valued if it co-exists within the broader boundaries of culture.

Tilak and Singh illustrate many points of inadequacy and failure of mission to Hindu India. Both were sadly separated from their families and society. The only option they had when they found Jesus was to align themselves with the church/mission that already stood 'outside the Hindu culture'. It called Hindus to it rather than going to them and incarnating among them. The biblical pattern for mission is to enter another space and culture and inhabit it and be clothed by it. Years from the short lives and precious mission work of both these men were wasted in exile from their family and society.

Conclusion

Tilak and Singh might seem strange and eccentric people to many, but to me they model the idea of 'the water of life in the Indian cup'. Their model is not unproblematic, but it presents to us a different way of thinking about

---

[5] SK George, *Gandhi's Challenge to Christianity* (Ahmedabad: Navjivan Publishing House, 1960), 12-13.
[6] E Stanley Jones, *The Christ of the Indian Road* (Nashville: Abingdon Press, 1925), 91-92.
[7] Ignatius Jesudasan, *A Gandhian Theology of Liberation* (Maryknoll, NY: Orbis Books, 1984), 127.

Christian life, something akin to the heart-beat of India and Jesus himself. They were steeped in their cultures, and deeply respectful of their ancient traditions and scriptures. Their faith in Jesus preserved this flavour as they nurtured continuities and linkages dismissed by the often arrogant missionary enterprise. Mission was not for them something they did or thought about, it was part of their Christian life – they lived and breathed it with Jesus.

Three further comments should be made. First, it is an anomaly of history that India as a deeply divided and religiously complex region has managed to remain a single democratic republic. This is a subject for research by historians, political scientists and sociologists. What is relevant for us here is the recognition that a vast variety of spiritual impulses have deeper roots from antiquity than the universalising and neat notions of 'Hinduism', 'Buddhism', 'Sikhism', and 'Jainism'. These notions were externally imposed or/and acquired and remain secondary to the fundamental facts of religious preferences: philosophical (theological/doctrinal) [*Gyana*], activist [*Karma*] and devotional [*Bhakti*]. People belonging to different sets of identities often transcend their particularities to subscribe to these. There cannot therefore be a single approach to relating with 'Indians'. Christian life and practice in India must pay serious attention to this diversity of preferences – all considered legitimate 'paths' or *marga*.

Secondly, the notion of a strictly defined, theologically delimited religion was an import within India. Christianity and Islam for this reason seemed strange 'beasts' to Indians and it intrigued them when they were described as 'Hindu' or 'Sikh'. Indians in general had and have no problem in living happily with differences and even contradictions but if these seem associated with things foreign they tend to be suspicious and distant. Despite its age, Christianity in India has been criticised for being foreign in its pedegree and practice. It is not surprising that in about 2,000 years Christianity in India is still a tiny minority (even less than Islam which appeared about 1,000 years later).

Thirdly, in matters of faith, generally most Indians prefer the devotional route – particularly one that encompasses the ideals of sacrifice, renunciation, and the simplicity of the person of the *guru-sanyasi*. They appreciate rituals and theological debates but are suspicious of the specialists who, like Brahmins, might use knowledge (doctrines, theology, philosophy and their expressions in ikons, arts, buildings etc.) as a means of power. *Bhakti* was and is a powerful equaliser – it enables people to transcend differences. This means a 'crossover' from a particular local identity to another would not seem starkly like the rejection or abandoning of one identity, history, culture, family etc., but rather like progressing on to something one can value as the fulfillment of their inner aspirations – fulfillment of their own faith tradition or a personal preference or choice.

Jesus is no threat to India and to the high-minded Hindus. Indians are expansive and open-minded. Jesus would be revered and followed if he incarnated as an Indian and lived as an Indian and died as an Indian. What Indian Christianity lacks is the principle of incarnation. No true translation is possible without this. Singh and Tilak remain fine examples of this.

MISSION IN THE CONTEXT OF FILIPINO FOLK SPIRITUALITY: *BAHALA NA* AS A CASE IN POINT

Tereso C Casiño

Filipino spirituality is a product of a conglomeration of religious worldviews and value systems.[1] It is no surprise then for Filipinos to be known for their religious and spiritual devotion in both 'lived experience and as reflections on that experience'.[2] One good example of valuing a 'lived experience' from a religious perspective is the famous People Power Revolution, which sent former President Ferdinand E Marcos to exile in February 1986. In hindsight some Evangelicals and Catholics in the Philippines interpret the People Power Revolution as an indigenous form of Filipino spirituality.[3] In the Filipino context, that which provides an indigenous framework for Filipino 'lived experiences' is the traditional concept of *bahala na*.

Christian mission in the Philippines began with Catholic missionaries in the 1500s. This was followed by a surge of Protestant missions at the turn of the twentieth century when Spain ceded the Philippines to the United States of America. However, almost 500 years of Christian presence across the archipelago have not dislodged the fatalistic bent of Filipino spirituality, which evidently hinders authentic Christian discipleship among millions of Filipinos. This chapter seeks to assess the interface between authentic Christian discipleship and the Filipino paradigm of folk spirituality known across the country as *bahala na*. This fatalistic bent is the epitome of Filipino folk spirituality that continues to baffle missionaries today. This chapter will identify major religious worldviews that provide the framework for solidifying a fatalistic mentality among Filipinos. Overall, the study investigates various aspects of fatalism and its effect on and implications for Christian discipleship within the larger context of mission spirituality.

---

[1] An earlier version of this theme is given fuller treatment in my essay, '*Bahala Na*: A Critique on a Filipino Paradigm of Folk Spirituality,' *Asia Pacific Journal of Intercultural Studies* 1:1 (January, 2005), 145-60. Many of the insights from this present essay were taken from this article, unless noted otherwise.
[2] Bernard McGinn, John Meyendorff, and Jean Leclercq (eds), *Christian Spirituality: Origins to the Twelfth Century* (New York: Crossroad, 1985), xvi.
[3] See for instance, Jose C Blanco, 'The Gospel of Absolute Respect: A Spirituality of People Power', in Douglas J Elwood (ed), *Toward a Theology of People Power: Reflections on the Philippine February Revolution* (Quezon City: New Day, 1988), 103-09.

Major Components of *Bahala Na*

The Filipino *bahala na* may be derived from the Hindu concept of *Bathala* or the Sanskrit word, *bhara*, which means, 'load'.[4] In the early times, the shift from /r/ to /l/, and in this case, from *bhara* to *bhala*, was a common linguistic phenomenon. 'Load' could mean 'responsibility,' which seems to be the closest linguistic meaning of *bahala*. Filipinos speak over 80 major languages, but the phrase, *bahala na*, appears to have a nationwide linguistic acceptance.[5] The fatalistic connotation of *bahala na* is expressed similarly in the Spanish phrase, *que sera, sera* (whatever will be, will be).[6]

Bahala na evolved from four major religious worldviews, namely, animism, Hinduism, Islam, and Catholicism. A fifth may be added, Chinese religion, but the Chinese influence on Philippine society, both ancient and contemporary, is basically confined to economics, trade, and material culture with no dent on the common religious psyche of Filipinos. Of course, there is an emerging trend in some parts of the Philippine society to embrace the practice of *feng shui* in Philippine modern architecture.[7] But this lacks nationwide acceptance in the contemporary Filipino society.

The four major religious traditions continue to have a strong influence on Filipino religious consciousness and spirituality. The first stream of Filipino spirituality is animistic in essence and form. Animism remains the bedrock of Philippine religious experience. Ancient Filipinos practised spirituality by worshipping celestial beings and nature, including ancestral spirits.[8] The breadth of animistic influence continues to manifest itself even in present-day Catholicism, and to some extent, Filipino society as a whole.

The second major stream of spirituality came when Hinduism reached the Philippines as early as 900 AD by traders from India and nearby islands. The Hindu traders brought with them social, economic, and religious systems. Filipino anthropologist, F Landa Jocano, notes that *bahala na* is traceable to the ancient Filipinos' highest-ranking deity known

---

[4] Leonardo N Mercado, *Elements of Philosoph* (rev ed, Tacloban City, Philippines: Divine Word University Publications, 1976), 183.

[5] Mercado limits the word *bahala* ('responsibility') to the Tagalog dialect. However, in Cebuano, *bahala* also connotes 'responsibility'. For example, one could say, *O sige, ikaw na ang bahala dinha* [Alright, take responsibility there!]. Similarly, the Ilongo dialect gives the same weight to the word: *Ti, ikaw na gid ang bahala dira, ha*?

[6] Evelyn Miranda-Feliciano, *Filipino Values and Our Christian Faith* (Mandaluyong, Philippines: OMF, 1990), 14.

[7] Sonia M Zaide notes that the early Chinese visited parts of the archipelago to 'buy and sell only' (*Philippine History and Government* [4th ed, Quezon City: All-Nations, 1989], 46).

[8] See F Landa Jocano, *Philippine Prehistory: An Anthropological Overview of the Beginnings of Filipino Society and Culture* (Quezon City: Philippine Center for Advanced Studies, 1975), 215-16.

as *Bathala*, believed to be of Hindu origin.[9] *Bathala* was known to be a powerful yet benevolent deity. Anthropologists assume that the reassuring benevolence of this deity accounts for the dominant risk-taking and adventuresome trait of the Filipinos. Regardless therefore of what will happen to them in the future, Filipinos believe that *Bathala* is available to lend assistance and help. Apparently such belief in *Bathala* became a dominant element in the fatalistic consciousness of ancient and contemporary Filipinos.

The third stream developed upon the arrival the Islamic faith in 1380 AD through a visit by a Muslim missionary named Mukdum.[10] The Muslim influence on the Filipino *bahala na* seems to account for the predeterministic consciousness of Filipino life. The Islamic philosophical system allows one to resign himself or herself to fate (*kismet*) according to the will of Allah. When facing life's crises and adverse circumstances, a Filipino concedes, 'If this is my lot, what can I do?'[11] *Bahala na* reinforces the belief that every event and circumstances in the universe emanates from the will of Allah. Of the Islamic concept of predeterminism, David L Johnson observes, 'When a man acts, God creates in him the will, the power, the intention to act. Yet a man is responsible for what he does. God acts through a man, but a man acquires the responsibility for the act.'[12] This extreme predeterministic attitude best expresses the core of Filipino folk spirituality.

The fourth religious stream began with the arrival of Catholic Christianity in the 1500s. When Catholic friars arrived in the archipelago, they discovered that Filipinos already had existing religious representations. So they simply assimilated these religious expressions in their missionary work. The result was the baptizing of local deities with Christian names. As a matter of fact, folk Catholicism developed by giving local deities equivalent functions and powers with patron saints. As the Spanish brand of Catholicism spread across the archipelago, it affected little the traditional fatalistic Filipino concept of *bahala na*. Over the centuries, Filipino Catholics, and later, many Protestants, embraced the concept without critical objection. They seem to find in *bahala na* the Christian equivalent of the believer's prayer of 'Thy will be done'.[13] The common practice of

---

[9] F Landa Jocano, *Folk Christianity: A Preliminary Study of Conversion and Patterning of Christian Experience in the Philippines* (Quezon City: Trinity Research Institute, 1981), 5.
[10] Zaide, *Philippine History*, 47.
[11] Wilfredo C. Paguio, *Filipino Cultural Values for the Apostolate* (Makati, Philippines: St. Paul, 1991), 135.
[12] David L. Johnson, *A Reasoned Look at Asian Religions* (Minneapolis, MN: Bethany, 1985), 157.
[13] Miranda-Feliciano admits that the issue of the difference between 'God's will' and *bahala na* is important because 'Christians seem to have retained the *bahala*

combining *bahala na* (fatalistic worldview) with 'Thy will be done' (faith worldview) produces the Filipino experience of 'split-level spirituality'.[14]

From a sociological perspective, *bahala na* allows Filipino individuals to connect with others. As a form of trust, a Filipino facing adversities in life would say, '*Bahala ka na sa pamilya ko*' (Take charge of my family).[15] Thus *bahala na* takes a sociological function when used to relate to others, especially in terms of trust, responsibility, and stewardship. When invoked, *bahala na* becomes a binding covenant through which people commit themselves to help or to care for one another. The concept then becomes a boundary-marker for interpersonal relations among Filipinos. Nevertheless, *bahala na* may also encourage Filipinos to embrace an unproductive perspective. Resigning totally to the work of *kapalaran* or *suwerte*, the Filipino may appear indifferent in the face of graft and corruption as well as welcome personal misfortunes impassively. The Filipino behaviorist, Tomas D Andres, pointedly writes:

> *Bahala na* works against individual and social progress. The Filipino takes on a posture of resignation to the fact: *Talagang ganyan ang kapalaran*. It harnesses one's behavior to a submissiveness that eats up one's sense of responsibility and personal independence. It provides one with a false sense of self-confidence to proceed with an unsound action in the belief that somehow one will manage to get by.[16]

Bahala na functions as a psychological mechanism, combining both negative and positive points. The downside of *bahala na* lies in its fatalistic bent where a Filipino leaves everything up to *kapalaran* (destiny); doing so would free a person from human responsibility. However, *bahala na* could pad the Filipino ego against failure and disappointment.[17] Similarly *bahala na* mitigates a Filipino from becoming a 'mental hospital patient.'[18] In daily

---

na! mentality, *only using more religious-sounding jargon*' (italics mine, *Filipino Values*, 14).

[14] Jaime Bulatao, a Filipino Catholic priest, coins the term 'split-level Christianity' to characterize the form of Christianity common across the Philippine archipelago ('Split-Level Christianity', *Philippine Sociological Review* 13 [1965], 119-21). Religious fervor among Filipino Catholics does not wane even with the introduction of modernity and secularization. See for instance, 'The Black Nazarene', http://www.gmanews.tv/story/143183/The-Black-Nazarene#; accessed 21/1/2009).

[15] Wilfredo C Paguio explains, 'We say that these words imply complete charge of a person over another or over something because it usually happens that, if a person gives this right to another and the 'giver' still meddles with the affair, the 'given' gets angry and says: 'Pinamahala ako, pagkatapos pakikialaman!' ('He has given me the charge over it yet he still meddles with the affair')' (Paguio, *Filipino Cultural Values*, 137-38).

[16] Tomas D Andres, *Understanding the Filipino Values: A Management Approach* (Quezon City: New Day Publishers, 1981), 132.

[17] Socorro C Espiritu et al, *Sociology in the New Philippine Setting* (Quezon City: Alemar-Phoenix, 1977), 76.

[18] Cited by Miranda-Feliciano, *Filipino Values*, 14.

practice though, *bahala na* is considered undesirable because Filipinos tend to use it as a negative psychological justification for their failure to take up human responsibility and accountability in times of hardships and crises. Still, others use it as a psychological defence mechanism to cope with adversities and failures.

Many in the Philippines view *bahala na* as the 'spirit to take risks'.[19] A fitting illustration is that of Sarah, who, at the tender age of 14, left the Philippines to work as a maid in a Middle East country.[20] The risk-taking spirit epitomized by *bahala na* is characterized with hope because many Filipinos, even in extreme difficulties, hope for the best.[21] When conditions are tough, the Filipino spirit of courage blends well with strong hope. In worst times the Filipino spirit is unbending and tends to dare the impossible. This daring spirit is expressed in local songs, poetry, and proverbs.[22] Given the Filipino daring spirit, *bahala na* serves as a reservoir of psychic energy and functions as an effective psychological prop on which one leans whenever life's situations get tough. Jose M. de Mesa stresses, '*Bahala na* provides Filipinos the capacity to laugh at themselves and the situations they are in. It reflects, in addition, the oriental philosophy to be in harmony with nature. While it may appear passive, it is nevertheless dynamic without being coercive.'[23]

The heart of the traditional Filipino spirituality lies in the bipolar religious potential of *bahala na*.[24] This means that *bahala na* possesses both positive and negative religious dimensions. Religiously speaking, *bahala na* operates on the belief that somewhere a cosmic force exists (not necessarily a Supreme Being) that controls the flow of the events in the universe. It is common for a Filipino to believe that his or her life is lived according to a fixed blueprint, which was designed by a cosmic force.

Paradoxically, the notion of an existing cosmic force that controls earthly life produces an element of trust.[25] As a result, *bahala na* serves as a religious tool through which one's life may be interpreted. There is

---

[19] Mercado, *Elements of Filipino Philosophy*, 183.
[20] Sarah is a pseudonym but the girl cited here is real.
[21] Jose M de Mesa, *In Solidarity with Culture: Studies in Theological Re-Rooting*, Maryhill Studies 4 (Quezon City: Maryhill School of Theology, 1987), 164.
[22] One particular song was written by the Cebuano song writer, Yoyoy Villame, in tribute to the fearless Filipino guerilla captain, Francisco Dagohoy, who refused to surrender although his men ran out of ammunition during a battle against the Spaniards. For an analysis of this risk-taking attitude in the light of Villame's song, see Carolyn O Arguillas, 'Letter from Mindanao', *Philippine Daily Inquirer* 9 September 1991, 1, 4.
[23] De Mesa, *In Solidarity with Culture*, 162.
[24] This section is primarily derived from Casiño, '*Bahala Na*', unless otherwise noted. 152-53.
[25] See Paguio, *Filipino Cultural Values*, 138-42. For a list of proverbs related to Filipino fatalistic resignation, see Leonardo N Mercado, *Elements of Filipino Theology* (Tacloban City, Philippines: Divine Word Publications, 1975), 68-74.

therefore an element of optimism in *bahala na* despite its strong fatalistic orientation. Filipinos, for instance, who live in abject poverty, still hope that one day the wheel of life (*Gulong ng buhay* or *kapalaran*) can still turn in their favour no matter how long it may take. If *suwerte* (luck) does not come to the parents, it might come to their children or grandchildren. The Cebuano proverb puts it aptly, *Sa likod sa itom nga panganod, aduna baya'y pag-laom* (Behind a dark cloud is a ray of hope).[26]

Optimism, however, which is produced by a *bahala na* attitude, could be taken to the extreme. Filipinos who put their trust in *kapalaran* (fortune) tend to be complacent about their work or future. Added to this is the view that time is elastic, which makes it difficult for many Filipinos to enforce a sense of urgency in their daily life. Oftentimes, the common dictum, 'There is always a tomorrow', makes many Filipinos work leisurely.[27]

Furthermore, the kind of spirituality informed by the *bahala na* worldview could function as a religious escape mechanism whereby Filipinos shy away from being active participants in the events of life. In many cases, *bahala na* translates into a religious 'I-don't-care' attitude. Under the influence of spiritual apathy, the Filipino says, *Hindi naman kami pababayaan ng Maykapal* ('The Supreme Being will not at all abandon us'). Even though *bahala na* develops an attitude of passive resignation, it does help an individual to accept misfortune acquiescently. This makes *bahala na* functional as a religious 'shock absorber', whereby a Filipino protects himself or herself from experiencing potential or actual impact of failures and fears in life. *Bahala na* thus functions to 'maintain one's sanity in the presence of actual difficulty'.[28]

The Essence of Bahala Na Spirituality

Even before Spanish Christianity came to the Philippines, the inhabitants of the archipelago were deeply religious as they worshiped the sun, moon, stars, trees, rocks, and other sacred objects. Islam and Hinduism notably influenced the religious consciousness of the pre-Spanish Filipinos. When

---

[26] See Tomas D Andres, *Management by Filipino Values* (Quezon City: New Day, 1985), 15-19.

[27] From the standpoint of work ethic, Andres explains, 'The attitude stems back to the time of the Spaniards when they exported Christianity to us. The kind of faith they taught the Filipinos was one which encouraged indolence. They taught us to pray for everything we needed and they made us understand that God would do everything for us. The *bahala na* attitude would probably not be a part of our culture had they taught us to work for our needs and ask God only for help' (Andres, *Management by Filipino Values*, 5).

[28] Elma Buguen, cited in an interview by Valentino L. Gonzales, 'Understanding the Dynamics of the Filipino Family: Pastoral Care Perspective' (a paper presented to the Faculty of Asia Baptist Graduate Theological Seminary, Philippines, October, 1983), 15.

Spanish Christianity arrived in the archipelago, this religious consciousness became deeply entrenched in the psyche of the inhabitants.

One notable aspect of the religious consciousness that is buried in the depth of the Filipino psyche is the courage to accept or face adverse circumstances. In the Filipino psyche, the world is a series of *karma*, an ethical predeterministic system of cause-and-effect. Anything, then, that happens to a Filipino (whether good or bad) is attributed to a cause, that is, an impersonal force known as *suwerte* (luck), *tsamba* (chance), or *kapalaran* (destiny). *Suwerte, tsamba, kapalaran* – all of which are non-ethical in nature – and *karma*, which is ethical, account for the Filipino's unbending spirit amid crisis and bad circumstances. In this connection, a Filipino's response to crisis and hardships is epitomized by the expression, *bahala na*.

Against this backdrop, *bahala na* evolves as a religious tool or device in which a Filipino copes practically with the adverse demands and circumstances of life. In order to survive, a Filipino toys with fatalism as a means of easing the pain of his or her circumstances, as well as lessening the burden of his existence. In such a case, *bahala na* functions as a convenient theodicy for Filipinos. Ironically, *bahala na* suggests to a Filipino that he or she is a mere automaton whose existence is at the disposal of the impersonal forces, namely, *suwerte* or *kapalaran*. In this context, *bahala na* operates as a paradigm for traditional Filipino spirituality.

The spread of Catholic Christianity in the Philippines did not correct the traditional fatalistic Filipino concept of *bahala na*. In many instances, Filipinos who have been converted to Christianity (whether Catholic of Protestant) retain the traditional concept of *bahala na*. Interestingly enough, many Filipino Christians have adopted the concept without critical objection and seem to interpret it as equivalent to the Christian notion of 'Thy will be done.' This syncretistic tendency poses a challenge to many Filipino Christians who simply hang up on the issue because they do not know what to do with it. These opposing paradigms construct in the contemporary Filipino religious experience a syncretistic form of spirituality.

The Clash between *Bahala Na* and Christian Spirituality

Friends call him Bunso, an intimate word for the youngest in the family. Bunso spoke gently as he narrated his experience. He worked in a Middle East country for years but suddenly lost his job because of the economic crunch that hit even the oil-rich countries of the Persian Gulf. Instead of returning to the Philippines, he decided to go to Kish Island, a territory of Iran, where he waited for his next entry visa to Dubai. At first he was optimistic that the visa would arrive in 10 days, but weeks passed so quickly and the days rolled into 20, then 40, and the counting never ends. By the time Bunso survived the island for more than 70 days, the hotel had enough of him because he could not pay his bills. So the hotel management had him deported. The night he was deported, he was confused but did not lose hope. Friends stood by him. Saying goodbyes, tears rolled down his cheeks, knowing what would happen next to him. Yet, his courage was there, a combination of *bahala na* and God's will.[29]

Filipinos confront two frameworks of spirituality in their daily life. They either live in a life of faith in a personal God who cares for them or abandon themselves to fate and simply wait passively on their fortunes or misfortunes. Of course, they can also decide to combine faith with fate, which seems to be common in Philippine society. Many, however, equate the two without critical objection and reflection, which results in a syncretistic form of spirituality.[30]

As noted, *bahala na* survives almost 500 years of the presence of Christianity across the Philippine archipelago and the onslaught of secularism and modernization. It has become a popular expression to cope with the pressing demands of life. *Bahala na* has become a paradigm of folk spirituality and functions as a theodicy in the Philippine society through which a Filipino lessens the pain of his or her adverse circumstances. In strict sense, *bahala na* worldview offers a kind of spirituality that is fatalistic in orientation and execution. This poses problems to missionary work across the archipelago as messengers of the gospel teach that God acts within and through human history, and that God is very much interested in the daily affairs of human beings. Interestingly, many Filipinos equate Christian spirituality, expressed in the prayer language, 'Thy Will be Done', and *bahala na* easily, taking the two without critical reflection and theological objection.[31] This results in a confused understanding and experience of spirituality, and poses theological and missiological problems. This uncritical acceptance and interpretation resulted in a unique blend of spirituality from animistic, Hindu, Islamic, and folk Catholic traditions. Contemporary Filipinos face an impasse regarding the issue of knowing when they have already crossed the boundary that gulfs between the Christian

---

[29] This is a true story. Many Filipino Christians continue to face similar painful situations and find themselves crying out, *Bahala na,* echoing 'Thy will be done.'

[30] For further discussion on the syncretistic tendency of Folk Catholicism in contradistinction with folk Protestantism in the Philippines, see Jae Yong Jeaong, 'Filipino Pentecostal Spirituality: An Investigation into Filipino Indigenous Spirituality and Pentecostalism in the Philippines' (ThD thesis, University of Birmingham, August 2001), 205-09.

[31] Insights in this section are derived primarily from Casino's '*Bahala Na:* A Critique on a Filipino Paradigm of Folk Spirituality', *Asia Pacific Journal of Intercultural Studies* 1:1 (January, 2005), 154-58; ' "Thy Will be Done": A Framework for Understanding Christian Spirituality', *Asia Pacific Journal of Interdisciplinary Studies* 2:1 (February, 2005), 56-63, unless otherwise noted.

version of God's will and *bahala na* spirituality, or whether both paradigms of spirituality are either complimentary or dissonant.[32]

Bahala na derives from a fatalistic worldview. The vague conceptualization of God by pre-Spanish Filipinos resulted in a belief that is still prevalent in the contemporary Philippine society. Accordingly, everything that happens is predetermined by an impersonal force or supernatural powers. On the basis of predetermined events, Filipinos try their best to forecast future events in order to avoid the curse of *palad* (fate). Because *palad* is faceless, Filipinos struggle to find ways to cope with life's inevitable events and circumstances. So they end up surrendering to the impersonal forces of the universe. Fatalism operates within the broader spectrum of Philippine society, and many Filipinos view *bahala na* as a psychological necessity more than a philosophy of life. Others perceive *bahala na* as primarily an ethical spirituality – a proper religious behavior in line with the will of an impersonal force known as *Bathala*. However, Filipinos conceptualize *Bathala* in plain anthropomorphism, an impersonal force that possesses 'a will'.[33] Whenever people face difficulty in determining *Bathala's* will, they exert extra efforts to maintain proper behavior. In this sense, a Filipino may know that he or she conforms to the will of *Bathala* by reading and interpreting one's *karma*, a practice that is mostly done on a trial-and-error basis.[34]

In contrast, Christian spirituality operates on the basis of a knowledge and experience of the providential will of a personal God.[35] In the Judeo-Christian tradition, God relates himself to creation actively, purposively, and personally. In this manner, faith serves as the Christian's response to

---

[32] On 'dissonance' see Leon Festinger, Henry W Reicken and Stanley Schacter, *When Prophecy Fails: A Social and Psychological Study of a Modern Group that Predicted the Destruction of the World* (New York: Harper Torchbooks, 1964). The authors write, 'Two opinions, or items of knowledge are *dissonant* with each other if they do not fit together – that is, if they are inconsistent, or if, considering only the particular two items, one does not follow from the other. . . . Dissonance produces discomfort and, correspondingly, there will arise pressures to reduce or eliminate the dissonance'

[33] Agaton P Pal writes, 'When the people are faced with difficult situations, they stoically say: '*Bahala na*' – This is an expression of the belief that '*Bathala* wills the happening of every event'. ('The People's Conception of the World', in Socorro C. Espiritu and Chester L. Hunt (eds) *Social Foundations of Community Development: Readings on the Philippines* [Manila: R.M. Garcia, 1964], 392).

[34] Pal notes, 'Everything which happens to man is the will of *Bathala*. Birth, marriage, death, good crops, poor crops, accidents, and other personal events happen because *Bathala* allows or wills them to be. Favorable events happen because his behavior has been displeasing. The occurrence of a preponderance of favorable events is a sign that a person has earned *panalangin* of unfavorable events, that he has earned *gaba*' ('The People's Conception', 392).

[35] For an excellent introductory study on Christian spirituality, see Alister E McGrath, *Christian Spirituality* (Oxford: Blackwell, 1999).

the creative acts of the personal God in and through history. Christians understand faith as a 'personal trust in God on the basis of knowledge' of his will.[36] This being the case, Christian spirituality finds fulfillment in a theistic worldview that guarantees an informed basis of a person's faith in God. Here the formation of one's faith results from a personal encounter with the God whose providence continually reaches out to humanity. 'To know and experience the power of God in our lives,' explains Evelyn Miranda-Feliciano, 'is superior to the derring-do of *bahala na* because our confidence to act does not arise from desperation but from a firm belief that ours is the right action. Of course, such assertion assumes that our faith is both biblically well-formed and well-informed.'[37] The heart of Christian spirituality lies in the conviction that God discloses his will to humanity as the guide, framework, and potential for personal growth and creative possibilities in one's life. The grammar of this disclosure is the will of God, something that could be 'communicated to and acted upon by human beings'.[38]

Common among many Filipinos is the belief that impersonal forces act behind the universal system and determine the events and affairs in the world. The notion of *Bathala* as impersonal rather than active, dynamic, and related reinforces this belief.[39] Over the centuries *Bathala* and other supernatural forces have been consistently depicted in non-personal languages.[40] Both the 1935 and 1973 Philippine Constitutions maintain the term 'Divine Providence' in the Preamble, attesting to the long history of a belief in vague identity of supernatural forces or a supreme being. Culturally, the category, 'Divine Providence', appears equivalent to the Cebuano usage of *Bathala* which, interestingly, bears equal status with *Panahon* (time). One may say, *Ang panahon ra gayod ang magbuot kung*

---

[36] Morris Aschraft, *The Will of God* (Nashville, TN: Broadman, 1980), 30.

[37] Miranda-Feliciano, *Filipino Values*, 18.

[38] Garry Friesen and Robin Maxson, in their book, *Decision Making and the Will of God: A Biblical Alternative to the Traditional View*, identify three meanings of God's will: (1) Sovereign: 'God's secret plan that determines everything that happens in the universe'; (2) Moral: 'God's revealed commands in the Bible that teach how men ought to believe and live'; and (3) Individual: 'God's ideal, detailed life-plan uniquely designed for each person ([Portland, OR: Multnomah, 1980], 29-44).

[39] Leonardo N Mercado has an excellent treatment of this idea in 'The Filipino Image of God,' *Philippiniana Sacra* 26:78 (September-December, 1991), 401-15, specifically 404, 409.

[40] To solve this vague concept of 'God' in the Filipino psyche, Benigno P. Beltran recommends a new look at Christology. He writes, 'Filipino Christology should elaborate an idea of God consistent with the Christian belief that God acted in history through Jesus of Nazareth.... One can only speak about God himself as one talks about Jesus – Christology begins with Jesus in order to find God in him' (*The Christology of the Inarticulate: An Inquiry into the Filipino Understanding of Jesus Christ* [Manila: Divine Word Publications, 1987], 232).

unsay mahitabo kanato ('Only time can determine what will happen to us').[41]

Interestingly the 1986 Philippine constitution made a major shift. Rather than imploring the aid of the 'Divine Providence', which is impersonal, the 1986 Constitution now invokes the aid of the 'Almighty God', using relational language.[42] This departure from the traditional notion of a cosmic force shows that the worldview that supports *bahala na* is no longer adequate to meet the religious needs of contemporary Filipinos. *Bahala na* promises only a manipulative fatalistic form of spirituality that commits Filipinos to the control of impersonal supernatural forces. Nonconformity to the 'will' of impersonal forces could result in misfortunes and bad events. Thus, behavioural orientation depends largely on adapting oneself to nature rather than the mastery of it. In times of fortunes and misfortunes, Filipinos look up to a transcendental reference point: '*Bathala* has caused it.' This cause, however, appears to be a human personification rather than a portrayal of a personal deity.

In contrast, Christian spirituality stresses a relational bonding between God and the believers, a relationship that is consummated in a covenant. As a moral relationship, God and believers bond in a covenant that allows the exercise of respective 'wills.'[43] The moral aspect that underlies this covenant relationship shows a stark contrast between Christian spirituality and *bahala na*. Christian spirituality then hinges on the 'will of God' in contradistinction with the impersonal grounding of the spirituality which *bahala na* offers.[44] While Filipinos seek to experience harmony with nature, and, consequently, conform to the 'wheel of fortune', the Christian seeks to establish a sound relationship with an all-wise, all-powerful, all-

---

[41] When an average Filipino says he or she trusts in God, there is a suspicion that the concept of God is not personal or related but impersonal, i.e., 'Time' and 'Providence.' See Onofre D Corpuz, 'The Cultural Foundations of Filipino Politics,' in Socorro C Espiritu and Chester L Hunt (eds) *Social Foundations of Community Development: Readings on the Philippines* (Manila: R.M. Garcia, 1964), 420-23.

[42] See Jose N Nolledo, *The Constitution of the Republic of the Philippines* (Manila: National Book Store, 1986), 1, xvi.

[43] Gordon D Kaufman notes, 'A covenant relationship is one that can be obtained only between moral wills, i.e., between beings who are capable of setting purposes for themselves and who can take responsibility for realizing those purposes, beings who are capable of determining themselves and their activities with respect to the future' (*The Theological Imagination: Constructing the Concept of God* [Philadelphia, PA: Westminster, 1981], 108).

[44] Cf Mercado, *Elements of Filipino Philosophy*, 187. Mercado notes, 'If there is Fate, both Christians and Buddhists agree that man holds the steering wheel of his life, that man is responsible for his own actions. Hence the Filipino is no less a fatalist than other people, for he is also very conscious of his own freedom. The Filipino is no less a fatalist than a devout Christian who believes that God's will is supreme, and that resignation is often the wisest course' (187).

loving providential God. In the strictest sense, cosmic order is achieved through a personal relationship with God.[45]

Christian spirituality discloses a personal reality that orders the world not from within but from beyond, while *bahala na* portrays an impersonal reality that orders the world from within and is in itself subject to that order.[46] The impersonal supernatural force of *bahala na* is directly accessible to and knowable by Filipinos by their actions and behaviors as determinant factors. Christian spirituality, on the other hand, points to an orderly universe that roots itself in God's providential will, something that is accessible to and knowable by faithful believers.[47] Thus, Christian spirituality depicts two wills – God and humanity – that interact dynamically with each other within the boundaries of a covenant. But *bahala na* portrays an impersonal supernatural force whose 'will' is vague and could be experienced basically through a series of fortunes and misfortunes.

An impersonal ethic characterizes *bahala na* spirituality, stressing that human life is executed according to *gulong ng palad* (wheel of fortune). The traditional Filipino psyche holds that 'Life is like a wheel, up today, down tomorrow'. To many Filipinos, the wheel metaphor is a blueprint for one's destiny, something that is directed by a supernatural force, either personified as *Bathala* or the impersonal categories of time or providence that controls the 'wheel of fortune'.[48] Such worldview rules out any concept of purpose or goal in life as time is the bringer of one's fate and destiny. Even *Bathala* and other supernatural forces, which many Filipinos perceive as the ones that control cosmic affairs, do not have the freedom within the system that they themselves supposedly created.[49] Future events then become predictable, and the impersonal cosmic forces do not have the power to alter them. Although *bahala na* necessitates proper action in order to conform to the 'will' of *Bathala*, there is limited freedom on the part of the Filipinos to experience authentic existence. Spirituality here becomes a burden rather than a blessing to many Filipinos as the blueprint of life does not change according to the *bahala na* worldview. *Bahala na*, laments Miranda-Feliciano, 'means that life is determined by an impersonal force

---

[45] Within a Judeo-Christian worldview, observes Kaufman, 'order is personal in origin and character; it is an order established by will and through purposive activity' (Kaufman, *The Theological Imagination*, 107).

[46] See Gordon Kaufman, *God the Problem* (Cambridge, MA: Harvard University Press, 1978), 219.

[47] Mercado admits that, 'although God for the traditional Filipino has been apersonal, Christianity ushered in the personal concept. So we find a continuum of Filipinos: those who still adhere to the apersonal God on the one hand, those who worship a personal God on the other hand, and those in between the continuum' ('The Filipino Image', 409).

[48] See de Mesa, *In Solidarity with Culture*, 150-53.

[49] For a list of Philippine indigenous pantheons, see Jocano, *Folk Christianity*, 4-17.

called *palad*, *suwerte* or fate. Destiny has no face. It is unfeeling, disinterested and bears a stamp of unmoving finality.'[50]

Aimlessness and fixation become trademarks of *bahala na*, which operates effectively within the Philippine concept of a cynical, impersonal ethic of time and history.[51] Many Filipinos see repetitive patterns in the blueprint of their lives, which control one's life and future events. This explains the Filipino plight of struggling within a belief system that relegates them to being pawns of the cosmic forces that rule and determine the events in the world. Having resigned to the notion that they lack the power to counter-control the forces of the universe, many in the Philippines simply adopt an escapist attitude in life saying, *Ito na talaga ang buhay ko* ('This is indeed my lot').[52]

Christian spirituality, however, operates on a goal-oriented vision of God's activity in and through history. It offers a vision that is pre-figured proleptically in the resurrection of Jesus. To Christians, the universe is open-ended; it is not, as the fatalistic *bahala na* spirituality suggests, a closed-ended cosmos where everything happens according to the whims and wishes of impersonal forces like *suwerte*, *tsamba*, and *kapalaran*.[53] Spirituality that is oriented by the will of God presupposes a definite goal, new possibilities, a new horizon, and works within the context of novelty based on the new act of God. In contradistinction with the fatalistic orientation of a 'wheel of fortune', Christians look up to God for a personal divine in-breaking into human time and history. Apparently an open-ended

---

[50] Miranda-Feliciano, *Filipino Values*, 14.

[51] For an extensive discussion on the Filipino concept of time and history, see the works of Mercado, *Elements of Filipino Theology*, 30-35, 105; *Elements of Filipino Philosophy*, 107-118.

[52] Tomas D Andres points out that *bahala na* accounts for the indolence of the Filipinos. He writes: 'He [Filipino] starts when he wants and he ends when he wants. Time for the Filipino is any time; so abundant commodity that one can waste it away' (*Understanding the Filipino Values*, 126).

[53] For an excellent discussion of the themes 'open-ended' and 'close-ended' universe from a sociological perspective, see Peter L Berger, *The Sacred Canopy: The Elements of a Sociological Theory of Religion* (New York: Anchor, 1967) 105-26. In a closed-ended universe, human life is completely controlled by external powers or gods. Glen Lewandowski, in his survey of how the peoples of ancient times in the countries surrounding Israel expressed the inability/ability to change their life situation, graphically notes: 'Each individual and even whole nations were subject to the arbitrary decision of the gods. No one could break out that closed, enslaving circle. One had to choose either to resign oneself passively to one's predetermined 'destiny' or to bribe the gods with the gifts and vows so that the gods would do them, no harm' ('God's Future', *Word-Event* 13:51 [February, 1983], 13). The notion of an open-ended universe introduces an encounter with a transcendent reality (i.e., God) not as a threat but as a challenge. In this case, the universe is seen, as Paul D. Hanson points out, 'as organically participating in one unified creative and redemptive act' (*Dynamic Transcendence* [Philadelphia. PA: Fortress, 1978], 17).

universe facilitates a dynamic interaction between God's providential will and responsive human will within the confines of freedom. In a Judeo-Christian worldview, God radically relates to time, history, and creation.

It is crucial then for Filipinos to understand that Christian spirituality points to God who works purposively in and through human history without depreciating human freedom. God's providential will forms the basis of order in the world, which is sensitive to human freedom and human responsibility. Human history has meaning, purpose, and direction when God's will and human freedom come into active interplay and thereby maintain actual relations.[54]

Furthermore Christian spirituality, although inclusive of the past and the present, has an apocalyptic mooring as it anticipates God's new acts in the future.[55] As Christians endeavor to live up to God's will, they enter into an apocalyptic consciousness resulting from their fresh encounter with the living God. For in the Judeo-Christian worldview, history is purposive and moves toward a grand climax, and human beings are 'free' and undetermined in the face of history. However, this has to be understood from the perspective of God whose freedom is unrestricted and cannot be curtailed by events in the world. God, in relation to human freedom, cannot be bribed but rather acts to fulfill the best for humanity. Here history becomes a reality to humanity, a matrix of God's new acts and freedom rather than as a slaving cycle of *karma* or *suwerte*. In other words, future, and the contingent events of history, can be seen as 'the free actions of God'.[56] In this sense, history translates as 'redemptive history' in contrast with an enslaving history that *bahala na* proposes.[57]

In a polytheistic-oriented framework of spirituality like *bahala na*, the gods are subject to the cosmic order that they themselves created; hence, there is no room for adherents to open up to a new horizon and face up creative possibilities in life.[58] In this case the forces that control a fatalistic

---

[54] Langdon Gilkey writes, 'If God is to redeem history as history, and give its own meaning, it must be through a wayward freedom and not over against it, through participation in the full human condition and not through the eradication of it' (*Reaping the Whirlwind: A Christian Interpretation of History* [New York: Seabury, 1981], 282).

[55] Of apocalyptic consciousness, Paul D Hanson writes: 'Apocalyptic describes a firm of literary expression employed by people knocked off balance by crisis in life and groping edge of abyss. It is further characterized by the fact that explanation and hope are found not within the context of historical events, but by reference beyond this world to an order above or below, the realm of heaven or the realm of arcane' (*The Diversity of Scripture: A Theological Interpretation* [Philadelphia, PA: Fortress, 1982], 41).

[56] See Wolfhart Pannenberg, *Faith and Reality* (London: Search, 1977), 18-19.

[57] See Oscar Cullmann, *Christ and Time: The Primitive Christian Conception of Time and History*, trans. Floyd V Filson (Philadelphia, PA: Westminster, 1950), 121-11.

[58] See Kaufman, *Theological Imagination*, 101-08.

universe are static, barren, and too impersonal. But Christian spirituality accentuates the God who could be 'encountered as the One who perpetually opens up to novel dimensions of creativity'.[59] The dynamic will of this personal and relational God serves as the centre of genuine and authentic spirituality, working in and for human history with purpose.[60]

Conclusion

The indigenous form of folk spirituality epitomized by *bahala na* offers both challenges to and opportunities for Christian mission across the Philippine archipelago. The interface between *bahala na* and the Christian understanding of God's will continue to exist. The clash between these two forms of spirituality will go on. The fatalistic bent inherent in Filipino folk spirituality will continue to baffle missionaries and messengers of the gospel. This is because the indigenous concept of *bahala na* is imbedded in the Filipino religious psyche and operates within a fatalistic framework of distinguishable religious worldviews like animism, Hinduism, Islam, and folk Catholicism. *Bahala na* depicts a Filipino as a mere automaton whose existence is at the disposal of impersonal forces like *tsamba*, *suwerte*, or *kapalaran*. The worldview surrounding *bahala na* folk spirituality presupposes a radical fatalism that operates within a fixed and closed-ended universe. This produces only an environment of fear and uncertainty that is prevalent among fatalistic Filipinos today. The Christian response to *bahala na* is 'Thy Will be Done', a spirituality that portrays a personal God who seeks to establish covenant relationship with those who are willing to exercise their faith and trust in his providential will.

---

[59] Hanson's contribution to see the dramatic unfolding of a notion of God's activity as 'Dynamic Transcendence' is worth noting. 'Dynamic transcendence' views God as 'the creative and redemptive, sustaining and purifying Reality at the very center of life' (*Dynamic Transcendence*, 21).

[60] Hanson concludes, 'God... is not seen as a static Being over against life, to which life against the very nature must conform. God is rather seen as dynamic Reality at the heart of all reality, encountered in life in its manifold forms, and yet transcendent as that upon which all that is and will be is utterly dependent' (*Dynamic Transcendence*, 21).

THE BACK TO JERUSALEM MOVEMENT: MISSION MOVEMENT OF THE CHRISTIAN COMMUNITY IN MAINLAND CHINA

Kim-kwong Chan

Introduction

Christianity first appeared in China in the seventh century through the efforts of Nestorian missionaries from Central Asia, followed by Catholic missionaries. The Protestant form of Christianity arrived in China in the early nineteenth century along with the colonial expansion of western countries in Asia.[1] The Protestant Community in China grew from humble beginnings with just a handful of converts in the early 1850s, to almost a million in 1949 after a century of labour by tens of thousands of missionaries sent from the west. These almost one million Chinese Christians were an insignificant group in the midst of a Chinese population of 450 million at the time when the People's Republic of China was formed in October 1949. The majority of Christian-operated social institutions, such as schools and hospitals, still heavily relied on financial support from western mission boards and agencies. The Christian community in China, like all other religious groups, went through harsh periods of political suppression under the Communist regime of the People's Republic and eventually ceased to exist in public. It was not until 1979 when the Chinese Government began to allow sanctioned religions to operate in the open, albeit with many restrictions, that Christian activities began to reappear. Since then Christians in China recorded phenomenal growth,[2] from a mere

---

[1] There was a Christian presence in China for centuries prior to the coming of the Protestant missionaries. Nestorian Christians first arrived in the seventh century (see Li Tang, *A Study of the History of Nestorian Christianity in China and its Literature in Chinese* [Frankfurt am Main; New York: Peter Lang, 2004]), followed by Franciscans in the fourteenth century. The Jesuit missions began in the late sixteenth century (see Michela Fontana, *Matteo Ricci: Un Gesuita alla Corte dei Ming* [Milano: Mondadori, 2005]) and Russian Orthodoxy in the eighteenth century. Finally, Protestant missionaries appeared on the scene with the arrival of Robert Morrison in 1807.

[2] This chapter deals only with the Protestant community in China. The smaller Catholic community is, like the Protestants, split into recognized and unrecognized sectors, which in the Catholic case are dominated by the complicated issue of the diplomatic tension between the Chinese state and the Vatican.

three million in 1982,[3] estimated by the government, to anywhere between 18 million[4] to 80 million[5] to the extremely high figure of 130 million.[6] A reliable working figure is 35 to 40 million, including both registered and unregistered Christian groups.[7]

During this period of rapid Christian growth, China as a nation emerged from economic obscurity with virtually no engagement with world trade and a large segment of population living under the absolute poverty line. By 2004 it had transformed itself into the world's third largest import-and-export entity;[8] and by February 2009 was the largest holder of foreign reserve in the world with almost two trillion dollars.[9] During the past 25 years, the economic growth of China generated some astonishing figures: GDP went through a 15-fold increase, exports increased 55-fold, and foreign reserves multiplied by almost 5,000.[10] The rise of China had global impact, with 'Made-in-China' goods flooding the world market and China's economic tentacles reaching into virtually every country. With the recent global 'financial tsunami', China is in the limelight as apparently the only major economic entity with sufficient financial capability to jump-start the global economy.

If we look at China's economic development and Chinese Christians' growth, we cannot ignore the possible ramifications on global mission as we compare the experience of Korea in church growth and economic

---

[3] Central Committee of the Communist Party of China, Document # 19. *The Basic Viewpoint on the Religious Question During Our Country's Socialist Period*, 31 March 1982, cit. Donald MacInnis, *Religion In China Today: Policy and Practice* (Maryknoll: Orbis Books, 1989).
[4] Amity Foundation, 'Church Statistics' section in *Amity News Service* at http://www.amitynewsservice.org/page.php?page=1230.
[5] David B Barrett, and Todd M Johnston, *World Christian Trends* (Pasadena, California: William Carey International University, 2001).
[6] Qwei Ya, 'The Equivocal Relations Between the Chinese House Churches and Chinese Government', in *Voice of America*, January 28, 2009, as quoted by China Aid Association, 27 February 2009, see www.chinaaid.org.
[7] From the mid-1980s to the mid-2000s, the China Christian Council and the Chinese Protestant Three-Self Patriotic Movement Committee, also known as the Three-Self Church, Official Church, or Registered Church, printed 30 million copies of the Bible and overseas Christian groups brought in at least another 10 million copies. See Kim-kwong Chan, 'Chinese Protestant Three-Self Patriotic Movement Committee' in J Gordon Melton and Martin Baumann (eds), *Religions of the World: A Comprehensive Encyclopedia of Beliefs and Practices*, 1: A-C (Oxford: ABC-CLIO, 2010), 251-252.
[8] W Gong, 'Our Country's Exports has, the first time, exceeded USD 1,000 billion', in *Remin Ribao* [People's Daily] 15 November 2004, see http://news.sina.com.cn/c/2004-11-15/04444423719s.shtml.
[9] X Wang. 'Imports to Get Forex Fund Boost', in *China Daily*, 19 February 2009, see http://www.cdeclips.com/en/nation/fullstory.html/?id=15655.
[10] China President Hu Jintao's speech at Yale University on 22 April 2006, see http://www.peacehall.com/news/gb/intl/2006/04/200604220826.shtml.

growth since the 1970s. Is it possible that the Korean experience in mission development – backed by strong economic and ecclesial growth during the 1970s, iconized by the Seoul Olympics in 1988, resulting in Korea becoming one of the largest missionary-sending countries in the world in recent years – can be applied to China? Some already speculate that the Christian community in China may one day become the world's largest exporter of missionaries, and that this mission force may be the one that will finally Christianize the 'last frontier' in missions.[11] This last frontier is popularly known in evangelical Christian circles as the '10/40 window',[12] an area which embraces the predominantly non-Christian region stretching from East Asia to the Middle East and North Africa.

The missiological notion that Chinese Christians will be the key players in the final hurdle of global evangelization runs parallel with the socio-political notion that China will be the ascending nation of the twenty-first century, dominating global affairs as the USA did during the twentieth century. As China exports shoes, refrigerators, television sets, language schools and construction labourers all over the globe, so the Chinese Christian communities will send missionaries to spread the good news to every frontier in this world! Is this wishful missiological thinking based on the Korean paradigm of mission development *vis-à-vis* its contemporary national and ecclesial growth? Or could this missiological vision be merely a nationalistic desire of Chinese Christians, fueled by nationalistic aspiration of a strong China reclaiming her former glory as the centre of the world, hence paralleling a Chinese church that would fulfill the Great Commission as the catalytic element ushering in the *eschaton* of Christian hope?

This chapter examines a current mission movement, originating in the Chinese church and advocated by overseas mission agencies, which seems to promote such missiological vision. The 'Back To Jerusalem' (BTJ) movement has been promoted by unregistered church networks in China, and promoted by western Christian supporters, with the original aim of sending 200,000 Chinese missionaries to the Muslim world within ten years.[13] It has attracted attention among mission agencies worldwide, some of whom support this immensely ambitious project and regard it as the final

---

[11] David Aikman, *Jesus in Beijing: How Christianity is Transforming China and Changing the Global Balance of Power* (Washington, D.C.: Regency Publishing Inc., 2003), 285-292.

[12] The 10/40 Window extends from 10 degrees to 40 degrees north of the equator, and stretches from North Africa across to China, containing the bulk of the non-Christian population of the world, see http://1040window.org/main/whatis.htm.

[13] Paul Hattaway, *Back To Jerusalem: Called to Complete the Great Commission* (Carlisle: Piquant, 2003). This book, along with the www.backtojerusalem.com website, is the main advocate of this movement. In 2003, the BTJ website proposed the mobilization of 200,000 Chinese missionaries within 10 years. In 2006 this figure was reduced to 100,000.

leg in the global evangelistic relay of missionaries beginning with Occidental missionaries and now by Oriental missionaries before the End Time. It is the first major initiative among the Chinese Christian community in China to do cross-cultural and overseas mission work. The BTJ has already captured the imagination of mission leaders and has now become a growing movement with dozens of training centers and scores of students in various stages of training, with many already serving in the mission field. Further, what fascinates missiologists is that the whole movement is a totally clandestine operation, operating under the radar of the Chinese Government.[14] It is involved primarily with non-registered Christian communities in China, hence technically all illegal and underground, and has field operations in countries that ban all missionary activities.

Given the difficult political and social context of Christian existence in China, namely the high degree of governmental control on Christian activities and a highly regulated media that is allowed to publish only politically correct material (even those Christian materials available in the officially-sanctioned Christian communities), many sources used are from oral interviews and from personal observations with little or no 'printed' record – this is for security reasons, as all of the activities of this BJM are technically illegal in the eyes of the authorities. There are some published materials, but details such as names and places are omitted or are altered to protect the current operations. For ethical and political reasons, it is often necessary to respect the confidentiality of some sources. Despite the high degree of secrecy surrounding BJM, there are sufficient materials to attempt a preliminary analysis of the mission discipleship of this movement, and to assess its missiological implications. It is hoped that this sensitive fieldwork can shed valuable light on the contributions of Chinese Christian communities – often living under severe restrictions – to the global mission endeavour.

Origin and Background of the 'Back to Jerusalem Movement'

Chinese from the more developed central and coastal areas seldom traveled to the poorer western border areas until the Sino-Japanese War of 1937-1945 when millions of Chinese, especially students, were displaced to the hinterlands as the Chinese Nationalist Government retreated into interior provinces from the advancing Japanese Army. As many Chinese began to realize the underdevelopment of these regions, they organized programmes

---

[14] For the Chinese Government's policy and regulations on religion, see Kim-kwong Chan and Eric R Carlson, *Religious Freedom In China: Policy, Administration, and Regulation – A Research Handbook* (Santa Barbara, California: Institute for the Study of America Religion/Hong Kong: Hong Kong Institute for Culture, Commerce and Religion, 2005).

to help develop the 'backyard' of the country as the base to build up defence capacity against the invading Japanese forces. It was also perhaps the first time that many Chinese Christians had first hand experience of the living situation of the northwestern border regions of China – which once had been a prosperous region of the Silk Road but were now desolated due to desertification. This region includes the contemporary Qinghai, Gansu, Ningxia, Inner Mongolia, Tibet and Xinjiang, mostly inhabited by national minorities such as Tibetans, Mongolians, Kazaks and Uygurs. Few Han Chinese would live there as this region was regarded as a frontier area, a wilderness for exiles, bandits and minorities, and ruled by local warlords. The largest among all these administrative regions is Xinjiang, with more than 1.6 million square kilometres bordering Tibet, Kashmir, Afghanistan, Russia and Central Asia countries.[15] There were a few brave foreign missionaries living in these regions and a few gospel outposts dotting the Silk Road.

About the same time in the 1940s, several Chinese Christian mission groups, without knowing of each other, began to organise evangelistic teams heading towards the northwestern part of China. Some were targeting the Western Region or bordering regions in general, others were focusing on the northwestern part in particular. These people were mostly from either the coastal areas like Shanghai or Shangdong Province, or from the Central areas like Henan or Jiangsu Provinces where Christianity was prospering. This chapter will mention the few major ones, and study the last one in detail since it is critical to the missiological vision of 'Back To Jerusalem' which later became the legendary basis for the current BTJ movement.

The Northwest Spiritual Band (Xibei Ninggong Tuan) was established by Revd Zheng Guquan from Shangdong Province. He called upon people to dedicate their life to serve God – living by faith, sharing all things in common, and with a vision to share the gospel on China's frontier, namely the northwestern region.[16] They had no formal support from any church or organization but relied solely on what God provided as they travelled towards the northwest. They did not require any formal training from their members, but just a dedicated spirit. This mission endeavour in the form of a spiritual band or spiritual fellowship was rather popular at that time. Chinese Christians generally thought that a spiritual band was spiritually superior to conventional mission groups, since conventional mission groups often relied on regular church or denominational support. Further, it was

---

[15] This region has undergone tremendous political changes including the rising and falling of nations, changes of names of places and cities, and re-drawing of administrative boundaries. For the sake of convenience, this chapter uses the current name and political boundaries with parenthesis to include the former name of a particular location.

[16] Personal interview with Cu Hongbao, the surviving co-worker of Revd Zhang Guquan, Urumiqi, July 2002; and later personal letter from Cu dated 15 July 2002.

also a reaction against foreign missionaries by Chinese Christians as most of the missionaries enjoyed generous financial support from their home board or churches and lived in luxury compared to ordinary Chinese church workers who received a very meagre salary from their missionary bosses.

The Northwest Spiritual Band would stop at towns and villages along the route and hold evangelistic meetings for a few days before moving on. They had no fixed itinerary, but rather a general sense of going to northwestern areas, relying on the guidance of the Holy Spirit. Most of them experienced many hardships yet, from their hymns, they regarded these sufferings and hardships as something that they were proud of, and a necessary cost to pay in order to save souls for God.[17] There was no specific goal or direction except a vague sense of evangelizing the whole world by pressing westward. In fact, few, if any, knew what lay beyond the next town, much less beyond the border of China, as none of them carried any map![18] By the late 1940s they were arriving in Xinjiang, the vast frontier area inhabited mostly by Uygur Muslims who speak a Turkish dialect. The team members then scattered to different parts of Xinjiang to spread the gospel if no church was established, or to help out the local church if it was already present. They worked among the Han Chinese, with virtually no work among the local Uygurs as none spoke the Uygur language. Almost all of the perhaps few dozen members were arrested by the new Chinese government in the early 1950s, and many served long jail sentences as 'anti-revolutionary elements' and some died in jail. A few are still alive and in their 80s. Some of their descendants carried on this evangelistic zeal, continuing the work of their parents despite the cost.[19]

The Christian Native Evangelistic Crusade, CNEC (later renamed the Christian National Evangelistic Crusade), was established in 1942 at the then Provisional Capital of China, Chungking, with financial support from Christians in the US and mission work operated by Chinese Evangelists. Two of their members, Li Kaiwan and his wife Ze Mingxia, originally serving in Yunnan Province, had requested to transfer to Xinjiang in 1945, just at the end of the Second World War. They felt the call to serve in northwest China. They joined the CNEC but raised their own support, as Li was a senior official of the Postal Service in Yunnan. Later Li became Commissioner for the Postal Service of the Xinjiang Province. With a donation from the Governor of Xinjiang, General Zhang Zizhong, also a Christian, they established the first Christian Church in Urumuqi (then called Dihua), the capital of Xinjiang. Eventually the CNEC sent in more people, all were well trained in theology, and established at least seven

---

[17] Kim-kwong Chan and Alan Hunter, *Prayers and Thoughts of Chinese Christian* (London: Mowbray, 1990), 71-72.
[18] Personal Interview of a surviving member of the Band, Elder Zheng Jinting, at Hami, Xinjiang, July 2004.
[19] Tetsunao Yamamori and Kim-kwong Chan, *Witnesses to Power: Stories of God's Quiet Work in a Changing China* (Carlisle: Paternoster, 2000), 1-7.

churches in Xinjiang by the end of 1950.[20] They became the largest Christian group in the province, giving shelter to other mission groups.

All these churches were mainly composed of Han Chinese with very few Uygurs. The CNEC was described in a prayer letter published by an American missionary in late 1950 as follows: "They are very closely associated with Mr and Mrs Li, whose ministry at Tihwa (or Dihua, now Urumuqi) will, we believe, if ever it is published, prove to be one of the most glorious chapters in the history of the Chinese church... they are a group of fine consecrated men and women, most of whom have been trained in Bible school."[21] Paul Li was ordained in 1946, the first Chinese ordained pastor of this province. Before the Lis were arrested in the mid-1950s, they managed to run a small theological institute and many of the students were later arrested by the government and sent as internal exiles to remote parts of the province as factory labourers. Some managed to establish Christian community at places hitherto there had been no Christian presence, and eventually developed these communities into a church, such as the church in Altay on the Russian border.[22] Paul Li spent some years in jail, like most of his colleagues, and later died in the 1960s. All of the churches established by the CNEC in the 1940s are still flourishing today.

The Chinese Christian Mission is a mission group, started just after the Second World War, based in Shanghai. By 1949, they had about a hundred missionaries all over China. Many of their missionaries were from Shangdong Province. In 1947, they began sending workers to the northwest and worked alongside with CNEC and The Spiritual Band. By the end of 1950, they had affirmed their mission goal in Xinjiang as mainly to target the Uygurs, not Han Chinese, as they observed that many other mission groups, such as The Spiritual Band and the later mentioned BTJ group, were evangelizing primarily among the Chinese, not those ethnic minority Muslims.[23] They made several evangelistic trips into remote parts of Xinjiang. They worked strategically, undertaking language studies and adopting such methods as medical mission to evangelize the Uygurs. Their

---

[20] Li Kaiwan, 'Church Report of Xinjiang', in *Zengdao (True Way)* Magazine, 30 November, 1950, back inner cover. Liu Songsan of Chinese Christian Mission also reported the work of CNEC in 1950, confirming Li's report of continuous church development in that province, see Liu Songsan, 'Evangelistic Journey in Xinjiang', *Evangelism Quarterly* 14, 23-26.

[21] HR Thompson, *Chinese Back To Jerusalem Band News Letter* No. 11 (April, 1950), 7.

[22] For example the Church in Altay was established by a lady, a student of Paul Li, who was arrested as a Christian and sent to a remote town on the Sino-Soviet border. She worked at the local shoe factory and spread the gospel in secret. She is now the head of the Altay Church, personal interview, name withhold for security reasons, July 2004.

[23] Liu Songsan, 'Who will save the descendants of Ishmael?' *Evangelism Quarterly* No. 13 (October 1950), 25.

work was terminated in the early 1950s as the Communist regime put a halt to all mission work in China. Nevertheless, this group was perhaps the only one that made practical plans as well as focusing on the local population as their mission target.

A small but significant mission was started by Revd Mark Ma in 1943 at a Bible School in Shaanxi after he received a series of visions indicating that the Chinese church should assume responsibility to take the gospel to Xinjiang and, in order to complete the Great Commission, to the rest of the world. The pathway of the gospel has spread in a westward direction, from Jerusalem to Antioch to all Europe, to America, then to the east, from Southeast China to Northwest China, and should carry on from Northwest China all the way back to Jerusalem. The remaining territory is under the power of Islam and the hardest place to embrace the gospel. This area was kept for the Chinese church as a portion of inheritance, so that the Chinese church can claim it when the Lord returns. As the Chinese missionaries take the gospel back to Jerusalem, they will stand on Mount Zion witnessing the return of Jesus Christ.

Based on his vision, Revd Ma challenged the students at the Bible school to join and they formed a small Gospel Band called 'The Band that Spreads the Gospel all Over The Place' (*Pinzhuan Fuyin Tuan*). The constitution noted Matthew 24:14 as the Band's motto, and the sphere of works was to spread the gospel first to the seven provinces in the northwestern region of China, then to the 'seven countries on the borders of Asia: Afghanistan, Iran, Arabia, Irak, Syria, and Palestine.'[24] In the last stanza of their Band's hymn, it was stated that: 'The gospel will be proclaimed back to Jerusalem with triumphal hymns. As we look upon from Mount Zion, we praise the Second Coming of Christ.'[25] Soon an American missionary in China, Helen Bailey, who heard of Revd Ma's groups, began to promote this group in the USA and UK by circulating newsletters via her friends with news of this group translated into English. It is in her first newsletter for this group that she called this Band the 'Back to Jerusalem Band'. Since then it has been known by this name in the English Speaking world, but not in the Chinese church.

Out of the few dozen who joined this Band, only three made any mention of Jerusalem as their mission desire or calling: Revd Mark Ma Ke (Ma Ke is Mark in Chinese), Ms Grace Ho (or He Enzhen), and Mr Mecca Zhao Maijia (Maijia is Mecca in Chinese). Revd Mark Ma Ke started briefly in Xinjiang and later settled in the interior part of China, Sichuan, for several decades. He never travelled anywhere further west than Urumuqi. Both Zhao and Ma noted in their testimonies that they had visions from God for reaching Jerusalem and desired to meet the Lord

---

[24] H Bailey, *The Chinese Back To Jerusalem Evangelistic Band, A Prayer Call*, mimeograph, nd (cira, 1950), 6.
[25] AJC Wang, *Silk Route Mission: Story of a Heroic Couple* (Taipei: Campus Evangelical Fellowship, 2003), 184-185.

there.[26] Zhao went to Kashgar in 1949[27] and Ho joined him later. Zhao and Ho later married and felt the call to travel further west than other Band members, although still without a clear destination in mind. In 1949-1950, they planned to go to Afghanistan because the local people had told them that that was the nation just west of China. However, the furthest they reached was Kashgar, still within China and several hundred kilometers from the Afghan border.[28] They both died a few years ago without ever leaving China. When this author interviewed Grace Ho in 2002, she had no idea that the Band's name was translated as 'Back To Jerusalem Band' in English, much less the current BTJ movement which claimed to be a continuation of the vision of this Band! However, a month after my interview with Ho, several BTJ movement advocates visited Ho and subsequently published a book describing Zhao and Ho's experience in Xinjiang as an attempt to realize their dream of preaching the gospel back to Jerusalem.[29]

One of the original members of this group, whom I interviewed in detail, suggests that the Band had no particular destination in mind to begin with. They simply moved in a generally westward direction as they 'felt the call', without maps, travel plans or information on the region. He suggested that the reference made on preaching the gospel back to Jerusalem in the band's hymn was merely a slogan (cf Matt 24:11) than a strategic objective of the Band. Despite their geographical and political naivety, more than half of them managed to reach and stay in various parts of Xinjiang. However, none of them had studied the local language since they had no particular ethnic 'target' group in mind.[30] The exception perhaps was Mecca Zhao as he later studied Uygur not for so much for evangelization but for something more practical in mind, he was re-trained as a seal carver and Kashgar is a bi-lingual city with Chinese and Uygur.[31] Eventually all mission activity came to a halt in the early 1950s in Xinjiang.

Back to Jerusalem Movement and Current Status

One Member of the Northwest Spiritual Band, Simon Zhao, spent almost 20 years in jail in Xinjiang. When he was released, he became something of

---

[26] Bailey, 6-7. Also Mecca Zhao had claimed to have three Divine revelations on the fate of the Band and of some of their colleagues including Ms Helen Bailey, recoded on p. 11. All of his prophecies were wrong!

[27] HR Thompson, *Chinese Back To Jerusalem Band News Letter* No. 10 (December 1949), 3.

[28] Personal interview with,Grace He Enzhen, in Kashgar, Xinjiang, August 2002.

[29] Wang, *Silk Route Mission*.

[30] Interviews by the author with Revd Huang Ziqing, an original member of the BTJ Band, in Xinjiang in August 2002, August 2003 and August 2006, and in Liaoling in April 2004.

[31] Personal interview with Grace Ho Enzhen, 2002.

a legend in Christian circles in Xinjiang because of the hymns and poems he wrote reflecting his many years of suffering for his faith which became a great source of comfort and encouragement for other believers.[32] Many came to him for spiritual advice. In the late 1990s at one of the unregistered church meetings in the province, Simon Zhao claimed he had a vision from God that the Chinese church should preach the gospel to the Islamic world eventually back to Jerusalem with theological justifications similar to those advanced by Revd Mark Ma almost half a century earlier. In the mid 1990s, the Chinese church was experiencing rapid growth and at the same time was under extreme government restriction. No one would have thought of doing mission outside of China as almost all efforts were for the survival of the Chinese Christian community under an atheistic regime hostile to Christianity. It seems to be the first major cross-cultural and cross-border mission initiated by the Christian community in China, a significant development especially in light of the fact that initiating bodies are all clandestine Christian groups operating in an underground manner.

These leaders of the unregistered churches made contact with Chinese churches abroad and, eventually with evangelical mission agencies, such as the Great Commission Center International.[33] A significant figure in this movement was Liu Zhenying, also known as Brother Yun or the Heavenly Man,[34] who claimed to have united several unregistered church networks and to spread the 'Back to Jerusalem' vision. Following his escape from prison in China and escape to Germany in 1997, his vision has been popularized in evangelical circles outside of China through the writings of New Zealand missionary Paul Hattaway,[35] and was promoted by some independent mission agencies, such as the Open Door. In addition, the BTJ vision has been disseminated through hymns, books, websites, and enthusiastic discussions at mission conferences. In the process, the original idea of evangelizing the Muslim world has been transformed into a call for Chinese Christians to evangelize not only the Muslims but also all the people-groups between China and Jerusalem.

Many North American Chinese church leaders acted as brokers, linking the leaders from unregistered Christian groups in China with western mission agencies eager to promote the BTJ vision. This called for massive mobilization of Chinese Christians, as many as 200,000 in a ten-year period, to be sent to evangelize the Muslim world as the last hurdle of the Great Commission. At the same time, the western mission agencies wanted provide financial support and training resources. A joint-venture outsourcing model began to emerge. Captivated by this fascinating idea, some groups have organized 'secret' international conferences to promote as well as to co-ordinate this movement. The secrecy reflects the

---

[32] Chan and Hunter, *Prayers and Thoughts*, 18-19, 26-27.
[33] See www.gcciusa.org.
[34] Brother Yun and Paul Hattaway, *The Heavenly Man* (London, Monarch, 2002).
[35] Hattaway, *Back to Jerusalem*.

clandestine nature of groups from un-registered churches in China, as well as the often-illicit nature of evangelization work in most of the targeted Muslim nations. Therefore most of the discussions of these conferences are not available other than as material circulated among the core players of the movement. But it would be correct to say that BTJ is a *movement* with a plurality of individual and institutional *agents* and a certain unifying *ideology*. There is no real centre to this movement as no one single group can stake an exclusive claim to it.

Currently there are at least two dozen mission agencies actively involved in this movement, with more than a dozen training centers in China and at least another ten abroad, training potential BTJ missionaries. Most of these training centres are funded by western-based mission agencies. Many BTJ Chinese missionaries are already in Middle Eastern countries, and some 'vanguard teams' are in the Middle East establishing support bases and so-called 'caravan stations'. By 2009, Chinese BTJ missionaries could be found in at least twelve countries, mostly Islamic nations, with many more graduates from various training centers ready to be sent out. Their status in the host countries includes that of student, tourist, business people, agriculture worker, beautician, shopkeeper, and contract worker.

The Assumptions of the Current BTJ Movement

The enthusiasm for the BTJ vision outside China seems to be a confluence of the centrality of Israel as a motif in evangelical millenarianism, especially in the United States, and western fascination with the rise of China and its huge population especially with the reported high number of Christian converts ready to be deployed in mission fields. After 9/11, Christendom has also devoted much more attention to the Islamic world. The BTJ implicitly regards this Chinese movement as the 'last change of the baton' of global missions; the gospel that travelled from the Middle East to Europe, and on to North America and thence (via western missionaries) to East Asia, will now be returned to its starting-point at Jerusalem by Chinese missionaries. In so doing, it will literally complete the mission-mandate of preaching the gospel to the whole world by circling the globe. This is not exactly a new idea for Chinese Christians, because some Chinese church leaders in the diaspora had promoted a similar ethnocentric missionary theme as early as the 1970s.[36] However it is a fresh idea for Christians in the unregistered churches.

---

[36] The last stanza of CCCOWE theme song (Chinese Coordination Center of World Evangelism founded in 1976 by Disaporic Chinese Christians) suggests that the Chinese Christian would carry the last baton of this global evangelism task from the western missionaries before the final triumph of the Lord – see www.cccowe.org The Great Commission Center International (www.GCCUISA.org) also advocates such a theme by portraying the global missions movement as encircling the world,

The advocates, represented by Hattaway's book and website for this movement, put forward several arguments to justify this Chinese BTJ movement regarding the Chinese missionaries as the last baton-carriers of global mission.[37] They are summarized as follows. Politically, China has no major political adversaries and is on good terms with virtually every nation. China does not label any other country as part of an axis of evil, and does not engage in name-calling towards any other nation. It can do business simultaneously with Cuba and USA, Iraq and Iran, the Palestinian Authority and Israel, Libya and the UK, North Korea and South Korea. Chinese nationals can go to countries where westerners have difficulty gaining access, especially in the Islamic world.

Experientially, Chinese Christians (especially those from the unregistered sector) have long endured harsh government suppression and developed a sophisticated form of ecclesial existence to conduct clandestine activities. Such a form of ecclesial existence would be rather suitable for new Christian converts in Islamic countries as most of these countries would regard such conversion as illegal and such religious activities to be suppressed by civil authorities. Therefore, the Chinese Christians can offer their experience to the Christian community in Islamic countries of how to avoid detection by the civil authorities.

Ecclesiastically, it is suggested since Christians in China practise a simple form of Christianity devoid of elaborate liturgical, diaconal and institutional structures, such an ecclesial form would therefore be simple to operate, flexible, and cost-effective. Such a model of church operation would be suitable for planning new churches in an environment which is hostile to Christianity, such as Islamic countries. Therefore, by having Chinese missionaries, the mission field can operate a stripped down form of church life ideal for the field situation.

In terms of human resources, the Chinese church also has an ample supply of experienced 'church-planters', as witnessed by the rapid growth of churches even in the hostile environment of Communist China. In addition, even though Christians are still a small percentage of the Chinese population, the absolute numbers are huge, creating a virtually endless supply of potential missionary candidates. This huge pool of missionary 'labourers' can be easily tapped into and will continue to supply the demand from the field.

Economically, these Chinese missionaries are used to living frugally as most of them are living in the rural areas in China with a low standard of living. They have also experienced economic hardship and can still manage to survive and to serve. Lifestyle and living standards of western missionaries in the field are often at par with western expatriates in general.

---

with the last leg being directed by Asians from the Far East, Front Cover, *Great Commission Bi-Monthly*, No. 48, February 2004.
[37] Hattaway, *Back to Jerusalem*, 94-134.

Such living standard may become a heavy financial burden for the mission-sending agency. With the same amount of money, a mission agency can easily employ a far greater numbers of Chinese missionaries to serve in the field, an ideal way to maximize the money.

Spiritually, Chinese Christians have also long accepted suffering as a part of Christian reality and are ready to be martyred without hesitation. In fact, one of the advocates, Brother Yun (the 'Heavenly Man') has even suggested that he is prepared to accept 10,000 Chinese martyrs in the first decade of the BTJ operation in order to crack open the Muslim world to the gospel.[38] One thing that fuels this disposition for martyrdom is Adventist belief: there is an eschatological assumption that Jesus will return once the gospel has been preached around the world ending in Jerusalem.

Missiologically, the idea of tens of thousands of Chinese missionaries roaming the Middle East North Africa (MENA) region evangelizing in secret is extremely attractive to many western Christians who are frustrated by the relative fruitlessness of western mission endeavours among Muslims. As one veteran missionary in a Middle Eastern country told me, 'We have been so lonely labouring for many years with little result. We are so frustrated that we are tempted to jump at any idea, however berserk it may seem.'[39] Is it not time to turn over the mission field from the hands of the missionaries of the older churches to the missionaries of the younger churches, such as the Chinese? Since missionaries from the older churches have already had their chance for more than a century with little result, should they now allow others to have a hand in this field? Among the mission agencies, BTJ has been getting an increasing amount of international attention and financial support, especially from pro-Israel Christian Zionist mission groups.[40]

Finally, the BTJ movement also draws some geopolitical attention, especially in the post-9/11 geopolitical context. In a hypothetical 'clash of civilizations' scenario between the west and the Islamic world, China would become a highly important 'third player' with which the United States wishes to be allied. David Aikman in *Jesus in Beijing* suggests that the BTJ movement could be instrumental in allying the USA and China to counter the global expansion of Islamic influence if (a) Christians in China increase to a point that China becomes a Christian-influenced or even a Christianized nation, like the USA, and (b) China sends out tens of thousands of missionaries to Christianize the current Islamic region from Central Asia to the Middle East. Since the rapid increase of Christian population is not an idea so far from reality, Aikman would therefore

---

[38] Editor, 'Interview with Paul Hattaway – A Captive Vision', in *Christianity Today*, April 2004, 84.

[39] Interviewed in April 2004 (name and place withheld for security reasons).

[40] For security reasons, identity of organization, individual and places are not mentioned except those with consent from the individual or those which had already appeared in open publications.

advocate the BTJ idea so that the geopolitical pattern in future would be the opposite of Samuel Huntington's original formulation of the 'clash of civilizations' thesis: instead of western (Christian) culture confronting an alliance of Middle Eastern (Islamic) and Eastern (Confucian) cultures, the Muslim world might have to confront an alliance of east and west, both outside and within its own borders.[41] The US would team up with China to check the growth of Islamic influence using Christianity as the force to change the global balance of power.

Reflections on these Assumptions

The BTJ movement has drawn divided opinion. Some regard it as a hoax[42] while others see it as a new mission mandate for 'Christendom'. In spite of the many accusations and refutations,[43] mainly regarding the handling of finances and claims of authority over the movement, it has drawn endorsements from a growing number of mission agencies worldwide.[44] With the increasing attention paid to evangelization of the Muslim world, the BTJ movement has gained momentum, especially among overseas Chinese and in the unregistered churches in China. There are also international conferences – often held somewhat confidentially due to the sensitive nature of the content – to promote and coordinate efforts among agencies within the movement.[45] This chapter now proceeds to analyze the theological roots and arguments of this movement and to ponder the possible implications, should the movement achieve a fraction of what it intends, for world Christianity and international relations.

It is true that the Chinese churches have a vast supply of potential missionaries. Furthermore, the increasing surplus of Chinese farm workers, perhaps the largest bloc of unemployed or under-employed labourers in the world (numbering 150 million in 2008), may facilitate recruitment of missionaries among rural Christians. But church leaders in the Middle East have stressed that future missionaries to that part of the world should acquire some sort of professional status and have in-depth understanding of

---

[41] Aikman, *Jesus in Beijing,* 194-206.
[42] The word used spontaneously by a leading historian of Chinese Christianity, name withheld, upon hearing mention of the BTJ during an academic conference in 2006.
[43] BTJ Foundation UK, *The Back To Jerusalem Foundation: Statement,* mimeograph, (December 2005), 1-4.
[44] For example, *China Source* (a mission bulletin on missions and China) devotes an entire issue to the BTJ (vol. 7, no. 1, Spring 2006).
[45] Participants in these conferences agree not to divulge information about the content of the sessions or the identity of the other participants, because of the sensitive nature of mission work in Islamic nations. Therefore the author, who has attended some of these conferences, is unable to enter into sensitive details beyond the generic information given in the text.

Islamic culture.[46] There are few Chinese Christians who meet those two criteria, especially with regard to quality training in cross-cultural issues.

My personal observation of many BTJ trainees suggests that they are mostly young people from 20 to 25 years of age with an average education of junior school to senior high school. Only a few have some college education. Most of them come from rural areas with little experience of city life, and almost none have had any cross-cultural experience outside of China prior their joining the programme for training. Almost all lack any professional skill. Also almost all of them, though rich in church ministry experience, have virtually no experience in the secular work place. When this author asked them what they would do in the field, most replied that God would provide them with a suitable status. Some suggested that they would like to be a vendor because most of the Chinese in the Islamic world, if they have some money, open small businesses such as shops and restaurant. If they lack professional qualifications and money, they would become vendors, or cheap labourers, usually illegal, for small businesses or sweatshops. A missionary recently told me that he had encountered in Iraq a group of BTJ missionaries from rural China. To his surprise, they had no knowledge of Iraq and certainly none of Arabic. Furthermore, they were pig farmers, not the best profession for gaining acceptance in the Muslim world![47] Finding it difficult to get work in their only profession, they subsequently left for another Middle Eastern country.

Some of those involved in training BTJ candidates have echoed such doubts about the suitability of many of their charges.[48] Other highly optimistic movements to mobilize huge numbers of global southern missionaries (such as Filipino overseas workers) have simply not achieved the expected results.[49] The long history of mission agencies reminds us that candidate selection is crucial to the success of any mission endeavour. Quality, not quantity, seems to count for more in the success of cross-cultural mission work. The potential impact of the BTJ on the Islamic world, at least in the immediate future, will be severely restricted by the limited availability of qualified candidates.

---

[46] Anonymous, 'Interview from the Land of the Pharaohs', *Back To Jerusalem Bulletin* 2 (December, 2004), 7-8.

[47] Personal communication, 31 January 2005 (identity withheld).

[48] For example, there have been many trainers of BTJ candidates in a Southeast Asian country (names withheld). In addition, in 2006, 2007 and 2008 I interviewed many trainers studying in various BTJ training centers. Most of them commented that candidates from rural areas lack the basic skills for living in urban environments. While many have rich ministerial experience, few are able to acquire the professional skills which would enable them to get secular jobs in foreign cities. In 2007 and 2008, I also visited many BTJ mission candidates in the mission field.

[49] There is a high level of missionary activity among Filipino workers in Hong Kong, with at least 80 churches, but little if any has gone beyond the Filipino community.

There are also political and commercial repercussions. If thousands of Chinese BTJ missionaries, perhaps posing as vendors, do in fact flood the bazaars of MENA countries selling Chinese goods, giving testimonies, having home-based worship meetings and passing out tracts, will the local authorities turn a blind eye? Such an influx of missionaries would probably lead them to tighten restrictions on foreign activities in general, and on Chinese in particular. The result could be intra-Chinese tension in such countries between those who are genuine merchants and those who are really missionaries. The negative impact on Chinese commercial activities, and the Chinese presence in general, in the profitable Middle Eastern market might prompt the Chinese authorities to take steps not to lose that lucrative market, which might in turn curb the flow of BTJ missionaries from the China side.

The spirit of missionary martyrdom emphasized by the BTJ, accustomed to persecution in China, might make them fearless in the face of the local authorities. But if any Islamic nation took severe measures against apprehended Chinese missionaries, such as execution, the result would be an international outcry, as well as international media coverage that would embarrass the Chinese government. Muslim fundamentalist groups might take some of those missionaries hostage, as in the recent case of Korean missionaries in Afghanistan, leaving the Chinese government no alternative but to use all diplomatic means available to rescue them, as the Korean Government did. Should several such scenarios occur, China would have to deal with these issues affecting its relations with the Islamic nations, upon which China depends for oil. The Chinese authority would certainly not trade the loss of Middle Eastern oil in exchange for Chinese Christian missionaries' right to evangelize in those countries. After all, China does not encourage religious development and strongly endorses economic development. The Chinese government might then find excuses to clamp down on Christian activities to which they are currently turning a blind eye, and resort to shutting down BTJ training facilities in China as well as restricting the exit of potential missionaries from China. All these measures would have endorsement from the general public, just like the condemnation from the public at large towards those missionary-sending churches in Korea when the Korean Government had to bail out the captured missionaries in Afghanistan.

The BTJ is also subtly ethnocentric, if not racist. It claims the right for the Chinese to own the God-given honour of carrying the baton in the final leg of the round-the-world evangelistic relay marathon. Some Korean Protestants have claimed a similar right, based on their high number of missionaries. Such ethnocentric visions of missionary 'chosen-ness' lack a sound foundation in Christian theology, for the mission mandate is given in the New Testament to all races of all nations in a co-operative manner. By interpreting divine calling as an exclusive Sino-centric privilege, or the so-called inheritance from God, there is a danger of repeating the racial superiority complex of the 'White Man's Burden' which influenced nineteenth century western missions.[50] Would this BTJ movement be a form of a 'Yellow Man's Burden,'[51] likely to generate tensions on the mission field similar to those associated with the 'White Man's Burden' in the past? Currently, some mission leaders are trying to modify the BTJ movement into a general call for the Chinese unregistered churches to do foreign mission. They also try to downplay the Sino-centric element by stressing cooperation between east and west on this final leg of the global mission mandate.[52] However, such a Sino-centric tone is still a strong flavour of this movement.

The BTJ seems to emerge as a Christian analogue to the figure of China rising in the global international order. Domestically, the rise of Chinese nationalism, enhanced by the Beijing Olympiad, empowers the Chinese with a sense of confidence to encounter the world, with more involvement in global affairs and more responsibility for global challenges than obtained in the closed-door policy in the past. The sending of Chinese Naval forces to protect the merchant fleet near the Somalia coast, and the Chinese peace keeping forces in Sudan, are current examples. Such nationalistic aspiration with global concern and global responsibility may easily translate into the evangelistic concern of Global Mission among the Christians in China, a form of nationalism in the Christian context.

Internationally, the increasing influence of China and the idea of China as a politically neutral nation[53] suitable for global involvement, may also encourage Chinese Christians to position themselves in global mission to co-work, if not to replace, the western missionaries currently in the field. However such an assumption would be valid if China is perceived as a neutral and non-threatening international force. Unfortunately, the increase of China's commercial presence in Islamic countries from Afghanistan to Mauritania, sometimes involving practices conflicting with Islamic tradition,[54] has already generated an increasing amount of Sino-phobic sentiments out of fear of Chinese market dominance and of a deterioration

---

[50] SL Duffy, 'Nineteenth Century Colonial World', see http://www.loyno.edu/~seduffy/imperialism.html 2006.

[51] Pal Nyiri, 'The Yellow Man's Burden: Chinese Migrants on a Civilizing Mission', *China Journal* 56 (2006), 83-106.

[52] In an international BTJ conference held in August 2006, participants (both Chinese and non-Chinese) from various mission agencies and church networks agreed that the BTJ is more a challenge to Chinese Christians to do cross-cultural mission rather than just to preach along the route from China to Jerusalem.

[53] See Erik Izraelewicz, *Quand La Chine Change Le Monde* (Paris: Editions Grassel et Fasquelle, 2005).

[54] Many Chinese restaurants in the Middle East sell alcoholic drinks and some, like those in Kabul, also operate brothels using the restaurant as a front. Most of the patrons are expatriate workers with the UN or with relief and development agencies. For example, see Justin Huggler, 'Chinese Prostitutes arrested in Kabul "Restaurant Raids" ', in *The Independent* (online) 10/2/2006.

of socio-religious values.[55] The Chinese Government's support to some of the regimes, such as Sudan and Zimbabwe, may cause resentment from the local population against the Chinese as well. Such fears will work against the Chinese BTJ missionaries, making it harder for them to be welcomed by local populations. It seems that mission work hitching on seemingly favourable political conditions may easily backfire once the political tide has turned.

The argument of endless supply of missionary candidates seems to be based on China's economic advantage of a massive pool of cheap labour translated into the mission context. This functions as a 'push' factor for the BTJ: in the job market tens of millions of Chinese peasants, with insufficient land to till at home and unable to settle in urban China, are 'available' for any kind of job available to make a better living than idling in the village. So Christians among this rural population would go any place so long as there is a chance of a better livelihood, just like their non-Christian fellow peasants. Currently already several million Chinese legally or otherwise have left China to seek a better living in more than 150 countries since the mid-1990s, as China relaxed its exit requirement for its citizens. The Chinese peasants may have paid up to USD 20,000 for various middle men and bribes to get to a MENA country as contract labour, and he or she will have to pay back the loan with high interest through the first few years of hard labour before this worker can save any money. Should an opportunity arise for these rural Christian to serve overseas, as 'missionaries' and all paid for by mission agencies, there would certainly not be any shortage of applicants. In fact, most of these trainees whom I have encountered experienced such opportunity to be selected for overseas mission that there was extensive competition among applicants. How can the selection process be able to check the motive of the mission candidates to screen off those who just want a free ticket out of China?

From the economic perspective, the BTJ movement talks of a highly cost-effective scheme which is attractive to hard-pressed western mission agencies eager for quick and sensational results which might elicit donor support. The financial cost of supporting one western missionary (plus family) can easily hire at least half a dozen Chinese BTJ workers! Outsourcing cheap labour-intensive jobs to labour pools of developing countries is a commercial trend to cut cost. Can this commercial method be employed in the mission field? In fact, this outsourcing method has been in practice since 1943 in the mission field of China[56] as US donors contributed money, and the Chinese church provided mission labour to reduce the cost

---

[55] Anti-Chinese sentiment has been observed in Muslim countries such as Mauritania, Mali and Niger, where Chinese operate brothels under the façade of restaurants. D Tao 'Afghan expels 'Chinese Restaurant-Brothel', *Phoenix Weekly* 24:229 (25 August) 44-46.

of sending US missionaries to China. The debate was more rhetoric than administrative, over whether those locally hired native staff are considered to be missionaries or not. However, the BTJ movement goes beyond the practice of hiring local labour to do the ground job, but hiring foreign (hence cheaper) labour for local work, a mercenary model indeed. Should that be the case, and if it is already happening in the mission field, is it a new form of international co-operation in mission modeling after the commercial world? This 'cost-effectiveness' idea has two problems: first, is it another form of racism as if Chinese BTJ missionaries could not have the same standard of living as the western missionaries are currently enjoying? Are not all Christians created equal, and do they not all deserve equal treatment? Secondly, would the mission agency replace those Chinese BTJ workers if a cheaper source were available, say, from Vietnam or Nigeria? If one takes this 'cost-effectiveness division of labour' idea a step further, would it not develop into a contract bidding system for a mission project where the job would go to whichever church group that can provide the best mission service with the lowest cost... say ten missionaries for ten years in A country with ten churches built with at least 100 converts per church for x amount of money, including penalty cost lists? And the church group that won such bid could sub-contract it to various groups? Who really owns the mission?

There is also the issue of legality. I have observed some of these BTJ missionaries enter a field illegally and remain so; others remain illegally after gaining their legal entrance. Some even use counterfeit travel documents to exit China and to enter other countries. Their good conscience about breaking or bending the laws is an extension of the legally dubious status of their churches within China itself. They often justify their dismissal of the legal system by referring to the New Testament injunction to 'obey God rather than men', as many of them disregard the need to respect the law if such law hinders the spreading of the gospel. How would this ethical issue be treated as these BTJ missionaries are operating illegally, trying to build up a clandestine group of converts who would themselves be arrested as criminals if known by the authority and prosecuted under the law? Where would we draw the line?

Conclusion

China is undoubtedly emerging as a major economic and political power in the international community. The Christians in China, together with others from the younger, hence mostly non-western, churches may in future write the next chapter in the story of world Christianity. However, the Christian community in China is but a minority group among 1.3 billion in the diverse Chinese population. Unlike Korea, it is still far from being an influential social group, even within the Chinese social milieu, as most of them are rural people with limited education and professional skills.

Although some may wish for a high figure of Christians in China, there remains the possibility that a community high in quantity may not be high in spiritual quality. It takes time to develop the spiritual maturity of a community.

The global mission initiative of the Chinese churches is still in its infancy, having begun with this BTJ movement originated more than a half a century ago by a handful of enthusiastic Chinese evangelistic with the misnomer of 'Back To Jerusalem' as its popular slogan in the west. This legacy, almost forgotten, is recycled by current Chinese church leaders, perhaps anachronistically, to become the historical justification that God had long intended Chinese to take up this honourable task at the End Time. There are a few similarities which link the past and the current BTJ movement: a Sino-centric wish, a vague strain of Christian Zionism, a proactive millenarianism, and perhaps a hint of Apostolic Catholic Movement. It has an undefined mission objective, other than the idea of ending up eventually in Jerusalem, and is unclear about what is involved in evangelizing people along the route all the way from China to Jerusalem.

The current BTJ movement differs from the previous one by incorporating the current global marketing trend, a business model, the political ascendency of China, and the shifting of Christianity's centre to the younger churches. Further, this movement is further fueled by enthusiastic promotions, personal visions, and a secular business model rather than on serious theological reflection and critical missiological and spiritual considerations.

There are many serious issues yet to be tackled. For example, the increasing presence of large numbers of missionaries from mainland China in Muslim-dominated areas may cast a different picture, for such proselytizing activity is currently regarded as illegal within the context of these nations. Eventually there will be conflicts between these missionaries and civil authorities, and with local religious communities. These conflicts involving Chinese citizens may well force Chinese authorities to face a political dilemma: to protect its citizen as a responsible nation, or to keep strategic political relationships with these nations. Seemingly religious incidents, such as trial or execution of such missionaries, may lead to legal action and end in political and diplomatic crisis. It could also lead to some embarrassing questions: would China defend religious liberty by protecting its citizens as they conduct proselytizing activities in other countries, like most developed nations do? Yet at the same time, China's record on religious liberty is far from ideal! It appears that the consequence of this BTJ movement may easily go beyond the religious, and enter into the complex realm of international politics, a situation that its original advocates might not have considered.

The severe lack of qualified pastoral workers within China due to the rapid growth of Christianity in the past 20 years, compounded with the strong governmental control on normal development of churches, also hinders the availability hence of recruiting of qualified BTJ candidates. The dubious motives of many of these mission candidates within the current Chinese social trend of migration overseas, the clandestine style of operation lacking accountability and transparency on financial and administrative matters, and the ethical issues with the law both in China and in the mission field – all these are factors which further cast doubt on the idea that the BTJ movement will bear strong influence on the development of global Christianity. It appears that the current BTJ movement is founded more on enthusiastic desires of western mission groups, nationalistic aspirations of the Chinese, opportunistic mission leaders, the threat from expanding Islamic influence, and the mythologized Christian community in China, with the political hedge on the rising of China as the new global power. It will require a lot more serious missiological and spiritual groundwork before it can become a credible and sustainable mission movement bearing impact on global Christianity.

THE HOLY SPIRIT AND MISSION SPIRITUALITY: THE CASE OF YOIDO FULL GOSPEL CHURCH

Younghoon Lee

Beginning with just five church members fifty years ago, Yoido Full Gospel Church – referred to as YFGC hereafter – has become the largest church in the world with a membership of 780,000 (as of the end of 2008). Such remarkable growth of the church may be the result of practising fervently the Pentecostal Holy Spirit movement and emphasizing mission and evangelism both domestically and abroad.

The mission of YFGC has two dimensions. First of all, the church has made every effort in mission in its narrower sense: namely, evangelism for the salvation of souls. At the same time, however, it has also been alert to social issues and willing to take its social responsibility not only in Korea, but also in the wider world.

In this chapter, I would like to review the history of revival and growth of YFGC during the past fifty-four years, and present its theology and practice of mission. The first section will demonstrate that the theology of mission of YFGC is firmly based upon Pentecostal spirituality. The next section will explain how the Pentecostal spirituality and the theology of holistic salvation that are peculiar to YFGC have constituted two dimensions of the church's mission: i.e., mission as personal evangelism and mission as social salvation. I will then introduce a variety of spiritual training programs that keep providing the mission practice of YFGC with fresh motivation.

I. The Theology of Mission of YFGC

1. The Holy Spirit as the Spirit of mission

The modern Pentecostal movement, which began in the U.S.A. early in the twentieth century, has been focusing on the experience of the baptism of the Holy Spirit and the ministry of the early church that are described in the Apostles of Acts. For instance, the characteristics that are distinct in Pentecostal theology, such as the baptism of the Holy Spirit, which is distinguished from the experience of conversion, have deep roots primarily in Acts.[1]

The Holy Spirit in Acts may be understood as the 'Spirit of mission.' The Holy Spirit makes mission plans, and initiates and leads mission. Furthermore, the Holy Spirit empowers the people for mission. Pentecostal theology understands the purpose and meaning of the baptism of the Holy Spirit as being thoroughly for the sake of mission. Based upon their reading of Acts 1 and 2, the Pentecostals indeed assert that the baptism of the Holy Spirit is an event of empowerment for mission.[2] Likewise, the Pentecostals take the events that the Book of Acts recounts as the norms for church so that they may consider evangelization of the world as the goal of their ministry. This is the point which differentiates them from the charismatic movement that appeared after the 1960s. The charismatic groups tend to limit their role to accomplish the spiritual renewal within their own denominations rather than to pursue the global mission.[3]

As a Pentecostal church, YFGC has been also deeply rooted in the model church and mission ministry that Acts prescribes, and endeavors to evangelize the world relying on the Holy Spirit who is the Spirit of mission. Our church believes that every Christian should receive the gift of the Holy Spirit so that he/she may live a life of witness to Jesus Christ in his/her life situation. Moreover, it urges each church member to be a 'little Jesus' who takes after Christ so that he/she may bear plenty of the fruit of the Holy Spirit, and live out the Gospel.

2. Missional Church

The church in the Book of Acts is never a community that is separated from the world. The church enthusiastically participates in mission towards those who are out of the Gospel. All the activities of the church should be

---

[1] William W. Menzies and Robert R. Menzies, *Spirit and Power: Foundations of Pentecostal Experience* (Grand Rapids, Michigan: Zondervan, 2000), 43. There used to be some criticism against putting the theological basis upon narratives such as Acts within Evangelical circles. However, as the result of hermeneutical change within the Evangelical theological circle, the perception that the biblical narratives also can be normative no less than the parts containing direct exhortations has spread. For more details, see Menzies, *Spirit and Power*, 37-61.

[2] Menzies offers two elements as the examples for understanding the baptism of the Holy Spirit from the perspectives that are different from Pentecostalism: i.e., one is the position of the Methodist and Holiness movements that regard the baptism of the Holy Spirit as what is introverted—namely, something for holiness—the other is that of the charismatic movement that ambiguously explains the baptism of the Holy Spirit only as the concept of 'power' or 'spiritual gift' almost missing out its missionary implications.

[3] Menzies, *Spirit and Power*, 32.

essentially mission-centered, and closely connected with mission.[4] The concept of the 'missional church'[5] – a term that has recently attracted attention – understands church principally as an assembly of those who are sent. Church is thus intrinsically missionary. David Bosch remarks, 'Since God is a missionary God, God's people are a missionary people.'[6] Mission is not just a part of a church's ministry. The church itself exists for the sake of mission.

The identity of YFGC as a Pentecostal mission-centred church, with a ministry shaped by the Book of Acts, has been demonstrated whenever the church has had to make an important decision. For instance, unlike the custom of general Korean churches, YFGC built a building for world mission, not education, next to the construction of the main sanctuary. Moreover, although the budget of the church has been inevitably reduced on a large scale since Pastor Yonggi Cho – the founder of the church – retired in 2008, and twenty regional chapels of the church around the Greater Seoul area were separated from the 'mother church' – i.e., YFGC – with 346,000 members, our church has taken the decision to increase the budget for missionary work.

3. Application of the threefold blessing to mission

With a holistic theology of threefold blessing, YFGC has been devoting itself to mission. As the threefold blessing testifies to God's blessing upon 'all aspects of life,' it also emphasizes the salvation that is realized in the present and the kingdom of God that is experienced in this world. Whereas traditional Protestant theology has understood the atonement of Jesus Christ primarily in connection with the salvation of soul, the Pentecostal theology of YFGC stresses that the influence of the atonement of the cross reaches not only the soul but also the body and the circumstances of everyday life.[7]

The theology of holistic salvation expressed in the threefold blessing has influenced the direction of YFGC's mission engagement. As a theological basis, the threefold blessing has inspired YFGC to dedicate itself to personal evangelism, proclaim the divine healing of physical and mental

---

[4] David J. Bosch, *Transforming Mission: Paradigm Shift in Theology of Mission* (Maryknoll: Orbis Books, 1991), 119-20.
[5] For the concept of the 'missional church,' see Darrell L. Guder, ed., *Missional Church: A Vision for the Sending of the Church in North America* (Grand Rapids, Michigan: Eerdmans, 1998).
[6] Bosch, *Transforming Mission*, 372.
[7] Volf rightly points out that Pentecostal theology argues for the material aspect of salvation that can be experienced in this world, whereas traditional Protestantism has sharply distinguished salvation from this-wordly blessings. See, Miroslav Volf, 'Materiality of Salvation,' *Journal of Ecumenical Studies* 26 (1989): 453-54.

diseases as well as embark on social services, and make every effort to transform society according to the Christian Gospel and values.

YFGC's belief in God's blessing has emphasized that Christians should not be satisfied simply with God's blessing in their lives. The point in God's blessing for the believers is for them to share it with their neighbors for the glory of God and use it for mission. The last article of the 'Seven Beliefs of YFGC,' i.e., the 'belief of sharing and caring' clearly epitomizes the church's communal understanding of God's blessing. A genuinely blessed church cannot hold the blessing to itself. It comes to acquire a genuine willingness to share what God has given with their neighbours in need, proclaiming blessing to the whole world, and setting an example of how to be a recipient of God's blessing. In this sense, the message of the threefold blessing has a holistic, social, and intrinsically missionary connotation.[8]

II. Mission Engagement of YFGC

As stated above, YFGC's mission engagement has two dimensions: i.e., personal evangelism and social salvation. Since the church's vision of holistic salvation intrinsically encompasses a social dimension, while still putting its priority on evangelization for saving souls, the church has been also able to carry out a mission of social involvement. Such a combination of two types of mission engagements resonates with the assertion of John Wesley, the founder of the Methodist church, who already put emphasis not only on individual sanctification, but also on social sanctification. It is also in the spirit of the fifth article of the Lausanne Covenant that affirms the importance of Christian social responsibility.[9]

---

[8] 'The Gospel of Blessing' as a part of the fivefold blessing is unique belief and theology of YFGC. The fivefold blessing of YFGC—i.e., regeneration, the fullness of the Holy Spirit, divine healing, divine blessing, and the second coming of the Lord—may look similar to the fourfold gospel—namely, regeneration, sanctification, divine healing, and the second coming of Jesus Christ—yet the former has replaced the latter's 'sanctification' with 'the fullness of the Holy Spirit.' YFGC's fivefold gospel is also distinguished from the traditional Pentecostal fivefold gospel. Donald Dayton presents regeneration, sanctification, the baptism in the Holy Spirit, and the eschatological expectation as five core beliefs of Pentecostals (Donald Dayton, *Theological Roots of Pentecostalism* [Grand Rapids, MI: Baker Academic, 1991]). Note that this version of the fivefold gospel does not include the gospel of blessing. See, Frank Macchia, *Baptized in the Spirit: A Global Pentecostal Theology* (Grand Rapids: Zondervan, 2006), 208. For more about YFGC's fivefold gospel and the threefold blessing, see Younghoon Lee, *The Holy Spirit Movement in Korea: Its Historical and Theological Development* (Oxford: Regnum Books International, 2009), 100-102; idem, *Cross, the Root of the Full Gospel Faith* [Korean] (Seoul: Institute for Church Growth, 2011), 16-37.

[9] For Lausanne Covenant, see C. R. Padilla, *New Face of Evangelism: An International Symposium on the Lausanne Covenant* (Downers Grove: IVP, 1976).

1. Mission as personal evangelism

1. SAVING SOULS

Through the empowerment of the Holy Spirit at Pentecost, church leaders and believers of the early church changed into daring evangelists. YFGC regards such change as the standard for evangelism and mission. The church has thus raised up many Spirit-filled evangelists to save souls.

2. CHURCH GROWTH AND CHURCH PLANTING

Since it was founded in 1958 with only five church members including Pastor Yonggi Cho himself, YFGC has been growing rapidly through the message of the fivefold gospel and the threefold blessing that brought hope and encouragement to those who were in need through the power of the Holy Spirit. As a result, the church's membership reached 100,000 by 1979, 200,000 by 1981, 500,000 by 1985, and 700,000 by 1992. This dramatic growth was the result of YFGC's single-hearted dedication to evangelism in its effort to carry out the Great Commission of Jesus Christ. This experience of evangelism and the resultant growth of YFGC has inspired many churches in Korea and abroad.

Moreover, YFGC also has been so active in church planting so that it has planted and supported 439 churches throughout the nation as of October, 2012. Besides, since the leadership transition of the church in 2008, the church has begun to put its twenty regional chapels, located throughout the Greater Seoul metropolitan area, on their feet to encourage them to more effectively evangelize their local communities. Their status of full independence was finally granted in January 2010. The total church membership of those chapels amounted to 346,000 at that time.

3. EVANGELIZATION OF THE WORLD

Pastor Yonggi Cho envisioned YFGC's evangelization of the world from the very early phase of his ministry. He founded Full Gospel World Mission to accelerate that vision. YFGC has so far sent about 700 missionaries to 65 countries, and its missionaries have planted 792 churches. In addition, Pastor Cho has for a long time conducted mass crusades around the world. In September 1997, more than 1.5 million people attended his Sao Paulo crusade. As the successor to Pastor Cho, I am also focusing my efforts on evangelizing the world.[10]

---

[10] The Committee for the 50 Year Annals, *A 50 Year History of Yoido Full Gospel Church: 50 Years for Mission, A Great Journey* [Korean] (Seoul: Yoido Full Gospel Church, 2008), 132-133.

2. Mission as social involvement

1. SETTING SOCIAL AGENDA AND RAISING CHRISTIAN LEADERS

YFGC founded *The Kukmin Ilbo Daily*, a newspaper company, in 1988 for the purpose of setting a social agenda from the Christian worldview. This is one of the most conspicuous projects YFGC initiated for social salvation. The *Kukmin Ilbo Daily* includes a section called 'Mission Today' as a vehicle for diagnosing social problems and proposing solutions from the Christian perspective. The newspaper has been cooperating with various NGOs in its efforts for social transformation, and it has been very active in raising funds to help disaster areas in Korea and abroad.

YFGC launched an organization called 'The Full Gospel Holy City Environment Movement' in 2009 to cope with the environmental crisis caused by global warming from the perspective of Christian belief in God's creation. The movement is promoting campaigns such as more usage of mass transportation and energy conservation.

Another aspect of YFGC's social involvement is education. YFGC contributes to raising Christian leaders for the 21st century through Hansei University in Gunpo-city, Full Gospel Youngsan Theological Seminary in Seoul, and Bethesda Christian University in California, U.S.A.

2. SOCIAL WELFARE PROJECT

YFGC established a welfare complex called Elim Welfare Town in Gunpo-city, Gyeonggi-do in 1988, which is one of the largest welfare facilities in Asia and began to implement the outreach programs for the underprivileged youth, and the elderly people with no one to rely on. Afterwards, it has continued to expand its welfare mission by establishing Elim Mission Center, a vocational school, and a specialized care home for the elderly.

YFGC has served its poor neighbours beyond borders, religion and ideology through a UN-affiliated international NGO named 'Good People' since 1999. The local projects include a medical clinic for children, health care through the medical service corps, child protection through cooperation with a local centre for children and support programmes for senior citizens who live alone, the handicapped and child-headed households. In addition, the church opened an institute called 'Free Civic College' to help North Korean refugees' successful settlement in Korea. As a result, 15 convenience stores are currently run by North Korean refugees throughout Seoul. Meanwhile, YFGC are laying foundations for mission overseas through activities such as the support of educational facilities, development of drinking water systems, environmental amelioration, medical service and construction of hospitals in the so-called 'third world'.

In addition, since 1984 YFGC has been supporting free surgery for children with heart disease. The number of Korean and foreign children supported as patients by the church now exceeds 4,500. In 1982, our church established the 'Sharing Movement' so that it distributed the necessities to orphanages, nursing homes, urban slums, Sorok-do – a special area for people suffering from Hansen's Disease – and rural churches across the nation. Since 1992, it has been helping the underprivileged in the society through a movement of donating old clothes and, since 1993, through a campaign of collecting waste paper. In 2003, it opened the Full Gospel Medical Center to provide medical services in the villages without doctors as well as to foreign workers, the handicapped, and people from rural churches.

3. THE SUPPORT OF NORTH KOREA FOR HUMANITARIAN REASONS AND THE ESTABLISHMENT OF INFRASTRUCTURE IN PREPARATION FOR REUNIFICATION

YFGC has been helping the North Koreans through the 'Good People' NGO by sending corn seeds and fertilizers, supporting meals for children, and donating medicine for tuberculosis. In 2007, the church began construction of the 'Yonggi Cho Cardiologist Hospital' in Pyongyang for the treatment of children with heart disease. This can be the basis of the reunification of Korea, going beyond the dimension of humanitarian economic support.

III. The Mission Training and Faith Training of YFGC

It is because the faith training programmes of YFGC are designed and practised in a mission-oriented fashion that the church keeps on inspiring a missionary ethos among its church members and sustains its identity as a missional church.

1. Mission-oriented worship service

The worship service of YFGC is mission-oriented. Above all, the preaching which takes place in the worship service is based on mission spirituality. The message of Pastor Cho regarding hope emphasizes that hope delivered through the gospel should be disseminated in local areas, in the wider society, and in the wider world, as well as in the personal life of believers. I also highlight in each sermon that the mission of the church is evangelism and charity, and all church members should live a mission-oriented life to testify to the gospel and to share love. Immediately after the preaching, YFGC has a time for altar call. This also demonstrates how much the worship service of YFGC focuses on the salvation of unbelievers, and on mission. In addition, we pray for others, all churches, leaders, nations, peoples and social issues as well as for personal matters during the unison prayer session, which is a significant part of our worship service as. This demonstrates that all church members participate in mission as evangelism and mission as social involvement.

2. Sharing of testimonies for the missionary work

Sharing of testimony is a characteristic of the Pentecostal tradition. Mission reports and the testimonies of missionaries are introduced through almost all activities of the church such as the public worship service, church newspapers such as the *Invitation to Happiness* and the *Full Gospel Family Newspaper*, a monthly magazine called *Plus Life*, and cell meetings. For instance, whenever Pastor Cho or I make a mission trip to overseas or domestic areas, our church airs a short video presentation about the mission trips in a public worship service to make the congregation recognize that each one of us should live as a witness of Jesus Christ, and to emphasize that the purpose of the church's existence is mission.

3. Mission conference

An annual mission conference is held for a week – either in the third or fourth week of May – at YFGC. Many missionaries dispatched by YFGC return to Korea with their family members during this period, and worship God under the warm welcome of the congregation. They also have a time to replenish their spiritual, psychological, and physical strength. In addition, missionaries may introduce their missionary work through the many worship services that are held during the conference, and they may have opportunities of fund raising.

A mission conference is a session for all church members to pledge offerings for mission as well as an opportunity to encourage missionaries. Whenever mission conference is held, the church members renew their sense of mission and recognize that the church exists for mission by watching the films that introduce the mission ministry in various regions of the world and by listening to special praise songs from overseas.

4. 'The World Mission' and 'The Revival Korea'

YFGC provides various outreach programs inside and outside the country every year. The Youth and Collegiate Department of YFGC plays a main role in this. 'The World Mission' – a short-term overseas mission trip program – provides young adults with opportunities to participate in various ministries by participating in the mission fields where YFGC's official missionaries are serving. In 2012, about 320 young people participated in this program in 21 countries. 'The Revival Korea' – a short-term, domestic mission trip programme – gives opportunities to serve the churches that YFGC planted around the nation. In 2012, around 900 church members took part in the programme. In addition, a great number of young people in YFGC are eager to engage in domestic evangelism so that they help grow many rural churches, and bring lost souls to Jesus Christ. The young people who become involved in such programmes develop a mission-oriented faith by directly experiencing YFGC's existing mission ministry inside and outside the country.

5. FMTC or Full Gospel Mission Training Course

The Mission and Church Planting Department of YFGC has run a programme called Full Gospel Missionary Training Course (FMTC) for pastors since 1994, and for the laity since 1995. The laity course consists of 12 weeks of lectures including theories of mission as well as mission reports from missionaries to various regions and cultures. It also includes two training camp sessions for reinforcement of team ministry and spiritual development. The trainees then take a short-term mission trip. The pastors' course is mandatory for all pastors of YFGC. This program is also included in the curriculum of the new pastors' training programme. All in all, the FMTC helps sustain the identity of YFGC as a missional church.

6. Crusade for the Asian Christians in Korea

The Crusade for the Asian Christians in Korea has been held every year since 1989. More than 4,000 Chinese-speaking Christians came from twenty different countries in 2012. The participants attend revivals and prayer meetings at Osanri Prayer Mountain, a Friday all-night prayer meeting and Sunday worship services of YFGC. Moreover, those pastors and church leaders visit some cell group meetings of YFGC, and have fellowship with the cell members. Through such a crusade, many church members of YFGC get chances to serve and have fellowship with the participants. Furthermore, they come to have more interest in mission, and pledge their continuous commitment and dedication to the mission work of YFGC.

7. CGI or Church Growth International

YFGC's extraordinarily rapid growth has increased international interest in the Pentecostal movement and church growth. This led Pastor Yonggi Cho to found the Church Growth International (CGI) in 1976. It provides education and training on church growth for its interdenominational members in more than 180 countries. There are many cases of pastors who enabled their church to grow rapidly by researching YFGC's revival through the CGI, or learning from Pastor Cho. A CGI conference is held every other year. The latest one was held in 2011.

IV. Conclusion

As stated above, YFGC makes every effort to carry out its mission as a missional church based on the mission spirituality of Pentecostalism and the Book of Acts. The message of the threefold blessing of YFGC has implications for mission, because it is a theology of holistic salvation as well as a social expression of the gospel. The blessing that Christians get from their threefold salvation has not only an individual dimension, but it is also extended to the realm of community and society.

Mission engagement of YFGC has been practised through the dynamic relationship between two emphases – namely evangelism for an individual's salvation, and social engagement modeled on the almsgiving ministry of the early church. Historically speaking, it can be argued that since the mission as evangelism resulted in saving souls and church growth, the capacity which this generated has made mission as social engagement possible.

I was elected and inaugurated as the second senior pastor of YFGC in 2008. Defining the ministry that YFGC has to pursue as mission and almsgiving, I emphasize in my preaching and teaching both dedication to preaching the gospel to the ends of the earth, and living a life to share God's blessings with our church and with each church member.

SPIRITUALITY AND CHRISTIAN MISSION: THE JOURNEY OF YOUNGNAK PRESBYTERIAN CHURCH, SEOUL, KOREA

Chul-shin Lee

What does it mean to have motivation for mission? Both the Apostle Paul and the Rev Kyung-Chik Han of South Korea had unique motivation in regards to mission which will be evaluated here. After discussing both the Apostle Paul and the Rev Han, I will offer my own personal perspective on mission as a pastor of a large church in South Korea.

Paul's Motivations

The Apostle Paul has exercised immeasurable influence on Christianity. In the Book of Acts, the story of Paul's conversion is mentioned three times: in chapters 9:1-12, chapter 22, and chapter 26. The first was written by himself and is a sharing of his own personal experiences, while the other two were confessions given through testimony. His testimonies were inspired by his assurance of the gospel through repentance, a vision that he received, and his passion.

Through his conversion, Paul came to believe that Jesus Christ was the Son of God. He said that he had met Jesus Christ, the one that he had been persecuting. This was something that he had never thought possible. His attitude changed and he no longer considered himself to be the most righteous. Paul spent time repenting after meeting Jesus Christ.

1 John 1:9 states that if we confess our sins, we are given grace and are forgiven. Verse 17 talks about the fullness of the Holy Spirit and that if you are assured of your forgiveness then the Holy Spirit will be present and active. In other words, when one repents of one's sins, one can experience the grace of forgiveness and can receive the fullness of God. Being certain about the grace that comes from forgiveness causes one to recognize that God has forgiven sin through the cross of Jesus Christ. Finally, there is an acceptance of Jesus Christ as Lord. Paul mentions several times in his epistles that through meeting with Jesus Christ, he became a new creature.

Paul's assurance of the gospel is crucial. A medical doctor can work to heal patients with their medical knowledge. A doctor becomes more confident as they receive clinical training and experience of helping patients. However, doctors can help patients heal even without full knowledge or experiences that bring them a deeper assurance of their profession.

Similarly, a pastor can be involved in the spiritual care of his people. They can teach biblical knowledge and theology that can have an impact on the recipients. However, being a witness of the gospel means that they need a personal assurance of the gospel – without it there will not be any spiritual change or healing. Paul's assurance of the gospel and conviction that Jesus Christ was his Lord and Savior was what started his devotion to mission. This is how the Apostle Paul was able to start his missionary work.

In Acts 9:15, it is written that Jesus told Ananais what sort of ministry Saul was going to have. Saul, who became Paul, followed the vision that was given to Ananais and witnessed to the Gentiles in Antioch and Asia Minor. In Acts 16, Paul goes to Macedonia. He would also go to Europe and in Acts 19 Rome was his final destination. The other apostles were active in witnessing, but imagining witnessing in Rome and across Europe could have been a lofty ambition. However, Paul had a vision for the Gentiles and it was through that vision that people all over the world, for centuries, have come to faith in Jesus Christ. Those who call themselves Christians are the fruit of Paul's endeavors.

As Paul had assurance of Jesus Christ and the gospel, he was able to persevere. In Acts 9:16, Jesus said that he would show Paul how much he would have to suffer in his name. As Paul would go to many different regions, he would also deal with various kinds of suffering. In 2 Corinthians 11:23, he writes about the sufferings he experienced on his journeys. He suffered beatings, went to prison, and even starved after a shipwreck. However, this suffering did not stop him from continuing what he felt like he was called to do. Why did Paul decide to endure in his suffering? It was his passion. The assurance of Jesus Christ and the gospel started a fire in his heart and he felt that he needed to continue. Until the end of his life, he was able to witness to many people who would come to call themselves followers of Jesus Christ.

The Motivations of the Rev Kyung-Chik Han (1902-2000)

Rev Kyung-Chik Han was the founder of the church at which I currently serve, Youngnak Presbyterian Church in Seoul, South Korea. He dedicated his life to his pastoral ministry but it was not limited to one or two churches. His ministry had a lasting impact on many churches in Korea. Dr. Nak-Jun Baek stated, 'He has faithfully done exactly what has been needed to bring the gospel to this country.'[1] While evaluating Rev Han, Rev

---

[1] Byung-Hee Kim (ed), *Han Kyung-Chik Moksa (Rev Kyung-Chik Han)* (Seoul: Kyujang Moohwasa, 1982), 128.

Hyang-Rok Cho stated, 'He has been a pastor that included the whole race and the nation in the realms of his ministry'.[2]

Rev Kyung-Chik Han was born on 29 December 1902 in a farming village northeast of Pyongyang as a farmer's son. Rev Han started attending church at an early age and began studying the Bible. His father had not sent him to a traditional school, but brought him to Jin Kwang School that was operated by the church. At school he studied science, Confucianism, and Chinese characters. He also learned about Christian faith and thinking at church and at school.

On his path to school, he walked by the front gate of a wealthy family's home. This home had the passage John 3:16 written on it: 'For God so loved the world that he gave his only begotten son, that whosoever believeth in him should not perish, but have everlasting life' (Jn 3:16 KJV). Seeing this passage frequently caused him to memorize it and it had a very significant impact on the shaping on the foundation of his faith. The verse was still planted deep on his heart during the later years of his life.[3]

As he had an interest in further studies, Rev Han worked as an assistant doing secretarial work under missionary William N Blair in order to fund his tuition. He then entered Soongsil University and majored in science. He felt that studying science would enable him to serve his nation and his people. He put a lot of effort into his studies and was even able to win a prize in a speech contest. Vacations were spent going on trips with the Christian Students Association to preach and share the gospel.

During a summer break from university, he was assured of his faith while working for William N Blair. Korea was under Japanese occupation at that time. While working, he changed his mind and believed that science was not what was going to bring radical change. Rev Han said his time was devoted to one prayer, 'How can I ultimately serve the people?'[4] He described in his writings how he spent one day praying while walking. He felt that it was during this time that God gave him a new vision and a purpose in life. He believed that this was when he was chosen by God to be used as a vessel. His thinking had changed and he said, 'It was good to study science and serve the people, but there is a need to see a fundamental renewal of the people. In order to see a renewal, the gospel must be spread.'[5] All of this would result in a decision to change his field of study to theology.

After graduation from a university in Korea, he went to study liberal arts at Emporia State University in Kansas. He then went to study theology at Princeton Theological Seminary and graduated in 1928. While preparing to

---

[2] Kim, *Han Kyung-Chik Moksa*, 159.
[3] Sungbae Kim (ed), *Youngnak Church 35 Years* (Seoul: Youngnak Church Press, 1983), 49.
[4] Mahn-Yol Lee, 'Talk with Rev Han Kyung-Chik', *The Korean Church and History* 1 (1991), 138.
[5] Lee, 'Talk with Rev Han Kyung-Chik', 139.

start a doctorate at Yale University, he developed symptoms of tuberculosis – at the time this was a fatal disease that could not be healed.

He could not find treatment and was told to try to find a place to relax and to allow for a natural recovery. He then spent two years in a treatment centre in New Mexico. The time in New Mexico was another time to focus on prayer and also to read many books. He came to feel that spending the last days of his life studying would be a sin, as he felt that he had debts to repay to the different people who had helped him. He prayed to go back to Korea for a period of three years and asked to be allowed to spend his final moments there.[6] His prayer had two parts. First, he confessed his sin. He did not feel that it was a sin to study but it was his ambition as a student that was sinful. It was this desire for his name to be known and for wanting a successful life. Wanting these things was a pursuit that consisted of loving worldly things. Second, he asked for an opportunity for ministry. He committed his life to God. He then spent some more time in recovery in Denver, Colorado until he was able to return to Korea in 1932.

His return to Korea was met with persecution. Korea was still under Japanese occupation and Japan was also engaged in war with the United States. As Rev Han studied in the United States, the Japanese saw him as a threat. The Japanese Government blocked his position as a professor at Soongsil University. He was also investigated by the Japanese for his pastoral ministry at Sinuiju City and was put in prison after interrogation and torture by the Japanese.

Eventually, during 1942, he was forced to resign as a pastor. He then ministered for three years until the end of the war in a welfare facility called the Borinwon that was responsible for aiding orphans and widows. After the Japanese surrendered in 1945, Russian soldiers came and settled in North Korea. They brought in communism and seized control. American soldiers came to South Korea. The country would then be divided into the North and the South. In October 1945, Rev Han escaped to South Korea to flee from communism in the North. Through experiencing Japanese imperialism and then Communist rule in the North, Rev Han understood how precious one's nation actually was. This confirmed his belief that the gospel was the only thing that could meet the needs of people and uplift them.

Youngnak Church was planted by Rev Han and those who escaped with him from the Communist North. Even with all the sufferings he endured, Rev Han kept his passion for ministry. He ministered to his new church with a vision that included evangelism, education, and service, with a goal to evangelize to the whole nation.

---

[6] Won-Sul Lee, Seung-Joon Lee and Joong-Sik Han, *Just Three More Years to Live! The Story of Rev Kyung-Chik Han* (Seoul: Rev Kyung-Chik Han Memorial Foundation, 2005), 85.

He aided in the planting of 600 churches in South Korea. At that time South Korea was still a young and under-developed country and he was a pioneer who contributed to service in the community. Youngnak Church continues its work and still runs non-profit organizations and facilities for orphans, the disabled, widows, and the elderly. Education was also a large part of his vision. Secondary schools and universities were built and the church currently operates nine schools. Rev Han also focused on military evangelism as all able-bodied Korean young men are required to serve in the military. All these ministries, facilities, and organizations contributed to the overall purpose of evangelizing the whole of the South Korean nation.

One crucial part of his work was with evangelization of North Korea. Strong emphasis was placed on this in the 1990s. Rev Han was presented with the Templeton Prize in 1992 and said that that the whole of the prize money, equivalent to nearly one million dollars, should be used for missions in North Korea.

Rev Han helped plant the foundation of Christianity in South Korea. Even at the point of his retirement, he had another vision to evangelize the whole continent of Asia and established the Asian Church Development Foundation. His assurance of the gospel and his love for his country and people gave him the passion to continue to minister throughout his life.

My Motivation

I would like to also share my story. I was born into a Christian family in which my father was a pastor. I consider it a blessing to have grown up in the church. I was an active participant at my church and was in the choir and volunteered as a Sunday School teacher. I felt satisfaction with my church and spiritual life.

As the end of the winter vacation of my first year of high school, I went to a revival service in which the pastor shared a powerful sermon on repentance. Many of the individuals there repented and shared how their lives were changed. However, I did not do the same. I felt that I didn't have any sins to repent. I felt that I lived a life that was a good example and thought that those who repented were the ones who committed terrible sins.

However, since I was surrounded by those who repented, I was curious about their experiences and asked them about their coming to repentance. One man told me to read the Ten Commandments. I read them all, away from all the people since I did not want any possibility to feel embarrassed. I did not want my sins to be exposed.

I started reading each commandment carefully. Still, I did not feel like I found any sins. After repeating the reading, I started to think about my sins and I felt the Holy Spirit bring to my mind the sins that I never wanted to recall. I had wanted to hide them and I certainly did not want to expose them. I wanted to continue to be ignorant. I rationalized my sins by saying that others were doing them as well so it was not important. I could not deny them anymore. I saw them clearly in front of me. It was that moment I realized that although I wanted to think I was righteous, I was actually an awful sinner.

I confessed my sins and I also received assurance that my sins were forgiven. I was certain that I was a new creature and had a new life in Christ. I was then confident that Jesus Christ was my personal Savior and the Lord of my life. After that experience, I continued to serve in my church but was no longer serving for my own satisfaction or to prove my own diligence. The assurance gave me a passion and I was filled with thanksgiving to God.

I also have a vision to share the gospel with the Korean people. I am still working with my church to plant and nurture churches and work with schools, the military, and local communities. I also desire to see the young generation find assurance of the gospel. When they are assured of the gospel, I hope that it will fire up their vision and passion in their souls to continue in missions.

North Korea is also a key interest and a challenge for our church. More than 13,000 people have escaped North Korea and have come to the South. They are a key part of our ministry. Some are now studying theology and some are being nurtured to serve as the next leaders of missions to North Korea.

The people from the North find it difficult to adapt to the democratic and capitalistic way of South Korean society. We pray for them and aid them in finding work. There are Bible Study groups that are trying to nurture the faith of those who have come from the North. The differences of their ideas and their verbal expressions make it difficult to easily adapt to an existing group.

We also aid those in the North by sending supplies and necessary aid. Our current policy is that we aim to help children and patients in North Korea through goods and supplies and not through cash donations.

My personal motivation in regards to mission is like that of the apostle Paul and Rev Han – the assurance of the gospel. I have been saved in the midst of my sin. I am assured that Jesus Christ is my personal Savior and the Lord of my life. Obtaining assurance of the gospel brings forth passion to witness. I see this in my own life and especially in the lives of Paul and the Rev Han.

GRACE KOREAN CHURCH, CALIFORNIA, USA: MISSION FROM THE MARGINS WITH LITTLE NOTICE (OF COURSE!)

Wonsuk Ma

What Was Not Present in Edinburgh 1910

The celebration of the centenary of the Edinburgh Missionary Conference of 1910 clearly revealed that several fundamental elements of Christian mission have drastically changed. This study is to illustrate these changes by identifying a surprise mission agent and its process of becoming missional. From hindsight, looking back on the 100-year development of world Christianity, we note that there are several things that were not present not only in the conference, but more importantly in the world of Christian mission.

The first was the absence of the churches from the global south (the 'southern church' in a short form). Less than 20 of the 1,200 delegates represented the mission field, and Latin America and Africa were almost completely missing. Equally missing was any real expectation that these 'heathen' churches would one day become a missionary force.

The second absence was the charismatic Christianity that had risen from the fringes of social and ecclesial structures. The Pentecostal movement, popularized by African-American Holiness preacher William Seymour in downtown Los Angeles between 1906 and 1909, was not represented at the Edinburgh conference. Its doctrines were too controversial and its leaders insufficiently credentialed to be considered for the gathering. There is no doubt that some leaders of the conference had knowledge of this controversy. This movement in its ever-increasing diversity of forms has outgrown all the Protestant believers put together, and it does not show any sign of slowing.

The third absence was any notion that the ever-powerful western church might lose its strengths, resources, and leadership in world Christianity and Christian mission. At the height of colonial imperialism, the west, as a political and ecclesial power, had all the reasons why evangelism of the world could be completed within their generation. The notion of the 'white man's burden' was widely and genuinely shared by the western church. Thus, world mission was accepted as a historic calling which God had placed on western Christianity.

The fourth absence is migration and its unique implications to mission. Although there are several other important developments that have serious implications to mission in the twentieth century, the increasing mobility of people en masse has introduced a lasting effect in several areas. The rapid Islamisation of Europe is often attributed to the church's dwindling dynamism and increasing Islamic population through migration and natural births. At the same time, migrant churches have the potential to re-energize the western host society and church.

A Case of New Mission Players from a New Margin

My search for a case to illustrate these changes is naturally directed to the southern churches, such as those found in Korea, China, Latin American Evangelicalism or African Initiated Churches. The Pentecostal-charismatic orientation of these growing churches has been well researched. My candidate is an Asian immigrant church in Southern California, south of Los Angeles. Grace Korean Church (GKC) in Fullerton has never called itself Pentecostal, but like many large Korean churches, the GKC is extremely Pentecostal in its theology, worship and ethos. Although it is formally a Presbyterian church, Rev Keehong Han, the current senior pastor of the church, frequently uses typical Pentecostal expressions such as 'full of fire' and 'baptism in the Holy Spirit', while he regularly prays for healing and exorcism in almost every worship and prayer gathering. Han, the current leader of GKC, characterizes the life of the church in two areas: the work of the Holy Spirit and mission.

With its 4,500 membership and a vast 26.2-acre 'campus', the church forms a distinct landmark in the city. With another large Korean church less than 1.5 miles from GKC, Fullerton has witnessed a significant Korean Christian presence in the last decades. However, the church's presence and its activities have been mysteriously hidden to mainstream society and media, except for a few nearby ministers, some missiologists and several short reports in the *Orange County Register*, a local newspaper. City authorities have become well aware of GKC through their unbending resolution in their prayerful and persistent pursuit of difficult building and planning permits.

This hiddenness has to do with the GKC's exclusive association with other Korean churches in the area and in the country (as well as in Korea). Although there is an English-speaking congregation, primarily made up of second-generation Koreans, the core group is the Korean-speaking, first-generation immigrant believers. Understandably, no English literature has been available to properly introduce the church and its impact to society and mission.

Why the GKC?

I am not an insider participant of this church. My first acquaintance with the church was through the GKC's widespread reputation as a single-minded missionary church during my studies in Southern California in the early 1990s. The GKC was not the largest among the Korean immigrant churches, nor was the broadcast preaching of Rev Kwang-shin Kim, its founder, impressively eloquent in delivery or profound in its theological content. Nonetheless, Kim was generally known as an unusual leader who had successfully mobilized his church for mission. Some of his missionary episodes became legendary as they defied many common-sense missiological rules. My visit to their rented school facility affirmed the rumors of him and the church, in spite of the large size of the congregation. My good lunch-meeting with Kim further confirmed his single-vision missionary commitment. Their missionary feat is truly impressive, and so are their mission players. Above all, the GKC and Kim represent a surprising new missionary player from a social and ecclesial fringe that has potential to influence the Christianity of the host nation and its missionary work.

This study is first of all descriptive, as the story of the GKC is not widely known outside of Korean-American Christian circles. It includes a look at Kim, the founder, the growth of the church, and the development of its missionary work, particularly its missionary enterprise in the former Soviet Union states. The second aspect of the study is a critical analysis of the GKC's mission-thinking and practices. Both perspectives are fully integrated together. The study concludes with evaluations, contributions, concerns and suggestions for the future of its mission work.

As indicated, there is not much literary work available. There are only two books, printed in Korean: the first one is an eclectic collection of stories, particularly on the GKC's mission to the former Soviet states,[1] and the second is a Korean book recently published with three distinct components: a synopsis of the construction of the Vision Center; an autobiography of Kim; and an autobiography of Keehong Han, the successor to Kim.[2] To them, two additional sources can be mentioned. The Grace Mission International (GMI), the new umbrella mission network, an outgrowth from GKC, but now including many 'daughter' churches in the States and in Korea, published a mission handbook listing its missionaries and a brief description of their ministries.[3] Also Yang, the GKC's mission pastor, wrote a Doctor of Ministry research project on the GKC's

---

[1] Hee-sung Park, *Gara Ganda: Mission Story, Expansion of the Kingdom of God* [in Korean] (Seoul: Gwang-ya, 2001). *Gara* in Korean is an imperative form of 'go', while *ganda* is a response form meaning, '(yes) am going'.
[2] Seung-hwan Baek (ed), *The Traces of Jesus: Miracle Story of Grace Korean Church* [in Korean] (n.p.: Yechan, 2009). This book is treated as a compilation and the three major sections, as well as several short pieces, will be identified by their authors.
[3] Grace Mission International, *To the Ends of the Earth* (Fullerton, CA: GMI, 2008).

missionary work.[4] Rev Han kindly arranged for his two mission leaders to be available to respond to my inquiries for documents and information.[5] Although it is useful to see the extent of the GKC's missionary work, it does not provide any useful data to unearth their mission motivation, mission approach nor to assess their effectiveness. In fact, the objectivity of all the presentation and the validity of the data cannot be established, and there is sufficient reason to detect the promotional nature of some parts of the sources. This study, therefore, attempts to 'read between the lines' in light of various personal comments I have received, especially from those who are either a part of the church or close to its mission operation. The primary purpose, however, is, as stated above, to uncover this 'hidden' missionary gem in the heart of a western society, and its potential contribution to the Christianity and society of its host nation.

Kwang-shin Kim

Kwang-shin Kim was born in 1935,[6] about ten years before the liberation of Korea from the harsh Japanese annexation of the country. He must have spent a few of his primary school years under the Japanese assimilation curriculum which denied Koreans their language and culture. His experience with the Korean War as a teenager greatly impacted him. He volunteered to serve in the army although he had not reached the required age. His early years are not known, but he must have witnessed, if not indeed gone through, the decades of poverty and political struggle under military dictatorship.

He graduated from the prestigious Seoul National University and served as an English teacher at Sookmyung Girls' High School in Seoul. There is no doubt that he went through an elite course as a man who endured the turbulent period of the nation. For an unknown reason, he migrated to Argentina and then to the United States. What he did in the States before his seminary education is not stated.

He had a radical conversion experience when he was 42, although he had been a church-goer and even a choir conductor, through his brother-in-law who made an intentional trip to share his experience of God's radical healing of a cancer. This triggered a chain of events which eventually led to Kim's encounter with God's reality. He was also baptized in the Holy

---

[4] Tai Choul Yang, 'A Study on the Mission Strategies of the Grace Korean Church in the Light of the Selected Five Modern Missions Strategies' [in Korean] (Doctor of Ministry Dissertation, Midwest University, 2009).

[5] I am grateful to Rev Tai Choul Yang, Mission Pastor, and Elder Steve Hong, a member of the GKC's Missions Committee for their help in obtaining necessary information.

[6] Nowhere can it be found where he was born; but his Korean accent strongly suggests Kyungsang Province of South Korea. However, he was in Seoul when he was 15 years old.

Spirit. He claimed that several spiritual gifts accompanied this series of events, including seeing a 'weeping Jesus' in his vision. Although he did not specify what he had been doing, two years later he began his seminary education at Biola. He founded the GKC in 1982 upon completion of his theological education. The first meeting had three families in attendance. When the church celebrated its 28th anniversary in 2010, the membership of the church had reached 4,500. The church now has around 6,000 registered members with various ministries. It currently owns an extensive infrastructure on its 26.2 acre property in Fullerton, Southern California.

Kim's vision of a local church was, and still is (even under new leadership), a community of believers empowered by the Holy Spirit to fulfill the Great Commission. This mission-centered ecclesiology was born of Kim's vision of a weeping Jesus in his early Christian life.[7] His life's journey as an immigrant in a 'foreign land' may have contributed to this sense of a missional call.[8] This dual theological pillar of GCK is attested by Rev Kee-hong Han, Kim's successor since 2004.

> From the beginning of the GKC, there has been a special anointing of the Holy Spirit. Many are healed, words proclaimed through Kim convict and convince hearts and lives through the power of the Holy Spirit; and many ardent atheists experience the presence and power of God as they enter the church. For the past 27 years, through the Spirit's anointing, the consistent calling of the GKC has been 'world mission' according to the Great Commission.[9]

This priority of mission is visibly, tangibly demonstrated by several realities. The first is a conspicuous banner that greets everyone in the main lobby of the Miracle Center, the main sanctuary. It reads, 'Mission is Prayer, War, and Martyrdom'. This not only demonstrates how the church understands mission, and their resolution to fulfill it, but more importantly shows mission as the very reason for the church's existence. The second is the way mission is financed. The church has consistently spent over 50% of its gross income on mission, and sometimes close to 60%. What is revealing is the reflection on the *modus operandi* of the church's mission finances by a key lay member of the GKC's mission committee.

> It is often said that the GKC spends 60 to 70% of its annual budget for mission, but it is not accurate.... No time was there a ready fund for mission; each time voluntary collection is made to meet urgent needs of mission. In this way, by the end of a year, the church has spent a high proportion of its finance on mission.[10]

---

[7] Kwang-shin Kim, 'Rev Kwang-shin Kim: Apostle of the Gospel with Passion', in *The Traces of Jesus*, 153-54.
[8] An important window to this motivation would be his sermons.
[9] Kee-hong Han, 'The Construction Story of the Vision Center', in Baek, *The Traces of Jesus*, 21. All the Korean translations are the author's.
[10] Suk-koo Hong, an untitled reflection in Baek, *The Traces of Jesus*, 172. The 2008 figures are $10 million mission spending out of $19 million annual budget.

The priority of financial resources given to mission has been demonstrated in the manner in which the church set financial priorities. It was widely known that the remuneration packages for the senior pastor and other ministers on the pastoral staff were equal. Also, for the first 22 years of the church's existence, in spite of rapid growth in numbers and resources, Kim refused to allow the church to own a property. It was argued, by assumption, that owning property distracted the church's attention and financial resources from mission. However, today there is an enormous burden to pay for the 40 million dollar International Prayer Center, completed in 2009. The third is a general perception which Kim was able to shape among the minds of the congregation that missionary service is the best way a Christian can live his or her life. Most members have participated in several short-term mission trips. When Kim suggests a member consider a full-time missionary career, in spite of dreaded fear, this is taken as the eventual climax of one's Christian life at the GKC.[11] Peter Wagner's glowing commendation may reflect Kim's powerful leadership impact on the whole church, and the unusual commitment to, and achievement in, mission: 'I believe David Kim is one of the most significant missionaries and apostles to be counted among them [mission heroes such as William Carey, Hudson Taylor, and David Livingstone]'.[12]

Mission of Grace Korean Church

To illustrate the theological assumptions that motivate its activities, two case studies may be useful. The first is the beginning of the GKC's missionary work in Russia.[13] It is reported that Kim had wept in prayer for five years for the Soviet states with little knowledge of or contact with them. He began to focus his prayer on 450,000 Korean descents scattered widely. In 1990, a 33-member missionary choir was organized, including many youths. With very little missionary experience whatsoever, the first missionary team of the GKC conducted gospel concerts interspersed with Korean folk songs in Sakhalin, Habarovsk, Moscow (Russia), Tashkent (Uzbekistan), and Almata (Kazakhstan). With the grip of Communism still strong, the itinerary came with enough challenges from state and local bureaucracy, the host's strong suspicion of the visitors' motives, a medical emergency, and a tight schedule and budget. Challenges were always overcome through total trust in God's intervention, the sheer determination of Kim and the team, and more importantly, a mind-set of martyrdom. Each formidable challenge proved to be a mere stepping stone for a spiritual and emotional breakthrough in each place. Evangelism was glowingly

---

[11] Kim interprets this to be the full meaning of an 'award-winning Christian': Park, *Gara Ganda*, 24, 26.
[12] C Peter Wagner, an untitled contribution to *The Traces of Jesus*, 167.
[13] A detailed account is found in Park, *Gara Ganda*, 41-70.

successful, although there is no independent report to support the church's publication.

Several immediate fruits were evident. First, in almost all the cities where the initial gospel concert was held, a local congregation was eventually established. Second, all the participants experienced deep missionary commitment, and years later several of them became career missionaries. Third, the church radically entered into a new mission era with intensified awareness. Their experiences were repeatedly shared through preaching, debriefing sessions, small group prayers, and the like. In the same year, ten were officially appointed as missionaries to 'Soviet' cities, while the GKC's 'Soviet' mission plan' was soon expanded beyond the ethnic Koreans. It was popularly known that the church chartered a jumbo jet from Los Angeles to Russia for a follow-up missionary trip. Throughout the flight, the whole team spent time in fasting, prayer and praise.

The second case study concerns Dushanbe Grace Church in Tajikistan which began in 1992 during the civil war period in this recently independent Muslim state.[14] The initial contacts were among 500 ethnic Korean descendants in Dushanbe, the capital city with 600,000 people. Yoon-sup Choi is one of the early GKC missionaries who pioneered a congregation, Dushanbe Grace Church. The church launched an aggressive evangelistic program with various approaches, including a martial arts studio for the city youth and eventually high ranking government officers and police. This sports program has attracted from 20 to 100 daily participants. As with all the church's programs, it begins with a time of prayer and a 15-minute presentation of a Christian message before a Taekwondo session. The church also began a daily feeding program for an average of 300 people, and conducted 30 or 40 short-term medical services (perhaps from the mother church, but without further clarification) for an average of six weeks.

However, at the heart of the evangelistic campaign are prayer and a straightforward presentation of the Christian message of repentance and salvation. Every day, an average of 70 members spend about five hours daily in prayer for the evangelization of the city and the entire nation. Choi organized and trained about 50 members with daily prayer for an hour, and personal evangelism by twos throughout the region. Great results were reported, particularly in rural villages where Muslim leaders accepted the Christian message and as a result entire villages turned to Christ. It is claimed that an estimated 150,000 have heard the presentation of the gospel, although the number cannot be verified. By 1999, the church grew to over 1,000 worshippers with a host of daughter churches throughout the country.

---

[14] The record of this amazing ministry is found in Park, *Gara Ganda*, 230-253.

When the church was bombed in 2000 during a Sunday worship service, 10 were killed and around 100 injured. This revealed several important facts. First, the church's rapid growth and its impact were perceived as a threat to Islam, the state religion. Second, its aggressive evangelistic activities represent a behavioral pattern of religious fundamentalism, which is likely to be met by a radical religious response from the dominant religion. Third, contrary to the intention of the perpetrators, this incident further consolidated this fundamentalist form of Christianity and its religious convictions. The heightened level of religious commitment among the members and the subsequent numerical growth of the church are clear indicators of this response. This also provides an unusual occasion for the GKC to reinforce its commitment and support to mission by offering special prayer sessions, dispatching support groups to the site, and mobilizing resources for the treatment of the injured and support for the families of the dead. It is not quite clear whether this incident has influenced public perception of Christianity or strengthened Muslim fundamentalism. Regardless, it is quite evident that the Christian presence in society was strongly felt.

One can hardly find any articulated theological reflection on the GKC's mission engagement. However, Kim's (and thus the GKC's), mission theology is discernible in sermons, church policies and mission operations. Missionary practices securely anchored on firm theological groundings can ensure the sustainability and consistency of the church's missionary future. Three such theological assumptions are noteworthy.

First, Kim has developed an extremely functional ecclesiology: the very reason for the church's existence is to carry out the missionary mandate. Hence, the spiritual formation and pastoral care is not an end itself, but a means for the building of a missionary community. Kim believes that the numerical growth of the congregation, which broke the 1,000-mark in its third anniversary, is a natural outcome of this mission-oriented nature of the church, and also God's resourcing of the church in order to fulfill the missionary mandate and expand its missionary enterprise.

The second is Kim's missionary pneumatology. His theology is not without controversy, as he assumed a popular Pentecostal-like theological framework, as many Korean churches have done.[15] Prayer for, and expectation of, supernatural manifestations of the Holy Spirit, such as healing, miracles, hearing God's voice, and the like, is an integral part of worship and spirituality at the GKC. The experiential dimension of Christian life, therefore, is greatly emphasised. However, the seriousness of pneumatology in mission takes a very different path from the popular 'wealth and health' theology of modern charismatic Christianity. The power of God through the empowerment of the Holy Spirit is to respond to

---

[15] Officially the GKC is affiliated with the Bosu Hapdong Presbyterian Church in North America.

a missionary call, and take up a lifestyle which includes suffering for the sake of mission. This surprise understanding of 'charismaticity' is a good contrast to the triumphalism for which Pentecostal mission has often been criticized. This pneumatology is closer to the precarious life of Jesus, and the portrayal of the suffering Servant for God's mission (eg, Is 42:1-25).

The third is the subtle eschatological orientation of the church. It is not the millennial kind of urgency which drove early Pentecostals to mission, but the sojourner imagery of human life in this world. It is possible that the unique social makeup of the immigrant congregation may have contributed to this orientation. Combined with a strong sense of purpose, things of this world (be it life, health, possessions or mission opportunities), are all viewed as part of God's providence to fulfill a God-given mandate. This utilitarian view of life also motivates sacrificial offering of what one has, including life.

How Kim, the GKC and its members have understood mission can be illustrated by several characteristics of their mission activities and expressions. The first is the primacy of soul-saving, the typical evangelical trait of mission. At the core of their missionary activity is the presentation of human sinfulness, the atoning work of Christ and the acceptance of Jesus as personal Savior. The 'presentation', however, can take various forms, including an extremely subtle form as seen in the first missionary campaign in the former Soviet locations. The choir's repertoire included old Korean folk songs to touch the emotional depth of multi-generational immigrants in harsh social environments. At the climax of any gathering is a straightforward presentation of Kim's simple message of salvation through Christ. The success of the first mission trip motivated the church to organize many large gospel celebrations in key former Soviet locations. In retrospect, such large-scale gatherings and well-planned 'cultural' presentations (with songs and dramas) proved to have filled social and emotional vacuums left by the collapse of communism. However, this 'cultural' packaging was intended to initially attract people to the eventual presentation of the gospel. The visible end-goal of the GCK's mission, therefore, is evangelism, and this is born of the theological conviction that sin is the fundamental root of all human and social problems. Consequently, their missionary approach is extremely spiritual, including intercessory prayer, belief in supernatural manifestations of God's power through healing and miracles, seeking the Spirit's guidance, and the like. Understandably any social component such as relief work, social services, and cultural interests, are to facilitate the evangelistic and church-planting work.

Also noticeable is the strong orientation to 'foreign' mission, that is, mission that involves the distinct element of 'going', preferably crossing geographical, cultural and religious boundaries. Naturally the church has prioritized its mission to the 'unreached people groups'.[16] The bigger the gap between 'home' and 'over there', the more commitment and sacrifice are demanded, and thus a more desirable mission field. No one raised any question about the neglect of the vast Hispanic population in Southern California as its mission priority. It is possible that, as first-generation Korean immigrants, harsh memories of the Korean War and the ensuing Cold War era, which put Korea in an international hot spot with tensions with communist North Korea, may have caused their enthusiasm for mission to the former Soviet locations. This 'going over there' has been deeply rooted in the Great Commission (Matt 28:19) along with the notion of reaching 'all the nations' and 'to the ends of the earth' (eg, Act 1:8).

Therefore, mission is extremely narrowly defined, and this in part explains the concentrated and focused energy in mission. My quick survey of the *Orange County Register*, the most popular local newspaper, had several reports published. But considering its huge size, both in the size of membership and the magnitude of its campus, its impact to the city of Fullerton and its highly concentrated multi-racial constituencies and its minimal impact on its immediate 'world' may be illustrated by this scanty media appearance. The GKC's mission has not touched many important broader mission agendas.

The above illustrations suggest that the church has adopted a strong 'faith mission' principle. In fact, in my judgment, the mission operation of the GKC is 'faith' mission in its truest meaning, practically stepping into the unknown with expectation of God's presence, guidance, provision, and intervention.

It is almost logically expected that prayer plays a key role, forming the firm bedrock of the church's mission operation. This applies both to the church as a whole, and missionaries in the field. Expectation of God's supernatural manifestation in divine healing and miraculous provision are part of their prayer life.

It is also important to unpack the notion of a missionary 'call'. Most of the early missionaries were not formally trained either in missiology or theology. Many of them are former businessmen, who were deeply committed in mission. When one is 'called' by Kim to go to mission, this is considered God's call to mission. The business is sold, and the house is now on the market. Often the husband will leave for mission, while the rest of the family clears themselves to later join the husband. As mid-career people, once their children's education is complete, many members seriously contemplate a missionary career. In fact, the most important criterion for missionary appointment for the GKC is one's conviction of the call and resolution 'to give life' for the call. Often missionaries go through an unimaginable change of life, from the comfort of North American

---

[16] Yang, 'A Study on the Missions Strategies of the Grace Korean Church', 14-23 notes the priority of unreached people groups in the GKC's strategy.

prosperity to a social context where one's very 'freedom of speech and faith' is not an entitlement, something one cannot take for granted. The level of determination and sacrifice to fulfill the call requires strong conviction of the calling and commitment to it.

This sense of call has been exemplified by Kim himself, as he does not spare any resources in mission settings through his own investment of financial resources and physical energy. Hong, who often accompanies Kim on mission trips, likens his *modus operandi* to bungee jumping, giving out everything to the end, and yet bouncing back.[17] Although there is no data available for the church, the drastic change from migration opens up a new openness to and interest in religion. Many are first-generation Christians who experienced an adult conversion, often characterized by a radical encounter with the reality of God. This is further reinforced by the experience of the Holy Spirit, often called baptism in the Spirit. Pentecostals interpret this crisis experience as the empowerment of the Spirit for missionary work (Acts 1:8), and the GKC seems to have adopted this understanding, as many Korean Christians would do. All of these result in a strong sense of call, and resolution to bring others to the blessing of eternal salvation through the preaching of the gospel.

A comment on the administrative structure may be important. The administrative structure is extremely agile and flexible, not only for the support of the deployed missionaries and their ministries, but also for swift decision-making and an immediate response to rising demands of the mission field. The mission structure does not sit on a big budget, as voluntary contributions toward *ad hoc* circumstances (such as the Dushanbe bombing) are made not only to the church but also directly to the mission field and missionaries by members. The deployment of human and financial resources is often spontaneous and reactionary. As military language is frequently used in the promotion of mission, so is Kim's role as the field general for combat troops. As expected, however, such an operational structure lacks stability and predictability and is therefore devoid of long-term planning and objective assessment.

Since the opening of the missionary era with the 1990 Soviet excursion, two decades have passed. This provides a time span long enough to establish the pattern of the GKC's mission work. Several significant areas of development and change are discernible. First, Kim retired in 2004 from pastoral responsibility for the GKC, and Keehong Han, a home-grown leader, assumed the helm of pastoral leadership. The process of leadership succession was extremely smooth, which many viewed as a reflection of Kim's unselfish attitude. Kim, now 'retired', has been relocated to Korea and has established another 'daughter church' of the GKC. The missionary structure has expanded, as daughter churches have multiplied. The missionary structure and resources of the GKC gave birth to an

---

[17] Suk-koo Hong, an untitled reflection in Baek, *The Traces of Jesus*, 174.

international mission network in 2008, the Grace Ministries International (GMI), which now functions as a corporate clearing house for missionary work of all the congregations in the network. Kim serves as the chairman. In reality, therefore, Kim continues his mission leadership over the GKC and its affiliate congregations, even though he has ceased to exercise pastoral leadership. A 2010 report claims that the GMI have now sent 270 missionaries (and 246 in 2009), and has established 1,500 congregations in the former Soviet states. Its mission field has also expanded to include China, Vietnam, Bangladesh, East Africa, Japan, as well as European and Latin American countries. These claims, however, cannot be independently verified.

Conclusion

My immediate task was to make the missionary story of the GKC known to others, to churches in the United States as well as throughout the world. The GKC is not a typical immigrant congregation even by Korean standards. Among Korean-American churches throughout the country, the GKC stands out as one of a kind. Kim has been genuinely revered, both within and without the church, for his incredible work ethic, sheer dedication and unorthodox creativity. His simplistic lifestyle and missionary vision have attracted a large number of gifted and committed Christians, and has partly contributed to the growth of the GKC as a congregation and its mission enterprises over the years.

My next task is to call for various concerned parties to seriously ponder the unique role they can play in nurturing or even strengthening such an unusual missionary gift. Here the 'parties' are the missionary thrust of the church, the Christian communities in the United States, and global mission circles. This concluding reflection is based on an assumption that each party has shared a strong desire to uncover new mission paradigms that will empower the missionary movement of the next generation, most likely emerging from unlikely margins, including the former missionary-receiving churches, immigrant communities, and unconventional groups in the west. The story of the GKC's mission should not only continue and be further developed, but also become a powerful case of how the Lord has been preparing his missionary people. At the same time, in my view, the GKC also badly needs help from wider mission communities so that it can read any undesirable signs to curtail its missionary work, and lend any assistance for the church to overcome challenges.

Personally, reflecting on the celebration of the Edinburgh 1910 Missionary Conference, the case of the GKC clearly demonstrates how we have been diligent in digging into the past, but sometimes forgetting the signs of God's future. The 'hiddenness' of the GKC, and many other creative mission groups unknown to the outside world, illustrates the mutual efforts needed: both by the church itself and the mission watchers. It is extremely unfortunate that the church's mission is 'from here to there' and completely ignores its powerful potential in resourcing the host US churches and its neighboring immigrant communities, such as Hispanic, Vietnamese, Cambodian, and many others. The church has produced only one English-language mission resource; it hardly shares anything unique about their mission motivation, or spiritual dynamics that trigger the whole church's involvement in mission; or its experiences, both positive and negative. As a typical first-generation immigrant congregation, it is difficult for the church to feel competent to present themselves to the host church and its mission thinking. This internal deficiency is further worsened by the complete lack of interest among mission watchers. The only one known is C Peter Wagner's short statement, which appears to be a patronizing over-gloss. Nonetheless, someone like him has been diligently unearthing many examples of the hidden work of God in past decades, and the world of mission badly needs more of this sort of mission thinking. This hiddenness will seriously deprive the churches, both the host and immigrant, of fresh new models of missionary 'success', while they search everywhere for new and viable ways of doing mission.

The mission publication industry, among others, has been suffering from the shortage of research on new mission initiatives. Those of non-western experiences will hardly find their way to a wide audience, except the stories of popular figures, as publishers have to survive by carefully selecting only market-worthy titles. At the same time, it is extremely encouraging that some Christian mainstream publishers have begun to produce more titles by non-western authors and from new missionary contexts. Surging interest in research on newly-developing areas is equally encouraging, as witnessed in the overwhelming response of the recent Templeton research initiative on global Pentecostalism. This significant interest by the western world should be commensurate by a similar level of commitment by mission actors in the new 'margins', such as the GKC. It is now clear that it lacks willingness to share its experiences with the wider world.

No one would question my conviction that the GKC represents a powerful case of a new missionary possibility. At the same time, how long it will be able to sustain the initial level of missionary zeal and commitment is anyone's guess. Within its two decades of missionary engagement, several important new mission paradigms and also new missionary impetus are evident, and they have strong potential to empower many others. At the same time, there are also several alarming developments which give cause for concern. These will require deep critical reflection so that the GKC's missionary achievement will go a long way, beyond the first-generation congregation and also beyond its Korean confines.

The first foundation block I would suggest for the long-lasting mission of the church is the construction and articulation of its mission theology. I cannot shrug off a lingering impression that the GKC's mission has been planned, executed and maintained by extremely pragmatic rules. This is coupled by a charismatic decision-making process. Its achievements therefore can be attributed to this agile and responsive management structure. Nonetheless, while its missionary structure and engagement has grown rapidly, consistency and long-term planning is lacking. The process of accountability and evaluation has not found its place and the church's missionary involvement has been extremely reactionary. The most fundamental theological question has not been seriously pondered and reflected such as, 'What is mission as we understand it?', 'What has motivated the way we have been doing mission?', 'What is the meaning of doing mission together?' and 'What are areas of mission to which the church has not paid attention?' etc. For example, now the church needs to ask a serious question as to what motivated its change from the policy of no property ownership, to the purchase and construction of a multi-million dollar property. If this is purely a management decision, the missionary legacy of the church will leave little for the next generation and the world to learn from its experience.

The second is a critical and evaluative analysis of its short mission history. A good history will reveal not only strengths and weaknesses, but will also place the church and its mission within the large historical and social context. When we fail to learn history, we tend to repeat the same mistakes. The GKC's missionary work can be compared to a sprinter, with unbelievable energy and determination. However, the church now needs to plan a long-term reality, and this requires everyone's help. A third-party research project will be one way to undertake such a work.

The third is a strategic thinking process for the future of the GKC's mission, based on the first two areas of deep reflection. At least one internal and yet serious look at the GKC's mission praxis is available, although mostly in Korean. By this stage, I hope the church will have acquired confidence to collaborate in research and that a good network of 'friends' will be in place to provide valuable consultancy. Southern California is a burgeoning hub for mission thinking, and the GKC's place could not be more ideal for bringing missiologists, mission strategists, and mission organizations together. This will truly bring the church's mission potential to its height in its own mission engagement, but more importantly in its contribution to a much wider mission world.

This is not to ignore some important initiatives which the church took over the years. For example, the GKC and its current pastor are deeply involved in the KimNet, a strategic mission network among Korean immigrant congregations in North America. The construction of the new world prayer center is another expression, I believe, of its commitment to an impact on the broader society.

If fundamentals are solidified, the model of the GKC can have a huge impact on both immigrant and mainstream Christianity in the United States. Its dynamic 'primal spirituality', single-minded dedication to mission, its mobilization of the entire church, and equally impressive achievements in its mission fields represent an impressive feat. If we borrow Hanciles' model of immigrant Christianity, the GKC model can present a concrete example of the Eli-Samuel model where the fresh dynamic of young immigrant Christianity can influence and restore the dwindling and ageing mainstream Christianity.[18]

However, this exceptional picture can be a reality only when the missionary motive of the church remains consistently pure as it began two decades ago, although strategies can change. There is need to consider critical questions, such as: 'What expenses are included in the 60% missions budget figure?'; 'Who are included in the published number of missionaries?'; and, 'How many congregations they claim to have established which continue to remain vibrant?' The glowing presentation of the GKC's mission work in its three published documents is not altogether convincing, as it seems to repeat the follies of old missionary literature by promote one's achievement, while conspicuously omitting critical assessments. There are good reasons why one should not simply assume that the past will be repeated in the future. If there is the slightest sign of inflation to maintain the reputation of the church, the GKC is already falling into a 'success trap'. It will not be easy to resist the temptation to maintain the reputation of being number one by devious means. With the changing circumstances of the church, including new leadership, the rise of a new generation, and the inclement financial picture, the church is forced to rethink its missionary motivation and *modus operandi*.

The very elements which made the GKC's mission such a great success can also cause its downfall. It is in everyone's interest to face the question of long-term sustainability. After two decades of missionary enterprise, the operation still remains strictly first-generation led. Unless the next generation (often born in the States) successfully inherits its mission conviction and legacy, the future will not be much brighter. Even at the current stage, without a proper training mechanism, evaluation process, and structure to ensure transparency and accountability, no one can guarantee that the two decades of impressive achievement will last. As its mission has been completely dependent upon the leader's charismatic vision and commitment, the new leader will inevitably now shape the mission theology and praxis of the church. The process of leadership succession was extremely smooth and by itself attested to the soundness of the church's structure. Now he will have to show how the church will take another significant leap forward in the development of its missionary work.

The most challenging and immediate threat to the GKC's two-decade old missionary legacy looks heavy upon the church leadership. The completion of the multi-million dollar international prayer center appears to

---

[18] The four models of immigrant churches are found in Jehu J Hanciles, *Beyond Christendom: Globalization, African Migration, and the Transformation of the West* (Maryknoll, NY: Orbis, 2008), 326-28.

be an Achilles Heel for the church and its missionary commitment, as it simply limits the resources available for mission. But more importantly it betrays the church's celebrated insistence on no-ownership of property to give its utmost priority to mission. As an immigrant church, this 'pilgrimage' type of ecclesiology was admired, especially given its resourcefulness. In fact, the new leader has to test his leadership and the church's missionary commitment, when the church is financially hard pressed. In fact, the heavy burden of its debt-service has potential not only to significantly reduce its missionary investment, but more fundamentally to undermine the very existence of the church. This may be the only way for the church to rediscover its unique missionary vision, although no one wants this pain. On the other hand, if the church weathers this financial challenge successfully, this impressive facility itself can provide a platform for his multi-racial and international missionary vision.

This well-guarded mission secret right at the heart of North America is now revealed. In many ways, the GKC has provided many critical clues for the restoration of vibrant Christianity and mission to North America. It also shows how a pragmatic operation can take the church into turbulent waters. Its mission, as with any congregation, is far from perfect. In fact, it has many uneasy problems, real and potential. Nurturing and strengthening its missionary success is in everyone's best interest, and ultimately for the kingdom's sake.

CONCLUSION:
SPIRITUALITY AS THE BEATING HEART OF MISSION

Kenneth R. Ross and Wonsuk Ma

While spirituality has never been absent from the experience and expression of Christian faith, it may be that the twenty-first century is proving to be a period when it is the primary mode of Christian mission. The centenary of the Edinburgh 1910 World Missionary Conference has provided an opportunity to draw comparisons across the span of one hundred years. One feature which stands out is that mission in the late nineteenth and early twentieth century took a strongly institutional form. Mission stations, schools, colleges and hospitals gave expression to the missionary movement, to the extent that a perennial question was whether the demands of funding and managing such large institutions detracted from the fundamental evangelistic purpose of Christian mission. A century later many of the institutions created by the missionary movement still exist in one form or another but it can be argued that they are less central to worldwide Christian witness. What has emerged, on the other hand, is what William Temple in mid-century described as the 'great new fact of our time': a truly worldwide grassroots Christian church.[1] With local churches worldwide taking a growing share of responsibility for Christian witness, their spiritual quality has become an increasingly decisive question.

Movements of spiritual renewal have therefore exercised great influence, none more than the Pentecostal/charismatic movement whose adherents have increased from very small numbers in 1910 to an estimated 614,000,000 by 2010.[2] They have placed a premium on authentic spirituality in discipleship and mission, and in this way have offered a witness which has proved compelling in many different contexts around the world. It is particularly evident that people in many parts of the southern hemisphere have found western forms of Christianity over-cerebral but have discovered that the religion comes alive for them when they put the accent on spiritual experience. As Kwabena Asamoah-Gyadu persuasively argues, 'Pentecostalism is an experiential religion *par excellence...*' and 'Pentecostal churches are thriving in Africa and among African communities in the western context primarily because of their emphasis on

---

[1] William Temple, *The Church Looks Forward* (London: MacMillan & Co, 1944), 2-3.
[2] Todd M. Johnson and Kenneth R Ross (eds), *Atlas of Global Christianity 1910-2010* (Edinburgh: Edinburgh University Press, 2009), 103.

belief, experience, conviction and commitment to what the Spirit of God is doing in the world.'[3]

Nicta Makiika's chapter on the African Instituted Churches often found at the margins of society underlines this point. In this diverse movement of faith, each church has its own founding vision, but a common feature is critique of the Christianity brought to Africa by European missionaries for its lack of spirituality. Whether a particular African Instituted Church was inspired in its origins by political resistance to colonialism, by sympathy with African culture, or by the spread of the global Pentecostal movement, an emphasis on the power and gifts of the Holy Spirit is something they all share. Illness and misfortune are met, primarily, not by building hospitals or educational institutions but by the conviction that healing and empowering come from the direct action of the Spirit of God. Faith is born and deepened less through intellectual engagement and more through the immediate experience of visions and dreams through which the character and purposes of God are made known. Community is formed by those who are marginalized by their societies but who find dignity and resourcefulness through the impassioned life of prayer in which they share. While there may be scope for the AICs to deepen their theology and extend the range of their social witness, there is no mistaking the fact that the move they have made to re-discover the spiritual dimension of Christianity has had massive and sustained appeal among poor and marginalized communities in Africa.

Meanwhile the historic churches which arose from the work of western missions have also been engaged in a process of inculturation, translating the gospel into terms which make sense in the local context. This is well illustrated by Michael Okyerefo's consideration of Ghanaian Catholicism, and the Asante and Ho Dioceses in particular. Motifs from traditional Asante acclamation of the king have been adopted for use in the celebration of the kingship of Christ. Traditional practices for naming or 'outdooring' a new-born child have been adopted as part of the Christian celebration of the sacrament of baptism. Christian faith therefore acquires a distinctively Ghanaian flavour yet, as Okyerefo is careful to emphasise, it does so without losing its universal character. Catholics from other parts of the world could still find the liturgy recognizable and feel able to participate comfortably. Many other parts of the world have witnessed a renewal of Christian faith and spirituality as a process of inculturation has taken place, allowing the faith to find expression in terms which resonate with local culture. In this way spirituality develops in a way which includes elements of both the local and the universal.

It might have been expected that the extraordinary revival of Christianity being experienced across sub-Saharan Africa would have resulted in a public and political life marked by Christian values. In fact, as Matthews Ojo demonstrates, the reality is quite the reverse. Corruption, nepotism,

---

[3] Kwabena Asamoah-Gyadu, chapter 2.

ethnic conflict and under-development have all too frequently been the dominant features in many African countries. Celebration of the advance of vibrant Christian faith across the continent is tempered by the sober reality that the prevailing values in the public sphere fall far short of Christian ideals. There has been a failure to translate Christian commitment and conviction into policy and conduct in the public sphere. This stands as an indictment of the historic mission churches which had the initiative for most of the nineteenth and twentieth centuries. Now the new force in African Christianity is the movement of charismatic renewal. How will it fare in meeting the challenge of poor governance and weak economic performance? Ojo gives evidence of its vigour and determination to meet this challenge through the power of prayer and passionate Christian commitment. Its unyielding focus on the spiritual dimension of Christianity brings a new point of engagement with the stubborn realities of corruption and abuse of power. With its ethic of participation and its relentless quest for integrity in every aspect of life, it may be that the Pentecostal/charismatic movement is equipped to make the connection between passionate faith and political reality.

Serah Wambua draws on the recent experience of the Anglican Church Mission Society-Africa to demonstrate how African Christians today are taking the initiative to engage the social, economic and political malaise of the continent. On her analysis, African churches have been greatly handicapped by a dualistic ideology, alien to traditional African thought, which has kept church life separate from other dimensions of the life of the community. There is need, first of all, for critical engagement at the level of worldview where positive elements in the African tradition can be retrieved and damaging ones confronted. This frees the African churches to engage in a much more integral, wholistic form of mission. This can be illustrated by the Sheep Care project in the Soweto slums of Nairobi, where a local church is mobilizing resources to meet the needs of the community, ranging from education for children through to kitchen gardening, improved nutrition, income generation and ecological awareness. Another case in point is 'business as mission' – developing businesses which model the values of the kingdom of God, are a force for poverty-reduction and a platform for evangelism. Spirituality is no longer regarded as something for the church sphere only. It is actively related to every dimension of life. To be a disciple of Jesus is to be a force for transformation and there is no restriction on the sectors within which that transformation may take effect.

Inter-generational dynamics present further challenges when it comes to faith crossing barriers. In a time of rapid technological and social change, youth culture often becomes far removed from the world that is familiar to older people. Drawing on primary research conducted among young people within the Catholic Church in Bolivia, Rosauro Lopez Sandoval highlights the extent of their frustration with church life and discourse which makes little or no attempt to connect with the world in which they are living.

Several strategies can be proposed to help to bridge this gulf. The most important, however, is the lived experience of the góspel, which has the power to communicate across the generational divide. Above all, the young people are yearning for authenticity and are ready to respond positively when they see the faith being lived out with integrity. This in turn becomes a base for the spiritual formation of the young people so that they themselves become a force for evangelization among their peers.

Drawing on long experience in the structures of the ecumenical movement, Moses Morales emphasizes that it is at the level of personal spirituality that ecumenism takes effect today. During the twentieth century the drive of the movement came to be focused on doctrinal and ecclesiastical matters which were addressed in a heavily institutional way. Dialogues, agreements, programmes, instruments, councils gave expression to the response of the churches to the gospel imperative of unity. Today, however, there is a fresh appreciation of the fact that the ecumenical vision stands or falls by the quality of the personal and communal spirituality which upholds it. It is through personal transformation, internal conversion, that the ecumenical vision is brought to fulfillment. If it fails to engage this level it quickly becomes sterile and moribund. Those who cherish the ecumenical calling of the church are therefore impelled to put a premium on the training and formation which shapes ecumenical persons. It is through cultivating the personal qualities of love, forgiveness, mutuality and passion for justice that the ecumenical movement finds its integrity and energy. Ecumenism today finds its grounding and inspiration in spirituality.

There can be few contexts presenting a more daunting challenge to Christian spirituality than the conflict between Israel and Palestine. From a perspective of long-term participation in the life of the Palestinian community, Andrew Bush proposes that the key to authentic Christian witness is the *kenosis* (self-emptying) of Jesus Christ. Applying the way of Christ to national identity will lead to nationalism being so transformed that it is defined by an inclination towards the well-being of others instead of being bent towards individual and communal uniqueness and privilege. Notwithstanding the problems entailed in applying a theology of self-emptying to an oppressed and suffering people, the servant-hood which marked the life of Christ suggests a radical option for Christians located in the heat of the Israeli-Palestinian conflict. They are best placed to access the way Christ chose and to bring it to their current situation today, opting to aim not for the destruction of their enemy but for the latter's welfare and flourishing. As was the case with Jesus, this will prove to be a costly option, but it is one which will yield the prophetic witness which may hold the key to breaking the deadlock in which all are currently confined. Might it be one of God's surprises in the contemporary world that the long-sought solution to the Israeli-Palestinian conflict is found not in the political, diplomatic or military realms but in the living out of authentic spirituality?

Conclusion

The fall of the Communist regime in Russia in the early 1990s introduced an unprecedented situation for the Russian Orthodox Church. No longer persecuted and enjoying a revival of many of its parishes and institutions, nonetheless this church, which for centuries had been almost synonymous with the Russian nation, found itself operating in a context where decades of state-driven atheism had left many people completely disconnected from the church and the Christian faith. Historically it had regarded mission as an internal matter of building up the life of the church to which practically the entire population already belonged. Now it faced the question of how to respond to the new context where many Russians have little or no knowledge of the Christian faith or connection with the life of the church. Valentin Kozhuharov, drawing on his experience as a Bulgarian missionary working in Moscow, outlines the response of the Russian Orthodox Church to the new context. An energetic programme of outreach, particularly focused on eastern Russia, has stimulated fresh reflection on the church's self-understanding in relation to the missionary challenge it faces. The spirituality it seeks to promote is strongly ecclesial, centred particularly on participation the eucharist as the church's defining act of worship. It is conscious, certainly, of the need to find points of connection for those to whom the life and worship of the church appears remote and irrelevant. Yet its guiding conviction is that it is through the authenticity of its worship that mission will take effect and the good news of Jesus Christ will touch people's lives profoundly and transformatively.

Despite the long history of Christianity in Asia it remains very much a minority religion among the people of the world's most populous continent. One reason often suggested is that it has appeared to be a foreign religion, lacking connection with the life-rhythms and aspirations of the great majority of the people. For the Catholic Church in Asia the *aggiornamento* of Vatican II, understood as 'opening the windows' of the church to the fresh air of the Spirit has presented an opportunity for a new missionary engagement based on dialogue with the Asian context. It is, in fact, as Clemens Mendonca suggests, a triple dialogue: dialogue with the poor of Asia, dialogue with the religions of Asia and dialogue with Asia's diverse cultures. Working sensitively across these three dimensions the church seeks to be attentive to the deep yearnings of the peoples of Asia. It is open to the construction of indigenous contextual theologies and ready to be informed by the rich experience of other religions. It looks to identify opportunities for collaboration and takes a clear stand against oppressive systems which hinder the people in their quest to flourish. Above all, this fresh missionary engagement with the peoples of Asia seeks to operate on a spiritual level. It recognizes that it is the action of the Spirit of God which will empower the triple dialogue and bring about authentic encounter and transformation.

A significant challenge for Christian mission is its lack of impact in the Indian subcontinent. Despite a long history and the emergence of vibrant

Christian communities in modern times, the proportion of the population adhering to Christianity remains very small. David Singh suggests that the point of connection for Christian faith in the Indian cultural context might be found at the devotional level. He cites the early twentieth century ministries of Sadhu Sundar Singh and Narayan Vaman Tilak. Both men distanced themselves from the institutional church and enjoyed great success as they engaged directly with the public. They emphasized the immediacy of their experience of Jesus Christ which they presented in a way which carried resonance in the context of Indian devotional traditions. They offered 'the water of life in an Indian cup' and found many who were ready to drink. Doctrine, ecclesiastical organization and an institutional appearance have limited appeal in the Indian context. It is the spiritual dimension of Christianity which strikes a chord. David Singh therefore suggests that the approach taken by Sadhu Sundar Singh and NV Tilak might be the one most likely to prove effective today. It is through cultivating and communicating its devotional life that the Christian community will be effective in commending the faith in the Indian context.

Perhaps the most exciting development in world Christianity in the past fifty years has been the translation of the faith into terms and concepts familiar to the societies to which it has been taken through the missionary movement. Translation, however, is always a risky matter and, while much can be achieved through faithful and accurate translation, there is also the possibility of moving in the direction of being inaccurate and misleading. Tereso Casino's careful study of the Filipino concept of *bahala na* provides an illustration of a very familiar indigenous concept which, at first sight, seems to be equivalent to Christian confidence in the will of God, as exemplified in the petition found in the Lord's Prayer: 'The will be done'. On closer examination, however, it is apparent that *bahala na* carries notions of an impersonal god and of a matters being determined by a fate over which human beings have no control. This easily leads in the direction of fatalism and determinism at the expense of the trust in a personal God which is the hallmark of Christian faith. Therefore using *bahala na* as a filter through which to understand Christianity leads to distortion and inhibits the emergence of mature Christian faith in the Filipino context. Such a process of critical discernment has a vital role to play if spirituality is to take an authentically Christian form.

Kim-kwong Chan's thoughtful study of the 'Back to Jerusalem' movement in China reveals how the 'go' dynamic inherent in Christian faith continues to find expression in today's world. Clearly mission is no longer 'from the west to the rest' but a geographical framework is proving motivational for a new generation of Chinese missionaries. Chan's penetrating analysis deconstructs the movement, showing that its spiritual, missionary and adventist character does not necessarily protect it from becoming compromised with political, cultural and economic currents which may distort its impact. Appealing to Chinese national pride, riding a wave of Chinese economic expansion and fulfilling long-held western hopes that Christendom might outflank the Muslim world, the movement constitutes a potent cocktail of influences which could lead it in a variety of unwelcome directions. Chan calls for critical missiological thinking, perhaps to enable 'Back to Jerusalem' to avoid the kind of complicity with alien ideology which handicapped western mission in the colonial period. There appears to be a long way to go before the movement will have the sensitivity needed in order to be effective in cross-cultural mission. Nonetheless, the passionate spirituality which drives the movement shows how traditional missionary zeal can find fresh expression in a movement inspired by Chinese Christianity.

One finding of the Edinburgh 2010 process was that initiative in mission today lies increasingly with local churches.[4] It is fitting therefore that this volume concludes with three studies of local congregations, all Korean, two in Seoul and the other in southern California. Younghoon Lee writes as senior pastor of Yoido Full Gospel Church, reputed to be the largest church in the world. He traces its development from its beginnings with just five members in 1958 through to the point where its membership reached the 780,000 mark in 2008. Consideration of the ministry of Rev Paul Yonggi Cho reveals that a strong Pentecostal theology of the Holy Spirit and a focus on the life of the early church, as recorded in the Book of Acts, have formed the core identity of the church. This has led to the cultivation of an outward-looking spirituality finding expression equally in evangelism which is aimed at the saving of souls and a holistic witness which seeks to shape society according to the values of the kingdom of God. This spirituality finds expression both nationally in the Korean context and internationally through missionaries sent to as many as 65 different countries. All of this springs from the essential missionary impulse that every member of the church is encouraged to receive the Holy Spirit and to become a "little Jesus" in the way they live their lives. Thus it is expected that all members of the church will have a vibrant mission spirituality motivating their lives. No one who comes in contact with Yoido will be left in any doubt that "the church exists for mission".

In similar vein, Chul-shin Lee writes of the church where he himself is pastor, Youngnak Presbyterian Church in Seoul, tracing its journey from the flight of Christian Koreans from the Communist North in the aftermath of the division of the Korean peninsula and indicating the influence which it exercised on the rebuilding of the nation following the Korean War. At the heart of the life of the church he finds a spirituality which is deeply personal. The founding pastor of the church, Rev Kyung-Chik Han, was a man whose motivation for mission derived from his own passion for the

---

[4] See 'Local Church – Your Time Has Come', Kenneth R Ross, *Edinburgh 2010: New Directions for Church in Mission* (Pasadena: William Carey International University Press, 2010), 9-18.

gospel. Lee outlines the main features of Han's piety, using the experience of the apostle Paul as a frame of reference. Conviction of sin, an experience of repentance, assurance of faith and a passion for the gospel – these were the main notes of Han's ministry and continue to be sounded today in the ministry of Lee. Out of this experience at the personal level has risen a commitment to mission which finds expression in church-planting within South Korea, community service, diaconal ministry in North Korea, and missionary enterprise throughout Asia and indeed worldwide.

In today's world migration takes place on an unprecedented scale, bringing vast numbers of people across the globe to live and work in new contexts. Many bring their faith with them or find it on the way. Perhaps to their own surprise as much as everyone else's, they can quickly become part of a base from which new missionary initiatives can spring. This is seen very clearly in Wonsuk Ma's consideration of Grace Korean Church in southern California. This rapidly growing congregation of first generation Korean immigrants was marked from its earliest beginnings by a strong emphasis on mission. It has realized in practice the kind of mobilization for mission which was never more than a dream for the strategists of the western missionary movement of the nineteenth and twentieth centuries. Strong emphasis on spiritual life finds its central focus in the virtue of sacrifice for the sake of mission. Though characterized by a lack of theological maturity and a neglect of the missionary challenge of its own local context, the passion with which GKC members have embraced the vision to plant churches in new places has resulted in a significant impact being made. At a time when the missionary endeavour of long-established churches in North America and Europe is in decline, immigrant churches emerge as a new base from which initiatives in mission may be launched. Theological maturity and missiological depth may be conspicuous by their absence. However, passion to share the gospel, determination to cross intimidating frontiers and willingness to sacrifice oneself provide the ingredients for new initiatives in cross-cultural Christian mission.

The studies of Christian mission gathered in this book are diverse, both geographically and thematically. They span the globe and include a wide variety of both social context and ecclesial life. Together they demonstrate that today there is a renewal of the missionary impetus of the churches which is marked by its spiritual character. The outstanding case in point is the worldwide Pentecostal/charismatic movement which is having extensive missionary impact and is unashamed about its emphasis on the spiritual dimension. It has reminded Christianity of its original character, correcting the over-cerebral and over-institutional form which it took during the modern period when global ascendancy apparently lay with the western churches. A recovery of the spiritual dimension of the faith can be observed, however, in other streams within world Christianity as well. Wherever this occurs it functions as motivation for mission, moving people of faith to share the good news of Jesus Christ both within their own communities and by crossing frontiers to take the message to new contexts.

It has often been assumed that the missionary movement was a time-bound, culturally specific episode, closely associated with western colonialism. With the demise of colonialism, it was therefore expected that Christianity's missionary period would also come to an end. The facts on the ground today present a very different picture. World Christianity is discovering new vision and energy for mission, as abundantly demonstrated in the essays collected in this volume. Its vitality is widely dispersed across the continents, including within the migratory movements which form a major force shaping human history in our time. Christian faith discovers new bases from which missionary initiative can be launched, as well as identifying new frontiers – such as western Europe, which a century ago was complacently regarded as a permanent base for mission, but today calls out for a movement of re-evangelization.

This turn of events does not mean that Christian mission is now immune to compromise and distortion. As has been demonstrated in the essays collected in this book, it is still entirely possible for Christian mission to become complicit in projects which dilute or even undermine its true purpose. Nonetheless, there is much evidence of the Christian faith recovering its spiritual core and finding motivation for mission which arises out of its essential character. As a result churches in every part of the world are being re-energised to play their part in fulfilling the missionary mandate to take the good news of Jesus Christ 'to the ends of the earth'. Far from spirituality being an afterthought in missiology, to be considered only after the hard-core strategic and institutional issues have been settled, it emerges today as the beating heart of mission. It may be that Edinburgh 2010 will be remembered most of all for the pneumatological turn in the understanding of mission which is exemplified in this volume.

BIBLIOGRAPHY

Adubofor, Samuel B. 'Evangelical Parachurch Movements in Ghanaian Christianity c. 1950-early 1990s'. Ph.D. thesis, University of Edinburgh, 1994.
Adeyemo, Tekouboh. *Hope for Africa: Against All Hope.* Nairobi: Samaritan Strategy Africa, 2005.
Aikman, David. *Jesus in Beijing: How Christianity is Transforming China and Changing the Global Balance of Power.* Washington, D.C.: Regency Publishing Inc., 2003.
Allport, G. W. and J. M. Ross. 'Personal Religious Orientation and Prejudice'. *Journal of Personality and Social Psychology* 5 (1967), 432-443.
Anderson, Allan H. *African Reformation: African Initiated Christianity in the 20th Century.* Trenton, NJ: Africa World Press, 2001.
Andres, Tomas D. *Understanding the Filipino Values: A Management Approach.* Quezon City: New Day Publishers, 1981.
Appadurai, Arjun. 'Disjuncture and Difference in the Global Cultural Economy'. In Mike Featherstone ed. *Global Culture: Nationalism, Globalization and Identity.* London: Sage, 1990, 295-310.
Appasamy, A.J. *Sundar Singh.* Cambridge: Lutterworth Press, 1958.
Asamoah-Gyadu, J. Kwabena. *African Charismatics: Current Developments within Independent Indigenous Pentecostalism in Ghana.* Leiden: E.J. Brill, 2005.
Aschraft, Morris. *The Will of God.* Nashville, TN: Broadman, 1980.
Atienmo, Abamfo O. *The Rise of the Charismatic Movement in the Mainline Churches in Ghana.* Accra: Asempa Publishers, 1993.
Bach, Daniel C. *The Revival of Regional Integration in Africa.* Ibadan: IFRA, 1999.
Baek, Seung-hwan. Ed. *The Traces of Jesus: Miracle Story of Grace Korean Church.* N.p.: Yechan, 2009.
Balia, Daryl and Kirsteen Kim ed. *Edinburgh 2010: Witnessing to Christ Today.* Oxford: Regnum, 2010.
Barrett, David B. *Schism and Renewal in Africa.* Oxford: Oxford University Press, 1968.
Barrett, David B. and Todd. M. Johnston. *World Christian Trends.* Pasadena, California: William Carey International University, 2001.
Bediako, Kwame. *Christianity in Africa: The Renewal of a Non-Western Religion.* Edinburgh: Edinburgh University Press; Maryknoll, NY: Orbis Books, 1995.
Bediako, Kwame. *Jesus in Africa: The Christian Gospel in African History and Experience.* Akropong, Akwapim, Ghana: Regnum, 2000.
Beltran, Benigno P. *The Christology of the Inarticulate: An Inquiry into the Filipino Understanding of Jesus Christ.* Manila: Divine Word Publications, 1987.
Berger, Peter L. *The Sacred Canopy: The Elements of a Sociological Theory of Religion.* New York: Anchor Press, 1967.
Blanco, Jose C. 'The Gospel of Absolute Respect: A Spirituality of People Power.' In Douglas J. Elwood ed. *Toward a Theology of People Power: Reflections on the Philippine February Revolution.* Quezon City: New Day Publishers, 1988, 103-109.

Bosch, David J. *Transforming Mission: Paradigm Shifts in Theology of Mission.* Maryknoll, NY: Orbis Books, 1997.
Boyd, Robin H.S. *An Introduction to Indian Christian Theology.* Delhi: ISPCK, 1975.
Brown, Alistair. *I Believe in Mission.* London: Hodder & Stoughton, 1997.
Brown, Wesley H. and Peter F. Penner ed. *Christian Perspectives on the Israeli-Palestinian Conflict.* Schwarzenfeld: Neufeld Verlag, 2008.
Bush, Andrew F. 'Palestinian Christian University Students in Interfaith Discussion.' Dissertation, Princeton Theological Seminary, 2004.
Casiño, Tereso C. 'Bahala Na' A Critique on a Filipino Paradigm of Folk Spirituality'. *Asia Pacific Journal of Intercultural Studies* 1:1 (2005), 145-60.
Casiño, Tereso C. '"Thy Will be Done": A Framework for Understanding Christian Spirituality'. *Asia Pacific Journal of Interdisciplinary Studies* 2:1 (2005), 56-63.
Centre for the Study of Values in Public Life, Harvard Divinity School. *Religions and Values in Public Life.* Cambridge, Mass.: Harvard College, 2000.
Chan, Kim-Kwong and Eric R. Carlson. *Religious Freedom In China: Policy, Administration, and Regulation-A Research Handbook.* Santa Barbara: California: Institute for the Study of America Religion/Hong Kong: Hong Kong Institute for Culture, Commerce and Religion, 2005.
Chan, Kim-Kwong and Alan Hunter. *Prayers and Thoughts of Chinese Christian.* London: Mowbray, 1990.
Chia, Edmund. 'Interreligious Dialogue in Ecclesia in Asia'. *Jeevadhara* 30:177 (May 2000), 300-312.
Chia, Edmund. 'Towards a Theology of Dialogue, Schillebeeckx's Method as Bridge between Vatican's Dominus Iesus and Asia's FABC Theology'. Ph.D. thesis, University of Nijmegen, 2003.
Cleary, L. Edward and Hannah W. Gambino. *Power, Politics and Pentecostals in Latin America.* Boulder, CO.: Westview Press, 1998.
Collins, Paul M. *Christian Inculturation in India.* London: Ashgate, 2007.
Corpuz, Onofre D. 'The Cultural Foundations of Filipino Politics'. In Socorro C. Espiritu and Chester L. Hunt ed. *Social Foundations of Community Development: Readings on the Philippines.* Manila: R.M. Garcia Publishing House, 1964, 420-23.
Corten, André and Ruth Marshall-Fratani ed. *Between Babel and Pentecost: Transnational Pentecostalism in Africa and Latin America.* Bloomington: Indiana University Press, 2001.
Cox, Harvey. *Fire From Heaven: The Rise of Pentecostal Spirituality and the Reshaping of Religion in the Twenty-First Century.* Reading, Massachusetts: Addision-Wesley, 1995.
Cox, Harvey. 'Foreword'. In Allan H. Anderson and Walter J. Hollenweger ed. *Pentecostals after a Century: Global Perspectives on a Movement in Transition.* Sheffield: Academic Press, 1999.
Creel, Austin B. and Vasudha Narayanan ed. *Monastic Life in the Christian and Hindu Traditions: A Comparative Study.* New York: Edwin Mellen Press, 1990.
Cullmann, Oscar. *Christ and Time: The Primitive Christian Conception of Time and History.* Translated by Floyd V. Filson. Philadelphia, PA: Westminster, 1950.
Davey, Cyril J. *The Story of Sadhu Sundar Singh.* Chicago: Moody Press, 1963.

Dayton, Donald. *Theological Roots of Pentecostalism*. Grand Rapids, MI: Baker Academic, 1991.
De Gruchy, John W. 'Theological Reflections on the Task of the Church in the Democratisation of Africa'. In Paul Gifford ed. *The Christian Churches and the Democratisation of Africa*. Leiden, E. J. Brill, 1995, 47-60.
De Mesa, Jose M. *In Solidarity With Culture: Studies in Theological Re-rooting*. Maryhill Studies 4. Quezon City: Maryhill School of Theology, 1987.
Dempster, Murray W., Byron D. Klaus and Douglas Petersen ed. *The Globalisation of Pentecostalism: A Religion Made to Travel*. Oxford: Regnum Books International, 1999.
Dickson, Kwesi A. *Theology in Africa*. London: Darton, Longman and Todd; Maryknoll, NY: Orbis Books, 1984.
D'Sa, Francis X. 'Ecclesia Semper Reformanda aus der Sicht anderer Religionen'. In Erich Garhammer ed. *Ecclesia semper reformanda: Kirchenreform als bleibende Aufgabe*. Würzburg: Echter, 2006, 231-247.
D'Sa, Francis X. 'Missionarisch Kirche sein in Asien: Dialog der Religionen als Herausforderung'. In André Gerth and Simone Rappel ed. *Global Message – Weltmission heute*. München: Don Bosco Verlag, 2005, 53-74.
Dulles, Avery. *Models of the Church*. New York: Doubleday, 2002.
Dunn, James D.G. 'A Protestant response to Juan Sepúlveda, "Born Again: Baptism and the Spirit"'. In Jürgen Moltmann and Karl-Josef Kushel, ed. *Pentecostal Movements as an Ecumenical Challenge: Concilium*, 3 (1996), 109-115.
Espiritu, Socorro C., and Chester L. Hunt ed. *Social Foundations of Community Development: Readings on the Philippines*. Manila: R.M. Garcia Publishing House, 1964.
Farquhar, J.N. *The Crown of Hinduism*. London: Oxford University Press, 1913.
Festinger, Leon, Henry W. Reicken, and Stanley Schacter. *When Prophecy Fails: A Social and Psychological Study of a Modern Group that Predicted the Destruction of the World*. New York: Harper Torchbooks, 1964.
Flannery, Austin P. ed. *Vatican Council II Vol. 1: The Conciliar and Post Conciliar Documents*. Dublin: Dominican Publications, 1975.
Flannery, Austin P. ed. *Vatican Council II Vol. 2: More Post Conciliar Documents*. Collegeville, MN: The Liturgical Press, 1982.
Foli, Richard. *Church Growth in Ghana*. Accra: Methodist Book Depot, 2001.
Fontana, Michela. *Matteo Ricci: Un Gesuita alla Corte dei Ming*. Milano: Mondadori, 2005.
Francis, T. Dayanandan ed. *The Christian Witness of Sadhu Sundar Singh: A Collection of His Writings*. Madras: The Christian Literature Society, 1989.
Francisco, Juan R. *Indian Influences in the Philippines*. Manila: Benipayo Printing Co., Inc., 1965.
Frederiks, Martha. 'Kenosis as a Model for Interreligious Dialogue.' *Missiology* 33:2 (2005), 211-222.
Freire, Paulo. *Pedagogy of the Oppressed*. New York: Continuum, 2007.
Friesen, Garry and Robin Maxson, *Decision Making and the Will of God: A Biblical Alternative to the Traditional View*. Portland, OR: Multnomah, 1980.
George, S.K. *Gandhi's Challenge to Christianity*. Ahmedabad: Navjivan Publishing House, 1960.
Gerlach, Luther P. and Virginia H. Hine, 'Five Factors Crucial to the Growth and Spread of a Modern Religious Movement'. *Journal for the Scientific Study of Religion* 7:1 (1968), 23-40.

Gifford, Paul. 'Ghana's Charismatic Churches'. *Journal of Religion in Africa* 24:3 (1994), 241-265.
Gifford, Paul. *Ghana's New Christianity: Pentecostalism in a Globalizing African Economy.* Bloomington: Indiana University Press, 2004.
Gifford, Paul, ed. *New Dimensions in African Christianity.* Nairobi: All African Conference of Churches, 1992.
Gifford, Paul, ed. *The Christian Churches and the Democratisation of Africa.* Leiden, E. J. Brill, 1995.
Gifford, Paul. 'The Complex Provenance of Some Elements of African Pentecostal Theology'. In Andre Corten and Ruth Marshall-Fratani ed. *Between Babel and Pentecost: Transnational Pentecostalism in Africa and Latin America.* Bloomington: Indiana University Press, 2001, 62-79.
Gifford, Paul. *African Christianity: Its Public Role.* Bloomington, Indiana University Press, 1998.
Gilkey, Langdon. *Reaping the Whirlwind: A Christian Interpretation of History.* New York: Seabury, 1981.
Glasser, Arthur F. *Announcing the Kingdom: the Story of God's Mission in the Bible.* Grand Rapids: Baker, 2003.
Gonzales, Valentino L. 'Understanding the Dynamics of the Filipino Family: Pastoral Care Perspective'. A Paper Presented to the Faculty of Asia Baptist Graduate Theological Seminary, Philippines, 1983.
Green, Maia. 'Why Christianity is the "Religion of Business": Perceptions of the Church among Pogoro Catholics in Southern Tanzania'. *Journal of Religion in Africa* 25:1 (1995), 25-47.
Guder, Darrell L. ed., *Missional Church: A Vision for the Sending of the Church in North America.* Grand Rapids: Eerdmans, 1998.
Hackett, Rosalind J. 'Charismatic/Pentecostal Appropriation of Media Technologies in Nigeria and Ghana'. *Journal of Religion in Africa* 28:3 (1998), 258-277.
Hanciles, Jehu J. *Beyond Christendom: Globalization, African Migration, and the Transformation of the West.* Maryknoll, NY: Orbis, 2008.
Hanson, Paul D. *Dynamic Transcendence.* Philadelphia. PA: Fortress Press, 1978.
Hattaway, Paul. *Back To Jerusalem: Called to Complete the Great Commission.* Carlisle: Piquant, 2003.
Hauerwas, Stanley. *The Peaceable Kingdom.* Notre Dame: Notre Dame University Press, 2002.
Hollenweger, Walter J. *Pentecostalism: Origins and Developments Worldwide.* Peabody, Massachusetts: Hendrickson Publishers, 1997.
Hoerschelmann, Werner. *'Christian Gurus': A Study of the Life and Works of Christian Charismatic Leaders in South India.* Chennai: Gurukul Lutheran Theological College and Research Institute, 1998.
Hünermann, Peter and Margit Eckholt ed. *La juventud latinoamericana en los procesos de globalización: Opción por los jóvenes.* Buenos Aires: Universitaria de Buenos Aires, 1998.
Hunter, Alan and Kim-Kwong Chan. *Protestantism in Contemporary China.* Cambridge: Cambridge University Press, 1993.
Ilogu, Edmund. *Christianity and Ibo Culture.* Leiden: E.J. Brill, 1974.
Izraelewicz, Erik. *Quand La Chine Change Le Monde.* Paris: Editions Grassel et Fasquelle, 2005.
Jacob, Plamthodathil S. *The Experiential Response of N.V. Tilak.* Madras: The Christian Literature Society, 1979.

Jakonda, Sulaiman Z. *Your Kingdom Come: A Book on Wholistic Christian Development*. Jos: RURCON, 2001.
James, William. *Varieties of Religious Experience*. New York: Touchstone, 1997.
Jenkins, Philip. *The Next Christendom: The Coming of Global Christianity*. Oxford: Oxford University Press, 2002.
Jeong, Jae Yong. 'Filipino Pentecostal Spirituality: An Investigation into Filipino Indigenous Spirituality and Pentecostalism in the Philippines'. Doctor of Theology thesis, University of Birmingham, 2001.
Jesudasan, Ignatius. *A Gandhian Theology of Liberation*. Maryknoll, NY: Orbis Books, 1984.
Jocano, F. Landa. *Folk Christianity: A Preliminary Study of Conversion and Patterning of Christian Experience in the Philippines*. Quezon City: Trinity Research Institute, 1981.
Jocano, F. Landa. *Philippine Prehistory: An Anthropological Overview of the Beginnings of Filipino Society and Culture*. Quezon City: Philippine Center for Advanced Studies, 1975.
Johnson, David L. *A Reasoned Look at Asian Religions*. Minneapolis, MN: Bethany House Publishers, 1985.
Johnson, Todd M. and Kenneth R. Ross ed. *Atlas of Global Christianity 1910-2010*. Edinburgh: Edinburgh University Press, 2009.
Johnstone, Patrick and Jason Mandryk. *Operation World: 21st Century Edition*. Carlisle: Paternoster, 2001.
Jones, E. Stanley. *The Christ of the Indian Road*. Nashville: Abingdon Press, 1925.
Kalu, Ogbu. *African Pentecostalism: An Introduction*. Oxford: Oxford University Press, 2008.
Kaiser, Walter C. 'Israel's Missionary Call.' In Ralph D. Winter and Steven C. Hawthorne, ed. *Perspectives on the World Christian Movement*. Pasadena: William Carey Library, 1992, A-25-33.
Kaufman, Gordon D. *The Theological Imagination: Constructing the Concept of God*. Philadelphia, PA: Westminster, 1981.
Kerr, David A. and Kenneth R. Ross ed. *Edinburgh 2010: Mission Then and Now*. Oxford: Regnum, 2009.
Kim, Byung-Hee ed., *Han Kyung-Chik Moksa (Rev. Kyung-Chik Han)*. Seoul: Kyujang Moohwasa, 1982.
Kim, Kirsteen and Andrew Anderson. *Edinburgh 2010: Mission Today and Tomorrow*. Oxford: Regnum, 2011.
Kim, Sungbae ed. *Youngnak Church 35 Years*. Seoul: Youngnak Church Press, 1983.
Kozhuharov, Valentin. *Missionerskata deinost na Ruskata pravoslavna tsurkva dnes*. Veliko Tarnovo, Bulgaria: Vesta Publishing House, 2008.
Kozhuharov, Valentin. *Towards an Orthodox Christian Theology of Mission: An Interpretive Approach*. Veliko Tarnovo, Bulgaria: Vesta Publishing House, 2006.
Kürschner-Pelkmann, Frank. *Reinhard Bonnke's Theology: A Pentecostal Preacher and His Mission - A Critical Analysis*. Hamburg: EMW, 2004.
Lamb, David. *The Africans*. New York: Vintage Books, 1983.
Larbi, Emmanuel Kingsley. *Pentecostalism: The Eddies of Ghanaian Christianity*. Accra: Center for Pentecostal and Charismatic Studies, 2001.

Laryea, Philip T. 'Mother Tongue Theology: Reflections on Images of Jesus in the Poetry of Afua Kuma', *Journal of African Christian Thought* 3:1 (2000), 50-60.
Lee, Mahn-Yol. 'Talk with Rev. Han Kyung-Chik'. *The Korean Church and History* 1 (1991), 134-62.
Lee, Won-Sul, Seung-Joon Lee and Joong-Sik Han. *Just Three More Years to Live! The Story of Rev. Kyung-Chik Han.* Seoul: Rev. Kyung-Chik Han Memorial Foundation, 2005.
Lee, Younghoon. *Cross, the Root of the Full Gospel Faith* [Korean]. Seoul: Institute for Church Growth, 2011.
Lee, Younghoon. *The Holy Spirit Movement in Korea: Its Historical and Theological Development.* Oxford: Regnum Books International, 2009.
Lernoux, Penny. 'The Latin American Church'. *Latin American Research Review* 15:2 (1980), 201-211.
Leonard, Christine. *A Giant in Ghana: 3,000 Churches in 50 Years. The Story of James McKeown and the Church of Pentecost.* Chichester, England: New Wine Press, 1989.
Lewis, I.M. *Ecstatic Religion: A Study of Shamanism and Spirit Possession.* Second edition. London: Routledge, 1989.
Lincoln, Bruce. *Holy Terrors: Thinking about Religion after September 11.* Chicago: Chicago University Press, 2003.
Lynch-Watson, Janet. *The Saffron Robe: A Life of Sadhu Sundar Singh.* London: Hodder & Stoughton, 1975.
Mana, Kä. *Christians and Churches of Africa Envisioning the Future.* Akropong, Ghana: Regnum Africa, 2002.
Macchia, Frank. *Baptized in the Spirit: A Global Pentecostal Theology.* Grand Rapids: Zondervan, 2006.
Manus, Chris U. 'New Testament Theological Foundations for Christian Contribution to Politics in Nigeria'. *Bulletin of Ecumenical Theology* 2:1 (1989).
Manus, Chris U. 'The Use and Role of the Bible in Three New Religious Movements in Nigeria'. Paper read at the Symposium on the Interpretation of the Bible, Ljubljana, Slovenia, 18-20, September 1996.
Marshall, Ruth. 'Pentecostalism in Southern Nigeria: An Overview'. In Paul Gifford, ed. *New Dimensions in African Christianity.* Nairobi, All African Conference of Churches, 1992, 8-39.
Marshall, Ruth. 'Power in the Name of Jesus'. *Review of African Political Economy* 52 (1991), 21-38.
Marshall-Fratani, Ruth. 'Mediating The Global and Local in Nigerian Pentecostalism'. *Journal of Religion in Africa* 28:3 (1998), 278-315.
Matthews, Ed. 'Christ and Kenosis: A Model for Mission.' *Journal of Applied Missiology* 2:1 (1991).
Mazawi, Andres Elias. 'Palestinian Local Theology and the Issue of Islamo-Christian Dialogue.' *Islamochristiana* 19 (1993), 93-115.
McGinn, Bernard, John Meyendorff, and Jean Leclercq ed. *Christian Spirituality: Origins to the Twelfth Century.* New York: The Crossroad Publishing Company, 1985.
McGrath, Alister E. *Christian Spirituality.* Oxford: Blackwell, 1999.
Meeks, Wayne A. *The First Urban Christians: The Social World of the Apostle Paul.* New Haven and London: Yale University Press, 1983.

Mendonca, Clemens. *Dynamics of Symbol and Dialogue: Interreligious Education in India.* Münster: Tübinger Perspektieven zur Pastoraltheologie und Religionspädagogik, Bd.13. LIT Verlag, 2002.
Menzies, William W. and Robert P. Menzies. *Spirit and Power: Foundations of Pentecostal Experience.* Grand Rapids, Michigan: Zondervan, 2000.
Mercado, Leonardo N. *Elements of Filipino Theology.* Tacloban City, Philippines: Divine Word Publications, 1975.
Mercado, Leonardo N. *Elements of Filipino Philosophy.* Revised Edition. Tacloban City, Philippines: Divine Word University Publications, 1976.
Mercado, Leonardo N. 'The Filipino Image of God.' *Philippiniana Sacra* 26:78 (1991): 401-415.
Meyendorff, John. 'The Orthodox Church and Mission: Past and Present Perspectives'. *St Vladimir's Theological Quarterly* 16 (1972).
Meyendorff, John. 'Theosis in the Eastern Christian Tradition'. In Louis K. Dupre and Don E. Saliers ed. *Christian Spirituality: Post-Reformation and Modern.* New York: Crossroad, 1989.
Meyer, Birgit. '"Delivered from the Powers of Darkness" Confessions of Satanic Riches in Christian Ghana'. *Africa: Journal of the International African Institute* 65:2 (1995), 236-255.
Meyer, Birgit, '"If you are a Devil you are a Witch and if you are a Witch you are a Devil": The Integration of "Pagan" Ideas into the Conceptual Universe of Ewe Christians in South-eastern Ghana'. *Journal of Religion in Africa,* 22:2 (1992), 98-132.
Miller, Darrow L. and Scott Allen. *Against All Hope: Hope for Africa.* Nairobi: All Africa Conference of Churches, 2005.
Miller, Donald E. and Tetsuano Yamamori. *Global Pentecostalism: The New Face of Christian Social Engagement.* Berkeley and Los Angeles: University of California Press, 2007.
Miranda-Feliciano, Evelyn. *Filipino Values and Our Christian Faith.* Mandaluyong, Philippines: OMF Literature, Inc., 1990.
Mühlen, Heribert. *A Charismatic Theology: Initiation in the Spirit.* London: Burns and Oats, 1978.
Munayer, Salim J. 'Relations between Religions in Historic Palestine and the Future Prospects: Christians and Jews.' In Michael Prior and William Taylor, ed. *Christians in the Holy Land.* London: The World of Islam Festival Trust, 1994.
Nii, Darku Amoo. *Holistic City Evangelism: Accra Perspective.* Accra: Eshcolit, 2005.
Nyiri, Pal. 'The Yellow Man's Burden: Chinese Migrants on a Civilizing Mission'. *China Journal* 56 (2006), 83-106.
Obeng, J. Pashington. *Asante Catholicism: Religious & Cultural Reproduction Among the Akan of Ghana.* Leiden: E.J. Brill, 1996.
Oduyoye, Mercy Amba. *Daughters of Anowa: African Women and Patriarchy.* Maryknoll, NY: Orbis Books, 1995.
Oduyoye, Mercy Amba. *Hearing and Knowing: Theological Reflections on Christianity in Africa.* Maryknoll, NY: Orbis Books, 1986.
Ojo, Matthews A. 'African Charismatics'. In Stephen Glazier ed. *Encyclopedia of African & African-American Religion.* New York: Routledge, 2001, 2-6.
Ojo, Matthews A. 'Deeper Christian Life Ministry: A Case Study of the Charismatic Movements in Western Nigeria'. *Journal of Religion in Africa* 17:2 (1988), 141-162.

Ojo, Matthews A. 'Deeper Life Bible Church in Nigeria'. In Paul Gifford ed. *New Dimensions in African Christianity*. Nairobi, All African Conference of Churches, 1992, 135-156.

Ojo, Matthews A. 'The Charismatic Movements in Nigeria Today'. *International Bulletin of Missionary Research* 19:3 (1995), 114-118.

Ojo, Matthews A. 'The Contextual Significance of the Charismatic Movements in Independent Nigeria'. *Africa: Journal of the International African Institute* 58:2 (1988), 175-192.

Ojo, Matthews A. 'The Dynamics of Indigenous Charismatic Missionary Enterprises in West Africa'. *Missionalia* 25:4 (1997), 537-561.

Okullu, Henry. *Church and Politics in East Africa*. Nairobi: Uzima Press, 1974.

Okyerefo, Michael P.K. 'The Gospel of Public Image in Africa'. In Harri Englund ed. *Christianity and Public Culture in Africa*. Athens: Ohio University Press, 2011, 204-16.

Oldmeadow, Harry. *A Christian Pilgrim in India: The Spiritual Journey of Swami Abhishiktananda (Henri Le Saix)*. Bloomington: World Wisdom, 2008.

Omenyo, Cephas N. *Pentecost Outside Pentecostalism: A Study of the Development of Charismatic Renewal in the Mainline Churches in Ghana*. Zoetermeer: Boekencentrum Publishing House, 2006.

O'Mahoney, Anthony. 'Palestinian Christians: Religion, Politics and Society, c. 1800-1948.' In Anthony O'Mahoney ed. *Palestinian Christians: Religion, Politics and Society in the Holy Land*. London: Melisende, 1999.

Otieno, Nicholas. *Human Rights and Social Justice in Africa: Cultural, Ethical and Spiritual Imperatives*. Nairobi: All Africa Conference of Churches, 2008.

Otto, Rudolf. *The Idea of the Holy*. Oxford: University Press, 1923.

Padilla, C.R. *New Face of Evangelism: An International Symposium on the Lausanne Covenant*. Downers Grove: IVP, 1976.

Paguio, Wilfredo C. *Filipino Cultural Values for the Apostolate*. Makati, Philippines: St. Paul Publications, 1991.

Pal, Agaton P. 'The People's Conception of the World'. In Socorro C. Espiritu and Chester L. Hunt (eds.). *Social Foundations of Community Development: Readings on the Philippines* Manila: R.M. Garcia, 1964.

Panikkar, Raimon. 'In Christ There Is Neither Hindu Nor Christian: Perspectives on Hindu-Christian Dialogue'. In C. Wei-hsun Fu & G.E.Spiegler ed., *Religious Issues & Dialogues*. New York: Greenwood Press, 1989, 475-489.

Panikkar, Raimon. *The Intrareligious Dialogue*. Bangalore: Asian Trading Corporation, 1984.

Pannenberg, Wolfhart. *Faith and Reality*. London: Search Press, 1977.

Papanikolao, Aristotle. 'Person, *Kenosis* and Abuse: Hans Urs Von Balthasar and Feminist Theologies in Conversation.' *Modern Theology* 19:1 (2003), 41-65.

Pappe, Illan. *The Ethnic Cleansing of Palestine*. Oxford: Oneworld, 2007.

Park, Hee-sung. *Gara Ganda: Mission Story, Expansion of the Kingdom of God*. Seoul: Gwang-ya, 2001.

Peel, J.D.Y. 'The Pastor and the *Babalawo*: The Interaction of Religions in Nineteenth-Century Yorubaland'. *Africa*, 60:3 (1990), 338-69.

Philip, P.O. 'The Place of Ashrams in the Life of the Church in India'. *The International Review of Mission* 35:3 (July 1946), 263-70.

Quinn, Richard. 'From Development to Justice'. In Padraig Flanagan. *A New Missionary Era*. Maryknoll, NY: Orbis Books, 1979, 145-151.

Radhkrishnan, Sarvepalli. *Eastern Religions and Western Thought.* Oxford: Oxford University Press, 1940.
Raheb, Mitri. 'The Spiritual Significance and Experience of the Churches: The Lutheran Perspective'. In Michael Prior and William Taylor ed. *Christians in the Holy Land.* London: The World of Islam Festival Trust, 1995.
Ralston, Helen. *Christian Ashrams: A New Religious Movement in Contemporary India.* New York: The Edwin Mellen Press, 1987.
Richards, H.L. *Christ-Bhakti: Narayan Vaman Tilak and Christian Work among Hindus.* Delhi: ISPCK, 1991.
Richardson, Don. 'A Man for All Peoples.' In Ralph D. Winter and Steven C. Hawthorne, ed. *Perspectives on the World Christian Movement.* Pasadena: William Carey Library,1999, A-104-109.
Robertson, Roland and William R. Garrett ed. *Religion and Global Order.* New York: Paragon, 1991.
Ross, Kenneth R. *Edinburgh 2010: New Directions for Church in Mission.* Pasadena: William Carey International University Press, 2010.
Rudolph, Hoeber S. and James Piscatori ed. *Transnational Religion and Fading States.* Boulder, CO.: Westview Press, 1997.
Ruether, Rosemary Radford and Herman J. Ruether. *The Wrath of Jonah: the Crisis of Religious Nationalism in the Israel-Palestinian Context.* Minneapolis: Fortress, 2002.
Sanneh, Lamin. 'The Horizontal and Vertical in Mission: An African Perspective'. *International Bulletin of Missionary Research* 7:4 (1983), 165-71.
Sarpong, Peter. *Ghana in Retrospect: Some Aspects of Ghanaian Culture.* Tema: Ghana Publishing Coorporation, 1974.
Schmemann, Alexander. 'The Missionary Imperative in the Orthodox Tradition'. In Gerald H. Anderson ed. *The Theology of the Christian Mission.* New York: McGraw-Hill, 1961, 250-57.
Schouten, Jan Peter. *Jesus as Guru: The Image of Christ Among Hindus and Christians in India.* Amsterdam & New York: Rodopi, 2008.
Sepúlveda, Juan. 'Reflections on the Pentecostal Contribution to the Mission of the Church in Latin America'. *Journal of Pentecostal Theology* 1 (1992), 93-108.
Shenk, Wilbert R. 'Recasting Theology of Mission: Impulses from the Non-Western World'. *International Bulletin of Missionary Research.* 25:3 (2001), 98-107.
Smart, Ninian. *World Religions.* Cambridge: Cambridge University Press, 1998.
Smart, Ninian. *Dimensions of the Sacred: An Anatomy of the World's Beliefs.* Berkeley, CA: University of California Press, 1998.
Sparks, Kenton L. 'Gospel as Conquest: Mosaic Typology in Matthew 8:16-20.' *The Catholic Biblical Quarterly* 68:4 (2006), 651-63.
Stamoolis, James. *Eastern Orthodox Mission Theology Today.* Maryknoll, NY: Orbis Books, 1986.
Stark, Rodney. 'Why New Religious Movements Succeed or Fail: A Revised General Model'. *Journal of Contemporary Religion* 11:2 (1996), 133-46.
Stout, Jeffrey. *Democracy and Tradition.* Princeton, NJ: Princeton University Press, 2004.
Streeter, B.H. and A.J. Appasamy. *The Sadhu: a Study in Mysticism and Practical Religion.* London: Macmillan, 1923.
Sugirtharajah, Rasaiah S. and Cecil Hargreaves ed. *Readings in Indian Christian Theology Vol I.* London: SPCK, 1993.

Tang Li. *A Study of the History of Nestorian Christianity in China and its Literature in Chinese*. Frankfurt am Main; New York: Peter Lang, 2004.
Taylor, John V. *The Go Between God: The Holy Spirit and the Christian Mission*. London: SCM, 1972.
Temple, William, *The Church Looks Forward*. London: MacMillan & Co, 1944.
Ter Haar, Gerrie. 'Strangers in the Promised Land: African Christians in Europe'. *Exchange* 24:1 (1995), 1-33.
The Committee for the 50 Year Annals. *A 50 Year History of Yoido Full Gospel Church: 50 Years for Mission, A Great Journey* [Korean]. Seoul: Yoido Full Gospel Church, 2008.
The Sabeel Survey on Palestinian Christians in the West Bank. Jerusalem: Sabeel, 2006.
Tilak, L. *From Brahma to Christ: The Story of Narayan Vaman Tilak and Lakshmibal his Wife*. New York: Association Press, 1956.
Van Dijk, Richard. 'From Camp to Encompassment: Discourses of Transsubjectivity in the Ghanaian Pentecostal Diaspora'. *Journal of Religion in Africa* 27:2 (1997), 135-160.
Vandana, Sister (Mataji). *Gurus, Ashrams and Christians*. Delhi: ISPCK, 1978.
Volf, Miroslav. 'Materiality of Salvation.' *Journal of Ecumenical Studies* 26 (1989): 447-67.
Walls, Andrew F. *The Cross-Cultural Process in Christian History*. Maryknoll, NY: Orbis Books, 2002.
Wang, A.J.C. *Silk Route Mission: Story of a Heroic Couple*. Taipei: Campus Evangelical Fellowship, 2003.
Ward, Miriam. 'The Theological and Ethical Context for Palestinian-Israeli Peace.' In Rosemary Radford Ruether and Marc H. Ellis, ed. *Beyond Occupation: American Jewish, Christian, and Palestinian Voices for Peace*. Boston: Beacon Books, 1990, 171-82.
Waters, Malcolm. *Globalisation*. London: Routledge, 1995.
Weber, Timothy P. *On the Road to Armageddon: How Evangelicals Became Israel's Best Friend*. Grand Rapids: Baker, 2004.
Wilson, Bryan R. 'The Functions of Religion: A Reappraisal'. *Religion* 18 (1988), 199-216.
Winslow, J.C. *Narayan Vaman Tilak: The Christian Poet of Maharashtra*. Calcutta: YMCA, 1930.
Wraith, Ronald and Edgar Simpkins, *Corruption in Developing Countries*. London: George Allen & Unwin, 1963).
Wyllie, Robert W. 'Pioneers of Ghanaian Pentecostalism: Peter Anim and James McKeown'. *Journal of Religion in Africa* 6:2 (1974), 109-122.
Yamamori, Tetsunao and Kim-Kwong Chan. *Witnesses to Power: Stories of God's Quiet Work in a Changing China*. Carlisle: Paternoster, 2000.
Yang, Tai Choul. 'A Study on the Mission Strategies of the Grace Korean Church in the Light of the Selected Five Modern Missions Strategies'. Doctor of Ministry Dissertation, Midwest University, 2009.
Yannoulatos, Anastasios. 'Orthodoxy and Mission'. *St Vladimir's Seminary Quarterly* 8:3 (1964).
Yannoulatos, Anastasios. 'The Purpose and Motive of Mission from an Orthodox Theological Point of View'. *International Review of Mission* 54:215 (July 1967), 281-97.

Yun, Brother and Paul Hattaway, *The Heavenly Man: The Remarkable True Story of Chinese Christian Brother Yun.* London: Monarch, 2002.
Zaide, Sonia M. *Philippine History and Government.* 4th ed. Quezon City: All-Nations Publishing, 1989.

LIST OF CONTRIBUTORS

J. Kwabena Asamoah-Gyadu is Professor of Theology at Trinity Theological Seminary, Legon, Ghana.

Andrew F. Bush is Associate Professor of Mission at Eastern University, St David's, Pennsylvania, USA, whilst serving with the Palestinian Bible Society in the Palestinian Territories.

Tereso C. Casiño is Professor of Missiology and Intercultural Studies at Gardner-Webb University (School of Divinity) in North Carolina, USA, and serves as Chair of North America Diaspora Educators' Forum--Global Diaspora Network. He previously taught at Torch Trinity Graduate University in Seoul, South Korea.

Kim-kwong Chan is Executive Secretary of the Hong Kong Christian Council.

Valentin Kozhuharov is currently a freelance lecturer in Christian education and in Missiology in Plovdiv University (Bulgaria) and tutor in Missiology at the Institute for Mission Studies, Budapest (Hungary). For seven years (2002-2009) he has been missionary and lecturer in the Department for religious education and catechization of the Moscow Patriarchate of the Russian Orthodox Church.

Chul-shin Lee is Senior Pastor, Youngnak Presbyterian Church, Seoul, South Korea.

Younghoon Lee is Senior Pastor of Yoido Full Gospel Church, Seoul, Korea.

Wonsuk Ma is Executive Director and David Yonggi Cho Research Tutor of Global Christianity, Oxford Centre for Mission Studies, Oxford, United Kingdom.

Nicta Makiika is General Secretary of the Organisation of African Instituted Churches, based in Nairobi, Kenya.

Clemens Mendonca is Executive Secretary for the Office of Ecumenical and Interreligious Affairs at the Federation of Asian Bishops' Conferences.

Moses Morales is the former Executive Secretary of the Secretariat for Ecumenical Dialogue of the Catholic Bishops' Conference in Bolivia.

Matthews A. Ojo is Professor in the Department of Religious Studies, Obafemi Awolowo University, Ile-Ife, Nigeria.

Michael P.K. Okyerefo is a Roman Catholic priest and Senior Lecturer in the Department of Sociology at the University of Ghana.

Kenneth R. Ross is Church of Scotland minister at Netherlorn and Honorary Fellow of Edinburgh University School of Divinity. From 2001 to 2010 he chaired the Scottish 'Towards 2010' Council.

Rosauro Lopez Sandoval is a Bolivian missiologist, teaching at the Universidad Católica Boliviana San Pablo

David Emmanuel Singh is Research Tutor at the Oxford Centre for Mission Studies (OCMS) in Oxford, UK.

Serah Wambua is East African Regional Advisor and Team Leader for Economic Empowerment for the Church Mission Society – Africa.

REGNUM EDINBURGH CENTENARY SERIES

David A. Kerr, Kenneth R. Ross (Eds)
Mission Then and Now
2009 / 978-1-870345-73-6 / 343pp (paperback)
2009 / 978-1-870345-76-7 / 343pp (hardback)

No one can hope to fully understand the modern Christian missionary movement without engaging substantially with the World Missionary Conference, held at Edinburgh in 1910. This book is the first to systematically examine the eight Commissions which reported to Edinburgh 1910 and gave the conference much of its substance and enduring value. It will deepen and extend the reflection being stimulated by the upcoming centenary and will kindle the missionary imagination for 2010 and beyond.

Daryl M. Balia, Kirsteen Kim (Eds)
Witnessing to Christ Today
2010 / 978-1-870345-77-4 / 301pp (hardback)

This volume, the second in the Edinburgh 2010 series, includes reports of the nine main study groups working on different themes for the celebration of the centenary of the World Missionary Conference, Edinburgh 1910. Their collaborative work brings together perspectives that are as inclusive as possible of contemporary world Christianity and helps readers to grasp what it means in different contexts to be 'witnessing to Christ today'.

Claudia Währisch-Oblau, Fidon Mwombeki (Eds)
Mission Continues
Global Impulses for the 21st Century
2010 / 978-1-870345-82-8 / 271pp (hardback)

In May 2009, 35 theologians from Asia, Africa and Europe met in Wuppertal, Germany, for a consultation on mission theology organized by the United Evangelical Mission: Communion of 35 Churches in Three Continents. The aim was to participate in the 100th anniversary of the Edinburgh conference through a study process and reflect on the challenges for mission in the 21st century. This book brings together these papers written by experienced practitioners from around the world.

Brian Woolnough and Wonsuk Ma (Eds)
Holistic Mission
God's Plan for God's People
2010 / 978-1-870345-85-9 / 268pp (hardback)

Holistic mission, or integral mission, implies God is concerned with the whole person, the whole community, body, mind and spirit. This book discusses the meaning of the holistic gospel, how it has developed, and implications for the church. It takes a global, eclectic approach, with 19 writers, all of whom have much experience in, and commitment to, holistic mission. It addresses critically and honestly one of the most exciting, and challenging, issues facing the church today. To be part of God's plan for God's people, the church must take holistic mission to the world.

Kirsteen Kim and Andrew Anderson (Eds)
Mission Today and Tomorrow
2010 / 978-1-870345-91-0 / 450pp (hardback)

There are moments in our lives when we come to realise that we are participating in the triune God's mission. If we believe the church to be as sign and symbol of the reign of God in the world, then we are called to witness to Christ today by sharing in God's mission of love through the transforming power of the Holy Spirit. We can all participate in God's transforming and reconciling mission of love to the whole creation.

Tormod Engelsviken, Erling Lundeby and Dagfinn Solheim (Eds)
The Church Going Glocal
Mission and Globalisation
2011 / 978-1-870345-93-4 / 262pp (hardback)

The New Testament church is... universal and local at the same time. The universal, one and holy apostolic church appears in local manifestations. Missiologically speaking... the church can take courage as she faces the increasing impact of globalisation on local communities today. Being universal and concrete, the church is geared for the simultaneous challenges of the glocal and local.

Marina Ngurusangzeli Behera (Ed)
Interfaith Relations after One Hundred Years
Christian Mission among Other Faiths
2011 / 978-1-870345-96-5 / 338pp (hardback)

The essays of this book reflect not only the acceptance and celebration of pluralism within India but also by extension an acceptance as well as a need for unity among Indian Christians of different denominations. The essays were presented and studied at a preparatory consultation on Study Theme II: Christian Mission Among Other Faiths at the United Theological College, India July 2009.

Lalsangkima Pachuau and Knud Jørgensen (Eds)
Witnessing to Christ in a Pluralistic Age
Christian Mission among Other Faiths
2011 / 978-1-870345-95-8 / 277pp (hardback)

In a world where plurality of faiths is increasingly becoming a norm of life, insights on the theology of religious plurality are needed to strengthen our understanding of our own faith and the faith of others. Even though religious diversity is not new, we are seeing an upsurge in interest on the theologies of religion among all Christian confessional traditions. It can be claimed that no other issue in Christian mission is more important and more difficult than the theologies of religions.

Beth Snodderly and A Scott Moreau (Eds)
Evangelical Frontier Mission
Perspectives on the Global Progress of the Gospel
2011 / 978-1-870345-98-9 / 312pp (hardback)

This important volume demonstrates that 100 years after the World Missionary Conference in Edinburgh, Evangelism has become truly global. Twenty-first-century Evangelism continues to focus on frontier mission, but significantly, and in the spirit of Edinburgh 1910, it also has re-engaged social action.

Rolv Olsen (Ed)
Mission and Postmodernities
2011 / 978-1-870345-97-2 / 279pp (hardback)

This volume takes on meaning because its authors honestly struggle with and debate how we should relate to postmodernities. Should our response be accommodation, relativizing or counter-culture? How do we strike a balance between listening and understanding, and at the same time exploring how postmodernities influence the interpretation and application of the Bible as the normative story of God's mission in the world?

Cathy Ross (Ed)
Life-Widening Mission
2012 / 978-1-908355-00-3 / 163pp (hardback)

It is clear from the essays collected here that the experience of the 2010 World Mission Conference in Edinburgh was both affirming and frustrating for those taking part - affirming because of its recognition of how the centre of gravity has moved in global Christianity; frustrating because of the relative slowness of so many global Christian bodies to catch up with this and to embody it in the way they do business and in the way they represent themselves. These reflections will - or should - provide plenty of food for thought in the various councils of the Communion in the coming years.

Beate Fagerli, Knud Jørgensen, Rolv Olsen, Kari Storstein Haug and Knut Tveitereid (Eds)
A Learning Missional Church
Reflections from Young Missiologists
2012 / 978-1-908355-01-1 / 218pp (hardback)

Cross-cultural mission has always been a primary learning experience for the church. It pulls us out of a mono-cultural understanding and helps us discover a legitimate theological pluralism which opens up for new perspectives in the Gospel. Translating the Gospel into new languages and cultures is a human and divine means of making us learn new 'incarnations' of the Good News.

Emma Wild-Wood & Peniel Rajkumar (Eds)
Foundations for Mission
2012 / 978-1-908355-12-6 / 303pp (hardback)

This volume provides an important resource for those wishing to gain an overview of significant issues in contemporary missiology whilst understanding how they are applied in particular contexts

REGNUM STUDIES IN GLOBAL CHRISTIANITY

David Emmanuel Singh (Ed)
Jesus and the Cross
Reflections of Christians from Islamic Contexts
2008 / 978-1-870345-65-1 / 226pp

The Cross reminds us that the sins of the world are not borne through the exercise of power but through Jesus Christ's submission to the will of the Father. The papers in this volume are organised in three parts: scriptural, contextual and theological. The central question being addressed is: how do Christians living in contexts, where Islam is a majority or minority religion, experience, express or think of the Cross?

Sung-wook Hong
Naming God in Korea
The Case of Protestant Christianity
2008 / 978-1-870345-66-8 / 170pp (hardback)

Since Christianity was introduced to Korea more than a century ago, one of the most controversial issues has been the Korean term for the Christian 'God'. This issue is not merely about naming the Christian God in Korean language, but it relates to the question of theological contextualization - the relationship between the gospel and culture - and the question of Korean Christian identity. This book demonstrates the nature of the gospel in relation to cultures, i.e., the universality of the gospel expressed in all human cultures.

Hubert van Beek (Ed)
Revisioning Christian Unity
The Global Christian Forum
2009 / 978-1-870345-74-3 / 288pp (hardback)

This book contains the records of the Global Christian Forum gathering held in Limuru near Nairobi, Kenya, on 6 – 9 November 2007 as well as the papers presented at that historic event. Also included are a summary of the Global Christian Forum process from its inception until the 2007 gathering and the reports of the evaluation of the process that was carried out in 2008.

Young-hoon Lee
The Holy Spirit Movement in Korea
Its Historical and Theological Development
2009 / 978-1-870345-67-5 / 174pp (hardback)
This book traces the historical and theological development of the Holy Spirit Movement in Korea through six successive periods (from 1900 to the present time). These periods are characterized by repentance and revival (1900-20), persecution and suffering under Japanese occupation (1920-40), confusion and division (1940-60), explosive revival in which the Pentecostal movement played a major role in the rapid growth of Korean churches (1960-80), the movement reaching out to all denominations (1980-2000), and the new context demanding the Holy Spirit movement to open new horizons in its mission engagement (2000-).

Paul Hang-Sik Cho
Eschatology and Ecology
Experiences of the Korean Church
2010 / 978-1-870345-75-0 / 260pp (hardback)
This book raises the question of why Korean people, and Korean Protestant Christians in particular, pay so little attention to ecological issues. The author argues that there is an important connection (or elective affinity) between this lack of attention and the other-worldly eschatology that is so dominant within Korean Protestant Christianity.

Dietrich Werner, David Esterline, Namsoon Kang, Joshva Raja (Eds)
The Handbook of Theological Education in World Christianity
Theological Perspectives, Ecumenical Trends, Regional Surveys
2010 / 978-1-870345-80-4 / 800pp
This major reference work is the first ever comprehensive study of Theological Education in Christianity of its kind. With contributions from over 90 international scholars and church leaders, it aims to be easily accessible across denominational, cultural, educational, and geographic boundaries. The Handbook will aid international dialogue and networking among theological educators, institutions, and agencies.

David Emmanuel Singh & Bernard C Farr (Eds)
Christianity and Education
Shaping of Christian Context in Thinking
2010 / 978-1-870345-81-1 / 374pp
Christianity and Education is a collection of papers published in *Transformation: An International Journal of Holistic Mission Studies* over a period of 15 years. The articles represent a spectrum of Christian thinking addressing issues of institutional development for theological education, theological studies in the context of global mission, contextually aware/informed education, and academies which deliver such education, methodologies and personal reflections.

J. Andrew Kirk
Civilisations in Conflict?
Islam, the West and Christian Faith
2011 / 978-1-870345-87-3 / 205pp

Samuel Huntington's thesis, which argues that there appear to be aspects of Islam that could be on a collision course with the politics and values of Western societies, has provoked much controversy. The purpose of this study is to offer a particular response to Huntington's thesis by making a comparison between the origins of Islam and Christianity.

David Emmanuel Singh (Ed)
Jesus and the Incarnation
Reflections of Christians from Islamic Contexts
2011 / 978-1-870345-90-3 / 245pp

In the dialogues of Christians with Muslims nothing is more fundamental than the Cross, the Incarnation and the Resurrection of Jesus. Building on the *Jesus and the Cross*, this book contains voices of Christians living in various 'Islamic contexts' and reflecting on the Incarnation of Jesus. The aim and hope of these reflections is that the papers weaved around the notion of 'the Word' will not only promote dialogue among Christians on the roles of the Person and the Book but, also, create a positive environment for their conversations with Muslim neighbours.

Ivan M Satyavrata
God Has Not left Himself Without Witness
2011 / 978-1-870345-79-8 / 260pp

Since its earliest inception the Christian Church has had to address the question of what common ground exits between Christian faiths and other religions. This issue is not merely of academic interest but one with critical existential and socio-political consequences. This study presents a case for the revitalization of the fulfillment tradition based on a recovery and assessment of the fulfillment approaches of Indian Christian converts in the pre-independence period.

Bal Krishna Sharma
From this World to the Next
Christian Identity and Funerary Rites in Nepal
2013 / 978-1-908355-08-9 / 238pp

This book explores and analyses funerary rite struggles in a nation where Christianity is a comparatively recent phenomenon, and many families have multi-faith, who go through traumatic experiences at the death of their family members. The author has used an applied theological approach to explore and analyse the findings in order to address the issue of funerary rites with which the Nepalese church is struggling.

J Kwabena Asamoah-Gyada
Contemporary Pentecostal Christianity
Interpretations from an African Context
2013 / 978-1-908355-07-2 / 238pp

Pentecostalism is the fastest growing stream of Christianity in the world. The real evidence for the significance of Pentecostalism lies in the actual churches they have built and the numbers they attract. This work interprets key theological and missiological themes in African Pentecostalism by using material from the live experiences of the movement itself.

REGNUM STUDIES IN MISSION

Kwame Bediako
Theology and Identity
The Impact of Culture upon Christian Thought in the Second Century and in Modern Africa
1992 / 978-1870345-10-1 / 507pp

The author examines the question of Christian identity in the context of the Graeco–Roman culture of the early Roman Empire. He then addresses the modern African predicament of quests for identity and integration.

Christopher Sugden
Seeking the Asian Face of Jesus
The Practice and Theology of Christian Social Witness in Indonesia and India 1974–1996
1997 / 1-870345-26-6 / 496pp

This study focuses on contemporary holistic mission with the poor in India and Indonesia combined with the call to transformation of all life in Christ with micro-credit enterprise schemes. 'The literature on contextual theology now has a new standard to rise to' – Lamin Sanneh (Yale University, USA).

Hwa Yung
Mangoes or Bananas?
The Quest for an Authentic Asian Christian Theology
1997 / 1-870345-25-5 / 274pp

Asian Christian thought remains largely captive to Greek dualism and Enlightenment rationalism because of the overwhelming dominance of Western culture. Authentic contextual Christian theologies will emerge within Asian Christianity with a dual recovery of confidence in culture and the gospel.

Keith E. Eitel
Paradigm Wars
The Southern Baptist International Mission Board Faces the Third Millennium
1999 / 1-870345-12-6 / 140pp

The International Mission Board of the Southern Baptist Convention is the largest denominational mission agency in North America. This volume chronicles the historic and contemporary forces that led to the IMB's recent extensive reorganization, providing the most comprehensive case study to date of a historic mission agency restructuring to continue its mission purpose into the twenty-first century more effectively.

Samuel Jayakumar
Dalit Consciousness and Christian Conversion
Historical Resources for a Contemporary Debate
1999 / 81-7214-497-0 / 434pp
(Published jointly with ISPCK)

The main focus of this historical study is social change and transformation among the Dalit Christian communities in India. Historiography tests the evidence in the light of the conclusions of the modern Dalit liberation theologians.

Vinay Samuel and Christopher Sugden (Eds)
Mission as Transformation
A Theology of the Whole Gospel
1999 / 978-18703455-13-2 / 522pp

This book brings together in one volume twenty five years of biblical reflection on mission practice with the poor from around the world. This volume helps anyone understand how evangelicals, struggling to unite evangelism and social action, found their way in the last twenty five years to the biblical view of mission in which God calls all human beings to love God and their neighbour; never creating a separation between the two.

Christopher Sugden
Gospel, Culture and Transformation
2000 / 1-870345-32-0 / 152pp
A Reprint, with a New Introduction,
of Part Two of Seeking the Asian Face of Jesus

Gospel, Culture and Transformation explores the practice of mission especially in relation to transforming cultures and communities. - 'Transformation is to enable God's vision of society to be actualised in all relationships: social, economic and spiritual, so that God's will may be reflected in human society and his love experienced by all communities, especially the poor.'

Bernhard Ott
Beyond Fragmentation: Integrating Mission and Theological Education
A Critical Assessment of some Recent Developments
in Evangelical Theological Education
2001 / 1-870345-14-2 / 382pp

Beyond Fragmentation is an enquiry into the development of Mission Studies in evangelical theological education in Germany and German-speaking Switzerland between 1960 and 1995. The author undertakes a detailed examination of the paradigm shifts which have taken place in recent years in both the theology of mission and the understanding of theological education.

Gideon Githiga
The Church as the Bulwark against Authoritarianism
Development of Church and State Relations in Kenya, with Particular Reference to the Years after Political Independence 1963-1992
2002 / 1-870345-38-x / 218pp

'All who care for love, peace and unity in Kenyan society will want to read this careful history by Bishop Githiga of how Kenyan Christians, drawing on the Bible, have sought to share the love of God, bring his peace and build up the unity of the nation, often in the face of great difficulties and opposition.' Canon Dr Chris Sugden, Oxford Centre for Mission Studies.

Myung Sung-Hoon, Hong Young-Gi (eds.)
Charis and Charisma
David Yonggi Cho and the Growth of Yoido Full Gospel Church
2003 / 978-1870345-45-3 / 218pp

This book discusses the factors responsible for the growth of the world's largest church. It expounds the role of the Holy Spirit, the leadership, prayer, preaching, cell groups and creativity in promoting church growth. It focuses on God's grace (charis) and inspiring leadership (charisma) as the two essential factors and the book's purpose is to present a model for church growth worldwide.

Samuel Jayakumar
Mission Reader
Historical Models for Wholistic Mission in the Indian Context
2003 / 1-870345-42-8 / 250pp
(Published jointly with ISPCK)

This book is written from an evangelical point of view revalidating and reaffirming the Christian commitment to wholistic mission. The roots of the 'wholistic mission' combining 'evangelism and social concerns' are to be located in the history and tradition of Christian evangelism in the past; and the civilizing purpose of evangelism is compatible with modernity as an instrument in nation building.

Bob Robinson
Christians Meeting Hindus
An Analysis and Theological Critique of the Hindu-Christian Encounter in India
2004 / 987-1870345-39-2 / 392pp

This book focuses on the Hindu-Christian encounter, especially the intentional meeting called dialogue, mainly during the last four decades of the twentieth century, and specifically in India itself.

Gene Early
Leadership Expectations
How Executive Expectations are Created and Used in a Non-Profit Setting
2005 / 1-870345-30-4 / 276pp

The author creates an Expectation Enactment Analysis to study the role of the Chancellor of the University of the Nations-Kona, Hawaii. This study is grounded in the field of managerial work, jobs, and behaviour and draws on symbolic interactionism, role theory, role identity theory and enactment theory. The result is a conceptual framework for developing an understanding of managerial roles.

Tharcisse Gatwa
The Churches and Ethnic Ideology in the Rwandan Crises 1900-1994
2005 / 978-1870345-24-8 / 300pp
(Reprinted 2011)

Since the early years of the twentieth century Christianity has become a new factor in Rwandan society. This book investigates the role Christian churches played in the formulation and development of the racial ideology that culminated in the 1994 genocide.

Julie Ma
Mission Possible
Biblical Strategies for Reaching the Lost
2005 / 978-1870345-37-1 / 142pp

This is a missiology book for the church which liberates missiology from the specialists for the benefit of every believer. It also serves as a textbook that is simple and friendly, and yet solid in biblical interpretation. This book links the biblical teaching to the actual and contemporary missiological settings with examples, making the Bible come alive to the reader.

Allan Anderson, Edmond Tang (Eds)
Asian and Pentecostal
The Charismatic Face of Christianity in Asia
2005 / 978-1870345-94-1 / 500pp
(Published jointly with APTS Press)

This book provides a thematic discussion and pioneering case studies on the history and development of Pentecostal and Charismatic churches in the countries of South Asia, South East Asia and East Asia.

I. Mark Beaumont
Christology in Dialogue with Muslims
A Critical Analysis of Christian Presentations of Christ for Muslims from the Ninth and Twentieth Centuries
2005 / 978-1870345-46-0 / 227pp

This book analyses Christian presentations of Christ for Muslims in the most creative periods of Christian-Muslim dialogue, the first half of the ninth century and the second half of the twentieth century. In these two periods, Christians made serious attempts to present their faith in Christ in terms that take into account Muslim perceptions of him, with a view to bridging the gap between Muslim and Christian convictions.

Thomas Czövek,
Three Seasons of Charismatic Leadership
A Literary-Critical and Theological Interpretation of the Narrative of Saul, David and Solomon
2006 / 978-1870345-48-4 / 272pp

This book investigates the charismatic leadership of Saul, David and Solomon. It suggests that charismatic leaders emerge in crisis situations in order to resolve the crisis by the charisma granted by God. Czovek argues that Saul proved himself as a charismatic leader as long as he acted resolutely and independently from his mentor Samuel. In the author's eyes, Saul's failure to establish himself as a charismatic leader is caused by his inability to step out from Samuel's shadow.

Richard Burgess
Nigeria's Christian Revolution
The Civil War Revival and Its Pentecostal Progeny (1967-2006)
2008 / 978-1-870345-63-7 / 347pp

This book describes the revival that occurred among the Igbo people of Eastern Nigeria and the new Pentecostal churches it generated, and documents the changes that have occurred as the movement has responded to global flows and local demands. As such, it explores the nature of revivalist and Pentecostal experience, but does so against the backdrop of local socio-political and economic developments, such as decolonisation and civil war, as well as broader processes, such as modernisation and globalisation.

David Emmanuel Singh & Bernard C Farr (Eds)
Christianity and Cultures
Shaping Christian Thinking in Context
2008 / 978-1-870345-69-9 / 271pp

This volume marks an important milestone, the 25th anniversary of the Oxford Centre for Mission Studies (OCMS). The papers here have been exclusively sourced from Transformation, a quarterly journal of OCMS, and seek to provide a tripartite view of Christianity's engagement with cultures by focusing on the question: how is Christian thinking being formed or reformed through its interaction with the varied contexts it encounters? The subject matters include different strands of theological-missiological thinking, socio-political engagements and forms of family relationships in interaction with the host cultures.

Tormod Engelsviken, Ernst Harbakk, Rolv Olsen, Thor Strandenæs (Eds)
Mission to the World
Communicating the Gospel in the 21st Century:
Essays in Honour of Knud Jørgensen
2008 / 978-1-870345-64-4 / 472pp (hardback)

Knud Jørgensen is Director of Areopagos and Associate Professor of Missiology at MF Norwegian School of Theology. This book reflects on the main areas of Jørgensen's commitment to mission. At the same time it focuses on the main frontier of mission, the world, the content of mission, the Gospel, the fact that the Gospel has to be communicated, and the context of contemporary mission in the 21st century.

Al Tizon
Transformation after Lausanne
Radical Evangelical Mission in Global-Local Perspective
2008 / 978-1-870345-68-2 / 281pp

After Lausanne '74, a worldwide network of radical evangelical mission theologians and practitioners use the notion of "Mission as Transformation" to integrate evangelism and social concern together, thus lifting theological voices from the Two Thirds World to places of prominence. This book documents the definitive gatherings, theological tensions, and social forces within and without evangelicalism that led up to Mission as Transformation. And it does so through a global-local grid that points the way toward greater holistic mission in the 21st century.

Bambang Budijanto
Values and Participation
Development in Rural Indonesia
2009 / 978-1-870345-70-4 / 237pp

Socio-religious values and socio-economic development are inter-dependant, inter-related and are constantly changing in the context of macro political structures, economic policy, religious organizations and globalization; and micro influences such as local affinities, identity, politics, leadership and beliefs. The book argues that the comprehensive approach in understanding the socio-religious values of each of the three local Lopait communities in Central Java is essential to accurately describing their respective identity.

Alan R. Johnson
Leadership in a Slum
A Bangkok Case Study
2009 / 978-1-870345-71-2 / 238pp

This book looks at leadership in the social context of a slum in Bangkok from a different perspective than traditional studies which measure well educated Thais on leadership scales derived in the West. Using both systematic data collection and participant observation, it develops a culturally preferred model as well as a set of models based in Thai concepts that reflect on-the-ground realities. It concludes by looking at the implications of the anthropological approach for those who are involved in leadership training in Thai settings and beyond.

Titre Ande
Leadership and Authority
Bula Matari and Life - Community Ecclesiology in Congo
2010 / 978-1-870345-72-9 / 189pp

Christian theology in Africa can make significant development if a critical understanding of the socio-political context in contemporary Africa is taken seriously, particularly as Africa's post-colonial Christian leadership based its understanding and use of authority on the Bula Matari model. This has caused many problems and Titre proposes a Life-Community ecclesiology for liberating authority, here leadership is a function, not a status, and 'apostolic succession' belongs to all people of God.

Frank Kwesi Adams
Odwira and the Gospel
A Study of the Asante Odwira Festival and its Significance for Christianity in Ghana
2010 /978-1-870345-59-0 / 232pp

The study of the Odwira festival is the key to the understanding of Asante religious and political life in Ghana. The book explores the nature of the Odwira festival longitudinally - in pre-colonial, colonial and post-independence Ghana - and examines the Odwira ideology and its implications for understanding the Asante self-identity. Also discussed is how some elements of faith portrayed in the Odwira festival can provide a framework for Christianity to engage with Asante culture at a greater depth.

Bruce Carlton
Strategy Coordinator
Changing the Course of Southern Baptist Missions
2010 / 978-1-870345-78-1 / 268pp

This is an outstanding, one-of-a-kind work addressing the influence of the non-residential missionary/strategy coordinator's role in Southern Baptist missions. This scholarly text examines the twentieth century global missiological currents that influenced the leadership of the International

Mission Board, resulting in a new paradigm to assist in taking the gospel to the nations.

Julie Ma & Wonsuk Ma
Mission in the Spirit:
Towards a Pentecostal/Charismatic Missiology
2010 / 978-1-870345-84-2 / 312pp

The book explores the unique contribution of Pentecostal/Charismatic mission from the beginning of the twentieth century. The first part considers the theological basis of Pentecostal/Charismatic mission thinking and practice. Special attention is paid to the Old Testament, which has been regularly overlooked by the modern Pentecostal/Charismatic movements. The second part discusses major mission topics with contributions and challenges unique to Pentecostal/Charismatic mission. The book concludes with a reflection on the future of this powerful missionary movement. As the authors served as Korean missionaries in Asia, often their missionary experiences in Asia are reflected in their discussions.

S. Hun Kim & Wonsuk Ma (eds.)
Korean Diaspora and Christian Mission
2011-978-1-870345-91-0 / 301pp (hardback)

As a 'divine conspiracy' for Missio Dei, the global phenomenon of people on the move has shown itself to be invaluable. In 2004 two significant documents concerning Diaspora were introduced, one by the Filipino International Network and the other by the Lausanne Committee for World Evangelization. These have created awareness of the importance of people on the move for Christian mission. Since then, Korean Diaspora has conducted similar research among Korean missions, resulting in this book

Jin Huat Tan
Planting an Indigenous Church
The Case of the Borneo Evangelical Mission
2011 / 978-1-870345-99-6 / 363pp

Dr Jin Huat Tan has written a pioneering study of the origins and development of Malaysia's most significant indigenous church. This is an amazing story of revival, renewal and transformation of the entire region chronicling the powerful effect of it evident to date! What can we learn from this extensive and careful study of the Borneo Revival, so the global Christianity will become ever more dynamic?

Bill Prevette
Child, Church and Compassion
Towards Child Theology in Romania
2012 / 978-1-908355-03-4 / 377pp

Bill Prevett comments that "children are like 'canaries in a mine shaft'; they provide a focal point for discovery and encounter of perilous aspects of our world that are often ignored." True, but miners also carried a lamp to see into the subterranean darkness. This book is such a lamp. It lights up the subterranean world of children and youth in danger of exploitation, and as it does so travels deep into their lives and also into the activities of those who seek to help them.

Samuel Cyuma
Picking up the Pieces
The Church and Conflict Resolution in South Africa and Rwanda
2012 / 978-1-908355-02-7 / 373pp

In the last ten years of the 20th century, the world was twice confronted with unbelievable news from Africa. First, there was the end of Apartheid in South Africa, without bloodshed, due to responsible political and Church leaders. The second was the mass killings in Rwanda, which soon escalated into real genocide. Political and Church leaders had been unable to prevents this crime against humanity. In this book, the question is raised: can we compare the situation in South Africa with that in Rwanda? Can Rwandan leaders draw lessons from the peace process in South Africa?

Peter Rowan
Proclaiming the Peacemaker
The Malaysian Church as an Agent of Reconciliation in a Multicultural Society
2012 / 978-1-908355-05-8 / 268pp

With a history of racial violence and in recent years, low-level ethnic tensions, the themes of peaceful coexistence and social harmony are recurring ones in the discourse of Malaysian society. In such a context, this book looks at the role of the church as a reconciling agent, arguing that a reconciling presence within a divided society necessitates an ethos of peacemaking.

Edward Ontita
Resources and Opportunity
The Architecture of Livelihoods in Rural Kenya
2012 / 978-1-908355-04-1 / 328pp

Poor people in most rural areas of developing countries often improvise resources in unique ways to enable them make a living. Resources and Opportunity takes the view that resources are dynamic and fluid, arguing that villagers co-produce them through redefinition and renaming in everyday practice and use them in diverse ways. The book focuses on ordinary social activities to bring out people's creativity in locating, redesigning and embracing livelihood opportunities in processes.

Kathryn Kraft
Searching for Heaven in the Real World
A Sociological Discussion of Conversion in the Arab World
2012 / 978-1-908355-15-7 / 1428pp

Kathryn Kraft explores the breadth of psychological and social issues faced by Arab Muslims after making a decision to adopt a faith in Christ or

Christianity, investigating some of the most surprising and significant challenges new believers face.

Wessley Lukose
Contextual Missiology of the Spirit
Pentecostalism in Rajasthan, India
2013 / 978-1-908355-09-6 / 256pp

This book explores the identity, context and features of Pentecostalism in Rajasthan, India as well as the internal and external issues facing Pentecostals. It aims to suggest 'a contextual missiology of the Spirit,' as a new model of contextual missiology from a Pentecostal perspective. It is presented as a glocal, ecumenical, transformational, and public missiology.

REGNUM RESOURCES FOR MISSION

Knud Jørgensen
Equipping for Service
Christian Leadership in Church and Society
2012 / 978-1-908355-06-5 / 168pp

This book is written out of decades of experience of leading churches and missions in Ethiopia, Geneva, Norway and Hong Kong. Combining the teaching of Scripture with the insights of contemporary management philosophy, Jørgensen writes in a way which is practical and applicable to anyone in Christian service. "The intention has been to challenge towards a leadership relevant for work in church and mission, and in public and civil society, with special attention to leadership in Church and organisation."

For the up-to-date listing of the Regnum books see www.ocms.ac.uk/regnum

Regnum Books International

Regnum is an Imprint of The Oxford Centre for Mission Studies
St. Philip and St. James Church, Woodstock Road, Oxford, OX2 6HR
Web: www.ocms.ac.uk/regnum